CONTRACT MANAGEMENT: POST AWARD

Contract Management: Post Award

National Association of
Purchasing Management Professor
at George Washington University

Wordcrafters Publications
Gaithersburg, Maryland 20878

Printed in the United States of America
90 89 88 87   6 5 4 3 2 1

Library of Congress Catalog Card Number:
86-51609
ISBN 0-941448-02-9

Wordcrafters Publications
15804 White Rock Road
Gaithersburg, Maryland 20878

FOREWORD

Until now, there has been a severe scarcity of textbooks or other effective learning tools created to deal with the complex art of contract management. This scarcity has been extremely frustrating (1) for the many students who would like to know more about this profession and its countless nuances; (2) for their instructors who have been forced, for the most part, to rely upon a hodgepodge of generally substandard educational aids; and (3) for active contract management professionals who have searched, mostly in vain, for highly focused texts well suited to upgrade and expand their knowledge of the rapidly changing rules of the road for this career field. As a working professional, I am delighted that, by creating this book, Dr. Stanley N. Sherman has taken a significant step toward remedying this situation. As President of the National Contract Management Association (NCMA), I also take great pride in the fact that this organization committed financial resources and provided encouragement to Dr. Sherman to follow through and complete this substantial undertaking.

This book represents one of the first tangible outputs of NCMA's educational grant program. My distinguished predecessor, Ken Jackson (NCMA President 1983-1984), deserves considerable credit for his leadership in establishing these initial grants. Ed Phelps (NCMA Vice President, Education and Certification, 1983-1984) and John Green (who administered our NCMA grant program for several years) also were instrumental in our grant programs to date. Jack Higgins, Jim Neal, Dave Lamm, and Bill Pursch similarly have strongly supported this program, and finally, and most importantly, all NCMA members throughout the world and our governing body, NCMA's Board of Directors, should take great pride in this book, because its creation may have been curtailed or significantly delayed, absent their wholehearted and constant support of this grant program.

I congratulate Dr. Sherman for what he has achieved. This book most effectively distills his world renowned knowledge and original research with respect to the post-award phase of contract management, and presents this information in a style and format that is most readable and quite understandable. I predict this book will soon be acclaimed as a major advancement in source material concerning this critical phase of contract management, and, as such, will be widely read and appreciated by students, scholars, and experienced professionals everywhere.

Stan Wilker
President 1986-1987
National Contract Management Association

v

PREFACE

There have been few previous attempts to present, in a single volume, insight into the many challenges and issues that are regularly encountered in the administration of contractual undertakings. The post-award work of contract managers has not captured the attention of authors whose writing is designed to support presentation in an academic setting. It is the objective of this book to fill that void in the literature of management. Although purchasing and materials systems are the subject of numerous texts, the opportunities for creative leadership and the substantial ambit for managerial discretion associated with post-award phases of procurement have received little attention.

It is widely recognized that organizational buying consumes large sums of money and that the manager's work requires unique skills of negotiation generally practiced under limited time constraints. It is also widely recognized that contracting is essential to the welfare of every society because it provides a mechanism for taking immediate action to fill needs that arise in all kinds of situations, whether routine or urgent, whether vital or merely desirable. The purchasing system uses contracts as flexible tools for executing programs, and managers have found them to be irreplaceable mechanisms. But the attention of management writers has been focused on pre-award rather than post-award actions and on internal rather than inter-organizational relationships. Nevertheless, success in contractual undertakings is dependent on insight, action, and issue resolution that cannot be addressed until the contract exists and often cannot be resolved by internally oriented actions alone. Post-award decisionmaking carries implications for the manager that have not been fully understood. It is hoped that this book will encourage further study of the field.

Managers have recognized the importance of contractual agreements since the beginning of organized society, but most writing on the subject has been of a legal nature. It has been devoted to the analysis of cases already decided by legal authority and has largely been an aid to the preparation of litigation. Differing in approach, this work seeks to analyze management problems and challenges as the manager encounters them, looking to the future. The objective is to reduce the doubt and ambiguity with which the field is viewed, to aid study by students who would enter the field, and to meet the needs of practitioners who may wish to stand back from the pressures of immediate issues to view the process in its context as a vital force in corporate or agency management and as a part of the overall logistics system.

This book is a follow-up to *Government Procurement Management*, Second Edition, 1985 which addresses procurement (pre-award planning, policy and practice) by the United States government. *Contract Management: Post Award* focuses on the manager's responsibilities in the administration of contracts, whether employed by government or the private sector. The text attempts to view the process objectively, giving consideration to the roles of both buyer and seller in post-award actions. Throughout the book comparisons are made between government policy and practice and private sector actions. Cases drawn from both industry and government contract management experiences are included.

Readers should recognize that post-award administrative action is a part of the procurement process and has been most highly developed to support programs subjected to the project management system in government. But every purchasing arrangement requires administration, including actions ranging from minimal follow-up and expediting work to continuous interaction between buyer and seller personnel. Most large contracts are written in support of a defined product or project, and there are numerous overlaps, perhaps duplications, of responsibilities among managers. Many of the management systems and techniques pertinent to post-award functions (e.g., scheduling, estimating, cost accounting, reporting, and quality assurance) are used by several functional managers, and they are relied upon by both parties to the contract. Effective post-award management occurs only when the procurement process creates a contractual agreement that enables the buyer's and seller's managers to operate at arms-length yet cooperatively. This has proven difficult for many procurement actions, especially those funded by the taxpayer in which public exposure of discrepancies precedes full analysis of issues, with the consequence that a balanced study of the processes is seldom presented.

Truly effective contracting operations result only when the managers possess special talent in negotiations both before and after award. This book provides case illustrations and analyses that will aid managers in applying and developing that talent. Each chapter includes text followed by exercises or cases intended to illustrate related issues and decisions likely to arise during the performance period.

Chapters are organized in a natural sequence beginning with discussion of contract management as an essential discipline and continuing in chapters 1 and 2 with treatment of the overall objectives, contributions, and ethical factors affecting the contract manager. Chapter 3 examines approaches to organizing for contract administration, including the need for teamwork in order to bring together the necessary expertise to cover all facets of contract performance and interaction. This material is followed in chapter 4 by discussion of the initial stages of performance, including two-party review of requirements; initiation of plans, budgets, and schedules; and development of working relationships. The fifth chapter treats technical documentation and the vital post-award process of interpreting the contractual instrument to determine the specific intent of the parties at the time of their agreement.

Post-award functions performed by contracting personnel are summarized in chapter 6. The functions have been grouped into several categories that reflect the unique types of duties in which the contract manager must develop expertise.

Chapters 7 through 14 contain specific major subjects that have powerful leverage on success. Each of these subjects embraces numerous complex interactions that managers must appreciate, anticipate, and address. They include the multidimensional issues associated with property: its possession, use, nature, and implications for the contracting parties. This is followed by an examination of subcontracting and purchasing systems. A major issue in large contracts is progress assessment and projection of completion, the focus of chapter 9, which compares the government's approach to management systems (setting standards for, and conducting reviews of contractor systems) with the relevant internal management systems in use by private industrial firms.

Issues involving quality assurance--its relationship to technical documentation, to contractor internal quality planning, and to acceptance and warranty issues--are addressed in chapter 10. Chapter 11 describes the financial implications of working capital and explains the leverage buyers exercise through their funding and payments practices. The chapter includes an analysis of the special rules and procedures by which the government attempts to control the vast sums involved in its contractual undertakings.

Two topics tend to dominate the controversial aspects of contract management: change and delay. Change, the most perplexing yet essential process pervading the contract relationship, is the subject of chapter 12. It is followed in chapter 13 by examination of the most prevalent of all contract realities, delay. Both result in the need for a clearly defined contractual relationship, including provisions for orderly modification encompassed in the terms and conditions and price commitments. The preparation of adjustment proposals, development of positions on technical and price matters, and the negotiation of issues associated with change and delay is addressed in chapter 14.

In the fifteenth chapter the methods of contract completion are discussed beginning with normal completion and the associated delivery and acceptance and payment processes. Convenience termination, the unilateral discretionary right taken by the government, is then treated as a unique authority that warrants careful review by all parties. The chapter includes consideration of contract breaches and the special problems associated with determining whether a breach has occurred, and, if it has, determining which party is responsible--a particularly difficult problem if a high level of post-award interaction between the parties has been practiced.

Chapter sixteen integrates the discussion of post-award management with the overall logistics objectives of buyers. It compares the similar objectives, yet widely divergent policies and practices, of industry and government as each attempts to accomplish efficient and effective flow of information and material in support of organizational objectives. The chapter calls for greater reliance on the managerial capabilities and judgment of post-award and pre-award managers in government.

ACKNOWLEDGEMENTS

While many students, instructors, practitioners, and companies have contributed to the development of this book, the author recognizes the special importance of support given by the National Contract Management Association through its text and case writing research grant program. While the work has been in a formative stage for several years, it was the impetus provided by NCMA's participation that has brought it to fruition at this time. Similarly, the strong support of Norma Maine Loeser, Dean of the School of Government and Business Administration, George Washington University, during the research and writing phases of the work was invaluable.

A special debt of gratitude must be extended to my students who, over a period of years, have stimulated thought and expressed the need to treat post-award administration from the manager's perspective. This work attempts to respond to that demand. Consequently, much of the detail that accountants and lawyers might add to this work is omitted. It is the author's hope that this has been done without losing the essential principles that should guide the manager's decisionmaking.

Both corporate and government agency managers have given much to the preparation of this book. They have been willing to be interviewed, to provide documents in key areas, and to share their experiences so vital to writing the cases. In the interest of data security, most of these persons should not be mentioned by name, but I am deeply indebted to all. Special mention of several persons reflects their contributions of particular importance. Dr. David Lamm read the original manuscript and offered detailed comments that afforded balance and technical advice that I sorely needed. Curtis Cook undertook case research at my request and made an outstanding contribution by his original drafts of seven cases. Karen Porterfield and Mary Wengraf provided extremely helpful editorial input at critical times. There were also five instructors who have used the pre-publication bindings of the draft book. Each of them provided feedback on their practical experiences in the classroom which afforded me an opportunity to clarify and correct difficult passages and omitted explanations.

Of greatest importance of all is the work of my wife, Helen, in criticizing the manuscript and editing the roughest passages. In addition her patience and encouragement during the project has made it possible. Regardless, the errors, ambiguities and omissions that remain are mine.

Table of Contents

Contract management as a business system; Comparison of the
expediting and contract management subsystems; Objectives of
contract management; Definition of post-award contract
management; Relationship of procurement and post-award
contract management; Role of the supplier in post-award
management; Government contracts: the genesis of contract
management systems; Formulating contract management
relationships; Contract management and contemporary functions;
Make or buy decisions are causing growth in contract
management; A system in search of a theory; Summary; Topics
for discussion; Exercise 1-1, FAR and UCC Research

Adopting the service-to-customer orientation; Identity problems
in the contracting function; Responsibility assignments, identity,
and contributions of the contracting function; Pre-award
management; Competitive practices; Resource mobilization;
Post-award management; Transition of control from procurement
manager to contract manager; Ethical challenges and
perceptions; Contract-oriented actions to improve ethical
decisions; Perceptions that compromise ethical standing of
contract managers; Increased use of criminal statutes to
motivate ethical decisions; Legislative actions of 1985; Summary;
Topics for discussion; Case 2-1, Cajun A: Cajun and the Beta
Site Concept

The Detroit Edison approach; Government organization for field
administration; Defense Contract Administration Services;

technical data; Impracticability and impossibility; The interpretation process; Performance deficiency vs. document deficiency; Objective of contract interpretation; General and technical sources of the meaning of words; Implications of integrated agreements; Rules of interpretation; Order of precedence of contract documents; Use of extrinsic evidence; Oral statements and concurrent actions; Previous actions and understandings; Customary practice and uses of the trade; Resolution of ambiguity; Summary; Topics for discussion; Case 5-1, Saved by the Contracting Officer; Case 5-2, MultiElectro

Categories of contract management functions; Monitoring and surveillance functions; Reports and services to procuring office and contractor; Reviews and audits of contractor internal management systems; Formal decisions and actions affecting contractors; Directions, negotiations, and agreements; Program-sensitive contract management functions; Staffing requirements for contract management offices; Overall management; Financial and price management; Technical and quality management; Property and transportation management; Social and economic policy administration; Summary; Topics for discussion; Case 6-1, Simplex "A"

Mixed ownership of property; Classifications of property for contract purposes; Property accounting and management; Government standards for a property system; Scope of government property clause; Furnished property; Title; Use; Administration; Risk of loss; Equitable adjustments; Final accounting and disposition; Abandonment and restoration; Intellectual property; Overview of contractual uses of intellectual property; Government policy concerning intellectual property; Summary; Topics for discussion; Case 7-1, Dyna-Math Disclosure Dilemma; Case 7-2, Proserve, Inc.; Case 7-3, Electronic Systems, Inc.

Purchasing systems overview; Subcontracting policy; Contract clause flow-down; Purchasing systems: audit and review; Contractor procurement systems review; Summary; Topics for discussion; Case 8-1, The Management Circus; Case 8-2, DPG, Inc.; Case 8-3, Tak Technology; Case 8-4, Harrington Industries; Exercise 8-1, Contract Clause Flow-down Analysis

Management systems objectives for buyers and sellers; Buyer interest in supplier systems and operations; Growth of government interest in contractor management; Method of payment; Magnitude of public funds; Lack of firm pricing; Institutionalization of audit; Degradation of expected performance outcome; Contractual integrity; Sources of management information; Types of projects; Information gathering; Presentation formats; Advanced techniques for progress monitoring; Line of balance; Program evaluation and review technique (PERT); Cost schedule control systems criteria (C/SCSC); Historical notation; Objectives of C/SCSC; The earned value concept; C/SCSC equation; C/SCSC and earned value terminology; Criteria; Summary; Topics for discussion

Changing perceptions of quality verification responsibilities; Government implementation of quality concepts; Criteria for application of inspection; QA system levels; An alternative view of contract quality assurance; Quality assurance practices; Quality surveillance - administrative issues; Organizing to obtain quality compliance; Inspection and acceptance of end items; Application and usefulness of warranties; Summary; Topics for discussion; Case 10-1, Mobile Test Vans; Case 10-2, Rejected Parts; Case 10-3, RCI and the Data Warranty

Introduction; Funding and payments; Payment procedures; Progress payment requests; Payment of cost-reimbursement contracts; Payment of fixed-price construction contracts; Contract finance policies and practices; Private sources; Assignment of claims; Partial payments; Customary progress

1

Contract Management: An Essential Business Function

CONTRACT MANAGEMENT AS A BUSINESS SYSTEM

This book attempts to deal with the management implications of contractual endeavors. It examines the methods by which both parties influence or control activities affecting their vital interests, the techniques used to determine contract status, and the types of actions used to ensure timely delivery of intended products or services.

Contract management, pre- and post-award, is gaining stature as an important business system. The process of awarding and administering contracts, generally referred to as purchasing in private companies and as procurement or acquisition in government, provides a means for objectively evaluating alternate sources for organizational needs. It promotes competitive behavior among potential suppliers, internally as well as externally, and gives impetus to improvements in productivity. These trends have been stimulated by the growth of diversity in products, by shortages made evident by such events as oil embargoes, by the growth of project management as a method of managing, and by the emergence of the just-in-time (JIT) system of production.

Diversity in finished products promotes external sourcing because the varied production processes require a range of facilities, tools and specialized skills often unavailable internally. Shortages stimulated by the oil embargoes and pressure to reduce inventories promoted by JIT have emphasized reliability of supply sources and caused top management to take an active role in supply problems and to demand greater knowledge of supplier capabilities and objectives. Many have adopted project management as a means for concentrating attention on performance of complex (or merely different) undertakings that organizations seek to sponsor. When such projects fall outside the area of expertise of an organization, as is occurring with increased frequency, they are con-tracted out. These trends necessitate greater involvement and interaction between buyer and seller and strongly promote development of superior post-award management skills.

Pre-award and post-award contracting actions are complementary; each focuses on aspects of management not adequately addressed by the other. Pre-award actions are treated more fully in the literature of management because they appear to deal with larger issues of job defini-tion, investment, and risk. Post-award management, however, is con-cerned with a broader set of management decisions. It embraces per-formance, costing, scheduling, work direction and negotiation issues in which the procurement manager is often involved only indirectly. Well conceived and executed procurement can be defeated under inadequate post-award management. Similarly, superior post-award management can only partially overcome inappropriate or deficient purchase planning and documentation.

Successful procurement of specialized needs depends on the con-tinuing close attention which is achieved by establishing an effective contract administration system. Administration of contracts (the terms *administration* and *management* are used interchangeably throughout this book) does not easily fit into traditional organizational arrangements. The manager's success is based on ability to focus on specific contract related issues. These issues tend to be holistic, crossing functional and buyer/seller lines of authority. Beginning with the Second World War, contracting, including post-award management, has grown and has been redefined because advanced technology in fields such as aviation, elec-tronics, space systems, and nuclear power plants increasingly required skills no single organization or unit could provide. Additionally, as the economy developed and new products and services were introduced, estab-lished companies encountered competition that could not be met by their own expertise and facilities. These necessary capabilities could be supplied through external sources.

The importance of contract management as a business system will continue because executives in both government and industry increasingly depend on external organizations for expertise to perform complex, spe-cialized segments of their responsibilities. Today, senior managers are assigning diverse service, research, and production work as well as con-struction to external sources because the skills and facilities required are unavailable internally. Such work assignments are critical to corporate strategies and require post-award interaction between buyer and seller at a level not encountered earlier. This level of interaction may be unnec-essary for the standard purchase order or small purchase agreement used in large quantities by most organizations in our economy. Purchasing and procurement have been recognized for many years for their indispensable techniques in obtaining goods and services. There are no institutions or enterprises that are self sufficient; all depend upon external sources to some degree. However, the principal use of the standard purchase order is to procure well defined items and services, especially proprietary commercial items manufactured for stock by the production firm. This distinction--purchase of standard products and services as opposed to acquisition of specialized, complex, and partially defined capabili- ties--highlights the need for contract management as a recognizable function of the post-industrial economy.

COMPARING EXPEDITING AND CONTRACT MANAGEMENT SUBSYSTEMS

Chart 1-1 summarizes and compares the expediting subsystem with the post-award contract management subsystem. Both are subordinate to the overall external sourcing system which is commonly managed by a purchasing or procurement organization. The success of contractual action is strongly influenced by post-award management regardless of the attention initially given to it by senior management. Current trends associated with external sourcing, such as emergence of just-in-time man- ufacturing and reemphasis upon competition as a public policy theme, tend to mask distinctions highlighted in chart 1-1. While expediting and con- tract management activities tend to be indistinguishable at the margin, the concept of expediting and the concept of contract management stand at opposite ends of a spectrum of activities and involvements that follow contract award. When properly applied either subsystem becomes critical to the success of the sourcing decision.

The expediting subsystem is well understood and regularly practiced pursuant to purchase and delivery of externally supplied products. It commonly requires establishment of a system of records (suspense files) and follow-up actions to remind suppliers of their delivery obligation. The follow-up actions are largely confined to postal, telegraphic or tele- phonic contacts designed to elicit status information and to express con- cern regarding performance. Emergence of critical problems may cause expediters to visit facilities of supply sources and, occasionally, to bring pressure on delinquent performers.

The contract management subsystem is different. Managers become involved. The buyer's contract administrator devotes substantial time and energy to learning the characteristics of suppliers. Nothing is ignored within the supplier's system that may be critical to successful fulfillment of procurement objectives. The post-award manager develops specialized tools for verifying progress, incurred cost, and conformity to specifica- tion. While chart 1-1 highlights the existence of two post-award systems, the characteristics that determine the applicability of either are found in chart 1-2. Chart 1-2 formulates a framework for evaluation of an exter- nal sourcing question. It lists the key elements of the sourcing objec-

existence of two post award systems:

Chart 1-1
External Sourcing Methods

Gov.   *Proz. Mgr.*   *Contracts*

Acquisition System Qualities	Expediting Subsystem	Contract Management Subsystem
Goals and needs of buyer	Efficient goods production and distribution	Global competitive information based logistics system
Purchase method	Traditional purchasing support of marketing and production program	Proactive procurement participating in strategic planning with customer orientation
Post-award management method	Award Follow-up inquiries Schedule monitoring Delivery and acceptance Discharge	Post-award conference Information systems coordination Management systems verifications Fulfill objectives Adjust systems and schedules

Chart 1-2

**Comparison of Contract Management
and Expediting Systems**

characteristics that determine applicability:

Post-Award Management System Requirements

Elements of Concern	Expediting System	Contract Management System
Timing of work	Product defined and/or complete at time of award	Performance of work, including job definition, continues after award of contract
Job definition	One party defines and/or controls product	Buyer/seller interaction to define, design, specify, and control product
Terms and conditions	Standard provisions relatively simple	Provisions selected to match and control the business relationship throughout period of performance
Interaction	Minimal contact between parties during performance	Administrative arrangements tailored to facilitate interaction between buyer and seller for entire period of performance
Joint objectives	Limited or defined: delivery and acceptance	Strong commitment to the jointly defined result; success objective dominates action
Independence	Parties are fully independent	Parties conceptually independent, but they subordinate conflicting goals to joint objectives
Information flow	Encompasses defined information and data transfer	Maximum flow of information includes technical progress, problems, funds, schedule, need for system adjustments, etc.
Effects of error	Falls on party that creates the error	Adverse impacts likely to be split; source of errors often mixed

tive together with a description of the characteristics that require a simple expediting procedure and those that require a full-fledged contract management process. The level of follow-up activity actually established for a specific procurement is based on the manager's assessment of the need for inter-organizational involvement. This is not fixed but will vary with the nature and criticality of the end objective.

OBJECTIVES OF CONTRACT MANAGEMENT

Industry and government have come to rely on contracting for significant undertakings because the contracting system concentrates the performer's attention on meeting organizational objectives without creating irreversible commitments to work force and facilities. Instead, activities are performed in accordance with a specification or work statement contained in the contract, and work is done under the overall direction of the buyer but in accordance with the parties' agreement on management and business conditions. Overall direction does not include supervision or direct management by the buyer. Consequently, the level of involvement between the performer and the sponsor is defined contractually yet invariably contains ambiguity concerning roles and authority. These matters are formulated as a function of the terms and conditions of the contract. They are controlled by the agreement and are vital to creating long-term business relationships. Contracts often require significant sums of money and involve complex work that is critical to the sponsor's (buyer's) overall program.

Contract administration applies to a broad spectrum of undertakings from purchase of nuclear power plants by public utilities to construction of all kinds of lesser facilities. It is applicable to production, research and development, most service contracts, and to nearly all purchases that call for performance effort to begin after award of the contract. Project size, in the absolute sense, is not a criterion for application of contract management, although size relative to total operations may be an important element in staffing the effort. High levels of complexity and significance to overall buyer objectives are key factors that mandate application of the discipline. But it is not only the buyer who is concerned with contract management. The discipline is vital to the interests of suppliers. In summary, the objective of contract management as a discipline is to provide a practical way for top management to establish a definable level of control over operations it sponsors but assigns to an external source to be fulfilled. The post-award subsystem is central to this objective.

Definition of Post-Award Contract Management

Activities generally referred to as post-award contract management may be defined as the set of techniques, policies, and practices through which parties to a contract seek to ensure that specific work that has been assigned for performance by one party (an independent entity) is progressing and will be accomplished in accordance with the established agreement between the involved organizations. The goal of the contract manager is to ensure that performance meets objectives which are definable in terms of three categories of measurement: performance, schedule, and cost. These measurements are expressed with varying degrees of precision in the contractual arrangement.

Relationship of Procurement to Post-Award Contract Management

While post-award activity follows the award of a contract, it is not independent of the buying process. It imposes important considerations on the procurement planner because post-award issues and overall effectiveness are strongly influenced by decisions leading to contract award. It can be argued that post-award management is one phase of the procurement process, but the techniques, decisions, skills and knowledge required during post-award administration are different from those leading to solicitation and award. Whereas the procurement manager reduces expectations to agreements, the contract manager oversees and directs translation of agreements to products, schedules to deliveries, and misunderstandings to settlements.

Contract arrangements have many variations and applications, but this book treats only those transactions under which performance of necessary tasks occurs subsequent to execution of the instrument. For example, the ordinary purchase order, including follow-up to ensure delivery, is a substantially different type of action, even though in a legal sense contracts and purchase orders are similar. Although purchase orders may involve large sums of money, they are normally used to acquire existing products and services, or ones built to designs defined and produced by the supplier without detailed instruction or specification by the buyer. The ordinary implication of the contract differs in that the necessary effort is initiated by the agreement, and the buyer specifies or controls substantial aspects of the end result.

Size plays a part in determining the scope of post-award administration. Procurement involving large dollar commitments warrants the close attention of both parties, including daily monitoring. The buyer seeks an efficient information flow between the parties that allows its top management to participate in key decisions. The seller seeks to protect internal systems from excessive interference. An effective contract management system provides a framework that enables the parties to resolve these conflicting objectives. This seldom occurs without tension. Senior management of both buyer and seller retain responsibility for successful use of resources, but their perspectives differ substantially concerning the direction of work and application of resources. The many issues on which buyer and seller perspectives differ are addressed throughout this book.

Contract management, viewed as a function distinct from expediting work, is consistently practiced in procurement of facilities construction, services, research and development, and production of equipment or material when design is buyer controlled. It is a vital function whenever qualitative matters govern acceptability of performance and are subject to judgments made subsequent to initiation of work.

The skills needed for post-award management vary with the nature of the procurement, but skill in coordination and negotiation is always required. The administrator's knowledge of the underlying contract work is secondary to knowledge of contract terms, business relationships, and customer expectations. The range of knowledge essential to successful administration usually requires a team approach. The area of construction provides an example. The first major phase of a construction program employs a contract to procure architectural and engineering work (a service) to create the form and design of the project. Architectural and engineering work may be followed by a contract for construction, or the sponsor may approach the project using a construction management concept. Throughout these phases of work, the owner (buyer) interacts with the contractor to verify that the design and arrangements to which he is committing resources are in accordance with the intended program. In cases where a construction manager is placed under contract by the owner, overall responsibility for interaction with the construction firm and for related subcontracting is delegated to the construction manager. At each level throughout the entire effort, sponsor and performer are independent entities joined by a contractual relationship in an undertaking to create a structure that can be relied upon to meet owner objectives. The total system that may evolve is almost impossible to fully define prior to initiation of the contract.

Role of the Supplier in Post-Award Management

The practice of contract management tends to be viewed as a concern of buying organizations. This is misleading. The supplier is equally concerned with the progress being achieved. In many ways the performing organization is more involved and concerned with status, performance, and expected completion than the buyer. The performing organization has committed manpower, skills, energy, and managerial expertise to the successful performance of the contract (often to many contracts concurrently) and is intimately concerned with the effect of variations and problems on its own internal structure--its own people. The supplier's post-award administrator is therefore committed to act as an interface between internal personnel and buyer personnel as well as a coordinator of internal activities. Proper interpretation of contract terms for internal application (including, in part, preparation of internal work orders) may be the most critical job expected of the administrator by supplier management. This requires ability to understand and regularly assess performance in relation to contract obligations.

Regardless of the position from which it is viewed--as buyer, seller, or observer--effective post-award administration strongly influences the success of undertakings that are significant to the mission and well-being of both parties. Contracting personnel, pre- and post-award, are responsible for negotiations that establish or modify working arrangements under which the contracting parties must collaborate and exchange information. Complexity is introduced by perceptions of the separate interest groups as they formulate and execute cooperative activities. The special significance of contracting as a management discipline is rooted in the depth of involvement of one party in the affairs and the managerial processes of the other.

When a formal contract calls for actions at the supplier's facility to properly measure and assess performance and provides rules for making adjustments to the agreement, the buyer tends to become concerned with the internal management capabilities and systems of the performer. The performing party should be equally concerned and should seek to reassure his customer. Each party is concerned with the internal preferences and attitudes of the other and with the working relationships among all participants in the overall effort. The interactions between buyer and seller may best be described as delicate. Regardless, they are critical to contract success.

Much effort has been expended to develop in contracting personnel a sensitivity to working relationships as well as contractual rules and obligations. This is true for agreements between private parties and applies to acquisition programs sponsored by government agencies such as DOD, NASA, or DOE. Differences are found between private and public contracts primarily because public reaction to examples of error or improper contracting actions has generated substantial friction and controversy. While private sector contracting is not subject to the same level of public oversight concerning propriety of its actions, sensitivity to the rights of the other party is critical. Appropriate accommodation of internal practices to the needs of the contract is the hallmark of good post-award management, regardless of the program or parties involved.

GOVERNMENT CONTRACTS: THE GENESIS
OF CONTRACT MANAGEMENT SYSTEMS

Contract administration has developed a substantial track record as a management function among companies that deal with agencies of the United States government. This is a consequence of the nature of government purchases (research, development, services, construction, major systems) and the precision and detail contained in the terms and conditions of government contracts. Government regulations contain several thousand contract clauses and variations of clauses. This vast collection contains precise rules, policies, and procedures designed to protect the public interest or to express public policy in all manner of contractual circumstances. Chart 1-3 provides some insight into the topical areas covered by these terms and conditions. The high level of detail exists because the government enters into contracts with every industrial segment of the economy and sponsors many large and relatively undefined projects for which administrative action extends beyond the traditional expediting work associated with ordinary purchase orders.

In recent years, the need has increased for industrial buyers to participate in contract administration because they are purchasing technologically new products and services, because the technologies are constantly changing, and because of the critical scheduling needs imposed by movement toward just-in-time (JIT) production. Nevertheless, practices in the field have been strongly influenced by operations of the government. Many government programs can be performed only by contracting with industry and require large investments in technologically driven work, employing long-term business relationships. Whether sponsored by public or private funds, such programs require contractual coverage that supports interaction between the parties during performance and facilitates adjustment of the agreement to meet changing circumstances. In the case of contracts in which there is substantial, direct, post-award interaction between purchaser and supplier, the experience of government may exceed that of industry and has clearly established a much more complete record of practices employed.

Many government agreements use various forms of incentive and other cost-based types of contracts. This ordinarily has been done when it does not appear that the work is well enough defined to assign performance risks to the supplier. In addition, use of these forms of contracting provides a greater level of flexibility in direction and coordination during performance than using the traditional format of the firm-fixed-price contract. The terms and conditions associated with these types of arrangements mandate extensive post-award oversight by the government as a means of protecting the public interest. One should not be misled, however; this need for oversight activity is not unique to the government. All buyers whose contracts involve complex, long-term arrangements or critical dependence on their suppliers protect themselves by becoming involved in the technical and business management decision-making of their suppliers. Nevertheless, government has led in developing comprehensive clauses and staff capabilities for this purpose.

Once a contract is established on any basis other than firm-fixed-price, the parties must share responsibility for successful performance. Nominally, the supplier retains full control of his work force and other resources. Nevertheless, the buyer's interests cannot be divorced from decisionmaking because the buyer's budget is impacted by the supplier's decisions. Greater insight into these interactions will be gained throughout this book, especially in chapter 11 where financial administration of contracts is addressed in detail.

Government contracts have many characteristics that emphasize the importance of post-award management. As indicated by chart 1-3, a principal characteristic is their complex and sophisticated terms and conditions. With many years experience and substantial legal and contractual personnel resources at its command, the government has developed and refined its contract clauses and related policies and regulations to reflect the myriad situations it has encountered. The process of refinement continues unabated and seems to accelerate during times when revelations of inefficiencies or improper purchase actions are highlighted by the media.

Organizational factors (treated more fully in chapter 3) lend substantial credence to the assertion that government practices are the genesis of today's contract management systems. They are also indicators of some of the dysfunctional behaviors found in the system. Government contract administration operations are conducted worldwide, but its procurement capabilities for award of large dollar contracts are concentrated in key centers. Consequently, government organizations performing solicitation and award activities are geographically and organizationally separated from field administrative organizations. The following is a list of characteristics which may contribute to some of the difficulties encountered during post-award administration.

1. There are several independent field organizations.
2. Personnel resources are supplied by both military and civilian personnel systems.
3. Personnel performing contract management work are widely dispersed.
4. Some functional groups such as audit and investigative agencies operate as partially or completely independent entities.
5. Within contract management offices, certain groups such as quality assurance have adopted a posture of independence that affects coordination of the overall system.
6. Responsibility and authority for contract management action are divided between procuring and field organizations.

Chart 1-3

Scope of Terms and Conditions Used
by the Contract Manager

TERMS AND CONDITIONS APPLICABLE FOR ALL BUY-SELL ARRANGEMENTS (EXPEDITING OR CONTRACT MANAGEMENT):

- List and description of deliverable items
- Specification detailing character of deliverable items or statement of work for services
- Schedule for deliveries
- Price or other consideration
- Fund citation (government-sponsored contracts)
- Social/economic requirements (government-sponsored procurement)

ADDED TERMS AND CONDITIONS FOR CONTRACT MANAGEMENT:

- Rules to aid interaction between buyer and seller:
  - a. Method of ordering specification changes
  - b. Method of negotiating cost and schedule changes
  - c. Informal communication (technical direction)
  - d. Adjustment of delay (and evaluation of causes)
  - e. Securing approvals of work increments
  - f. Authorizing payments
- Rules to aid management systems reviews, analyses, and concurrence:
  - a. Security systems
  - b. Quality assurance or inspection systems
  - c. Accounting, estimating, and budgeting systems
  - d. Technical and schedule information gathering and summarization
  - e. Project organization and communication systems
  - f. Property management and control systems
  - g. Handling, delivery, and control of intellectual property
  - h. Purchasing and subcontracting systems
  - i. Progress and status information analysis systems
  - j. Reporting systems and definitions
  - k. Billing and costing systems
  - l. Engineering release and configuration management
  - m. Internal audit and control systems
- Rules to implement social and economic policy (government-sponsored procurement)
- Rules for securing special audit and inspection rights for buyer
- Rules for resolution of controversy, dispute

7. Contract management responsibility is divided between contract officials and project or technical officials in such a way that true decisionmaking power is difficult to pinpoint.
8. Technical administrators, administrative contracting officers, quality assurance personnel, audit personnel, procuring contracting officers, and other groups and offices essential to the administration of contracts frequently have little direct contact unless special arrangements are made.

Many other factors entering into the background of intensive government contract management will become evident in subsequent chapters. Regardless of these characteristics, it should be noted that the government has no monopoly on the concepts and practices associated with contract management.

FORMULATING CONTRACT MANAGEMENT RELATIONSHIPS

When organizing to accomplish contractual programs, one must consider work flow, personnel capabilities, and perceptual nuances within both the buyer's and seller's organizations. A major objective is to facilitate coordination and direction of essential work. Contract managers encounter an additional responsibility: they must assume responsibilities toward two independent entities--the buyer and the seller. It is not sufficient to perceive the organizational characteristics of only one contractual party. Suppliers employ entire staffs of contract administrators, as do buyers, and, while their overall objectives are similar, the assigned responsibilities are substantially different, and there is an inherent tension between the parties. We have already discussed their joint objectives--fulfillment of the obligations and duties encompassed by the contract agreement. While fulfilling joint objectives, the contract administrator has a primary obligation to learn to work with counterparts in his or her employer's organization, but this does not diminish the reality that success depends on the ability to work and coordinate with the other contractual party. The employer's interests and the administrator's position are advanced by cordial communications and cooperative actions as well as by performance of contract obligations. For the buyer the broad definition of success is on-time delivery of contract end items that comply with contractual specifications. For the seller this definition is slightly altered; success depends on timely performance of specified work acceptable to the buyer, and receipt of contractual compensation without delay. Cost factors--especially cost that varies substantially from the contract agreement--may alter the perception of success but are primarily a concern of the party that must fund the variance and even so, will be viewed as secondary. Implicit in these objectives is a set of specific duties and procedures that involve all levels and functions in the management spectrum. Chart 1-4 summarizes these duties.

A buyer's post-award contract administration structure is normally a subfunction under purchasing or procurement, but the manager is more directly concerned with progress in performing contract work and proper interpretation of performance in light of requirements. By contrast, the purchasing manager, working with a set of requirements, is more concerned with finding, qualifying, and attracting the interest of capable suppliers. In the simplest contractual relationship, a post-award manager's involvement with the supplier may be limited to accepting incoming deliveries and authorizing payment. Involvement increases one step if detailed inspection is required, and another step if follow-up and expediting communications are necessary. A giant upward step toward involvement occurs when on-sight visitation during performance is necessary. With fully developed long-term contract relationships, visitation gives way to residence at the supplier's facility. This is the normal condition when large and critical efforts are under contract, and its importance is increased when the work is technologically complex.

The administration of contracts may include a set of activities known as systems studies. Systems studies are activated without any necessary tie-in to specific contracts. They involve the buyer (government) in examining internal management capabilities and systems of the supplier (and potential suppliers). Systems studies may touch any of the normal subdivisions of a company. Examples--but by no means a complete list--include systems of accounting, estimating, compensation, procurement, quality assurance, property control, configuration control, budgeting, and scheduling. Corporate buyers may be reluctant to become involved in systems studies because they are costly and because suppliers may object, but when the government is the buyer, such studies are normal. There are few facets of an organization excluded from the reach of the post-award manager when circumstances warrant the expense and effort associated with the study.

CONTRACT MANAGEMENT AND CONTEMPORARY FUNCTIONS

Relationships between various management disciplines are becoming more complex and critical as our economy generates a larger variety of products and services. This variety is accompanied by greater specialization in management and business functions, but it has also increased the degree of overlap and the interdisciplinary nature of functional activities. This requires better coordination and has caused greater recognition of interdependence between functions. In response, many organizations have formed teams of management representatives charging them with responsibility for specified achievements and authorizing them to seek assistance from supporting fields of expertise and organizational functions. These teams respond to the need for direct communication among experts and enable organizations to operate with fewer levels of management. Whereas a few broadly defined departments have tradition- ally been considered adequate for the needs of most firms, large organi- zations adhering to that approach require multiple layers of management to cover all necessary subjects. A problem arises with such a structure whenever the knowledge base for effective workers expands. To function effectively, workers whose contributions are based on knowledge must have open channels of communication with those who are affected by or have an impact on ongoing work. Contract management is an informa- tion-dependent, multidisciplinary management function. It may be located in financial, legal, marketing, or purchasing departments but is able to perform effectively only if communication channels are open.

As with private companies, government agencies find it difficult to fill their requirements for personnel having the special knowledge, skill and attitudes needed by those who administer ongoing contracts. This difficulty may call for the government to reconsider recruitment and placement policies or to adjust the responsibilities assigned to post-award management personnel. All phases of contract administration demand an interdisciplinary orientation. Success requires the manager to develop, simultaneously, close working relationships with contemporary groups in his own organization and with those of the other party. With increasing variety and complexity of products and services, the manager is called upon to exercise independent thinking, yet fully coordinate actions to meet corporate goals. As a practical matter, this may call for use of a team arrangement. Contract issues impose on the team leader an obliga- tion to be fully prepared regarding long-term obligations and commitments as well as current problems and issues. This level of preparation requires thorough knowledge of contractual details and the precise concerns of all team members.

The post-award contract administrator may be independently respon- sible for contract monitoring or may work under a project manager. The work requires collaboration with each group and individual associated with the undertaking to ensure that contractual obligations will be met on time, and that action will be taken when necessary to resolve problems which may jeopardize that outcome.

MAKE OR BUY DECISIONS ARE CAUSING
GROWTH IN CONTRACT MANAGEMENT

The expansion of procurement since the 1940s affects the methods by which managers direct and control their projects. Procurement of work is quite different from the conventional purchase of products. The

Chart 1-4

CONTRACT MANAGEMENT SYSTEM POST-AWARD
RESPONSIBILITIES AND DUTIES OF MANAGEMENT GROUPS

Buyer (Government) Team Members

Contracting officer: (PCO, ACO, TCO), price analyst, audit, financial, legal	Program, project manager, technical officer, (COTR) and supporting disciplines
Provides contract and administrative leadership; coordinates and conducts post-award conferences; ensures participants understand requirements	Keynotes and promotes project at all levels in-house and among external support groups; provides leadership in technical and management areas
Coordinates in-house actions among central procurement, field offices, technical codes, audit and other units	Prepares and presents program and budget needs, including updates and revisions
Keeps informed of progress; notes and records events concerning technical, financial, and business matters	Maintains technical interface with user, contractor, field support activities
Takes contractual action on requests including subcontract consent, approval of specifications, test plans, data and report submissions, material reviews	Reviews and validates technical reports, specifications, test plans, drawings, etc.
Administers property and quality assurance programs; authorizes shipments, determines acceptance, authorizes payments	Maintains technical direction; verifies progress; evaluates proposals; controls configuration and testing programs
Requests, receives proposals; secures technical, audit reviews; prepares analysis of proposals; negotiates modifications	Secures, analyzes current data on incurrence of cost, schedule, revised work plans, and estimates to completion
Directs contract actions: specification changes, other modifications, compliance actions, sanctions	Reviews, controls technical actions: engineering change proposals, waiver and deviation requests, schedule adjustments
Seeks to maintain integrity of the contractual relationship	Carries responsibility for meeting program objectives

Chart 1-4 (Continued)

CONTRACT MANAGEMENT SYSTEM POST-AWARD
RESPONSIBILITIES AND DUTIES OF MANAGEMENT GROUPS

Supplier (Contractor) Team Members

Project, program manager, supporting staff and functional disciplines	Director of contracts, contract administrator/manager
Provides technical and managment leadership; manages and controls work force; directs, adjusts budget, schedule actions, work replanning, etc.	Supports marketing effort by consultation and negotiation; provides contractual and administrative leadership during post-award operations
Prepares, has prepared: reports of technical, budget, schedule status; specifications; test plans	Prepares work authorizations; coordinates pre-performance conferences
Coordinates with, meets customer needs; assesses progress; evaluates problems; corrects for deficiencies	Ensures preparation and timely delivery of submittals: specifications, test plans, technical and management reports
Responds to requests for engineering change proposals, revisions of funding, cost estimates, and schedule	Ensures that internal charges, pricing, costing, and schedules comply with contract; secures timely payments; coordinates customer visits
Seeks new business through change, identification of needs	Secures subcontract consent, waiver, change order action, other approvals; observes cost, schedule agreements, etc.
Directs work force toward meeting contractual obligations; ensures work performed complies with requirements	Establishes and maintains system of documentation to capture and record all significant events and actions; negotiates modifications
Meets profit and loss objectives and seeks to satisfy top management	Coordinates preparation and submission of engineering change proposals and proposals for equitable adjustments, etc.
Seeks overall customer satisfaction while protecting corporate interests	Ensures items offered for delivery meet contract commitments; obtains acceptance

broadened concept of procurement is that it provides an alternative method of performing any task. Research and development, diverse services, production, and construction are all eligible to be contracted out. Furthermore, management regularly decides to use outside organizations for key undertakings and does not limit purchase activity to acquisition of materials and parts for which in-house capabilities are not suited. The more critical purchases, however, are not bought with a standard purchase order. A higher degree of control by the buyer is essential when vital activities are to be entrusted to external sources. A comprehensive business relationship must be established, resulting in the writing of fully developed and uniquely designed contracts. Because of this, contract management has taken on special importance as one of the more recently developed management techniques.

The trade-off between internal and external sourcing is generally treated as the make or buy process. It is a standard and widespread procedure but one fraught with the pressures and concerns of affected groups and individuals. Many resist contracting out, including in-house labor groups, managers who want expanded roles and responsibilities, and individuals who prefer direct working relationships with counterparts. Nevertheless, economic advantages, and frequently the need for expertise unavailable internally, promote contracting out many business activities. Other pressures for contracting out have been the recent explosion of intellectually based products and services as well as computer and communications technologies, accelerated by the introduction of the microchip. Increasing diversity in our economy has made contracting an essential process in the competitive vitality of even the largest enterprises. Directing and controlling contractor performance without interfering in the contractor's managerial prerogatives is an art that challenges contract managers.

A SYSTEM IN SEARCH OF A THEORY

There exists today a paucity of research directed toward formulating the theoretical underpinnings of contract management. Academicians have not examined the subject in depth, although numerous books and articles have been published dealing with procurement. The existing literature emphasizes pre-award phases of organizational buying and materials management. Little attention is given to post-award managerial actions and perceptions associated with fulfilling expectations when subjected to the stresses of joining independent organizations to achieve difficult objectives. There are several plausible explanations for this lack of academic treatment. Perhaps one of the most important is that most challenges faced by contract managers are similar to those of managers in other disciplines. They have personnel, money, and schedule problems. They deal with investments and commitments that are at risk. So why set them apart for special study?

   This question doesn't lend itself to easy answers, but a few suggested lines of inquiry may be appropriate to introduce the subject. Much of what distinguishes contract management from other disciplines is perceptual. A contract creates legally binding agreements on how to proceed when change, delay, or failure arise. The agreement leaves each party with a vested interest in the method of accommodating or adjusting to these developments. The process of establishing the agreement through technical and price competition with other parties often leaves participants suspicious of their contract partner. Each assumes that the other party seeks an advantage or wants to escape some key element of his overall commitment. These perceptions are reinforced by communications restraints imposed during pre-award phases when competitive processes are designed to preserve objectivity. Attempts to be fair impede the flow of information. After award, the flow is impeded for different reasons. The parties now want to manage their own problems and avoid disclosing deficiencies that may be overcome internally or that may imply error or omission. These concerns are amplified in proportion to the sums at risk. They exist in both parties--buyer and seller.

   Another consideration is that contract managers are committed to mediating relationships between organizations. This commitment causes them to see issues from a perspective not evident to others within their own organization. A third consideration is the involvement and influence of management groups, such as project managers, engineers, and production managers, whose work is not viewed as contract management, yet whose goals are achieved through the contract. These factors inhibit formulating a consensus on the conceptual basis for contract management work. For example, engineers and scientists are oriented toward identifying with their disciplines, as are logisticians and managers of physical distribution, production, inventory control, and material. Persons in each of these fields of management activity tend to view their work as the center stage for management action. Additionally, functional group managers tend to view their field of activity in terms of its end result and procurement and contract management as support activities. Little thought is given to the factors that cause their dependence on these support activities. For example, the industrial purchasing people appear to be reluctant to adopt, as descriptive of their field, any characterization other than one headed by the word *purchasing*. Managers charged with responsibility for end results are reluctant to accept the concept that their work is essentially a contract management function, even though they recognize that achievement of those results must be through contractually defined procedures. These perceptions of various interest groups reflect educational background and attitudes and need not be dysfunctional.

A more fully developed theory of contracting, in the author's view, would benefit all groups working in the field. An important step toward such a theory would be to identify and reach a consensus on what constitutes the core function that contract management addresses. As indicated earlier, some direct relationship exists between longer term, larger dollar, and technologically complex undertakings and the need for a contract management discipline. Nevertheless, the earlier discussion does not provide a clear understanding of the conceptual framework within which the contract manager must work. Chart 1-2 suggests several elements of such a framework.

Another approach is that advocated by the Detroit Edison Company. For them, contract administration is a set of specific skills to be organized into training packages. The training packages become obligatory for those who are chosen to be construction supervisors. They apply this approach to many projects in addition to construction and have found it works. Their approach achieves a blend of the basic knowledge of industrial contract management practices with construction, engineering or other skills.

Other contributions to the formation of a framework for analyzing contract management are emerging. Two articles published in the *Proceedings* of the 1985 Federal Acquisition Research Symposium address the subject of formulating a consistent theory of contracting and acquisitions management. One of these articles by Williams and Arvis[1] contends that the establishment of a contracting science would allow for a systematized approach to gaining contracting knowledge and insight. The authors strongly advocate the use of scientific method in studying the contracting process and highlighted the tendency for contract research to be based on anecdotal material and essays with little use of empirical information. They argue that this kind of research generates a limited credibility. The authors also seem to believe that only through studies based on scientific method can basic truths and understandings about the contract discipline be developed.

A second article in the same proceedings by Waelchli[2] advocates establishing a sound theoretical basis for systems acquisition management. He attempts to apply Stafford Beer's 1966 organizational model (the "Self-Vetoing Homeostat") to the defense systems acquisitions process. Dr. Waelchli's article defines the core subject of his theoretical model in a specific and limited way. He adopts the special case of

---

[1]Williams, Robert F. and Arvis, Paul F., *Proceedings*, 1985 Federal Acquisition Research Symposium, Fort Belvoir, Virginia.

[2]Waelchli, Fred, *Proceedings*, 1985 Federal Acquisition Research Symposium, Fort Belvoir, Virginia.

acquisitions sponsored by the Executive Branch of the government, funded by the Congress, and executed through a contractual relationship with industry, as the generic model to which research should be addressed. This definition of a core subject area may be too limiting in scope to be of theoretical interest.

There is a more general fundamental process around which a framework may be developed that has theoretical significance to the economic and behavioral concerns of the acquisition community. It is defined in a less exclusive way, centering on the organizational buying process. Acquisition, after all, is a generic function throughout all economies regardless of the basic structure--whether free or controlled. Some systematic studies have been completed in the area of buyer behavior by personnel essentially concerned with the marketing equation. For example, the Webster and Wind model[1] carefully analyzes the behavior of buyers in the organizational context of a purchasing function sponsored by a corporate environment. The acquisitions process sponsored by the government, particularly the acquisition of defense products from industrial sources, has been analyzed by Peck and Scherer,[2] Danhof,[3] Fox,[4] and Gansler.[5] Of course it is fraught with some unique political and perceptual dimensions not present in the normal corporate purchasing process. These special circumstances do not alter the fundamental equation within which the contracting parties operate.

Particularly from 1981 to 1985, one of the factors which has stimulated concern for a better theoretical foundation for procurement work is the rising level of public criticism and apprehension focused on our government systems acquisition process. Although much of the criticism may be stimulated by the politically unpopular diversion of national resources into the defense sector, this series of revelations and pressures is keenly felt by the participants in government contract operations. The

---

[1]Webster, Frederick E. Jr. and Wind, Yoram, *Organizational Buying Behavior* (Prentiss-Hall, Englewood Cliffs, New Jersey, 1972).

[2]Peck, Merton J. and Sherer, Frederic M., *The Weapons Acquisition Process* (Harvard University, Boston, Massachusetts, 1962).

[3]Danhof, Clarence H., *Government Contracting and Technological Change* (The Brookings Institution, Washington, D.C., 1968).

[4]Fox, J. Ronald, *Arming America* (Harvard University, Boston, Massachusetts, 1974).

[5]Gansler, Jacques S., *The Defense Industry* (The MIT Press, Cambridge, Massachusetts, 1981).

rising level of concern has resulted in significant new statutory enactments and extensive regulatory modifications aimed at improving or
correcting perceived errors and deficiencies. This situation has caused
contract managers, project managers, and procuring officers of the
government as well as their counterparts in industry to be concerned with
the apparent lack of a framework and a theoretical conception of the
nature of their work. Most of these participants in the contracting
process believe that the government's system is very well managed and
extremely efficient and honest when viewed objectively. They are most
disheartened when, on a routine and daily basis, they are bombarded with
news reports and public statements which seem to say that the processes
in which they are engaged are at best, wasteful and deficient or at
worst, fraudulent and criminal. It is true that a significant proportion of
this criticism is justified by the public interest in achieving efficient and
economical expenditure of taxpayer dollars. However, the perception of
many practitioners in the field of government contracting is that the
criticism and corrective measures are causing the process itself to be
more expensive, less efficient, and less capable of producing and delivering the products, commodities, and services necessary to successful
operation of the government. With particular emphasis on the needs of
the Department of Defense, this potentially dysfunctional pathway could
be disastrous for the national defense effort. A better, more broadly
understood theoretical framework for executing procurement and contract
management activities could lead to greater public acceptance and understanding of the nature of both public and private acquisitions.

SUMMARY

Our purpose in chapter 1 has been to capture interest in the field
of contract management and to highlight its relationship to other management functions and to top management. Several points are covered.

- The similarities and differences between an expediting subsystem and a
  contract management subsystem, including discussion of the circumstances under which each is needed
- A definition of post-award contract management and comparison of the
  work with that of expediting and procurement
- The need of both supplier and buyer for a post-award contract management subsystem
- The relationship between pre-award and post-award managers
- The important role of government in developing and defining the scope
  of post-award management action
- As illustrated in chart 1-4, a summary of the specific, similar, yet
  clearly distinguishable work and responsibilities of buyer and seller

contract managers
● The need for people with a more broadly based theoretical understanding of the field.

TOPICS FOR DISCUSSION

1. Discuss the factors which have expanded the need for effective contract management subsystems.
2. What differentiates between an expediting and a contract management subsystem?
3. Explain the important similarities and differences between purchase orders and contracts.
4. Government has strongly influenced the development of post-award contract management. Discuss the reasons for this assertion.
5. Distinguish between the roles of technical managers and directors of contracts in the supplier organization.
6. What are the reasons for characterizing contract management as an interdisciplinary field of work?
7. Discuss the need for research to more fully develop the theoretical foundation for contract management.

EXERCISE 1-1

FAR and UCC Research

Contract administrators should develop expertise in handling problems related to numerous post-award issues that routinely challenge their resourcefulness. Although for many years post-award actions have been performed regularly by private and public sector personnel, the development of expertise is impeded by the lack of any standard reference to which all practitioners might refer for guidance and explanations. There are many diverse sources of information but only two that, individually, may be considered indispensable as resources for the contracting world. They are the Uniform Commercial Code (UCC) and the Federal Acquisition Regulations (FAR). When taken together, these sources approach the status of a standard reference of great value.

This exercise is designed to acquaint the student with those major portions of the UCC and the FAR that pertain to post-award contract management actions. Either of these documents may be purchased, but for purposes of this exercise, the student is advised to use library sources. The UCC, as prepared by The American Law Institute and National Conference of Commissioners on Uniform State Laws, may be found in *Uniform Commercial Code*, 1978, Official Text (Philadelphia, PA:

The American Law Institute, 1978). It may also be found in other reference works in law or major general reference libraries. The FAR is published jointly by the United States Department of Defense, the General Services Administration, and the National Aeronautics and Space Administration under authority established by the Office of Federal Procurement Policy Act of 1974, as amended. New issuances under the FAR system are published in the Federal Register. In addition, the FAR is published in cumulated volumes of the Code of Federal Regulations (softbound volumes) and in loose-leaf form. These sources may be purchased from the Government Printing Office but should be found in law and most research libraries. In addition, the Commerce Clearing House *Government Contracts Reporter*, available at law libraries and major research libraries, contains the complete FAR. The *Reporter* is a nine-volume loose-leaf service updated regularly.

Using any available source, find each of the following sections of the UCC and the FAR. Write a two- or three-sentence description of each assigned section. Prepare to advise your supervisor or class how you interpret the similarities of, and differences between, the two sources (UCC and FAR). Note: These assigned sections of UCC and FAR are selected; they do not constitute a comprehensive listing respecting any of the topical areas.

Exercise 1-1 (Continued)

UCC		FAR	
Topic	Section	Topic	Sub Part
Applicability	2-104	FAR system	1.1
Offers	2-205	Solicitations and offers	14.2, 14.3 15.4
Acceptance of offer	2-206 2-207	Awards	14.4, 15.6
Oral contracts	2-201	Authority, informal contract	1.6 50.3
Inspection	2-316(3)	Quality	46.2, 46.6
Payment	2-512	Payment	32.5
Breach	2-713	Termination	49.1
Warranties	2-313 2-314 2-315	Warranties	46.7
Accept/reject goods	2-607	Accept/reject	46.5
Care of goods rec'd.	2-601 2-602	Property	45.5

2

Contracting: Objectives, Image, and Ethical Behavior

The principal objective of post-award contract management should be to satisfy the expectations of customers. This objective is similar to that of the materials and purchasing system of which post-award management is a part. The customer may be internal (for example, in corporate contracting, a distribution manager in need of new vehicles) or external, such as an industrial consumer, a wholesaler or final consumer. The customer's position is unimportant if the system is successful because his needs will be satisfied. The important point is that objectives should be identified from the perspective of the customer--the individual or group whose activities depend on the products and services being produced. Customer interest is focused on a product or service that is produced on time, functions properly, and complies with cost expectations. Customers indirectly sponsor the contracting system but have little knowledge of it and seldom take an interest in it. Nevertheless, customers expect their needs to dominate the business systems of suppliers, including contract operations. Whether the post-award manager is employed by buyer or seller, satisfying these expectations is his or her proper objective.

Contract administrators tend to overlook the end objective of providing exemplary service to customers even though they have an integral part in creating the service. But post-award managers are twice removed from the customer. Although recognized as members of the procurement team, their responsibilities are acquired after the contract is formulated by the procurement manager. The procurement manager is already once removed from the customer by top managers, sales, or program managers whose charter is overall system delivery. This posture in relation to the customer is not unique for contract administrators. It is similar to the position of most functional management groups. It differs because contract actions are not merely advisory; post-award managers ensure delivery of service or product and, when necessary, may intervene to stop delivery.

In this chapter, we will concentrate on the relationship between the objectives and the image of contracting. Contracting objectives need clarification, and its image can be improved. The relationship between objectives and image is important to contracting practitioners' sense of identity, i.e., how they perceive of their contributions to success and the reception afforded these contributions by their contemporaries. We will also discuss ethical questions because they are fundamental to the concept of identity and are a problem for contracting managers, influencing the image of the function and the behavior of incumbents. Finally, we will examine recent moves in government to reduce the incidence of unethical conduct by imposing burdensome and (when indicated) punitive requirements on persons and companies involved in public contracting. These measures are also oriented toward reducing costs by eliminating certain categories of expenses from those that the government is willing to reimburse.

ADOPTING THE SERVICE-TO-CUSTOMER ORIENTATION

The concept of service to customers may be embraced by all organizations, public and private, and can be profitably assimilated by members of each functional management group. If managers at all levels and within each discipline, including contracting officers, purchasing agents, and contract administrators, adopt this as their primary goal, it will help them to maximize their achievements by encouraging optimization and reducing excessive concern over functional details. Focussing on broader objectives reorients the performance of functional duties to more fully meet customer needs. Adopting this concept before all others will lead to a favorable, forward moving purchasing organization.

The history of management reveals differential treatment of subordinate management functions by senior managers.[1] Some functions have been favored with greater attention, talent, and resources, while others have been ignored. Finance, marketing, and engineering have captured superior access to the top centers of power; manufacturing and logistics functions have not. One cause of this differential treatment has been the

---

[1]Reck, Ross R., "Reinterpreting the Purchasing Function Into Corporate Strategy: Implications For Purchasing Performance," (*Proceedings*, Purchasing/Materials Management Research Symposium, Tempe, Arizona, March 6-7, 1986).

tendency of entrepreneurs to retain leadership and control over the
expenditure side of their businesses as operations expand, while turning
over to others responsibilities such as market development and finance.
For this reason, managers of the retained functions, such as procurement,
have been slow to develop strong leadership roles, thereby limiting the
scope of their relationships with owners and senior managers.

Management development in government has led to a similar stature
for logisticians in general and particularly for procurement and contracting executives.   During the early years after World War II, the government contracting officer "was in fact the procurement manager, the
engineer, the fiscal manager, and the logistician."[1] This was before the
rise of the project management concept during the 1950s.   Since then,
the specialization of funding, scheduling, accounting, and pricing functions, together with the explosion of scientific and technological knowledge, have forced the contracting function outside the mainstream of
action sometimes leaving it little leverage over performance, while other
management core groups assumed center stage in management decisionmaking.   Some realignment or balancing of this state of affairs may be
needed.   Through sourcing activities and actions to match performance
with commitments, purchasing and contracting functions enhance the value
of products.   But the potential of these activities and actions for maxi-
mizing the customer's benefit can be realized only by more fully integrating the operating knowledge of purchasing and contracting managers into
planning and strategy formulation.

IDENTITY PROBLEMS IN THE CONTRACTING FUNCTION

Because the need for post-award administration is a logical consequence of purchasing action, it has been given little independent attention by corporate managers. The functions performed are varied and
complex yet are subordinate to the planning and definition functions
essential to pre-award actions. As a result, practitioners have not
reached a consensus as to the common set of purposes essential to developing a sense of identity, enabling them to reach beyond immediate goals
to conceptualize their broader objectives as members of the corporate
family. These objectives must be compatible with their daily tasks and
yet enable them to contribute more fully to creating a strategy for
corporate success. While purchasing (or procurement) executives may
have achieved recognition for their contributions to strategy, the contract
administrator has not. Purchasing executives make their contributions in

---

[1]Freeman, III, RAdm. R. G., "Executive Comment," (*Contract
Management*, May, 1986).

two ways. First, they help convert objectives from broad concepts to workable plans of action. Their requirements for presolicitation documentation bring about the translation of mission statements and technical goals into concrete schedules and costs. Having secured procurable definitions of work, they move to create sourcing options--to locate, solicit, and qualify external sources for evaluation as competitive alternatives. These contributions have a broad impact on productivity and innovation, which benefits the economy as well as the enterprise. The post-award manager has an important complementary role because contracts involve two-party management. He or she contributes operational insights that are essential to successful management of contractual undertakings. This includes the ability to observe and act upon unanticipated as well as expected events and complications that arise as a unique product of two-party management. The post-award manager has the continuing responsibility of negotiation and accommodation essential to merge the effort of independent entities but has not been present at strategic planning councils in either government or corporate hierarchy. This situation should not continue.

An element in procurement executives' (including contract administrators) limited success at top management levels is their tendency to focus on actions to the exclusion of goals. They write justifications, analyze costs, react to schedules, and emphasize regulations. Strategic issues such as market trends, economic forces, development of sources, productivity gains, technological change and new information flowing across organizational boundaries fail to capture their attention.[1] While problems of identity are often viewed as perceptual problems, not practical ones, they impact the ability of managers to operate effectively.

An impetus to review the status of the procurement function and to bring about changes arose when shortages of basic resources surfaced in 1973-74 and again in 1979. The oil crises of those years highlighted awareness of supply vulnerabilities and captured senior management attention. More recently, productivity retrogression has surfaced in the United States, stimulating more pressure to reevaluate the effectiveness of our productive systems, including the roles played by procurement and contracting personnel. In addition, during 1981 through 1985, continuous publicity given to apparent and real deficiencies in defense contracting brought about policy changes that altered the government's approach to contract award and administration. Simultaneously, industry's attention to the advantages of just-in-time inventory and long-term contracting have increased the demand for more effective management of relationships

---

[1]An excellent study of these factors by Robert Spekman and Ronald Hill is reported in "Strategy for Effective Procurement in the 1980s," *Journal of Purchasing and Materials Management*, Winter, 1980, p. 2.

between buyers and sellers. The impact of these changes is only beginning to emerge at this time. The procurement professional needs to
consider this climate of change and the opportunity it presents to revamp
his or her image. Executives are challenged to pay attention to their
larger role in achieving society's objectives as well as organizational
success.

RESPONSIBILITY ASSIGNMENTS, IDENTITY, AND CONTRIBUTIONS OF THE CONTRACTING FUNCTION

Assignment of organizational authority and evaluation of performance
are responsibilities of senior managers. If this staffing function is well
done, organizational success should be enhanced. The senior manager
needs a good understanding of the competencies essential to excellent
performance by those selected to receive authority. Pre- and post-award
procurement functions have not been well understood as factors in
achieving success, even though general expectations regarding the work to
be performed by contracting people are consistent from organization to
organization. Their work includes well known technical and coordination
activities throughout the planning, solicitation, award, and execution
phases of contracts. Inadequate functional identity causes problems to
arise, not with respect to the formal assignment of duties, but in clearly
expressing the contributions that contract managers make, or should
make, to the larger needs of the organization. If all contracting policies,
procedures, justifications, negotiations, administrative actions and decisions and are grouped together, what do they mean? There is no easy
answer, but it is evident that the nature of the work expected of contracting personnel changes with the phase of work involved. Expertise in
finding and qualifying sources of supply and in stimulating both productivity and innovation through creative management of the procurement
system is central to the pre-award mission. Fulfillment of contractual
objectives through cooperative yet arms-length oversight and negotiation
is central to the post-award mission. The little understood challenge
presented by contracting work is the duty to objectively mediate between
the perceptions and interests of the manager's employer and those of the
other party. Accomplishing this effectively is indispensable in contracting
work.

Pre-Award Management

Many economists have concluded that economic welfare and improvements in living standards for society as a whole are contingent on productivity gains. These ends are recognized as desirable by most people,

and it is implicit in the work of all managers that they assume some responsibility for productivity improvement. Pre-award managers of procurement have a unique role in this regard. Their contributions include ability to advance competitive practices and to mobilize external, independently owned resources for application to organizational goals. Through these capabilities, powerful stimulus is given to economically aggressive behavior.

Competitive practices. In most organizations, the procurement executive is expected to rely on competition in acquiring materials and services. Taking advantage of competition is part of the culture of the profession; its use is ordinarily required by corporate policy, and it is mandated in government by statute and regulation. These factors imply that competition is important, but the societal objective of productivity improvement is the source of competition's vitality through which the buyer stimulates a greater level of efficiency and economy in the production of goods and services. The need for ideas, designs, and technology, rather than merely price advantage, frequently forms the basis for competition. Encouraging competition sometimes requires short term-source restriction based on recognized proprietary standing, technical know-how, or investment. It may also require specific up-front investment by the buyer. These special efforts should be oriented toward cost savings, consistent reliable performance, or encouraging innovative vitality. This is partially accomplished when the buyer protects investments and innovation (including those made by independent sources of supply) while continuing to develop new alternatives. The challenge is for the buyer to distinguish between valid competitive advantage and inappropriate source restriction. While the success of competitive practices is normally measured in terms of dollar savings, the existence of reliable alternative sources provides advantages for the buyer in stimulating quality and delivery compliance. Effective buyers stimulate existing as well as potential suppliers to search for more effective and efficient ways to perform future work assignments. The forcing mechanism for existing sources is the possibility of losing future business. The procurement professional is charged with creating and fostering that possibility while maintaining a consistent posture that excellent performance will result in continuing, profitable business. Consequently, he or she should consistently seek ways to introduce or maintain a competitive edge in the quest for an adequate base of sources. This requires attention to both price and innovation and an ability to adjust emphasis to support current goals.

Resource mobilization. Regardless of the gigantic size of contemporary corporate and government organizations, many are finding that in-house resources are no longer sufficient to meet demands. It is becoming essential to reach beyond internal capabilities for technology and materials. This is a consequence of the knowledge explosion and of emerging demand and competitive production in Third World countries. It has added to the need for new solutions to sourcing problems. Management is looking carefully at potential needs for external sources and discovering that they are far more complex than those satisfied by ordinary material and routine services. The need is for specialized capabilities, facilities, material, equipment, unique know-how, financial depth, and technological skills. In sum, organizations need a much larger mixture of items and services than the in-house reservoir can provide.

The increasing diversity in products, technologies, and systems forces managers in their role as strategic planners to consider alternative methods by which they can mobilize capabilities to meet their assigned mission. Through the contracting process, they have the power to bring together almost any capabilities needed to support their operations. Furthermore, procurement processes allow this to be done rapidly relative to other methods of gathering capabilities, such as expanded payrolls and investment or acquisition by merger, consolidation, and so forth. These latter approaches work well but involve greater commitment, less flexibility to deal with change as it occurs, and reduction of alternatives for future decisions. Contractual systems avoid these effects and through competitive practices, may reduce costs of performance.

While contractual systems offer the foregoing advantages, they also present difficulties. It is inherently more complex to purchase a capability than to assign work internally. Internal resources have a common employer. Their work may be more easily coordinated using the well understood rules of the master-servant relationship. For purposes of their organizational life, the members of the organization have no independent objectives (except personal achievement and recognition). In contrast, dealing with external sources for the performance of organizational objectives introduces competing independent entities each with its own set of organizational objectives. These include profit, work force integrity, growth, continued influence, and independence. The effort to preserve these independent objectives creates much of procurement's complex image.

This complexity arises for several reasons. In awarding a contract, it must be negotiated, and in negotiation all facets of the ensuing business relationship must be considered. In a fashion similar to investment decisions in general, contract award is based on expectations of future performance. The outcome is often far removed in time from the decision. The contract must provide a mechanism for identifying a host of future problems and establish a means of resolving them. It must delineate all of the buyer's objectives and tie them to schedules and dollars. The procurement professional and his contemporaries within the selling organization tend to be caught up in the process of working out the details. As a result, contracting offices have acquired the unfortunate image of policeman, one who can stop progress and who is viewed as likely to do so. This image can be changed if the contract manager clearly presents the objectives and advantages of competitive practices. Articulation of these factors is an integral part of his or her role.

Post-Award Management

Contract managers hold responsibility for post-award actions and success in a manner that is analogous to that of product and project managers. (In industry this work is generally assigned to a director of contracts or a contract administrator; in government it is assigned to contracting officers.) Contracts are similar to programs in several ways. Both have a defined beginning and ending, a stated output, specified budget, stated schedule, and a method of measuring completion. These characteristics, along with business terms and conditions, are present for each contract, even those that are relatively small in value. The contract manager's job is to ensure that performance meets these parameters. Technical objectives are varied and range widely in magnitude. Many undertakings require the support of multiple contract actions. Management issues vary with personalities, budget, external interest in results, and the skill and experience of managers.

Contract administrators experience a disadvantage in developing relationships with senior managers because, in place of adopting single-minded loyalty to their employer, they are called upon to promote the common interests of the parties in the contract. Their problems begin when the contract is awarded, at which point goals and overall strategy decisions are already made. Success and the validity of pre-award decisions are now intertwined. Emergence of deficiencies is unwelcome, yet it is the post-award contract manager's job to discern whether acceptable performance will occur, if not--why, and to determine and highlight the nature of the problems and solutions, regardless of fault, as early as possible. This role and the potential conflicts that arise for the manager are examined in this book. The coincidence of common and independent objectives of the parties demanding impartial judgments by persons employed by one party, may result in conflicts over decisions. This is most likely to affect the short-term interests of the parties. Many of the dynamics of this work will be described in the chapters that follow.

TRANSITION OF CONTROL FROM PROCUREMENT MANAGER TO CONTRACT MANAGER

As part of acquisition strategy, the procurement manager is called upon to create a sourcing system that will achieve specified objectives. At a minimum, the strategy should include an approach to obtaining alternative sources, ensuring effective and timely performance, finding methods for analyzing cost effectiveness, stimulating innovative behavior, and providing for reliability assessment. The system must then be operated so that program goals are met; goal achievement becomes the measure of managerial performance. A decision to employ an external source, however, limits the tools by which the procurement manager can control performance, because the procurement process assigns performance responsibility and managerial control to the external entity. On close examination, we find that the pre-award procurement manager does not determine mission or goals; they are established by general management. Consequently, in external sourcing, the procurement manager may find himself in an inherently risky position, holding responsibility for the key sourcing decision but having control of neither preceding nor subsequent action. The post-award manager is similarly positioned without control over decisions in earlier phases of strategy development and with only limited control of contractor performance. Nevertheless, the system works well most of the time.

The model that follows (figure 2-1) represents the managerial structure encountered within both public and private procurement. It tends to heighten risk for managers at each stage. In addition to the risk of making a poor decision, each manager can inherit, or be forced to accept, those made by others. For example, during pre-award phases the manager may (unintentionally) select an unworkable or suboptimizing strategy, select an unqualified or unmotivated contractor, or impose unrealistic commitments for actions during performance. These decisions may jeopardize program success. At each stage, the decisionmaker lacks authority respecting earlier or later stages of the process. Each manager tries to reduce these risks but has limited knowledge and inadequate power for control.

In addition to constraints imposed by internal transfers of authority, the right to manage and direct the executory part of a contract is assigned to the contractor. Independence in decisionmaking is one of the strengths of contracting--a strength not to be lost by unintended conversion into a master-servant (i.e., employer-employee) operation. This is important to the parties and especially important to the buyer who must recognize the independence of the contractor and forgo direct supervision or control over those performing the work. The contractor must be allowed to perform in accordance with the terms and conditions of the contract. Although the authority to review and make decisions or approvals of specific actions may be retained, the general power to manage is transferred to the supplier. Because of this, the procurement manager must, in addition to the scope of work, decide the level of control to be retained and any constraints to be imposed on the method of performance prior to contract award. These decisions must then be expressed contractually. Furthermore, the contract should clearly identify who will exercise any management controls retained by the buyer. This

Figure 2-1

Flow Chart For Transfer of Contracting Authority

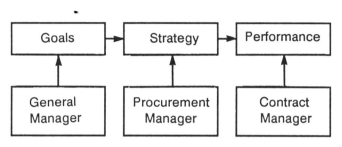

is particularly important in government contracting because several independent central and field offices may be interested in post-award decisions. Validation of the decisions remains uncertain until contract completion.

ETHICAL CHALLENGES AND PERCEPTIONS

Ethical behavior is a topic which has been treated systematically by many writers in theology and philosophy and cannot be fully addressed here. In general, individuals making decisions in business affairs, whether public or private, are expected to discern right from wrong and to consistently elect the proper course of action. In the following sections of this chapter, we will address the special pressures and complexities added by contract relationships. The sections examine recent codification of rules governing public procurement which have been designed to stimulate public reporting and to penalize infractions of correct ethical behavior.

Increased standards for making ethical business decisions are being demanded by Congress and by executive actions. These demands are not limited to public procurement. Indictments in the field of insider trading highlighted this general trend during 1986. The Levine indictment is illustrative of changing standards. It is an outstanding example because of its magnitude and the senior position of the defendant. The allegation concerned use of non-public information, partly obtained in the course of the defendant's role as a mergers and acquisitions expert in his investment banking firm, to garner an alleged profit of $12.6 million.[1] It can be argued that the indictment would not have been possible without the

---

[1]"Its War on Insider Trading," *Business Week*, May 26, 1986, p. 38.

extraordinary information gathering power of current day computers plus the commitment of substantial investigatory resources to ferret out the facts. This was followed by even larger insider trading revelations such as that of Ivan Boesky.[1] These cases are illustrative of public emphasis on initiatives to control white collar crime or abuse.

In federal procurement, initiatives by both the Executive Branch and Congress are seeking improvements through policy changes and investigatory practices that are less clearly beneficial and much more controversial than the insider trading actions. This point was made by Coleman Raphael, chairman and CEO of Atlantic Research Corporation at that time.[2] He pointed out that the Pentagon's hot line for reports of waste, fraud, and abuse received over 23,000 calls during a two-year period. Of these contacts, 7,000 inquiries were initiated and referred for action. One of the investigations produced a significant dollar savings ($800,000) which resulted from a change in an Air Force requirement for "hardening" a circuit. (No actual abuse or fraud existed.) The Inspector General's office claimed savings of $3.5 million from the hot line program over that same period. But as Raphael points out, 7,000 inquires could not have cost less than $200 each ($1,400,000), and telephone monitoring and answering could not have cost less than $50 each ($1,150,000). Consequently, the entire net savings from discovery of waste, fraud, and abuse produced by the highly touted hot line program was, at best, $150,000, not a very significant savings when arrayed against the Pentagon budget for two years.

Regardless of these kinds of results, ethical decisionmaking is essential to long-term success. A key to improvement is well designed, open channels for communicating to top executive levels instances of waste, fraud, and abuse and for objective and confidential examination of apparent improprieties. Approaches to this may include, for example, creating corporate board audit committees and selecting committee members from independent (outside) members of the board. If the committee is positioned so that employees have confidential access to its members, increased validity is lent to corporate assertions of high standards of conduct. In the public arena, hot lines and rules to protect whistle blowers may contribute as one means of surfacing unethical practices. However, the political and media processes examining public issues have a tendency to dramatize reports before the facts and implications are

---

[1]"Who'll Be The Next To Fall?" *Business Week*, December 1, 1986, p. 28.

[2]Coleman Raphael, "The Art of Demolishing World Trade," *Capital Ideas*. Presentations from the 70th Annual International Purchasing Conference, May 5-8, 1985. (NAPM, Oradell, N.J., 1985).

known. The process is similar to the media distribution of reports that 2,000 people were dead because of the Chernobyl nuclear disaster. Since the immediate toll of two persons (34 days later it had risen to 23)[1] was quite different, some legitimacy for confidential treatment, while facts are studied and implications reviewed, should be recognized as part of an ethical system.

Contract-Oriented Actions to
Improve Ethical Decisions

The following list summarizes actions taken during 1985 and 1986 that were intended to bring about more ethical decisionmaking by both government and private sector managers during government contract performance:

1. Increased staffing of audit and investigative agencies
2. Increased use of criminal sanctions in lieu of civil action in cost and pricing data cases
3. Increased certification requirements as a condition of obtaining payments under public contracts
4. Steps toward transferring the burden of proof to the contractor in cost allowability cases
5. Stringent restrictions on the right of former DOD employees to accept employment with DOD contractors
6. Increased reporting requirements for former DOD employees and their current employers
7. Encouraging and protecting *whistle blowers*

These actions were designed to increase the concern of government employees and contractors with the propriety of their actions and representations. They will cause contract management personnel of both parties to experience

1. a higher degree of exposure to investigative and audit surveillance,
2. greater risk of criminal prosecution for unethical business decisions,
3. detailed record keeping to support reporting,
4. reduced interest in competing for contracts with the government,
5. reduced interest in employment in government procurement and contract management positions.

----

[1]Bohlen, Celestine, "U.S. Doctor in Moscow Says Toll 23," *Washington Post*, May 30, 1986, p. A 25.

The actions undoubtedly will cause a more careful review of decisions for ethical implications and may reduce the incidence of misbehavior, but the amount of improvement will not be easy to measure. On the other hand, costs can be measured. They include increased study and review prior to submitting proposals; increased documentation to support claims and statements; new record keeping systems at agency, corporate, and individual levels to support reporting; loss of potential employees because of reduced future employability; and increased long-term institutional staffing of nonproductive activities for audit, employee counseling, investigation, and prosecution.

Perceptions that Compromise Ethical Standing of Contract Managers

Although the contract administrator's daily routine is filled with practical and usually urgent actions, managing ethical questions is a major challenge. Since contract management is a human system, the matter of ethical judgments is always present. Because there are two parties at interest in a contractual relationship, these judgments are easily misinterpreted and challenged. Daily administrative duties require personal contacts that can be seen as opportunities for exercising improper influence. For some outside observers, this may appear as a conflict of interest in making business decisions. Areas in which these temptations exist include compiling information for reports to the purchasing organization; preparing invoices; interpreting quality, technical and testing requirements; and deciding to blame the other party for events that may have caused delays, cost increases, or other adverse consequences. To illustrate the complexity of the perceptual problem, note that it is the responsibility of the seller's contract manager to ensure that all products offered for delivery and acceptance conform with the requirements of the purchaser in accordance with contract specifications. Many judgments in this area relate to questions in marginal technical areas and are not easily made, yet all are financially significant to both buyer and seller and especially to those responsible for successful task performance within the supplier's organization. Pressures to gain acceptance of end items in accordance with contract schedules are especially severe and are raised by the buyer's ultimate users, program managers, and contracting officers, and by the contractor's management team. Nevertheless, proper performance of the contract management task requires judgment in addition to systematic evaluation of the product in light of the contract's technical requirements. Questions arise even when both documentary and direct observations verify that the product is ready for delivery.

Chart 2-1 highlights contract management decisions from the buyer's perspective. It illustrates eight selected areas in which contract man-

Chart 2-1

Effects of Incorrect Decisions, Mistakes, and Unethical Behavior in Contract Administration[1]

Decision	Type A Mistake[2]	Type B Mistake[3]
Pay or withhold progress payment	Pay when refusal would stimulate better performance	Withhold when cash need is critical to performance
Disseminate or withhold information	Disseminate unnecessary information (generating cost for analysis work)	Withhold information needed for performance
Perform/omit in-process inspection	Omit when contractor quality assurance system is ineffective	Perform when contractor is adequately performing quality assurance
Accept or reject item	Accept without complete knowledge of compliance status	Reject a compliant product
Grant/refuse specification deviation	Grant when deficiency is unjustified or compliance is vital to program	Refuse when the need is validated and in interest of both parties
Grant/deny specification waiver	Grant when deficiency is unjustified or compliance is vital to program	Deny when history and necessity justify departure from specification
Direct/refuse technical direction	Direct when informality compromises control	Refuse when direction is essential to cooperation
Suspend/fail to suspend cost	Fail to challenge when allowability should be questioned	Suspend when payment is due and reasonable

----

[1]Regardless of which party is initially affected, erroneous decisions result in adverse cost, schedule, and/or performance effects on buyer and user (by means of the claims process in the case of type B mistakes).
[2]Type A mistake: initial adverse affect falls on buyer (government)
[3]Type B mistake: initial adverse affect falls on seller (contractor)

agers must exercise judgments which affect the financial and programmatic success of the parties. Mistakes occur continuously in these areas
because information is missing or inadequately analyzed. The chart
includes only ordinary decisions, made in good faith, to carry out responsibilities, but when error is recognized, it may be perceived as both
erroneous and unethical. It specifies two types of mistakes. The first,
type A, includes erroneous decisions with initial adverse effects on the
purchaser. Type B includes erroneous decisions with initial adverse
effects on the seller. The challenge in contract management is to avoid
mistaken decisions. Unfortunately, the differences between a correct
decision, a type A or B mistake, and an unethical decision are difficult to
perceive. The illustrated decisions require judgment concerning complex
factual circumstances and are difficult to classify. When challenged after
the fact they are even more difficult to justify.

Difficulties in assessing decisions reach beyond the question of the
contract manager's personal ethical behavior (and related gains and
losses). His decisions affect the image of his organization, of sponsoring
organizations, and of the organizations with which contracts are established. Most of the issues decided by post-award contract managers deal
with contract fulfillment questions affecting costs, prices, schedules, and
rights of the parties. Unfortunately, resolution of such questions reflects
upon decisions by others in the procurement process. Both economic interests and technical reputations may be jeopardized, causing all contributors to be concerned whether objectivity and forthrightness prevail.
Ethical questions can be raised in nearly all decisions involving interpretations of requirements, including design, quality and reliability,
accounting issues, property matters, data rights and patent rights questions, and other matters that affect the relative positions of parties to
the agreement.

Increased Use of Criminal Statutes
to Motivate Ethical Decisions

In 1982 publication of Gordon Adams' book *The Politics of Defense
Contracting, the Iron Triangle*[1] may have contributed to increasing apprehension in Congress and the press regarding ethical requirements. During
the years 1981 through 1985, a litany of public disclosures generally
implied that government contracts were subject to excessive failures of
confidence on the part of contractors. These disclosures have led to

---

[1]Copyrighted in 1981 by the Council on Economic Priorities, *The
Politics of Defense Contracting* was published by Transaction Books, New
Brunswick (U.S.A.) and London (U.K.).

stringent new measures designed to discourage improper behavior and to improve performance. Many new measures have found their way into legislative action; others have been taken by the Executive Branch, particularly the Department of Defense, which is the focus of much of the public criticism.

Broadened use of existing statutes has compelled greater attention to correctness of representations and certifications made by government contractors. These actions are pertinent to contractors' managers because they furnish required data, because the increased activity associated with verification and enforcement is post-award, because administrative expenses associated with the requirements are substantial, and because risk is heightened by the formality imposed on their judgments which must be recorded. By these measures, participants in public contracting have been subjected to increased oversight by audit and investigative agencies.

The government's attitude has changed toward certification and submission of data and information by contractors. Of the numerous categories of information and certifications, the cost and pricing data requirements are particularly important. It is a difficult area for contract managers because pricing data is associated with innumerable actions during administration of contracts and is broadly defined to include any factual information that could affect prices. Prior to 1985, virtually all cost and pricing data issues were handled under procedures codified under the Truth in Negotiation statute (10 USC 2306). Under that statute, no criminal penalties exist. As a result, if a contractor submitted defective data to the government, whether intentionally or by error, sanctions were limited to price reduction. No other penalty resulted. In an effort to increase pressure for better data submissions, the Executive Branch in recent actions has drawn on other statutory authority in addition to, or in lieu of, the Truth in Negotiation statute. These actions were based on one or more of the following statutes: the False Claims Act (31 USC 3729), the Criminal False Claims Act (18 USC 287), and the Criminal False Statements Act (18 USC 1001). Use of the statutes increases the exposure of contractors and their personnel who engage in unethical conduct. This form of inducement for managers to properly consider the accuracy and impact of their statements, representations, and certifications is summarized in chart 2-2. The impact of increased probability that government agencies would seek criminal sanctions for defective data on the basis of the false statements or false claims statutes is difficult to assess, but it has not improved the confidence of contractors. For the government, it increases the choice of sanctions. Because of the risk of greater penalties, it also increases the costs of defending against allegations of deficiencies regardless of outcome. These factors are important to both prime and subcontractor managers under government-funded programs.

Chart 2-2

Summary of Statutory Standards for Evaluating Statements, Data, Certifications, and Claims Under Contracts Issued by the United States

10 USC 2306	18 USC 1001	18 USC 287	31 USC 3729
Truth in Negotiations Act	**Criminal False Statements Act**	**Criminal False Claims Act**	**False Claims Act (Civil)**
Activated by submission and certification of data	Activated by making a statement	Activated by presenting a claim	Activated by presenting a claim
Certification no longer required; defective data tolls action	Concerns a matter within the agency's jurisdiction	Claim must have been made to the agency	Claim must have been made to the agency
The cost or pricing data must be shown to be defective	The statement was false and the party knew it to be so	The claim must have been false	The claim must have been false
The government negotiator must have relied on the statement for pricing purposes	Reliance on the statement is not a criterion	Whether the agency's action was based on the claim is not a criterion	Reliance on the claim is not a criterion for sanctions
Contract price must be shown to be higher because of the defective data	The statement must have had a material impact	Damages need not be proven to impose sanctions	Damages need not be proven to impose sanctions
Intent to defraud is not necessary to exact a price reduction	Intent to deceive (as indicated by knowingly making the statement) must be shown	Knowledge that claim was false or intent to defraud must be shown	Knowledge that claim was false or intent to defraud must be shown
Sanctions include interest for any period of overpayment and may include penalty equal to total amount of overpayment	Sanctions include $10,000 fine or five years or both	Sanctions include $1 million fine, five years or both	Sanctions total 3 times actual damages plus $2,000 per false claim and costs of litigation

LEGISLATIVE ACTIONS OF 1985

Several other procurement actions in addition to those taken by the Executive Branch under the false claims or false statements acts were made a part of Title IX of the Department of Defense Fiscal Year 1986 Authorization Act as adopted in Public Law 99-145. This legislation codifies behavior rules to dissuade practices that may appear unethical and strengthens the government's position in restricting payments for contractor expenses which Congress feels should not be paid as costs of government contracts. The new enactments increase the sanctions provided under both the civil and criminal false claims statutes. These current changes are reflected in chart 2-2, but continuing legislative concern assures further action.

The 1986 DOD Authorization Act introduced the following new policies:

1. Requires a report by uniformed or civilian government personnel who are employed in a *covered position* whenever they have employment-related contact with DOD contractors. A covered position is a position in a procurement function with a civilian grade GS-11 or military pay grade of 0-4 or higher that has any relation to
   a. the negotiation, award, administration, or approval of the contract;
   b. the selection of a contractor;
   c. the approval of changes in the contract;
   d. quality assurance, operation and development testing, the approval of payment or auditing under the contract;
   e. the management of the procurement program. (When such contacts occur, if not rejected, the employee must disqualify himself from participating in procurement relating to that contractor and initiate a report to the agency concerning the contacts.)
2. Imposes a penalty of imprisonment and fine if a presidential appointee, who acts as "a primary government representative" in negotiations or settlements with a contractor of the Department of Defense, accepts employment with the same contractor within a period of two years after the termination of those representation activities.
3. Modifies 10 U.S. Code by adding a new section 2324, which is designed to increase the government's leverage over its defense contractors. The section contains rules pertaining to cost allowability.
   a. Provides a criminal penalty (a fine) if a contractor knowingly includes unallowable costs in a proposal for settlement of incurred costs.

b. Requires DOD to issue new regulations that will specifically disallow any indirect costs from contractor settlement proposals that violate the applicable regulatory cost principles.

c. In addition to item b, requires the DOD to assess a penalty against the contractor equal to the amount of the disallowed costs plus interest accrued over the time of excess payment if the Secretary of Defense determines by clear and convincing evidence that the indirect cost is unallowable.

d. Requires the DOD to assess a penalty totaling three times the cost involved if the determination of the Secretary of Defense regarding unallowable indirect costs is made prior to the submission of the settlement proposal.

e. Makes specific costs unallowable under government contract reimbursement rules. These are costs associated with entertainment; the defense of civil or criminal fraud, if the contractor proves to be liable; any fines and penalties which the contractor must pay; the costs of lobbying; costs associated with alcohol, donations, promotional advertising, first-class air fare, dues, and gifts.

f. Constrains contracting officers' discretion by limiting their authority to settle contractor proposals concerning any costs included in the proposals that have been questioned by an auditor. The limitation requires a contracting officer to make settlement only after obtaining the opinion of the auditor and adequate documentation from the contractor regarding those costs.

g. Requires contractors to submit, along with their settlement proposals, a new certificate to the effect that the indirect costs are allowable to the best of the certifier's knowledge and belief.

h. When making settlements of questioned costs, requires contracting officers to reflect the amount of the specific individually questioned costs that will be paid under the settlement agreement.

i. Subjects requests for payment of costs to the criminal and/or civil penalties of the false claims acts, if the requested payments are for costs that are expressly unallowable under the procurement regulations.

4. Provides a modification of 10 U.S. Code 2313 by adding a new authority for the Director of the Defense Contract Audit Agency to subpoena the papers or the records of a contractor concerning matters under study by the agency. This authority is limited to those kinds of records to which the Secretary of Defense is entitled under 10 U.S. Code 2313(a) or 10 U.S. Code 2306(f).

5. Requires interest to be assessed for the period of overpayment when, under a DOD contract, overpayment is made that is caused by

submitting inaccurate, incomplete, or noncurrent cost and pricing data. If the submission was knowingly defective, an additional forfeiture equal to the amount of the overpayment is to be assessed.

These new enactments are pertinent to contractors whose contracts are "covered contracts." Such contracts are generally defined as contracts in excess of $100,000 unless issued on a fixed-price basis without any provisions for payment of cost incentives. This definition of covered contracts may be somewhat ambiguous, but it provides a clear indication to contractors that the Congress objects to, and would like to reduce, the number of contracts on which cost reimbursements are allowed since the punitive measures are applicable only to that category of contracts for which

1. cost and pricing data have been submitted, and/or
2. costs are reimbursable by the government to the contractor under the payment terms of the contract.

The new regulations are sufficient to cause contractors who may otherwise be very interested in obtaining cost-reimbursement government contracts to carefully consider options, such as ensuring that all accepted work is under a fixed-price arrangement, awarded on a competitive basis without submission of cost and pricing data, or is otherwise rendered not subject to these rules. This approach certainly is feasible for well defined projects, however, past contracts for research and development work have not lent themselves to the firm-fixed-price arrangement. This also has been the case for other projects insufficiently defined for rigid price commitments. Exploration may be needed to find approaches that would allow innovation oriented projects to be contracted on a competitive firm-fixed-price basis.

SUMMARY

Contract managers have a unique position in the management ranks of their organizations. Several reasons for this are examined.

- At times, contract managers must serve their employer by taking actions that appear to conflict with the employer's perceived short-term interests.
- The ability of contract managers to contribute to organizational success has been limited by an inadequately developed sense of identity, image, and ethics.
- Those in the field are beginning to fully develop their concepts of identity, image, and ethical behavior.

- The objectives of the procurement and post-award management functions have been formulated to focus on the strategic use of contracts for successful performance.
- The role of contract administrators is mediating viewpoints of the contractual parties to achieve ethical decisionmaking while performing work that presents opportunities for less than arms-length decisions.
- Special insight concerning ethical questions is attributed to public contracting personnel and has led to the recent introduction of new rules of behavior for personnel who deal with public contracts.

TOPICS FOR DISCUSSION

1. Evaluate the suggestion that contract managers should adopt a "service-to-customer" orientation as their overall professional objective.
2. Explain the relevance of "identity." How is it defined, and why is it important in the contracting field?
3. In what ways does the pre-award contract manager promote economic welfare?
4. Post-award contract managers contribute to economic welfare by applying special expertise and resourcefulness. Explain what makes their role challenging and complex.
5. Explain the concept of contractual relationships as compared with master-servant relationships.
6. Discuss and evaluate the actions which have caused increased attention to ethical decisionmaking by government and contractor employees.
7. Explain the significance of type A and type B mistakes made by contract administrators.
8. Consider the trend toward using criminal sanctions to secure a higher level of ethical decisions in government contracting. Are the recent statutory actions wise? Effective?

CASE 2-1

Cajun A: Cajun and the Beta Site Concept

Cajun Corporation designs systems and creates software as one of California's leading high tech companies. Its product line includes interactive graphics systems and software programs. Cajun's special expertise is creating computer systems that automate the operation of industrial production equipment. Cajun's major customers are industrial corporations, but the customer list includes many nonindustrial operations that are approaching the computer age with heavy emphasis on finding more efficient methods of performing their work. The key to Cajun's success is superior expertise in software development and the ability to analyze industrial processes for application of computer based controls. Cajun's superior work attracted major corporate interest, and the company was bought out by the General Supplies Corporation in 1981.

One of Cajun's functional management groups is contract administration headed by John Riverton. The following situation is drawn from Mr. Riverton's commentary on the operation of the contract administration group.

The success of Cajun's contract administration department is partially due to personnel who have extensive experience in contracting and who have developed close working relationships with the software engineers as well as customers and suppliers. Mr. Riverton is an engineer, but for many years has found greater satisfaction in managing the contractual interface between buyer and seller.

A general objective of contract administration at Cajun is to minimize the company's legal and financial risks. One way of meeting this objective is by providing support to the marketing personnel. The contract administration department negotiates terms and conditions of all new sales agreements. Part of the basis for their role in negotiating is their ability to ensure that personnel with expertise in the salient terms and conditions are present at negotiation sessions.

Some of the issues that must be covered in negotiations are corporate sales agreements, software licenses, clarification of exact performance as expected by the customer, and pricing. The pricing issues are handled fairly easily by using price books developed by the company which are based on experience in developing a wide variety of software products. The basic estimating work is done by the software design engineers who have substantial knowledge of many types of development efforts. Most of Cajun's expenses are incurred for labor. Preparation of bids requires estimating the manpower level and time to perform the systems effort. Software packages are licensed on the basis of price schedules based on price books. Equipment is selected from original manufacturers (Cajun does not fabricate equipment) and must be assembled and integrated into deliverable systems. The hardware components of systems are considered to be "products" and are sold to the purchaser. Product prices are strongly influenced by the amount of time required to integrate and install the whole system.

Keeping in the forefront of their industry is vital to Cajun. They accomplish this by devising methods of automating and improving industrial practices for standard and unique manufacturing processes. While Cajun has superior software engineering capabilities, the company searches for opportunities to define new applications of their systems expertise. This presents a challenge because the companies that engage in various types of manufacturing not only are ideal prospects as customers, but also are the best source of knowledge about the manufacturing methods that could be automated by Cajun. Cajun's success depends on intimate, detailed information exchange with these companies. In return, companies that cooperate with Cajun in the learning and development processes find that they acquire a substantial lead over their competitors in adopting the latest and most efficient technologies.

Because of this, Cajun has cultivated close relationships with many customers. Information flows in both directions. Once Cajun creates technology that will automate a specific industrial process, substantial new markets are opened. But study of actual processes is essential and generates the need for sophisticated, cooperative interaction with customers. This need for access to information sources for new applications caused Riverton to define the concept of Beta sites. To illustrate these points, John Riverton made this statement:

> Let's say there is a market that we want to penetrate--to use an actual example, mold flow design. We need to create a software package that will calculate hot metal flowing into a mold, including all stresses created by the cooling process. We want a way to control heating and cooling of the mold in segments to create less stress. The mold is intricate and the casting is critical, like that needed to cast turbine parts for the internals of a jet engine, where an absolute minimum of machining is to be applied after extracting the part from the mold. When we decide to penetrate that market, we ask the customer for permission to set up a Beta site. After reaching an agreement, the development of the new technology is accomplished by our people at the manufacturing facility. This requires close working relationships.

The Beta site customer is attracted to this arrangement because participation secures first use of the new technology and because it is acquired at a reduced cost. It places them far ahead of the competition. Since the Beta site is so important to this whole process, it must be carefully negotiated to set it up properly. It requires agreement on all the details, such as the flow of cash, manpower impact, security, use of the technology, working relationships, and appropriate distribution of benefits.

Upon successfully completing any new system, Cajun initiates a marketing program oriented toward sales to known potential users of the technology. Key aspects of the negotiation are corporate sales agreements and software license agreements. The agreements that Cajun proposes to customers are found at the end of this case as attachment A, Corporate Sales Agreement, and attachment B, Software License Agreement. Some customers, such as the U.S. government, negotiate vigorously to substitute their own terms and conditions regarding the key issues.

* * * * *

1.   From the foregoing situation, develop a schedule of negotiable issues
     and the potential content of an agreement to set up a Beta site for
     Cajun at Reynolds Engineering Corporation, a manufacturer of com-
     pact, high-thrust air vehicle engines.
2.   After considering appropriate FAR and FAR supplement rules and
     clauses, prepare a summary of issues that must be resolved to
     establish a sales arrangement for a Cajun system to a U.S. govern-
     ment-funded customer.

Attachment A

Corporate Sales Agreement

   This Agreement is made as of _____ between
CAJUN COMPANY, a California Corporation having its principal place of
business at 5155 Old Ironsides Drive, Santa Clara, California (herein
"Cajun") and _____ a_____
corporation having its principal place of business at_____
_____
(herein "Buyer").

   WHEREAS, Buyer intends to purchase Cajun interactive graphic
products and license Cajun software from time to time during the term of
this Agreement; and

   WHEREAS, in order to avoid repetitive negotiations, the parties
hereto desire to enter into this Agreement to establish the terms and
conditions which will be applicable to the sale of such products and the
licensing of such software.

   NOW, THEREFORE, in consideration of the mutual promises hereinafter set forth, the parties hereto agree as follows:

1.0 DEFINITIONS
     1.1   The term "Products" shall mean Cajun's interactive graphics
           systems, or any part(s) thereof, but shall include Cajun
           software.
     1.2   The term "Software" shall mean Cajun's software programs and
           related supporting materials.

2.0 OVERRIDING CHARACTER OF THIS AGREEMENT
     2.1   This Agreement shall apply to all Buyer's purchase orders
           accepted by Cajun (including its Western European subsidiaries)

which Buyer (including its subsidiaries, affiliates and facilities within the United States, Canada and Western Europe) may place during the term and within the scope of this Agreement. The terms and conditions of this Agreement shall apply to any such order, whether or not this Agreement or said terms and conditions are expressly referenced in the order or other documents of purchase. Unless otherwise mutually agreed to by both parties in writing for a specific transaction, no inconsistent or additional term or condition in any such order or other document of purchase shall be applicable to transactions falling within the scope of this Agreement, except for special terms, as described in Article 3 below, which are agreed to by both parties, and which are applicable only to specific transactions.

2.2   The parties agree to use reasonable efforts to place a legend on each order or other document of purchase within the scope of this Agreement substantially as follows:
"Subject to the provisions of the Corporate Sales Agreement dated _____." Nevertheless, this agreement shall apply under its terms regardless of whether any such legend shall have been placed on any such order or other document of purchase.

3.0 SPECIAL TERMS

3.1   Terms with respect to the following matters shall be as agreed to between Cajun and Buyer in connection with each individual transaction covered by this Agreement:

A.   The quantity and type of products to be furnished and Software to be licensed;

B.   Delivery schedule and shipping destination;

C.   Other special terms to which both parties specifically agree in writing.

4.0   TERM OF AGREEMENT

4.1   This Agreement shall have a three year term commencing on the date first above written, provided, however, either party may sooner terminate this Agreement by giving three months advance written notice to the other party.

4.2   Termination of this Agreement shall not affect its application to purchase orders placed and accepted prior to the date of such termination.

5.0   ORDERS WITHIN THE SCOPE OF THIS AGREEMENT

5.1   This Agreement shall only apply to orders placed by Buyer which have been acknowledged and accepted in writing by Cajun.

6.0   PRICES
      6.1   Prices for Cajun Products purchased and Software licensed
            within the scope of this Agreement shall be in accordance with
            Exhibit A entitled "Prices."

7.0   PAYMENT
      7.1   Cajun's price for the Products shall be paid to Cajun by Buyer
            in United States dollars without setoff as follows:
            A.   System Purchase:
                  1.   Fifty percent (50%) of the price within ten (10) days
                        of shipment of the Products from Cajun's California
                        factory;
                  2.   Forty percent (40%) of the price on the earlier of
                        (1) ten days after installation of the Products at
                        Buyer's facility, or (2) in the event installation is
                        delayed for reasons attributable to Buyer, thirty days
                        from the date of shipment of the Products from
                        Cajun's California factory;
                  3.   Ten percent (10%) of the price on the earlier of (1)
                        the date of Buyer's acceptance of the installed
                        Products (in accordance with Cajun's then current
                        acceptance procedure), or (2) thirty days after the
                        date of installation of the Products.
            B.   Add-on Purchases:
                  1.   Fifty percent (50%) of the price within ten days of
                        shipment of the Products from Cajun's California
                        factory;
                  2.   Fifty percent (50%) of the price on the earlier of (1)
                        ten days after installation of the Products at Buyer's
                        facility, or (2) in the event installation is delayed
                        for reasons attributable to Buyer, thirty days from
                        the date of shipment of the Products from Cajun's
                        California factory.
            C.   If the Products are delivered to Buyer in installments, the
                  pro rata price allocable to each such delivery shall be
                  paid by Buyer to Cajun in accordance with the terms of
                  Section 7.1A or 7.1B.
      7.2   Any Cajun invoices not paid when due will be subject to a
            monthly service charge of one and one-half percent (1.5%) of
            the unpaid balance, such service charge to be paid within ten
            days of receipt of Cajun's invoice.

8.0   TERMS AND CONDITIONS OF SALE OF CAJUN PRODUCTS
      The following terms and conditions of sale shall apply to any and all

Cajun Products purchased within the scope of this Agreement:

8.1   <u>Title and Risk of Loss</u>. Cajun shall deliver Products to Buyer FOB Cajun's California factory. Upon such delivery to a carrier at Cajun's factory, title to the products and all risk of loss or damage shall pass to Buyer.

8.2   <u>Shipment</u>. Cajun, acting on behalf of Buyer, shall ship the Products to Buyer freight-collect or prepay the shipping costs and bill Buyer for such costs.

8.3   <u>Warranty</u>.

    A.   Cajun warrants to Buyer that the Products delivered to Buyer, and any services performed by Cajun in connection with such Products, will be free from defects in title, material and workmanship for a period of:

        1.   One hundred twenty (120) days from the date of shipment of the Products from Cajun's California factory, or

        2.   Ninety (90) days from the date of installation of the Products whichever period ends first.

    B.   If the Products fail to meet the above warranty, Cajun, at its option, shall repair or replace the defective Products, provided that:

        1.   Buyer gives Cajun prompt notice of any defect and satisfactory proof thereof, and

        2.   Buyer has properly used and maintained the Products.

    C.   This Section 8.3 sets forth exclusive remedy for claims (except as to title) based on defects of the Products, or any services furnished by Cajun in connection therewith, whether the claim is in contract, warranty, tort (including negligence), or otherwise, and however instituted. Upon the expiration of the above warranty period, all such liability shall terminate. The foregoing warranties are exclusive and in lieu of all other warranties, whether written, oral implied or statutory. NO IMPLIED OR STATUTORY WARRANTY OF MERCHANTABILITY OR FITNESS FOR A PARTICULAR PURPOSE SHALL APPLY.

8.4   <u>Indemnity</u>

    A.   If notified promptly in writing by Buyer and given complete authority, information and assistance (at Cajun's expense), Cajun shall defend, or may settle any suit or proceeding brought against Buyer based upon a claim that any Products purchased hereunder constitute infringement of any United States patent, copyright or trademark. Cajun shall pay all damages and costs awarded in such suit or proceeding provided Buyer does not by any act (including any admission or acknowledgement) materially impair or compromise the defense of such suit or proceeding. If the Products in such suit or proceeding are held to constitute infringement and their use is enjoined, Cajun shall, at its own expense and option, either procure the right for continued use of the Products by Buyer, or replace or modify the Products so that they become noninfringing. As a last resort, Cajun shall accept return of the Products and refund the purchase price, less depreciation.

B.   Cajun shall have no liability to Buyer for claims of infringement based upon the use of Products in combination with apparatus or devices not supplied by Cajun.

C.   The foregoing constitutes the sole remedy of Buyer and sole liability of Cajun for patent, copyright or trademark infringement.

8.5 Proprietary Information.

A.   Cajun normally supplies information for the proper installation, test, operation and maintenance of Products. Portions of such information are proprietary and confidential in nature and will be so marked. Buyer agrees to abide by the terms of such markings and to use all such information, whether marked or unmarked solely for the installation, test, operation and maintenance of Products.

B.   If Buyer transfers title to or leases the Products hereunder to any third party, Buyer shall obtain from such third party a written agreement affording Cajun the protection set forth in Section 8.5A above.

8.6 Taxes. Buyer shall pay the gross amount of any present or future sales, use, excise, value-added or other similar tax applicable to the price, sale or delivery of any Products furnished hereunder or, alternatively, Buyer shall furnish Cajun with evidence of exemption from such taxes acceptable to the taxing authorities.

8.7 Excusable Delays.

A.   Cajun shall not be liable for delays in delivery or performance hereunder due to any cause beyond its reasonable control, including, without limitation, acts of God, acts of Buyer, strikes or other labor disturbances, inability to obtain necessary materials, components, service or facilities.

B.   Cajun will notify Buyer of any material delay excused by Section 8.7A above and will specify the revised delivery date as soon as practicable. In the event of any such delay, there will be no termination and the date of delivery shall be extended for a period equal to the time lost by reason of such delay.

8.8   Installation.

   A.   Cajun's quoted price for the Products includes the installation of the Products by Cajun's personnel at Buyer's facility. Buyer is required to provide, at its own expense, the electrical, heating and air conditioning environment specified by Cajun.

   B.   The Products will be deemed to be installed upon demonstration of the Products' capability of processing diagnostic software.

8.9   Termination by Buyer.

   A.   In the event Buyer terminates (cancels) any order for products prior to the requested delivery date of such order, Buyer shall pay Cajun as termination charges within ten (10) days of Buyer's termination notice:

      1.   Twenty-five percent (25%) of the order if Buyer terminated the order within the first third of the time period between Buyer's initial placement of the order (by telex, hard-copy purchase order, letter or otherwise) and the requested delivery date; or

      2.   Thirty-five percent (35%) of the price of the order if Buyer terminates the order within the second third of the time period between Buyer's initial placement of the order (by telex, hard-copy purchase order, letter or otherwise) and the requested delivery date; or

      3.   Forty percent (40%) of the price of the order if Buyer terminates the order within the last third of the time period between Buyer's initial placement of the order (by telex, hard-copy purchase order, letter or otherwise) and the requested delivery date.

8.10 Disclaimer of Damages.

   A.   IN NO EVENT SHALL CAJUN BE LIABLE FOR ANY CONSEQUENTIAL, SPECIAL, INDIRECT OR PENAL DAMAGES, INCLUDING, BUT NOT LIMITED TO, LOSS OF PROFIT OR REVENUES, LOSS OF USE OF THE PRODUCTS OR ANY EQUIPMENT OR SYSTEM, COST OF CAPITAL, DOWN-TIME COST, LACK OR LOSS OF PRODUCTIVITY, OR CLAIMS OF BUYER'S CUSTOMERS FOR SUCH DAMAGES.

   B.   If Buyer transfers title to or leases the Products here under to any third party, Buyer shall obtain from such third party a provision affording Cajun the protection set forth in Section 8.10A above.

9.0 CAJUN SOFTWARE

9.1   Any Cajun Software licensed to Buyer during and within the scope of this Agreement shall require Buyer's execution of Cajun's standard "Software License Agreement" in the text attached as Exhibit B.

10.0 GENERAL

10.1 This Agreement shall be governed and construed in accordance with the laws of the State of California.

10.2 Neither party may assign its rights or obligations under this Agreement without the prior written consent of the other party.

10.3 Any notice hereunder shall be in writing and shall be deemed properly delivered when duly mailed by registered mail to the other party at its address as first set forth above or other address as either party may by written notice designate to the other.

10.4 This Agreement may not be modified, amended or changed unless done so by written document signed by an authorized representative of both parties.

IN WITNESS WHEREOF, the parties hereto have executed this Agreement on the date first set forth above.

CAJUN COMPANY   _____COMPANY

By _____   By _____

Title _____   Title _____

Date _____   Date _____

Attachment B

Agreement No._____

Cajun Company
Software License Agreement

This Agreement is between Cajun Company, 1850 Kings Way, Santa Ana, California (hereinafter "Cajun") and

---

Name

Address
(hereafter "Licensee") for the licensing by Cajun to Licensee of the use of certain computer software programs.

I. LICENSE

A. Definitions

1. "Licensed Program" means a software program listed on a Schedule A and any updated, improved, or otherwise modified version ("Release") of such a program and any related materials, in machine readable and/or printed form, furnished to Licensee by or on behalf of Cajun, including any materials provided under any Cajun software service, and any full or partial copies of any of the foregoing.

2. "Designated Equipment" means, with respect to each Licensed Program, the specific central processing unit(s) ("CPUs") and workstation(s) listed on the same Schedule A, or, with respect to any subsequent Releases, the particular CPU and workstations for which Licensee has paid Cajun's applicable fee, if such fee is paid for only part of the equipment listed on such Schedule A.

3. "Schedule A" means a schedule in the form attached to this Agreement which has been made a part of this Agreement by execution by both parties.

4. "Cajun Program" means a Licensed Program which is owned by Cajun, or for which Cajun has the independent ability, including the right to use source code, to provide maintenance and support for its customers.

B. License Grant and Scope

1.   Subject to the terms of this Agreement, Cajun hereby grants to Licensee, and Licensee accepts, a non-transferable, nonexclusive license to use each Licensed Program only on the Designated Equipment for the Release in question. Licensee expressly understands that a Licensed Program cannot be transferred to, or used in connection with, any CPU or workstation that is not licensed by Cajun to operate the Release in question.

2.   Upon request, Cajun will license Licensee, for an additional license fee, to use the Licensed Programs in connection with additional workstations which Cajun determines to be compatible after conducting an inspection at Cajun's then

current charges. (Releases furnished after such inspection may not be compatible with stations not supplied by Cajun.) Other peripheral equipment may be added to Designated Equipment without a license from Cajun, but Licensed Programs may not be compatible with any peripherals not supplied by Cajun.

3.   Licensee may obtain Releases beyond those originally furnished for particular Designated Equipment by either (i) entering into a software support contract covering the Licensed Program and Designated Equipment, or (ii) placing a purchase order which identifies the Licensed Program, Release number and Designated Equipment (by System I.D. No., number of workstations and required system configuration), and in either case paying Cajun's applicable fee.

C. Assignment/Transfer

Neither the licenses granted hereunder nor the Licensed Programs may be assigned or transferred without the prior written consent of Cajun, and any such attempt will void the licenses. If Licensee desires to transfer the Designated Equipment to a third party for continuing use by such part, Cajun agrees, upon Licensee's request and subject to Cajun's reasonable approval, to offer to enter into a standard Cajun license agreement with such third party. After the third party and Cajun have executed an agreement covering the Licensed Programs(s), Licensee may transfer the Licensed Program(s) to such third party. In the absence of such an agreement, if Licensee transfers the Designated Equipment, Licensee shall promptly return to Cajun the Licensed Programs, including all copies which contain any portion of a Licensed Program, provided that Licensee may remove from such copies any modifications made by Licensee.

D. Modification/Copies

1.   Cajun grants to Licensee the right to modify and/or copy any Licensed Program in machine readable form as necessary for backup, archival or modification purposes only. Upon termination of the license for such Licensed Program, the license to use any modified Licensed Program is also terminated. Licensed Programs in printed form shall not be copied in whole or in part, but additional copies may be obtained from Cajun at its then standard charges. Licensee shall not reverse assemble or reverse complile any Licensed Program.

2.   Licensee agrees that any copyright notices and/or proprietary notices appearing on and in Licensed Programs will be reproduced and included on and in any modifications and copies, in whole or in part, of Licensed Programs.

E. Ownership

Cajun either owns or has the right to license Licensed Programs. As between Cajun and Licensee, Licensed Programs and all copies thereof, in whole or in part, including all portions of Licensed Programs contained in modifications, shall remain the sole property of Cajun.

F. Protection of Licensed Programs

Licensee agrees that Licensee and its employees will not provide or otherwise make available any Licensed Program or portion thereof in any form (including derivative programs) to any third party and will keep such materials in confidence. Licensee further agrees to limit availability of Licensed Programs only to those employees who need to use such Licensed Programs as permitted by this Agreement.

II. SERVICES

A. Initial Services For Cajun Programs

With respect to the first machine readable form of a Cajun Program furnished with a Cajun system, Cajun will physically place it on the Designated Equipment and will cause it to execute the applicable Cajun Standard Operational Test Procedure. If, for reasons not attributable to Cajun, the foregoing work with respect to any system requires more than three person days, Licensee will pay Cajun for the additional time at Cajun's then standard charges.

B. Other Services For Cajun Programs

With respect to each Cajun Program furnished with a Cajun system, Cajun will furnish, without additional charge, the services described below for a period of ninety days after the hardware portion of such system is first installed at the original installation site; provided, however, if such installation is, for reasons not attributable to Cajun, delayed to a date more than thirty days after delivery of such hardware by Cajun to Licensee, then the period shall be one hundred twenty days from the date of such delivery. (Such hardware will be deemed to be installed upon demonstration of its capability of processing diagnostic software provided by Cajun for purposes of such demonstration.) The services are:

1. Upon Licensee's written request and furnishing Cajun with all requested information, Cajun will provide services for correcting or working around variances between the function of a Licensed Program and Cajun's published user documentation, provided the variances occur on an unmodified version of Cajun's most current Release of a Licensed Program or the prior major Release made available by Cajun used on Designated Equipment in normal operating condition and with operating software and environment as specified by Cajun. Cajun will use reasonable efforts to correct or work around the variances described above, but does not represent or warrant that such variances will be corrected or worked around. If a problem is determined by Cajun to be of Licensee origin, Licensee will pay Cajun's then standard charges for work performed in responding to the problem.

2. Any new Releases of the Licensed Program generally released by Cajun to other licensees, with the exception of reconfiguration releases prepared to accommodate different hardware.

3. Any updates of applicable user manuals and new user manuals and guides generally released by Cajun to other licensees.

4. Consultation by telephone via a toll-free line within the U.S.A. to assist Licensee with the application of Licensed Programs.

5. Cajun's user publication and applicable software status bulletin.

C. Services For Non-Cajun Programs

With respect to each Licensed Program other than Cajun Programs furnished with a Cajun system, Cajun will use reasonable efforts (any litigation will be at Cajun's option) to require all suppliers of such programs to provide the services which they have contracted to perform for Cajun's customers and which Cajun has formally announced will be available at no charge, but Cajun will have no other responsibility with respect to non-Cajun Programs.

D. Protection Against Infringement Claims

Cajun shall defend, or may settle, any

suit or proceeding brought against Licensee based upon a claim that the use of a Licensed Program constitutes infringement of any United States patent, copyright or trade secret, if notified promptly in writing by Licensee and given complete authority, information and assistance (at Cajun's expense). Cajun shall pay all damages and costs awarded in such suit or proceeding provided Licensee does not by any act (including any admission or acknowledgment) materially impair or compromise the defense of such suit or proceeding. If the Licensed program is held to constitute infringement and its use is enjoined, Cajun shall, at its own expense and option, either (i) procure the right for continued use of the Licensed Program by Licensee, or (ii) if the performance thereof will not be materially and adversely affected, replace or modify the Licensed Program so that it becomes non-infringing, or (iii) accept return of such Licensed Program and refund the license fee allocable thereto. Cajun shall have no liability for claims of infringement based on use of any Licensed Program in combination with any equipment or software not supplied by Cajun. The foregoing states the entire liability of Cajun and sole remedies of Licensee with respect to infringement claims.

III. GENERAL

A. Term and Termination
Each license granted herein shall remain in force until Licensee discontinues use of the Licensed Program on the Designated Equipment or until Cajun terminates this Agreement or the license for such Licensed Program. Cajun may terminate this Agreement or any license hereunder: (i) effective immediately upon notice if Licensee provides or otherwise makes available to any third party any Licensed Program or portion thereof, or (ii) upon thirty days notice if Licensee attempts to use any Licensed Program or modification thereof on equipment other than the Designated Equipment for the Release in question, or attempts to transfer any license or assign this Agreement without the prior written consent of Cajun, or fails to perform any other material obligation under this Agreement, and does not cure such breach within such period. Immediately upon termination, Licensee shall return to Cajun the Licensed Program(s) and all copies thereof, provided that Licensee may remove from such copies any modifications made by Licensee.

B. Excusable Delays
Cajun shall not be liable for delays or failures in performing its obligations arising out of or resulting from (a) an act of God; (b) any other cause beyond Cajun's reasonable control, including, but not limited to, the inability to obtain necessary labor, materials, equipment, utilities, services or facilities; or (c) any act, failure to act, or delay in acting on the part of any governmental authority or of Licensee; strikes or other labor difficulties; accidents or disruptions such as fire, flood, civil disturbance or breakdown of essential machinery or equipment; or delays or shortages in transportation. In the event of any such delay, the time for Cajun's performance shall be extended by a period equal to the time lost by reason of such delay.

C. Limitations of Liability
1. The total liability of Cajun, its subcontractors and suppliers for all claims of any kind, whether in contract, tort

(including negligence),
48 strict liability, or otherwise, arising out of, connected with or resulting from Cajun's performance or breach of this Agreement or the Licensed Programs or services furnished hereunder shall in no event exceed the fee allocable to the particular Release of the Licensed Program which gives rise to such claims, or if no such allocation can be made, the price of the system with which such Release was furnished or a year's charges for the software services in connection with which such Release was furnished; provided, however, that in no event shall Cajun's total liability with respect to a system (including all hardware and software) exceed the price of the system.

2.   In no event, whether as a result of breach of contract, tort (including negligence), strict liability, or otherwise, shall Cajun, or its subcontractors or suppliers, be liable for loss of profits or revenues; claims of customers; loss of use of Licensed Programs or Designated Equipment or any other equipment, software, system, or facility; loss of data or information; lack or loss of productivity; interest charges or cost of capital; cost of substitute equipment, software, systems or services; cost of purchased or replacement power; downtime costs; or special, consequential or punitive damages of any nature. As Licensee has control over its use of Licensed Programs, Licensee shall indemnify Cajun, its subcontractors and suppliers against any claims of any kind made against them by any customer of Licensee.

3.   The Licensed Programs are not furnished for use in connection with the design, analysis, construction or operation of any part of a nuclear facility, and Licensee warrants that it shall not use the licensed Programs for such purposes or permit others to use them for such purposes. If, in breach of the foregoing, any such use occurs, neither Cajun nor its subcontractors or suppliers shall have any liability for any nuclear or other damages, injury or contamination, and Licensee shall indemnify them against any such liability, whether as a result of breach of contract, tort (including negligence), strict liability or otherwise.

4.   NEITHER CAJUN NOR ITS SUBCONTRACTORS OR SUPPLIERS MAKES ANY WARRANTY WITH RESPECT TO ANY LICENSED PROGRAM OR SERVICES FURNISHED HEREUNDER, AND NO WARRANTIES OF ANY KIND, WHETHER WRITTEN, ORAL, IMPLIED OR STATUTORY, INCLUDING WARRANTIES OF MERCHANTABILITY OR FITNESS FOR A PARTICULAR PURPOSE, SHALL APPLY.

D. Miscellaneous

1.   All notices hereunder shall be in writing and shall be deemed to have been duly given upon being delivered personally, or upon receipt if mailed by certified mail, return receipt requested, to the other party at the address set forth in the initial paragraph of this Agreement or such other address as a party may designate by written notice to the other.

2.   The validity, in whole or in part, of any provision of this Agreement shall not affect the validity or enforce-
48ability of any other provision hereof.

3.   Cajun's subcontractors and suppliers shall have the right to enforce this Agreement, including the provision for termination, with respect to their programs.

4.   Licensee shall pay all taxes or similar charges resulting from this Agreement or any activities

hereunder, exclusive of taxes based on Cajun's net income.

5.   Fees and terms of payment, shipment and delivery will be as provided in the applicable Cajun sales or service contract or quotation.

6.   This Agreement shall control and have precedence over the provisions of any purchase order or other document, constitutes the entire agreement between the parties respecting the subject matter hereof, and supersedes all previous and collateral agreements, representations, and warranties. No representation, warranty, course of dealing, trade usage, term or condition not contained or referenced herein shall be binding on either party. This Agreement may not be modified or amended except by a written document signed by a duly authorized representative of each party.

LICENSEE   **CAJUN COMPANY**

By:_____   By:_____
         Signature of Authorized   Signature of Authorized
             Representative   Representative

Name:_____   Name:_____
             Typed or Printed   Typed or Printed

Title:_____   Title:_____
             Typed or Printed   Typed or Printed

Date:_____   Date:_____

SCHEDULE A
TO
CAJUN SOFTWARE LICENSE AGREEMENT OR AMENDMENT

Agreement or Amendment No. _____

Effective Date: _____
(To be no later than delivery date of first Licensed Program)

LICENSED PROGRAMS FOR DESIGNATED EQUIPMENT LISTED BELOW

Item No.   Description

DESIGNATED EQUIPMENT FOR LICENSED PROGRAMS LISTED ABOVE

| | | Cajun System | No. of |
| Item No. | Description | I.D. No. | Workstations |

Licensee:_____   Cajun Company_____

By:_____   By:_____
  Signature of Authorized   Signature of Authorized
      Representative   Representative

Name_____   Name_____
  Signature of Authorized   Typed or Printed
      Representative

Title_____   Title:_____
      Typed or Printed   Typed or Printed

3

Organization for Administration of Contracts

Organization and personnel issues can hamper effectiveness regardless of the field of activity. Contract administration is no exception and because of geographical factors may entail a more complicated organizational problem than most management functions. We will examine three approaches to organizing administration for contract management: the concept developed at the Detroit Edison Company, the government's general approach as represented in the Defense Contract Administration Services (DCAS) of the Defense Logistics Agency (DLA), and the approach of the Naval Regional Contracting Center (NRCC) in Washington, D.C. Whether field administration should be established is an important element of this discussion because it requires substantial financial and manpower investment. Defense and non-defense government agencies and private companies follow different paths as they approach that question.

THE DETROIT EDISON APPROACH

Detroit Edison is a large investor-owned utility. The company performed virtually all work, including construction, in-house until around 1950. At that time they began to contract for the construction phase of major projects but continued to perform the engineering and procurement services in-house. In the early 1970s the company changed this approach by contracting for architectural and engineering (A&E) work. They included engineering, procurement, and construction services in the A&E duties.

While developing this comprehensive contracting-out program, the company began to assign a purchasing person to act as project purchaser for each major contract. The project purchaser was drawn from and expected to represent the general purchasing organization but was physically located with the project manager from whom he received daily work direction. The duties assigned to the project purchaser were extensive but, in total, were no less than those required for comprehensive administration of the major project contracts.

The position of the project purchaser has not been abandoned at Detroit Edison but has given way to a more comprehensive approach, wherein individuals are assigned to act as contract administrators for all awarded contracts, including materials, equipment and services, not just construction. The large number of people required for this made it infeasible for the company to draw its entire contract administration work force from its purchasing organization. Instead, the company sought a way to assign the role of contract administrator to personnel who were responsible for the work or requirement for which a contract is awarded. To do this, Detroit Edison developed a contract administration program whereby selected employees from the requisitioning organizational units receive training in the administration of contracts through a comprehensive, company-designed course. After completing the training phase, these persons become eligible for assignment as contract administrators for contracts appropriate to the individual's overall skills and knowledge. As contract administrators, they become the company contact with the contractor/supplier for normal day-to-day matters relating to the contract and are responsible for coordinating and administering all aspects of the contract. Their overall objective is to ensure that the company receives a satisfactory product, on time, and within budget.

This concept of administration is carried out without creating any new organizational entities or employing net additional staff. The company's program is designed on the basis that the responsibilities for administering contracts are added to the individual's normally assigned duties. Through the training program, administrators are provided with essential contractual knowledge and are briefed on administrative procedures associated with contracts. The capabilities developed become complementary to their existing expertise. They are challenged to make the contract a successful relationship, the results of which have pleased the company. Top executive personnel declare that their approach has exceeded all expectations in savings and improved relationships with contractors and suppliers.

The company's belief in this program has been strongly reinforced through five years experience in its use. In addition to their training program, they have developed a manual to guide the work of the administrator. Their contract administration training program includes the following highlights:

1. General orientation to contracts
2. Goals and planning techniques for contract administration
3. The essentials of contract interpretation
4. Rules governing contract types and their applications
5. Scheduling systems and techniques for monitoring progress
6. Contractual responsibilities of the owner/purchaser
7. Inspection and quality assurance responsibilities
8. Information gathering practices, methods of recording information, and techniques for controlling documents and data records
9. Invoice processing, time reporting, and progress payments
10. Evaluation of the contract, overall performance, and supplier capabilities
11. Situation analysis and problem resolution
12. Forms, logs, records, reports, and lists necessary to administer contract management

The purchasing organization played a lead role in developing this concept. It enjoyed the support of the president and the chairman of the board of directors. Although no separate entity for contract administration exists, approximately one thousand of the company's employees are trained in the practical applications, and many of them have current contract administration assignments. The company is strongly committed to the program and believes it meets their business needs.

GOVERNMENT ORGANIZATION FOR FIELD ADMINISTRATION

Defense Contract Administration Services

The largest organization devoted to contract administration is the DCAS, a part of the DLA. It has been integrated into the DLA structure but is designed to support administration assignments from all defense organizations and civilian agencies. At the headquarters level located at Cameron Station in Alexandria, Virginia, the contract administration functions are divided into two groups: Directorate of Contract Management and Directorate of Quality Assurance. These directorates report to the director of DLA and include the headquarters level functional responsibilities associated with contract administration. The thirteen DLA headquarters level staff offices provide support to the contract administration directorates in a manner similar to their support of the procurement, supply center, and logistics activities of DLA. Figure 3-1 illustrates this structure.

Field organizations of DLA include supply centers, depots, and service centers as well as the Defense Contract Administration Services

Figure 3-1

**Partial Organization of Contract Administration
for the Defense Logistics Agency**

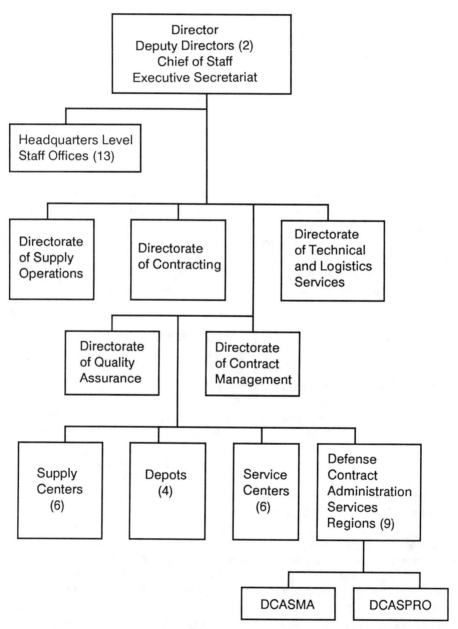

Regions (DCASR).[1] Contract management and field support for procuring centers are provided by nine DCASR. Under each DCASR there are several Defense Contract Administration Services Management Areas (DCASMA) and/or Defense Contract Administration Services Plant Representative Offices (DCASPRO). In addition, a number of residencies (offices with twenty or more personnel) are established at or near various industrial plants. The residency may report through or be supported by a DCASMA but provides a base of operations geographically closer to the contractor plants for which it is responsible than would otherwise be feasible.

Throughout the DCAS structure, quality assurance and contract administration are subdivided organizationally. The administrative contracting officer (ACO) is appointed within the contract administration structure, and quality assurance representatives are employed within the quality assurance structure. This subdivision has been advocated by the quality assurance community, reflecting the technical nature of their function and the necessity of locating much of their work at contractor facilities. Some observers of the overall contract administration process sense a degree of tension and possibly some communication weaknesses within DCAS associated with this organizational arrangement. All observers recognize the importance of quality verification including identification of deficiencies and resolution of differences of opinion between buyer and seller. These areas are often root causes of financial, delivery, and acceptance problems which post-award administrators must address.

Although DCAS has a highly structured approach to organization, there is no standard method for administering contracts government-wide. Approaches vary with budgets, personalities, and perceptions of needs. Agencies other than DOD seldom have adequate staff or funding for widely dispersed administrative duties and, in lieu of hiring necessary staff, usually draw upon the DOD capability on a cost reimbursable basis. Private companies generally do not enter into the comprehensive post-award processes of government. Instead, their arrangements tend to be ad hoc. They staff field administration work only for specific projects demanding close interaction with supply sources. The cost of field organizations constitutes a significant barrier to their establishment by the competitive private company. Cost is no less significant for the government procurement system. However, with purchases from every industrial group and in every geographical sector, the scope of government operations may justify its expense.

---

[1]See chapter 10 (especially charts 10-3 and 10-4) for additional information on the organization of field administration for quality assurance.

Special Factors in Organizing
Field Administration Offices

The DCAS structure is only one of the field contract administration organizations in government. Each military service has field administration organizations, and the Defense Contract Audit Agency (separately chartered and organized) exists primarily for its skill in examining and reviewing contractor books, records, and accounts in support of contract administration and pricing activities.

In organizing contract administration, government actions have been guided by two factors: the effort to achieve administrative economy, and efficiency and unwillingness to rely on executive discretion. This has resulted in an organization primarily designed to have checks and oversight functions; the management of contracting work is secondary. This orientation exists because the buying process provides opportunities for poor judgment, error, and fraudulent behavior. These opportunities are always present because key decisions both before and after contract award cannot be made on the basis of purely objective criteria. Every decision can be challenged; every decision can be interpreted as biased or based on inappropriate criteria. This is difficult for elected public bodies, such as Congress, to accept. Instances of waste or corruption, and even the unproven appearance of waste or corruption when public funds are involved, are cause for media highlighting and legislative correction. These factors have been an important influence on the organization and operation of public contracting.

Legislative sensitivity to apparent improper or misguided behavior by government or contractor personnel peaked during the 1981-1986 time frame, but it did not begin then; it has always existed. Some results are

1. separation of contract administration and contract audit;
2. semi-independence of contract administration and quality assurance;
3. establishment of the inspector general (investigative) function in procuring agencies;
4. adoption of policies patently designed to provide unique advantages to government in its relationships with suppliers, including
   a. data submission prerogatives and powers,
   b. unilateral directive authority,
   c. rules to avoid payment of contractor expenses normally included in private transactions but unpopular if government funded.

Benefits and Costs Resulting from Organizational Influences

The offices of DCAS, DCAA, and the Inspector General (IG), as well as approximately nine other types of administrative, investigative and oversight organizations, are a product of the influences just discussed. DCAS and DCAA were created as combinations of previously established administration and audit functions organized within each of the three military departments. The combinations occurred in the mid 1960s through a decision of then Secretary of Defense Robert McNamara and as a result of a study known as *Project 60*. An important factor in the adoption of the DCAS and DCAA structure was the "one face to industry" objective of ensuring that only one field administration office (in each category) would deal with any one contractor. In addition the combination promised economy and efficiency by permitting field administration organizations to manage larger volumes of contracts per manpower unit. Economy also is achieved by enabling the individual procurement agencies to limit their contracting staff to the number needed for pre-award planning, solicitation, and negotiation activities. To encourage their use instead of relying on administration personnel, the procurement regulations were altered so that, upon award, contracts normally are assigned to a field office. This approach avoided the specific selection and delegation of a field administration office by the procuring office. The IG was created in 1978 by the Congress because of publicity highlighting repeated instances of apparent and real fraud, waste, and abuse of procurement authority.

The government has made some progress toward the objectives of achieving economy in field manpower requirements and in creating administrative checks and balances. Even its "one face to industry" objective has been partially achieved. Recent moves have also increased the publicity given deficiencies found through its investigative actions. However, the complexity of post-award administrative activities imposes substantial manpower requirements and qualitative burdens on the government procurement system. Resulting problems can be summarized as follows:

1. *Procurement and contract administration personnel are unable to communicate fully.* This is because buyers and negotiators seldom directly observe performance problems and surveillance issues and do not comprehend the effect of pre-award decisions on administrative relationships. Similarly, field contract administration personnel are not privy to the nuances of pre-award negotiations and have almost no control over and little advance knowledge of workload being imposed by procurement actions.

2. *Responsibility for project success is fragmented.* Program management charters in government consistently assign this responsibility to project or program managers. However, since contracting authority resides with contracting officers, using field administration splits contract authority between procurement and administrative contracting officers. This increases coordination problems.

3. *Auditing and contracting personnel have different objectives, making
    communication difficult.* Nominally, the contract audit work force
    was established as a support function for contracting officers. Its
    job was to provide expertise in reviewing and examining contractor
    books and records. The need for advising contracting officers is
    apparent, since the agency (DCAA) can determine costs (a key func-
    tion in the case of redeterminable, incentive, and cost type con-
    tracts); review forward pricing, and final labor and indirect rate
    proposals; analyze cost and price data in contract proposals; and
    make special studies and reports concerning contractor estimating,
    accounting, and other systems. However, the independent status of
    auditing, and the top-level perception that contract audit should
    function not as a service in administration but as a review and
    check on administrative decisionmaking with a reporting and investi-
    gative support responsibility, have created tension within the
    contracting system. Tension arises because contract managers
    (including technical managers and contracting officers) strive for a
    cooperative working relationship with contractors in order to
    formulate agreement on events and their contractual impact during
    work performance. The support role of audit aids this process,
    while the reporting and investigative roles do not.

4. *Contracting officers feel constrained against compromise.* The
    practice of using audit capabilities as a tool for exercising control
    over contracting personnel as well as for verifying contractor data
    inhibits discretionary action and decisionmaking. Contract adminis-
    trators, sensitive to the likelihood that challenges from internal
    reviewers will be critical, avoid compromise, forcing issues into
    litigation.

5. *Communication failures occur between audit, quality assurance and
    contract administration personnel.* Of all the contract administration
    functions, audit and quality assurance are the most manpower inten-
    sive. Audit is specialized and separated. Quality assurance involves
    specialized technical orientation and to a limited extent has achieved
    independence within DCAS. It responds as an organization to ACO
    initiatives, generally restricting direct response by quality assurance
    personnel.

6. *Administrative contracting officer workload does not permit atten-
    tion to issues until significant problems have developed.* According
    to procurement regulations and their warrants (appointment certifi-
    cates), ACOs have authority to make decisions regarding contracts
    and contractor matters. They fulfill this responsibility to the extent
    feasible, but with contract workloads encompassing several hundred
    contracts with hundreds of individual contractors, ACOs have limited
    knowledge of individual contract situations. Since decisions con-
    cerning issues must be formulated after fully comprehending all

facts, "fire drill" mentality is encouraged. This workload environment is further amplified by the organizational reality that ACOs are non-supervisory and usually have one or no assistants. They must negotiate with other internal administrative groups to the extent they need specialized functional support. Similarly, when procurement contracting officer or audit support is needed, it must be requested--not directed.

7. *Direct access to contractor records and personnel by several government agencies causes strained relationships.* Contract management activities express support for the "single face to industry" concept. However, this does not alter the number of government entities that assert direct access rights to contractors during performance phases of procurement. The following is a list of these entities:

a. Defense Contract Administration Services (note: large contract management organizations continue within the Air Force, Navy, and Army and are assigned contract management responsibility in lieu of DCAS at many important contractor plants)
b. Procurement contracting officer and staff
c. Program/project manager and staff
d. Defense Contract Audit Agency
e. Office of Federal Contract Compliance Programs, Department of Labor
f. Agency Inspector General and/or
   1) Defense Criminal Investigative Service
   2) Navy Investigation Service
   3) U.S. Army Criminal Investigation Division
   4) Air Force Office of Special Investigations
g. General Accounting Office
h. Congressional committees and staff

Only the first five organizational groups listed have direct assignments pertinent to normal administration of government contracts, but all conduct studies and audits to develop information concerning contract progress, costing, and performance when needed for their policy, reporting, and investigative objectives.

To illustrate the government's organizational efforts, we will review the structure of the Naval Regional Contracting Center (NRCC) in Washington, D.C., and the relationship between contracting officers and project managers at another major procurement organization.

NAVAL REGIONAL CONTRACTING CENTER, WASHINGTON, D.C.

The Naval Regional Contracting Center (NRCC)in Washington, D.C., is a field activity of the Naval Supply Systems Command (NAVSUP). Operating since 1948 under various names, it assumed its current name in

1982 when it was accorded status as a command headed by a commanding officer.[1] This change reflected the increasing importance of contracting in the Navy. Since 1982 NRCC has continued to serve the naval community in the Washington metropolitan area by acquiring supplies, equipment, services, and research and development for the Department of the Navy. It has become a recognized producer of trained contracting personnel for the acquisition process of nearby systems commands.

Organizational Overview

The approach to contract administration taken by NRCC, Washington, D.C., differs from that taken by many government activities. Since contract administration is only one of several NRCC functions, a review of the overall organization will be helpful. The mission of NRCC, Washington, includes

1. contracting to support naval activities within the Naval District, Washington;
2. intra-Navy contracting assignments for metal working machinery, automatic data processing (ADP) equipment, and maintenance;
3. operation of a common bid room for the Naval Systems Commands;
4. functional management responsibility for procurement within the Naval District, Washington.

The NRCC supports more than 150 activities in the Washington metropolitan area and awards over 5,000 contracts annually. Contracts range from low cost items of supply to complex multimillion dollar research and development and service contracts spanning several years. NRCC frequently is asked to acquire supplies or services of a unique, unusual, complicated, and frequently critical nature by headquarters commands in the Washington, D.C., area.

Four regional contracting centers report directly to the Commander of the Naval Supply Systems Command. Figure 3-2 depicts this structure and shows the position of NRCC, Washington, in relation to the U.S. Navy organization at the time of this writing.

Figure 3-3 illustrates the organizational structure of NRCC, Washington. The commanding officer is responsible for accomplishing the NRCC mission, including contracting, management and administrative functions, and is aided by an executive officer who serves as his direct representative in maintaining the general effectiveness of the center.

---

[1]This section is based on research by Patrick O'Day while a student at George Washington University.

Figure 3-2

Relationship of Naval Regional Contracting Centers to U.S. Navy Organization

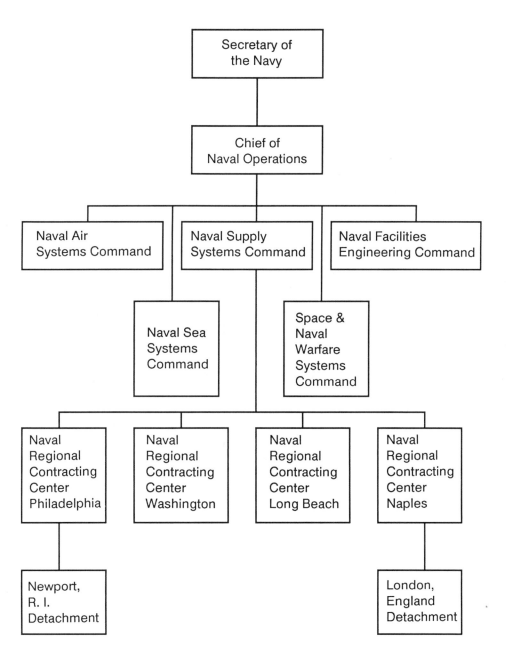

Figure 3-3

Naval Regional Contracting Center
Washington, D.C.

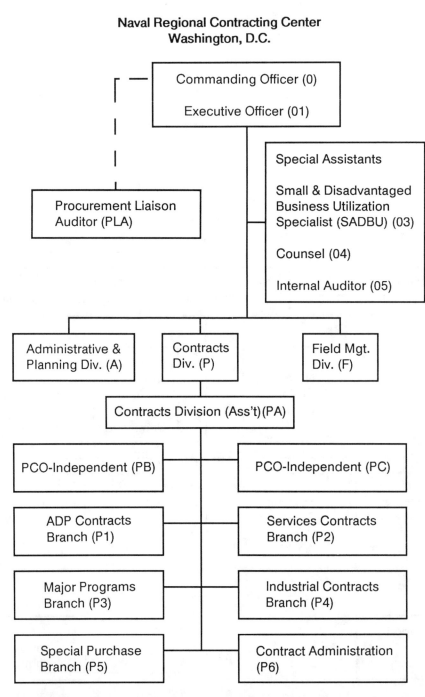

The Small and Disadvantaged Business Utilization (SADBU) specialist is responsible for maintaining NRCC's program to locate and make maximum use of small businesses, small disadvantaged businesses, and labor surplus business sources capable of supporting NRCC acquisitions.

NRCC's Office of Counsel is responsible for providing legal advice and determinations when required by NRCC's contracting and administration work. Counsel sends a representative to all Contract Review Board (CRB) meetings.

NRCC's internal auditor heads the NRCC Internal Review Program performing scheduled and specialized audits and conducting follow-up effort to implement audit recommendations. Reports are submitted directly to the commanding officer for review. The Procurement Liaison Auditor is responsible for overall audit assistance to Contracts Division personnel. This work includes developing cost analyses and acting as liaison to the Defense Contract Audit Agency (DCAA) offices in obtaining cost data.

An Administrative and Planning Division provides administrative, planning, financial, and contract support and computer functions for the center. The Field Management Division of NRCC is responsible for reviewing the procurement functions at Navy Field Contracting System activities in the Washington metropolitan area. This division is responsible for presentation of the Defense Small Purchase course and other procurement-related courses designed to assist field activity personnel such as contracting officers' technical representatives (COTR).

The director of the Contracts Division manages and supervises all contracting and contract administration operations of the center and distributes workload among the branches. Part of the director's job is to ensure that contractual actions are consistent with regulations and policy. Organization, staffing, and efficient use of contracting and administration personnel are key responsibilities. The Contracts Division is represented in Contract Review Board meetings and performs the full range of acquisition and contracting functions for supported activities. The division provides assistance in preparing contract requests and acquisition plans. Its assistance extends to determinations regarding the method of procurement, type of contract, solicitation preparation, bid and proposal evaluation, source selection decisions, and contract administration functions. Figure 3-3 includes the organizational structure of the division. One part of the Contracts Division, the Contract Administration Branch (Code: P6), is devoted to post-award actions.

The independent PCO (Code PB) functions as Deputy Command Competition Advocate. This person is responsible for developing acquisition strategies and innovative approaches for the elimination of sole source procurement, for acquiring complex automatic data processing equipment and services, and other actions demanding command attention. In a similar role, the independent PCO (Code PC) is also a deputy command competition advocate whose duties are identical to those of Code PB, but are directed toward acquisition of complex R&D, hardware and services, and those related actions generating command attention.

The ADP Contracts Branch purchases automatic data processing equipment including computers, minicomputers, mainframes (CPU), terminals, printers, and all associated hardware and software.

A wide range of support services is purchased by Service Contracts Branch. These tend to be contracts for high-dollar value services: food service for the U.S. Naval Academy; operation and maintenance services for worldwide Navy Communications Stations; training, software development, and conversion services; studies relating to operational deployment of ships, flight crews, and material; and studies to assess issues pertinent to the top levels of management within the Navy.

Research and development projects and hardware are bought by the Research and Development Contracts Branch. Their work includes purchase of rocket motors and bodies, propellants, explosives, urinalysis kits, technical studies, and special items such as telescopes, recreational boats, and galley kitchenware.

The Industrial Equipment Contracts Branch purchases heavy industrial hardware including automated material handling systems, all types of metal-working equipment, furnaces, propeller balancing machines, and other equipment used to repair aircraft, surface ships and submarines, both afloat and in overhaul.

The special Procurement Branch is responsible for purchasing small-dollar value ADP equipment and associated software from the GSA schedule. Its purchases include a variety of services and items not covered by the other contracts branches.

The Contract Administration Branch is the focus of this study. Its position within the contracts center is of interest because it differs from most government procurement structures. Its contract administration personnel are a part of the buying office yet are hired for their expertise in administration of NRCC contracts. However, the Contract Administration Branch does not handle all post-award types of actions such as exercising options, initiating new procurement modifications in excess of $100,000, and contract closeout services.

There are two general approaches to contract administration practices at NRCC, Washington. The first approach employs the Contract Administration Branch to closely integrate the duties of the procurement contracting officer (PCO) with those of the administrative contracting officer (ACO) for contracts in which this close relationship is highly valued. Using this approach, the Contract Administration Branch retains all contract administration functions normally assigned to field activities. The second approach is to assign functions to Defense Contract Administration Services (DCAS) activities.

The first approach is used for approximately 15 percent (750) of the

5,000 contracts awarded by NRCC each year. These contracts involve maintenance services performed at government activities for which the retained administration is viewed as the best and probably the only effective way to cover on-site inspection and acceptance of the work performed. When this approach is used, some of the retained administrative functions are delegated to the requiring activity (those for which it holds technical expertise). Code P6 of the NRCC performs the balance.

The second method employs normal assignment of contract administration. NRCC retains functions such as exercising contract options and issuing new procurement modifications. This method is used for the majority of contracts awarded by NRCC, but the Contract Administration Branch becomes involved in specific issues arising under contracts for which DCAS has been assigned administration. This occurs only when requested by DCAS activities, a requiring activity, or a contractor. The normal assignment of a contract to a DCAS activity is done based on geographical considerations in accordance with DOD 4105.59-H, *Directory of Contract Administration Services Component.*

The Contract Administration Branch at NRCC was established in 1982 to centralize the contract administration function. Previously, beginning around 1976, the contract administration function was the responsibility of the acquisition branches, but performance of the function suffered because of the relatively higher priority placed on timely award of contracts. Management's attention tended to be focused on award actions. As with most procurement offices, priorities were concentrated almost exclusively on pre-award and award with little emphasis on post-award functions. The result diminished effectiveness in administration. As an experiment, therefore, Contract Administration was established as a separate branch with exclusive contract administration responsibilities. This created a dedicated staff and allowed the acquisition branches to continue to concentrate on awarding contracts.

Contract Administration Branch

The Contract Administration Branch is comprised of ten employees, including one secretary. This represents approximately 12 percent of the total number of employees in the Contracts Division (80) and approximately 7 percent of the command complement (135). Excluding the branch head, the average level of contracting experience of each employee is fifteen years. The branch head assigns work within the branch, matching the more complex work with experienced individuals. Formal training in contract acquisition and administration is mandatory for new personnel during the trainee/intern phase. Subsequent to that phase, most training is on the job, although there are government and private institution courses and programs available to enhance mandatory and on-the-job training. For training purposes, an individual occasionally may be assigned a more complex case than experience would warrant. Personnel utilize the regulations and local guidance, develop contacts with appropriate personnel within and outside the command, and use their own knowledge and experience. As in many government offices today, the office is experiencing personnel shortfalls. Individuals are assigned approximately forty cases at one time. The current office work backlog is approximately two hundred routine, less complex actions. Work on these types of actions is often delayed as a result of urgent, more complex requirements. The branch head estimates that the addition of four more contract administration personnel would significantly improve productivity.

Lack of formal guidance is one of the difficulties--and advantages-- associated with performing contract administration functions. Issues normally have no clear-cut procedures or answers. Effectiveness depends on the knowledge, experience and judgment of the ACO. Actions are based on interpretation of individual contract clauses and provisions. Guidance is sought by review of the FAR, DAR Supplement, NRCC instructions and handbooks, and previous decisions on similar issues in other contracts. Most guidance is not explicit, leaving a major portion of the interpretation responsibility to judgment. Limited formal NRCC procedural guidance is available for contract claims and contract close-out. However, one key to effective contract administration is the flexibility allowed the ACO. Contract administration is full of uncertainties-- each situation is different. Since issues of differing magnitude arise concerning the numerous types of contracts, regulations and rules are less significant than a thorough understanding of the situation.

Interrelationships with Other Functions and Organizations

The Contract Administration Branch has extensive contact with other NRCC codes and other organizations. Communication is precipitated by contract questions or problems and is accomplished by telephone, visits, and written messages. In DCAS administered contracts, the branch handles most of the issues that require PCO action, such as decisions in termination and dispute cases. Additionally, the branch is NRCC's principal interface with DCAS activities whenever information is needed or contract problems arise. Contacts with requiring activities also arise; most are concerned with requirements interpretation. Calls are occasionally received from contractors who need assistance with payments and contract interpretation issues even though their contracts have been assigned to field administration.

In supporting all administered contracts at both DCAS and NRCC, the branch has direct access to the acquisition branch heads, the NRCC special assistant functions, and the Office of Counsel. Internal communication concerning relatively simple matters is accomplished orally and in writing when necessary. Branch personnel must ensure that the documentation of all actions is included in the individual contract file. The commanding officer, executive officer, and/or contracts division director enter into contract administration matters as necessary, particularly on major issues involving high-dollar value contracts. Prior to issuance, final decisions of contracting officers are submitted to the NRCC Contract Review Board for approval or disapproval. In claims decisions, the Contract Administration Branch coordinates all interested groups to ensure obtaining concurrence of NAVSUP and higher levels. Higher commands review and approve or disapprove NRCC final decision letters involving $3 million or more.

The performance of the branch is being carefully observed, since its establishment as a separate branch could be emulated if successful. It is believed that success largely depends on communications between the branch and outside organizations as well as the informal communications network between the branch and other NRCC functional organizations. Branch personnel consult with the Office of Counsel, SADBU, and acquisition branch personnel in their effort to make decisions that are fair, in the best interests of the government, and in accordance with contracting regulations. The branch provides an example of integrating contract management into the procurement activity while giving it the status of an independent operating function. Its value as a model may be important since contract administration is considered by acquisition office personnel to be a function that is secondary to buying. Within government there has been little experience using alternatives to field administration.

SUMMARY

Finding an ideal organization for the administration of contracts has proven difficult. The chapter presents the following points:

- A review is made of three approaches used to organize the administration of contracts: two by government and one by a large investor-owned utility.
- Each organization has extensive post-award operations and attempts to achieve maximum return for its investment in the required work.
- All three approaches share the challenge of giving close attention to post-award responsibilities, a task not easily done by personnel charged with pre-award duties.
- The work of contract administration differs substantially from that of procurement.
- A review of Detroit Edison's approach to contract administration provides an excellent overview of the work required by private

corporate buying organizations.

● An examination of the Defense Logistics Agency's organization of
  contract administration services provides a review of the special
  factors influencing organization of post-award administration in
  government.
● A study of the structure of the NRCC, Washington, shows the potential for including post-award management as part of the responsibilities of a buying office in a government setting.

TOPICS FOR DISCUSSION

1. Explain and evaluate Detroit Edison's approach to contract ad-
    ministration. Would such an approach be viable for government?
    For manufacturers?
2. In what ways has government organization for contract admini-
    stration been influenced by legislative sensitivities?
3. Several burdens have been imposed on procurement and field con-
    tracting activities of the government. Discuss these burdens and
    identify those you think are particularly important.
4. Discuss the features you think are unique in the organization of the
    Naval Regional Contracting Center.
5. Consider the general division of procurement and post-award con-
    tracting work into several independent organizations in government.
    What might be a more effective structure for this work?

CASE 3-1

Frigate Fracas[1]

The United States Navy's Naval Sea Systems Command (NAVSEA) issued a charter (NAVSEAINST 5400.49B) to establish responsibilities of the
ship acquisition program manager for its guided missile frigate (FFG-7).
The following is paraphrased from that charter.

The program manager is assigned full authority to conduct the program within approved performance, supportability, funding, and schedule
constraints and thresholds. He shall exercise authority over the planning,
direction, control, and utilization of assigned program resources and will

---

[1]This case is based on research by William Sumner while a student
at George Washington University.

provide direction to the program support effort being performed by other NAVSEA organizations. As the responsible executive, he is authorized to act on his own initiative in matters affecting the program. This authority implies complete responsibility and accountability for the total performance of his program. All operating relationships described in this charter shall be considered complementary to this fundamental concept. NAVSEA functional elements will provide technical assistance, contracting support, and administrative support to the program office. In this regard, the command headquarters organization manual applies.

According to the NAVSEA Command Headquarters Organization Manual (NAVSEAINST 5400.1B, Chapter 10), contracting officers perform the following duties:

1. In direct support of command managers, serve as contracting officer and plan, select, negotiate, award, administer, and terminate contracts for the commodities assigned
2. Provide advice and assistance to the deputy commander on all contracts matters for the commodities assigned
3. Participate in advance acquisition planning, determine overall contracts strategy and tactics, and advise program managers concerning matters relating to contracts
4. Ensure compliance with DOD FAR Supplement policies and procedures
5. Review and approve business clearances and other contract-related documents commensurate with the authority set forth in the DOD FAR supplement and Navy contracting directives, and with the delegation of authority for contract matters made by the deputy commander
6. Represent the deputy commander, as directed, to government and industry in division contract matters
7. Process extraordinary contractual actions under Public Law 85-804 (other than amendments without consideration)

These delegations of authority have an interesting set of overlaps. The program manager is responsible for utilizing resources and completing the assigned project. Success in fulfilling the charter--i.e., meeting the system construction schedules, performance, etc.--is the job assigned; career progress is at stake. Nevertheless, it must be done within the appropriate constraints that may be imposed by the contracting process. That process is rather clearly established as the responsibility of the contracting officer.

Working relationships and operating practices are established partly as a consequence of the assignments of authority. Tension and dysfunctional conflict sometimes arise between NAVSEA program managers and contracting officers. In late 1983 the Commander of NAVSEA began to hear complaints, and directed a board of senior officers to oversee a study to determine the nature of the conflicts and prepare a report summarizing the significance of the difficulties. The board conducted its study and prepared a report detailing numerous conflicts and complaints from the program managers and contracting officers. The report contained quotations from command executives, including those that follow:

1. The program manager does not inform me of his plans nor include me in meetings in which contractual requirements are established.
2. The contracting officer is not well enough informed on the technology involved in the acquisition. He doesn't understand the ball game.
3. The program manager is consistently tardy in providing specifications in time for proper review prior to issuance of solicitations.
4. The contracting officer delays the process. For example, he holds up the procurement request for additional justification when the sole source is obvious.
5. The program manager isn't informed about the regulations and requirements derived from congressional policy and doesn't particularly care.
6. The contracting officer holds too much authority, considering most of the negotiated issues directly impact the program.
7. The program manager issues technical directions without due regard for the integrity of the contract.
8. The contracting officer lets too many competitors enter into the competitive range, complicating and delaying the discussion phases of the procurement.
9. The program manager is not concerned about justification for sole source procurement and writes sloppy sole source memos.
10. The contracting officer's authority for the negotiation process is unrealistic because the principal issues at stake are budget and technical, and his expertise does not extend into that area.
11. The program managers issue technical directions that exceed their authority and create conflicts over informal changes.
12. The contracting officer attempts to extract dollars from the contractual agreement, even though it is established that the entire project is underfunded.
13. The contracting officer is slow in his reaction to changes. In fact, he batches the changes that occur, causing further slippage in the program and, therefore, unnecessary cost increases. We are informed that our industrial counterparts have no such problems of delay relating to their changes processes.

After reviewing the report, the commander directed his staff to set contracting officers, together with their appropriate staff members, would work out a complete coordination agreement establishing the working relationships between the offices. The commander specified that a coordination agreement be established for each project. He also specified that the following issues must be addressed in order to define the roles of both parties in the acquisitions and contract management processes.

I. Presolicitation Phase
Advance planning
Submission of purchase
  request
Obtaining sources
Sole source determination
Request for proposals

II. Solicitation and Evaluation
  Phase
Discussions
Technical evaluation
Business evaluation
Determination of
  competitive range

III. Negotiations and Award
Discussions with
  contractor
Selection of contractor
Contract preparation
  and award

IV. Contract Administration
Technical direction
Contract changes and
  extensions
Monitoring performance
Patents
Acceptance of final
  products
Payment of vouchers
Property administration
Administrative closeout

* * * * *

Assume you are the executive officer and are responsible for timely action on this directive. Detail how you would comply. As part of your plan to stimulate discussion at a conference on the subject, provide a pro forma statement of the proper roles (functions, duties, and responsibilities) that are appropriate for program managers and contracting officers in each phase of a new project in the command. State responsibilities and authority for

1. initiating action;
2. ensuring coordination (meetings, documentation);
3. supplying information; and
4. deciding on a course of action.

CASE 3-2

Armored Division-RCI

The Armored Division of the RCI Corporation is responsible for several of the corporation's major programs for the United States Department of Defense (DOD). The Division Manager, Robert Stimsonn, was gratified that, in 1985, his division had achieved an increasing share of business with the U.S. Army Material Command--particularly the Tank Automotive Command (TACOM)--and had secured significant sales sponsored by the U.S. Marine Corps. At that time, Stimsonn's largest program was production of the Land/Sea Personnel Carrier (LPC).

Stimsonn had spent many years devising an effective organization for working under contracts awarded by the United States government. He found that government agencies employed many separately authorized persons, each cognizant of specific matters. He also found that many of these government officials, though extremely knowledgeable of specific rules and technologies, were unable to fully coordinate all factors and interest groups within government in a timely manner. Consequently, the division's government business tended to be variable, subject to changing perceptions, complex, and frustratingly difficult to manage. It had nevertheless proven a profitable and rewarding business at Armored Division under his direction. He and his key managers enjoyed working out the scientific, technical, and contractual challenges constantly being placed before them.

At Armored Division, Stimsonn had created an organization he felt was extraordinarily effective for marrying high technology and heavy manufacturing operations necessary in developing and producing vehicle-mounted weapons systems for overland military missions. The basic structure of Armored Division under Stimsonn as it related to managing government contracts is depicted in chart 1. (Traditional staff and operating functions are omitted from the chart.)

This organization constituted the Stimsonn variation of program/ project management. It evolved in response to the conflicts arising over management and control of the large-scale, technologically complex programs that Armored Division captured. The division's several business managers were responsible for profit and loss for programs under their cognizance, interface with customer representatives, and business management of the project. The business managers reported to the Deputy Division Manager for U.S. Defense Business. They were considered to hold overall plenary responsibility for their respective programs. The business managers, however, did not control all aspects of production; project managers were also established for each specific program or project won by the company. The project manager was drawn from the division's engineering group and held technical management authority for assigned projects. Project managers reported directly to the Deputy Division Manager for engineering. In addition, the Director of Proposals, Contracts, and Negotiations reported directly to Stimsonn and had the responsibility for devising corporate strategy in proposal development and for negotiating and administering all contractual matters. Two groups were established under this director. The first was the operations group of contracts and proposals personnel who serviced the production and logistics activities of the division. The second was the engineering group of contracts and proposals personnel who serviced the division's developmental and engineering support projects.

Support of the proposal and negotiation processes by pricing personnel was provided by the Pricing and Financial Services Director who reported to the Division Comptroller. His pricing personnel were generally assigned as team members who developed prices and coordinated estimates. Teams were established under direction of the pertinent contracts and proposals group. Stimsonn liked this organizational concept, because he found that each of these functional areas represented power centers with independent viewpoints and positions that needed to be fully represented at top staff levels. He wanted managers who would aggressively state their attitudes and positions directly to him.

Some conflicts emerged from this structure. Project managers complained that they didn't have sufficient control over personnel and resources to fully meet design and development objectives. Some business managers argued that they should have fuller directive authority over contracts and financial support personnel. On several occasions even customer personnel had argued that control of project activity was not adequately centralized. Stimsonn, however, was satisfied that the organization not only enabled him to keep in touch with ongoing work, but also kept him informed of all sides of most issues as they arose.

* * * * *

Criticize this organization and suggest a more effective alternative arrangement based on your knowledge of program/project management and matrix management. Justify your suggestions.

Chart 1, Case 3-2

**Armored Division Organization
(Program Control Structure Only)**

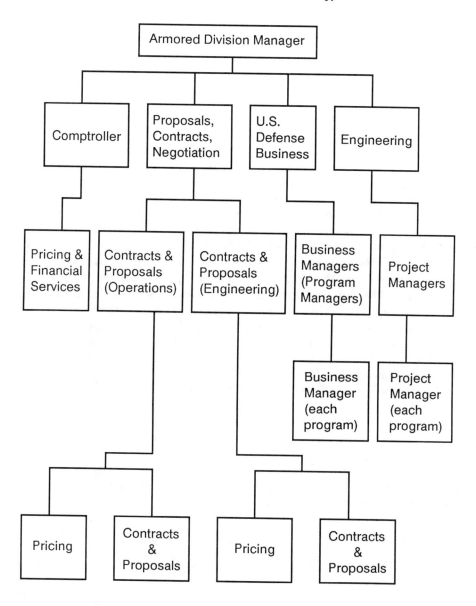

4

Initiating Performance: Translating Agreement Into Plan

The agreement, signature, and issuance of a new contract is accompanied by an air of celebration. Contractors feel it is a victory because they have won out over their competitors. Procurement managers and program personnel feel victorious because performance of work is thereby started, an event that often follows many months of pitfalls, delays, and frustrations. However, executing the contract only begins the executory phases of the procurement. Converting the new agreement into an operating plan is the responsibility of the contractor, but it is one in which the buyer's personnel have a great interest, since their program's success is at stake.

Procurement and contract managers must proceed with a degree of caution, because it is their responsibility to view contracts with a critical eye on practical performance challenges and to assess contractor capabilities. This is based on their disciplinary perspective and experience with a history of programs that seldom meet all planning objectives--technical, cost and schedule.

The viewpoint of corporate proposal managers is different. Their goal is to secure new business; therefore, their projections and estimates tend to be unqualified. This is in contrast to contract managers, especially in competitive organizations, who must ensure that company policies and assets are preserved and enhanced through the profitability of potential contract agreements. They approach the contract by carefully analyzing proposed terms and conditions.

DEVELOPING AN OPERATING PLAN

This chapter examines the process of converting the pre-award understandings and attitudes of buyer and seller personnel into viable operating procedures and practices designed to bring about successful contract performance. In doing this, it is valuable to examine the opinions of practitioners. The following description of the pre-award responsibilities and objectives of contract administrators was given by a contract manager at a major CAD/CAM company.

Contract administration provides support to the field sales people in dealing with the customer contractually. Sales people sometimes give things away; consequently, contract administration holds respon sibility for negotiation of the contract. Our objective is to minimize the company's legal and financial risks. We carry this out by negotiating the terms and conditions of all prospective contracts. The pricing and discounting responsibilities are carried by marketing people, but contract administration looks out for items such as FOB terms, payment terms, software licenses, and other contract features designed to protect the company. When a contract is awarded, the contract administration responsibility switches from negotiation to administration. Contract administration acknowledges the order and enters it into the company's data base as a sales order. This entry is done through a computer terminal, and the computer is programmed to aid in converting the sales order into manufacturing language. It takes the assembly numbers, the part numbers, and other data and explodes them into the various subassemblies, etc., necessary for production. A production work order is generated directly from the entry of the sales order. From that point on, the production work order controls internal operations.

The performance initiation process is similar at another company in which work is done principally for the Department of Defense. Upon receipt of a new contract award, the contracts manager is responsible for initiating work by writing a sales order. The sales order constitutes the internal directive used by the company to implement what the contract requires. The order is written by extracting essential technical and schedule information from the contract for use by research and production personnel. The extracted material is limited to the description of required work, quantities, prices, and delivery dates that are germane to performance. This approach eliminates unnecessary contractual details from the internal information system. Work does not begin until the contracts office issues a sales order.

A similar process is carried on by the contracts manager at an electronics manufacturing firm that pursues defense contracts. The contracts manager emphasizes the technical content of sales orders. She writes the sales order based on the contract, but not until she has read the specifications and related technical documentation. She views the specification as critical because she frequently discovers unacceptable provisions. For example, the company had received a contract to provide the electronic communications system for a helicopter. One provision of the specification required that the system, upon installation, would not impair the performance of the aircraft. The contract manager noticed that terminology. Because she felt that even one pound added to an aircraft would affect--perhaps impair--its performance, she concluded that the specification called for an impossibility. Having picked up that detail, she had the specification wording changed to read that the company would design the electronic system to operate within the performance envelope of the aircraft. As she explained it, the precise language was important because the more encompassing language could subject the company to additional unexpected risks. She noted that the program management personnel, including the engineering review group, failed to catch the provision, because they were too close to the project.

The approach of these companies reflects practices of many whose work is in accordance with customer-originated specifications and work statements. When a contract has been won, the initial authorization of work internal to the performing organization is accomplished by contract managers. The ease with which performance is accomplished and an acceptable end product completed is strongly influenced by how well the original internal work order is created and distributed to departments that must perform the work. Once an agreement is firm, contractor procedures for initiating work may vary, but self-interest dictates that a standard process be established and that a part of the operating routine include verifying the performance requirements and laying out an effective work plan. These are vital parts of the total performance challenge.

POST-AWARD ORIENTATION

Post-award orientation may be defined as a communication process whereby the parties verify that they hold consistent views of their agreement and ascertain that planned operations are likely to fulfill their expectations. A closely related but subordinate objective is to discover and resolve potential performance problems at the outset of the performance period. There are two primary methods used by the government for post-award orientation. The first is to hold a conference with the contractor. The second is simply to use a letter or other informal communication to advise the contractor of the government's principal concerns regarding successful performance. It is interesting that there is no standard government policy regarding the level of post-award performance orientation activity that should be conducted with contractors. However, the government's greatest concerns regarding these issues can be discovered by examining existing checklists and by referring to the regulations. An excellent source of information on this subject is the Federal Acquisition Regulation, Subpart 42.5.

From the buyer's perspective, one of the major constraints on post-award orientation is avoidance of commitments or implications that the post-award meetings would in any way alter the contract. This is particularly important under government policy designed to preserve the integrity of the competitive process. The orientation of a new contractor should clarify the roles of each member of the contractor's and purchaser's personnel teams. Team members need predictable, viable working relationships both internally and with their counterparts in the other party's organization. If a post-award orientation conference is used to achieve coordination, issues such as the mutual understanding of contract requirements should be addressed. Developing such an understanding may be particularly important in areas concerning spare parts, data and data rights, safety precautions, financial arrangements, rates of funding, planned production cycles, and expectations regarding the extent of subcontracting. The post-award orientation is certainly not limited to these factors, but they are important and likely to involve ambiguities and misunderstandings. The necessity for orientation conferences may be greater when the parties have not previously worked together and when the undertaking is large and complex.

A post-award conference is attractive to contractors because it gives them an opportunity to explore more fully their operating relationships with the customer, including--in the case of government--the technical director, the ultimate user, and the contracting officer. Additionally, such conferences afford insight into the relationships between the user, the technical people, and the contracting officer. For example, a contractor may be concerned with whether he or she should respond to the direction of the technical officer and, if so, whether the contracting officer will ratify the action if it requires additional sums of money. This is not an idle issue because government contract policy clearly states that only a contracting officer can authorize a change in the terms and conditions of a contract. Nevertheless, the meaning of technical direction and how it may be differentiated from formal change actions is not easily expressed.

A key issue here is the attitude of government contract managers toward their ability to accommodate work variations during performance. Many contractual projects are dynamic in the sense that unexpected decisions arise. For instance, during contract work, questions may surface that demand judgment as to whether the work is required and therefore already covered or is an addition to, or subtraction from, the existing contract. The parties need to know how smoothly contract interpretation issues will be approached and be able to confirm their own interpretations as they initiate work. Contractors want assurance that if a contractual variance requires an addition to the contract, this will be recognized.

The government perspective of the value of a post-award conference is somewhat different. There is concern with establishing a working relationship between the government and the contractor, but many issues deal with government policy implementation. Nevertheless, most of the areas to be discussed are judgmental. For government contracts, post-award orientation conferences are usually chaired by the administrative contracting officer; although when key technical understandings are needed, the procurement contracting officer may lead the conference. The contracting officer's role in this conference is to ensure the following points:

1. The contractor understands the procedures for notification, review and consent to subcontracts
2. The contractor is aware of the importance of the delivery schedule and the relationship of deliveries to other elements of the government program
3. An understanding exists regarding the sequence and scheduling of events in the production or development cycle as contemplated by the contract
4. Issues, such as the development of spare parts lists and the initiation of effort toward definition and pricing of spares support, have been addressed
5. The contractor is addressing safety issues, including compliance with hazardous materials policies

These issues are only the beginning. The parties are concerned with financing arrangements and requirements for presenting invoices. When cost type contracts are used, the parties look for elements of cost that need clarification to reduce doubt as to whether the cost is considered allocable and reasonable. The government is routinely concerned with the effectiveness of the contractor's accounting and cash management systems and compliance with policies such as equal opportunity, subcontract management, information systems, and reporting. All can become key issues during start-up operations. Government concerns often relate to policy and process issues, while contractor concerns are primarily oriented toward defining the practicability of operating arrangements for performing the job. Perhaps most critical to both parties is their need to know who speaks with authority for the other party and what degree of flexibility exists in the contractual relationship. Both parties want to define the risks involved in the working practices for a particular contract. Each needs to understand the internal operating relationships of the other party to the degree that those relationships have an impact upon their own interests. Finally, both need an operational understanding of what is acceptable and what will be paid for and when. These operational relationships, if successfully established at the outset of a contract, can facilitate the ease with which the two parties will work together for the duration of their relationship.

POST-AWARD ORIENTATION:
AN R&D BUYER'S PERSPECTIVE

The following paraphrased interview illustrates the perspective toward post-award conferences of a chief of procurement at a naval weapons research activity.

Please describe the work of your procurement division.
We award about two hundred new contracts each year. They are valued at about $100 million and about 90 percent are of the negotiated cost type. We buy primarily research and development.
I have seen little in the way of authoritative sources describing post-award start-up requirements. What sources are you aware of?
There isn't much other than the short statements in the FAR. DOD instruction 7000.2 may be of some help in certain circumstances. There isn't any specific requirement to hold a post-award conference. It is done when required, but it is discretionary to the contracting officer.
Who usually chairs the post-award conference?
The contracting officer or the negotiator. The way we are organized, the negotiator represents the contracting officer, and if he or she is a senior negotiator, the contracting officer might not go along. However, the contracts department always chairs the meeting.
When a conference is set up, do the instructions leave a great deal of latitude to the contracting officer?
Yes. But we hold only four or five conferences of that type each year. The decision to hold a conference really depends on the complexity of the program and the contract.
That's not very many, perhaps only 2 percent of your total contract awards.
Yes. Whether or not we hold a conference is affected by the process leading up to the award of the contract. If it is a competitive procurement, the kinds of discussions held with a contractor during the pre-award process are limited. You are able to cover only areas of strengths and weaknesses, and you can't get into the kind of detail often needed from the standpoint of a complete technical understanding. Furthermore, you can't discuss management and organization issues nor can you lead or direct the contractor during those pre-award time periods for fear that you would be aiding him in the competition, thereby violat-

ing your responsibility to the competitors. Consequently, in a competitive procurement, there are numerous things that need to be discussed during the post-award phase, and that's when the post-award conference becomes important. That's when we conduct such a conference.

The regulations explicitly state that provisions of the contract cannot be modified during a post-award conference. How do you handle this?

We never seek to reopen negotiations at the post-award conference. We do find out things--contractor interpretations--of which we were unaware; but it has worked out rather well. The discrepancies that we learn about at the post-award conferences have not been ones that require reopening of negotiations. If a discrepancy arises that is that big, we would have to initiate change action, but we would also conclude that we had done a rather poor job during the negotiations.

How do you document post-award conferences?

We aren't as concerned about the documentation as we are about the understanding developed. Keep in mind, we aren't modifying the contract. To have a successfully managed contract, you must understand exactly what the contractor is telling you during proposal and negotiation stages. We find we're able to do that if we have a sole source negotiation. So the post-award conference isn't as important in that situation. But in a competitive procurement, we are limited in the subjects we can discuss. We need to know how the contractor has organized his management team, what responsibilities the key people have, and what decisions they can make. We then get into the question of what decisions we will allow them to make without coming back to us for approval. We discuss the government management team and how it works. Also, we'll discuss cost in terms of each of the work packages.

Will all of this be contained in the minutes of the post-award meeting?

Yes. In general, we ask the contractor to prepare the minutes.

The FAR seems to indicate that the minutes are very important, yet you are letting the contractor prepare them.

Yes, the minutes are important; they set the stage. Nevertheless, we let the contractor prepare them, and we review them to see whether or not they have captured what we have agreed are acceptable operating practices.

Let's switch around for a moment. In your view, what are the things that the contractor seeks during the post-award conference?

They're worried about the authority for action, they want to know to whom they should talk, and they want to gain a feeling for the kinds of things we will approve. They want to know that, if they listen to the program manager, the contracting officer will ratify the action. I think they already know the answers to these questions, but they always want to hear them again. Then, they're concerned about funding--when it is going to be available. I also think that in these conferences, they are attempting to weigh the strength of the program manager against the strength of the contracting officer. Another thing we always get into is the statement of work. We review it at the conference. The contractor will make statements such as, "You didn't really want me to do that, did you? It's obvious we don't have enough money in the contract for that." So we have to reaffirm that what we intended is what was called for by the work statement. Then too, we always get into some small details like the format of reports and their timing.

In summary, how would you characterize the purpose of the post-award conference?

A lot can be done prior to award. That's the time to settle all of the issues unless doing so would infringe upon the fairness of the procurement process. Post-award activity should do no more than fine tune the arrangements. The objective is to make sure that there is a complete understanding of what the contractor is going to do, and that should be put in perspective with government requirements. I think both parties are really seeking the same thing, but I see the whole process as being no more than a fine tuning of the negotiations.

POST-AWARD CONFERENCE CHECKLISTS

One approach to managing post-award conferences effectively is to use checklists. Contract managers can develop checklists of topics pertinent to their specific contract workload, and several checklists have been developed by various government agencies. But there is no standard set of practices. From the government's point of view, there are only two general categories of substantive issues to be raised at the conference: technical questions (including quality assurance) and contract administration issues. The checklist that follows identifies most general topics pertinent to supply and service contract orientation conferences. Specialized technological matters specific to each contract should be added to the general list as required.

Post-Award Conference Checklist

I. Technical and Quality Assurance Issues
    A.   Quality assurance/inspection system compliance
    B.   Procedure for design drawing approval
    C.   Policy toward waivers and deviations
    D.   Procedure for pre-production samples
    E.   Qualification and environmental testing requirements
    F.   Approach to specification interpretation

G. Value engineering incentives/program questions
H. Inspection and acceptance
I. Data requirements and manuals
J. Adequacy and availability of facilities
K. Program-unique or specific issues of concern
II. Contract Administration Issues
  A. Personnel Matters
    1. Specific authority and responsibility of managers
    2. Key personnel
  B. Overall Management Issues
    1. Routing of correspondence
    2. Questions concerning terms and conditions
       (a) omissions
       (b) conflicts
       (c) explanations
    3. Space and accommodations for resident inspectors
    4. Planning reports
    5. Special reports
    6. Classification and security requirements
    7. Plant protection and security
    8. Foreign supplier procedures
    9. Duty-free entry certificates
    10. Insurance policy and questions
    11. Liability questions
    12. Industrial relations notifications
    13. Assistance regarding priorities and allocations
    14. Occupational safety/health/hazardous materials
    15. Modification of contracts
    16. Termination procedures
  C. Production and Progress Management
    1. Technical direction authority
    2. Work progress reports
    3. Production plans
    4. Milestone identification and report
    5. Production surveillance procedure
  D. Financial, Cost, and Payment Issues
    1. Financial reports
    2. Invoicing, billing procedure
    3. Funding schedule
    4. Payment and financing
    5. Overtime policy and approval
    6. Withholding rights and procedures
    7. Change order accounting
    8. Interdivisional transfers
    9. Allowability of cost

E. Intellectual Property Requirements and Rights
    1. Royalty reports
    2. Patent reports
    3. Technical data deliveries
    4. Technical data rights
F. Procurement and Subcontracting Matters
    1. Subcontract consent
    2. Procurement systems approval
    3. Subcontractor management
    4. Subcontractor cost and pricing data
    5. Subcontractor source inspection
G. Social and Economic Policy Objectives
    1. Small and disadvantaged business subcontracting
    2. SADBU reports
    3. Operation of labor statutes, as applicable
        (a) Davis Bacon
        (b) Work hours
        (c) Walsh Healey
        (d) Service contract
        (e) Anti-kickback
H. Property Management Matters
    1. Government property--types, schedule
    2. Property--maintenance, preservation
    3. Property--accountability, identification
    4. Property reviews and audits
    5. Property disposal
I. Transportation and Shipping
    1. Delivery of end items
    2. Transportation authorizations
    3. Place of delivery

CONTRACTOR'S POST-AWARD START-UP ACTIONS

In most respects, start-up activity following receipt of a new contract award is similar to that of internally sponsored undertakings. However, the existence of a contractual relationship affects the start-up operations because the client has an interest in, and may wish to influence, the approach taken by the supplier's manager. This desire to influence is expressed most strongly when the government sponsors the effort. Agencies recognize that contractors must plan and manage their own operations, but several factors cause the government to require its contractors to establish internal management practices that conform with government methods. These factors include the existence of a public source for funding, political and media oversight, and the vast accumulated experience of the government in managing and operating projects through the contractual method.

In addition to potential customer influence on contract start-up activities, the discretion of a contractor's manager respecting project planning is constrained by existing internal corporate policy, procedure, and practice. Consequently, steps toward organizing, staffing, and defining a project's operations may require negotiation to find a satisfactory fit within the existing management structure.

This section focuses on new contracts other than those for work that will be integrated into existing operations. It treats contracts for which a special management structure, such as a project office, is needed to increase the likelihood of program success. The actions discussed have been identified as key elements in the initiation of new projects. Ten major categories of project initiation activities to which contract managers, project managers, and corporate executives must give appropriate attention are identified. Descriptions of these categories of activities are not intended as comprehensive statements of all project initiation steps, but rather as an overview of the scope of project start-up activities. Additional topics should be added for specific types of projects; for example, a facilities construction project would contain added elements relating to site operations and logistics. Numerous book-length sources would be required to fully address many of the specific topics.

Project office and project team. Upon receiving a new contract, a company must complete a project plan. This may require appointing a project manager and, at a minimum, requires organizing the project office and assigning personnel to the project team. To the extent that the project has been organized prior to submitting the project proposal, this work already will have been completed. However, an update is necessary upon receiving the contract. A firm statement of required skills is needed along with a review of qualified internal and external personnel resources so that hiring requirements or necessary assignments or transfers can be identified. Project organization must include assigning specific tasks to named individuals, establishing close working relationships with the functional organizations supporting the project, and drafting or updating the project charter. Early responsibilities of the program manager include setting objectives for the project, providing adequate space, and assembling the necessary staff to carry out the project.

Project policies, procedures, and instructions. A new project requires an effective document processing system including adequate measures for control over the issuance, update, and change of policies and procedures. Any new policies and procedures must fit within and coordinate fully with those of the umbrella organization. At a minimum, the project system should ensure compliance with reporting requirements; the management issuance system for generation of work statements and specifications; policies concerning travel, trips, and conferences; security requirements; and intellectual property policies and procedures. Each of these areas is sensitive to customer requirements, and the planning should consider specific provisions of the contract and beliefs and attitudes of the customer with respect to the operating environment.

Project policy concerning budget, costing, and financial affairs. The new project should set up cost budgets for both direct and indirect expenses, initiate a release system for ensuring control over the entire funding process, set up a project charging system, and build or modify a chart of accounts for project use as necessary.

Project master plan, schedules, and task level budgets. Generating a project master plan is a major undertaking that should be done in the early weeks of the program. It is accomplished by analyzing the overall project requirements and contract specifications and by reviewing all internal and external resources available to the company. The major purposes of this planning process are to identify and schedule all major milestones to be achieved during the course of the contract, to define work activities to fit the format of a work break-down structure, and to schedule and budget all tasks required to complete the overall project. The project should generate a comprehensive scheduling system including, where appropriate, a complete project network that identifies critical items and the critical path and assesses associated risks.

Release system for initiation and control of individual tasks. Once an overall master plan has been developed, the project must establish a work order release system that ensures that budget allocations, starting and ending dates of task items in the schedule, definition of completion of tasks, and status reporting for each task are activated for the contract. The project should establish a purchasing and subcontracting authority within its control as well as a make-or-buy analysis system, and establish responsibility for monitoring subcontracts, including their compliance with customer policy. The purchasing system analysis is particularly important when the customer is a government agency.

Comprehensive reporting and evaluation system for internal information. The project manager should initiate an information needs study to identify the specific internal reports necessary for the project. These should include manpower, financial and progress reports and should define the need for updating both weekly and monthly. Reports should include task level and project level status reports, labor variance reports, and cost performance reports. The system should provide for updating data (using automated source code entry if feasible) and should provide charts to be used for management decisionmaking activities. In addition, an evaluation procedure should be established, including periodic data reviews and project review meetings. Reviews should be coupled with a system for corrective action when a deficiency is identified.

Client-customer interface and reporting requirements. Although internal reporting procedures provide those elements of information necessary to managing a project within the performing organization, provision must be made for reports that will flow through to the customer or client. Requirements for this should be set forth in the contractual agreement, and the principal responsibility during the start-up process is to ensure that project reporting procedures are responsive to both periodic and ad hoc requirements of the contract. Staffing of the project should consider manpower needs for the timely preparation and delivery of required reports. When comparing government-funded and privately sponsored contracts, a significant difference in the level and detail of contractual reporting will be found.

Specific contract administration duties. Communication channels must be established between the buyer and the seller on both an informal and a formal basis in a way that ensures the development of records of all significant contract actions. Such actions include requests for information, approvals of documents, contractor needs for property or data, and resolution of questions in which the customer must be involved. Project methods should be established for developing new business in the form of add-on work, changes, and other new developments, such as identifying bid opportunities. Methods used to handle deviations, waivers and change orders, including the negotiation of adjustments to the contract and coordination of technical information exchanges, are central to effective contract administration.

Systems engineering. Principal responsibilities of the systems engineering group include defining functional requirements of the system, providing for cost effectiveness studies, and developing appropriate priorities and trade-offs for all work activities. Systems integrity studies are the key to the success of this group. The group should be able to ensure that an operating system will be achieved upon the performance of all tasks encompassed within the program under contract. It should define approaches to all key project decision areas, identifying each decision process with regard to timing and sequence and relating it to performance objectives. To reduce risk and ensure the achievement of end objectives, the need for management reserves should be identified and established throughout the system. Systems engineering should also be responsible for searching out growth opportunities and objectives for the project. The group is responsible for establishing qualification and check-out objectives consistent with the contract and usable for guidance in engineering and quality assurance management.

Engineering work plan and product assurance system. These elements of a project represent the essential, grass roots efforts necessary to a development program leading to a successful manufacturing and production operation. The project office must assume the responsibility for establishing and staffing an adequate project engineering capability or assigning the work to functional supporting organizations. The objective is to perform design studies, write detailed equipment specifications, define subsystem interfaces, complete test planning, and write vendor specifications. Under this set of responsibilities, the project office should prepare a reliability assessment plan, provide for detailed qualification testing, provide for inspection and/or quality assurance, plan for evaluation of subcontractor performance, and make allocations of responsibility for the overall engineering and product assurance effort. The group should create a value engineering documentation system.

SUMMARY

A vital phase of post-award management is planning, organizing, and initiating performance. This chapter discusses the following points:

- Responsibilities assigned to supplier contract managers to convert new contract awards into internal work directives
- Issues associated with customer-controlled technical documents
- Orientation that enables the parties to develop a full understanding of their relationship, including special concerns of government
- An R&D buyer's view of orientation practices and their usefulness
- A range of topics that may need to be addressed during post-award conferences, including a checklist for conducting a conference
- Ten categories of start-up actions needed to initiate performance of a large-scale procurement

TOPICS FOR DISCUSSION

1. Summarize the principal roles of a supplier's contract manager during the post-award start-up phases of a new contract award.
2. Summarize the principal roles of a supplier's contract manager during the pre-award phase of contract activity.
3. Define and explain the concept of post-award orientation.
4. Under what conditions do you think a post-award conference should be mandatory?
5. For what reasons might it be argued that the government's approach to post-award orientation differs from that pertinent to most private sector contracting? In what ways would it be similar or identical?
6. Comment on the technical and quality assurance aspects of a post-award conference checklist. Discuss several issues that may be important at the conference and the circumstances under which they are likely to arise.
7. Differentiate between a reporting and evaluation system for internal control and a system for reporting to the customer.

CASE 4-1

**Technical Direction Policy for
the Strategic Defense Initiative**

John Jones was elated when selected to become the director of procurement for the newly established, high-priority, and highly visible Strategic Defense Initiative program. His enthusiasm for his new duties was somewhat tarnished, however, when he encountered a dispute over his proposed adoption of a specific format entitled "Designation of Contracting Officer's Technical Representative." The new format was to be issued by the contracting officer for each SDI contract. John's purpose was to provide for appointment and control of technical direction work. (His proposed format is attached.) The program director and technical staff members felt that the format was too restrictive and detailed, considering the nature of the research and innovation work required under the program. In his previous experience, John had used the format with great success, and he argued that reduced specificity or abandonment of the format would diminish program control.

* * * * *

Analyze and critique the specific provisions of John's format. Explain your support for each provision, and where you think a change is needed, propose new wording and state why you think the change should be approved.

DESIGNATION OF CONTRACTING OFFICER TECHNICAL REPRESENTATIVE

Procurement of _____

under the provisions of Contract No. _____, dated _____,

with _____.

1. This is to certify that _____ of _____

_____is hereby designated as the Contracting Officer's Technical Representative (COTR) for the above referenced contract.

2. This designation will be reviewed annually, effective _____ unless sooner terminated in writing by the Contracting Officer or successor, or by reason of your reassignment, resignation or termination.

3. The Contracting Officer is to be notified immediately if you receive notice of reassignment, or when you will be absent for an extended period of time or otherwise be unable to fulfill the responsibilities of this position. In your absence your immediate superior is to give notice.

4. AUTHORITY AND DUTIES: You are hereby authorized by this designation to take any and all action with respect to the following which could lawfully be taken by me as Contracting Officer, except any action specifically prohibited by the terms of the subject contract and paragraph 5, "LIMITATION," of this designation.

a. To monitor and to ensure that the Contractor performs the technical requirements of the contract in accordance with the contract terms, conditions, specifications and drawings.

b. To review, evaluate and comment on any aspect of the contract and its performance including problems, proposals, technical issues, and including written recommendations to the Contracting Officer.

c. To communicate and coordinate directly with the Contractor to the extent necessary to carry out your duties as COTR except as prohibited in paragraph 5, "LIMITATIONS," of this designation.

d. To attend post-award, pre-construction, negotiation, and other conferences.

e. To coordinate site entry for Contractor personnel.

f. To ensure that Government-furnished property, if provided in the contract, is available when required and proper documentation is obtained when such property is transferred.

g. To provide appropriate notification to the Contracting Officer in any instance when immediate or expeditious decision is required.

h. To perform or cause to be performed any inspections which are necessary to ensure compliance with all contract technical requirements and to require the Contractor to correct any deficiencies. A written report of any deficiency, delay or problem, and recommendation for corrective action, will be provided to the Contracting Officer.

i. To perform technical acceptance of completed work for the contract and to record inspection and acceptance on the "Material Inspection and Receiving Report," or other applicable form, and to ensure that this form is prepared and forwarded to the Contracting Officer.

j. To verify that the work completed or goods or services received are acceptable prior to partial or final payments, and to sign all invoices and return them to the payment office within two weeks or as otherwise stated on the invoice provided by the Financial Management Office (FMO). If the invoice cannot be verified, the COTR must notify the Contracting Officer immediately. Failure to adhere to this procedure may result in late charges being assessed to your budget. A copy of all verified invoices must be sent to the Contracting Officer. Verification date and full name of the COTR must be on every invoice.

k. To maintain all necessary records to document and describe the performance of your duties as COTR, and to distribute such records as applicable. You are required to submit a written report monthly (every 15 days on construction contract) to the Contracting Officer concerning the Contractor's progress and performance of the work or items delivered. If your designation is terminated for any reason before completion of the contract, you will turn over your records to the successor COTR or as instructed by the Contracting Officer.

l. To provide advice and assistance to the Contracting Officer in other areas of contract administration not specifically covered herein.

m. To submit requests to procurement for additional services/tasks.

n. To verify maintenance activities.

o. To establish priorities and expedite task orders.

p. To forward upon contract completion, to the Contracting Officer, all records, documentation, and any final report or product with respect to the contract.

5. LIMITATIONS: You are prohibited from taking any action with respect to the following:

a. To authorize commencement of work at the beginning of a contract or in circumstances involving an increase of work, unless and until the Contracting Officer has authorized the Contractor to proceed to work.

b. To encourage or approve, by word, actions, or omissions, any action by a Contractor which requires, but has not received approval from the Contracting Officer.

c. Written communications with the Contractor and documents shall be signed as "Contracting Officer's Representative" with a copy furnished to the Contracting Officer.

d. To award, agree to, or sign any contract (including delivery and purchase orders) or modification thereto, or in any direct or indirect way to obligate the payment of money.

e. To give instructions or to make any form of agreement which affects the unit price, total contract price, quantity, quality, delivery schedule, or scope of work. All instructions and agreements of this type can be made only by the Contracting Officer.

6. The COTR may designate an assistant to act as his/her representative as a result of his/her absence; however, prior approval of such designation must be received in writing from the Contracting Officer.

7. By signing below you certify that you have read, understand and agree to these instructions. You are required to acknowledge receipt of this designation (or termination) in the space provided below and return the original acknowledgement to the Contracting Officer for retention in the contract file. A duplicate copy is provided for your records.

RECEIPT OF THIS DESIGNATION IS HEREBY ACKNOWLEDGED. I HAVE READ AND FULLY UNDERSTAND THE AUTHORITY AND LIMITATIONS:

_____

COTR SIGNATURE   DATE

_____.

TELEPHONE NO.

THIS DELEGATION IS APPROVED

_____

CONTRACTING OFFICER   DATE

FOR CONTRACTOR USE: RECEIPT OF THE CONTRACTOR'S COPY OF THIS DESIGNATION IS HEREBY ACKNOWLEDGED. I HAVE READ AND FULLY UNDERSTAND THE AUTHORITY AND LIMITATIONS OF THE COTR.

_____

CONTRACTOR SIGNATURE   DATE

_____

TITLE

_____

COMPANY

THIS DESIGNATION IS HEREBY TERMINATED
EFFECTIVE_____ WITHOUT PREJUDICE TO ANY
ACTIONS TAKEN PURSUANT THERETO BY THE DESIGNATED COTR.

_____

CONTRACTING OFFICER SIGNATURE   DATE

RECEIPT OF TERMINATION OF DESIGNATION AS COTR IS HEREBY ACKNOWLEDGED:

_____

COTR SIGNATURE   DATE

CASE 4-2

The Spare Parts Problem[1]

Nobody liked doing it this way, but dealing with the government procurement system sometimes required extraordinary measures. Robert (Bobby) Jones, Contract Manager for MTB, Tactical Systems, had convinced his superiors nearly a year ago to "go out on a limb" by starting

_____

[1]Research and the original draft of this case were performed by Curtis Cook while a student at George Washington University.

work on the big U.S. Army spare parts order prior to receiving a formal contract. MTB had operated three months on its own funds before the contract finally arrived--and it was an unpriced, undefinitized order against a Basic Ordering Agreement at that. Now, in August, 1985, eleven months and three weeks later, the order was still not negotiated and the Army was claiming MTB's costs were too high. Bobby Jones had a choice. The terms of the Basic Ordering Agreement stated that unless the order was negotiated within one year of issuance, MTB was authorized to delay shipment of the spares. He knew the Army desperately needed the parts, but he also knew the company needed to negotiate a firm-fixed-price for the order that included the costs MTB had incurred in "financing" the order for three months before a formal contractual document was received. Government auditors did not want to recognize those costs. A further complication was the probability that MTB's final costs would exceed the "Not-to-Exceed" amount of the order--due largely to the circumstances surrounding the pre-contract costs incurred.

With only a week to go before the one-year deadline was reached, negotiations were just starting in earnest. The balance of the parts order was essentially ready to ship, yet Bobby knew if he released the shipment, he would lose what leverage he had to negotiate a fair and reasonable price for the entire effort. In retrospect, he wondered whether it had been wise to authorize work without contractual coverage. More pressing was the fact that Bobby needed a short-term negotiation strategy by tomorrow morning when face-to-face negotiations would begin.

General Company Background

Magnetic Transformation & Barometrics, later shortened to MTB, was founded in 1964 to design and develop specialized electronic reconnaissance systems for the government. MTB's initial business had two primary components: system studies and data analysis activities--resulting primarily in the delivery of reports, and system design and development of test models and one-of-a-kind operational systems. Over the years, technology fallouts from this strategic reconnaissance base were an important ingredient in building and expanding other business areas. In 1978 MTB became a subsidiary of DWS. By 1983 MTB had sales of almost $200 million with 2,500 employees in three locations: Sunnyvale, California; Hanover, Maryland; and Murray, Utah.

Authorization of Work without Contractual Coverage

Bobby Jones was responsible for managing all tactical systems contracts within the Advanced Military Systems Division of MTB. With several contract managers working for him on a variety of government programs, he had the authority to authorize work in advance of receiving formal contractual coverage, subject to the approval of the Director of Contracts, Project Manager, Business Manager, and Director of Finance. As a practical matter, these approvals were given when Bobby Jones recommended this action. From time to time, based on his expert judgment, experience with the customer, and risk assessment, he would decide it was in the best interests of MTB to authorize advance work. In those cases, and in accordance with MTB policy, he completed the proper form (see attachment 1, "Authorization of Work Without Contractual Coverage"). As can be seen by examining the form, Jones was required to evaluate the risks involved, the duration of risk, the estimate of costs to be expended by contract receipt date, how the contract would provide for recovery of pre-contractual costs, and why the individual government contracting officer was considered "reliable."

In the case of the current contractual dilemma, Bobby recollected the events that led up to early authorization of work. The program was the Army's TRAILBLAZER system, an advanced application of MTB's earlier direction finding sensor technology, which had become the production standard for the Army's tactical, ground-based communications intercept and direction finding systems. A local or remote controlled system, TRAILBLAZER provided real-time intelligence and combat information to commanders at division echelon and below. The TRAILBLAZER systems themselves had been developed, produced and fielded on an extremely tight schedule. According to the government's direction, spare parts production had taken a back seat to a production that would meet the initial operational capability date in the overall program management plan. As a result, the need for spare parts was critical.

About fifteen months ago, the Army had approached MTB with what was, unfortunately, a familiar story: The need was there, the funds were not. At the time, the Army was waiting for its quarterly allocation of funds for the TRAILBLAZER program. Until the funds were received, the Army could not execute a contract for the critically needed spares. The contracting officer had informally requested that MTB "support the program" by initiating some of the advance work on the spare parts order, such as ordering long-lead materials, etc. When the funds became available, the Army would issue an order against an existing Basic Ordering Agreement to fund the work, then negotiate the fixed price within 60 days, as required by government regulations covering undefinitized contractual actions. Bobby Jones had worked with this contracting officer before. He was sincere, honest, and well intentioned. It appeared the contractual order would be issued within a couple of weeks. Based on the facts at the time, he authorized the work using the attached form. All approvals were obtained as a matter of routine.

Things immediately began to go wrong. The technical specifications for the spares arrived late, unaccompanied by the anticipated formal contract. MTB was not sure whether these were the controlling specifications or an advanced set for guidance. Weeks passed with no official word from the contracting officer. When prodded for reasons for delay in issuing the order, the PCO responded that higher priority work had kept him from working on the MTB order. He did assure Mr. Jones that funds had been received to cover the not-to-exceed amount of the order.

Finally, three months after MTB had authorized the work, the formal provisioned item order arrived. It stipulated that if negotiations were not completed within one year after the date of the order (through no fault of MTB), MTB could withhold shipment of the balance of the spare parts. The order was dated with the current date. MTB continued to work on the spare parts, submitting progress payment requests in the customary fashion. As the weeks turned into months, Bobby Jones became concerned that the Army had not set a date for negotiations. Costs were accumulating as work progressed. On several occasions, Jones had asked the PCO when negotiations would be scheduled. The response was always the same: higher priorities were keeping the PCO from addressing the TRAILBLAZER situation. Then just a few weeks ago, Jones learned that the Army PCO would not be negotiating the price of the order. That responsibility had been delegated to the local Defense Contract Administration Services (DCAS) office.

As the one-year deadline approached, the Army was exerting pressure on MTB and DCAS to negotiate the total fixed price. Of course, the Army was concerned that Jones would withhold shipment of the spares. Meanwhile, DCAS was primarily interested in negotiating what it considered a fair and reasonable price, regardless of when the spare parts were delivered. With the likelihood that the price would exceed the original estimated value of the order, negotiations could be protracted. Tho precontract costs promised to be difficult to discuss, considering that DCAS was not a party to the original informal agreement.

Bobby looked at his watch, got a cup of coffee, and picked up the phone. He'd better tell his wife he wouldn't be home for dinner.

Attachment 1, The Spare Parts Problem

AUTHORIZATION OF WORK WITHOUT CONTRACTUAL COVERAGE

Proposal/Project Name_____Project Manager_____
Proposal/Project Number_____Contract Administrator_____

The following work has been authorized: Precontractual Work _____ Unfunded Contract
Work _____ Long Lead Time Procurement _____ Competitive _____ Sole Source _____

The work will be performed without contractual coverage in accordance with Corporate
policy #FI-16 and as defined on the reverse side of this form.
Description of work_____
_____
_____

Period of Performance _____Contract Type_____
Customer _____ Contracting Officer_____
Estimated Amount of Risk: This Authorization: $_____
                             Cumulative Authorization: $_____
Risk Evaluation:
       Duration of Risk _____ Weeks
Date Contractual Coverage is Expected _____
       Estimate of costs expended by contract receipt date $_____
How will contract provide for recovery of precontractual cost?_____
_____

Why is this contracting officer reliable? _____
Negotiation scheduled for_____
Negotiation will be impaired/enhanced by an early start because _____
_____
Explanation of necessity of performing without coverage _____
_____
Long lead time procurement (if applicable)   Estimated Commitment $_____
                                             Estimated Cancellation Cost $_____
Explanation of necessity for long lead time procurement _____
_____

Initiated by: Director of Contracts   _____
                (or designee)   Signature   Date
                Project Manager   _____
                                           Signature   Date
Approved By: Line of Business Manager _____
                                           Signature   Date
                Director of Finance   _____
                (Long Lead Time Procurement Only)   Signature   Date

CASE 4-3

Reston Development Corporation

Reston Development Corporation has an established reputation for excellent work in computer simulations applied to the replanning and redevelopment of blighted urban areas. Organized on a project basis, each job is acquired and managed by the systems leader. The company is staffed with several extremely competent systems engineers. There is no administrative staff except for three secretaries and Edward Tunlow, the president, who is also systems engineer and manager.

Based on the company's experience in computer simulation and as a result of several personal contacts, Edward Tunlow submitted an unsolicited proposal to the Army Corps of Engineers in early February, 1984. Reston's proposal involved development of a computer simulation model to assist the Army's urban studies land planners in the area of land use and analysis. Response was almost immediate. Roger James, a project officer at the Army Corps of Engineers, called Edward Tunlow within the week and suggested a meeting to discuss the ideas presented in the proposal.

Tunlow's proposal projected a cost of $75,500, but after discussions with the Army, he revised his plan and agreed on a completion price of $68,500. Roger James agreed to that figure. After some delay and further discussions, during a luncheon conversation in late February, Roger James advised Tunlow that the project should get under way. Throughout the spring, summer and fall, a team of several Corps personnel and two of Tunlow's staff had numerous discussions concerning the scope of work and its progress. By December, Reston completed the work, delivered the computer simulation model, and billed the Corps for $87,500.

The Corps was delighted with the new model since it greatly advanced their work. However, the contracting officer and disbursing officer for the Corps were puzzled over what to do with Reston's invoice, inasmuch as no contract existed.

5

Requirements,
Work Statements,
and Specifications

PRESUMPTIONS AND RISKS IN CONTRACTING

As the parties to a proposed contract approach their agreement, there are six presumptions which they should recognize as undergirding the effort. Whether implicit or explicit, these presumptions impact the subsequent success of the undertaking. If, in practice, they prove to have been invalid, the result will color the normal course of interpreting contract requirements. Each party expects that the agreement, when interpreted, will prove consistent with its understandings. This chapter examines these presumptions and formulates a practical approach for contract managers in determining the meaning of contracts. Emphasis is placed upon the parties' need to reexamine and reassess what their agreement expressly states until the meaning of their contractual responsibilities is clear.

Performance feasibility. The first major presumption is that it is possible to perform the proposed work. While this is not likely to be expressly stated, it is important. Many contractual agreements are not subsequently fulfilled because performing the work is impractical. Significant losses must be borne by either party when impracticability is not recognized early in performance. This subject, including both absolute impossibility and impracticability, will be examined later in the chapter.

Competency. It is presumed that the party who agrees to perform the work can and will do so competently. The buyer is responsible for making an appropriate source selection decision by examining and assessing the performer's capabilities. An obligation also exists for offerors to assess their own capabilities and offer to perform work for which they

111

have the necessary facilities, manpower, and technical expertise. Nevertheless, when performance problems arise, buyers regularly challenge the competency of the contractor.

Document soundness. The existence of sound contract documentation is an implicit but often violated presumption and can become a significant issue in interpreting many contracts. Contract documentation is the set of documents including terms, conditions, schedules, specifications, referenced documents, and other elements that comprise the written understanding of the parties. Contract documentation may include all or only parts of a contractor's proposal. The precise nature of all parts included within the scope of the contract documentation should be examined for each situation that arises.

Cooperation. A fourth presumption is that the parties will cooperate. This presumption imposes duties on the buyer which tend to be overlooked, yet at all appropriate stages during the performance period, the obligation to cooperate is placed upon the buyer. Usually, this will not be explicitly represented in the contract documentation. The seller also is obligated to cooperate, but this seldom becomes an issue, whereas the buyer's cooperativeness is often challenged. The buyer must facilitate normal performance and provide information necessary to perform work economically and efficiently.

Absence of mistake. As they enter into a contract, the parties presume that there is no material error or mistake on their part regarding the nature and objectives of the undertaking. This presumption is often not fulfilled. Mistakes are endemic in human relationships and do not disappear simply because two parties enter into a formal, contractual understanding. The particular situation and the nature of the mistake-- whether it is mutual or unilateral--determine the party who must absorb the impact of mistakes. The magnitude of burdens imposed by mistakes can be substantial.

Conscionability. Misunderstanding, optimistic analysis, and supervening events can lead to contract requirements that impose an unconscionable burden on either of the parties. An unconscionable burden, however, ordinarily bears most heavily upon the performing party. The existence of unconscionability is not easily assessed and would not be recognized by the parties prior to entering into the agreement. It is a situation which implies that the contractual agreement forces one party to perform work substantially against his interest, under circumstances where the cost of performance is not in proportion to the magnitude of the assumed obligations. In general, the consequences of an unconscionable performance would be disastrous to the economic well-being of the obligated party.

Contract administrators should recognize that failure of any of the six presumptions will jeopardize the success of the undertaking. Failure will result in overturning normal performance expectations and will require renewed interpretation of the contract. This could impact the normal course of performance. The likelihood that any of these presumptions are erroneous is a substantial source of risk to the parties.

THE CENTRAL PLACE OF TECHNICAL DOCUMENTATION IN CONTRACTING

The Foundation of Agreements

The formation of a contract requires gathering numerous ingredients, including business terms and conditions, schedule of performance, list of deliverable materials and data, designation of cost or price, payment arrangements, and the technical data package. Of these, the technical data package is most likely to be the source of controversy or misunderstanding. Because the other ingredients are the product of many prior applications, they are normally developed to the point where their meaning and implications are widely understood. This is certainly characteristic of the standard boiler-plate terms and conditions incorporated into most government contracts. Even so, interpreting contractual understandings is a matter of interpreting all elements that make up the contract. Controversies and misunderstandings associated with any element of a contract can become critical issues if problems arise subsequent to award.

Because each element of a contract is selected or written to support the undertakings defined by the technical data package, it becomes the foundation for most contractual misunderstandings. The data package works in concert with the deliverable item list to define the expected accomplishments of the performing party. While the deliverable item list is a summary of the products to be delivered upon completion of the contract, the technical data package defines all of the capabilities and configurations that must be built into those products. Furthermore, the technical data package sets the basis for evaluating the acceptability of the deliverable end item.

The technical data package is made up of several kinds of documentation, but it is usually keynoted by one of several possible types of specifications. It may contain lists of applicable data and drawings. It will frequently incorporate, by reference, other documents which control particular elements of the end product, such as related specifications and standardization documentation. In total, the technical data package may be comprised of voluminous descriptive material and criteria for acceptance. It requires careful, detailed examination by both parties to avoid problems arising in contract interpretation.

Basis for Competition and Contractual Integrity

Technical documentation provides the foundation upon which the purchaser seeks competition during formation of the contract. Its impact on competition is well understood by industrial and governmental buyers and by competitors. Competition creates variable pressures, depending upon the industry, stage of technological development, and number of competitors. Whether based on price, innovation, design or capability, competition is governed primarily by the relationship between the state of the art pertinent to the project and the complexity and clarity of the technical package provided to each competitor.

The objective of those preparing technical documentation should be to create a documentation package that can be understood in the same manner by all potential competitors. Failure to do this will lead to variations in approach that degrade the quality of the competition secured. If competitors do not offer to perform work that will result in identical output, any competition based on price will not be equal. Many times procurement is based on a data package that is new, changed, or contains other imperfections. Consequently, in a significant proportion of contract solicitation and award procedures, a common basis for competition is not present. This is probably most prevalent in government procurement involving major research and development or the manufacture of products which are new or have no prior record of success. Newness and lack of a production track record are characteristics of more complex and advanced undertakings. Creative approaches to drafting technical data packages coupled with procurement techniques that permit competition even without a track record are important elements in developing contract solicitation and award procedures.

Whether or not a competitive procedure has been used in formation of a contract, the technical data package remains a critical element in maintaining the integrity of the contractual relationship. Integrity of contract implies that the parties will fulfill their commitments developed at the time of contract award, that is, specific requirements will not be disregarded or unenforced during subsequent contract management activities. Contract managers are strongly oriented toward preserving obligations and commitments made at the time of contract formation. This orientation is reinforced when making an award under the influence of competitive pressures.

Causing Managers to State What is Wanted

As managers approach the release of technical documents for contract application, they must reduce their options to a set of decisions concerning the configuration and performance requirements to be incorporated into the contract. Final release of any technical data package compels decision, even though the manager may prefer to delay action. The contractual process enforces discipline upon all contributors to the project definition. For large and technically complex projects, this discipline is unwelcome, because it forces cutting off improvement in the product requirements. Unfortunately, this discipline applies only to contract definition; it does not alter the progress of technological advancement or the continuous discovery of better ways to approach and define end products. A continuous search for improvement leads to change and contract adjustment.

THE TIME FACTOR: CONTRACTS DON'T CHANGE

A contract represents a snapshot of technology at a point in time. It locks a particular set of definitions and capabilities into the technical data package. One function of a contract is to embrace and stabilize the parties' goals. Once contract commitments have been established, the technical data package cannot be changed without positive effort. If it is changed, it opens the contractual understanding to adjustment of schedule and cost parameters which otherwise would remain stable. This stability of the contractual commitment may be viewed as a key advantage of a contractual procedure because it forces the parties to define measurable outcomes which they believe are feasible within the resource and time obligations of the agreement. However, this stability is also a great handicap in performing major undertakings because it enforces a discipline on the developmental and change processes, severely inhibiting the free exercise of innovation and experimentation. The existence of a contract stimulates the parties to examine carefully the need for improvements in light of the learning processes continuing during work performance. Government contract clauses are designed to simplify changing the technical requirements. This subject is covered in detail in chapter 12.

Problems of Language and Semantics

Technical data problems begin during the drafting stage prior to contract solicitation. A principal objective is to create understandable language to convey the buyer's intentions. The engineer or technical writer seeks to establish an unequivocal basis for deciding the nature of the job, who will perform the work, and the method of measuring the end product. Clarity and precision characterize a good technical data package. Achieving that objective is extremely time-consuming. Since the principal purpose of drafting specifications and related data is to govern performance of a contract, superior writing skills and review procedures

are vital. Specification writers often fail in their effort to achieve
current, unambiguous, complete, and error-free contract documents.

Creating the Contract Base Line

The contractor uses a contractual data package as the basis for
developing a work plan which, in turn, controls his application of
resources. The work plan usually is documented in the form of an
internal work statement which records the intended sequencing and
scheduling of work in an effective manner and determines the required
application of facilities, manpower, material, and other needed elements.
Through this internal work statement, the technical data package governs
contract cost estimating and pricing and is a key element in defining the
risk associated with performance of the contract.
Although the contractor derives his work plan from the technical
data package, the package remains the basis for evaluating whether any
alteration in the work plan will require the negotiation of an adjustment
of contract price or schedule commitments. The technical data package
constitutes the formal base line for technical effort and is particularly
important in long-term contracts. The variety of events that may occur
during performance expands with the length of the performance period,
the stability of specifications or schedule, the magnitude of the job, the
number of related contracts, mixed ownership of property, and competing
demands for application of the buyer's funds. In many cases, the buyer
and seller view events as responsibilities of the other party. Their
differing viewpoints call for resolution of differences through reference
to the technical data package. The parties must develop a clear view of
the relationship between the requirements of the data package and the
actual performance that has been achieved. These issues should be
addressed in a timely fashion during performance.

Project End Objectives and Data Package Interpretation

Contract managers tend to overlook project end objectives. Their
principal concern is contract compliance as measured by the contract.
When contract requirements coincide with end objectives, contractual
effort is focused on meeting the mission. Without question, this is the
intent of the parties. Unfortunately, this coincidence may become
unclear with passing time. Contract requirements may turn out to be at
variance with the mission. Regardless, contract interpretation issues
emerge. This is an ever present concern, because the economic interests
of the parties may be at variance with fulfilling project end objectives.
When substantial cost or schedule growth occurs, this becomes a critical

issue. The root question is, who should shoulder the burdens--the buyer or the seller? One specific question is whether mission objectives are expressed in the technical data package. Another may be whether there has been misdirection of work. These issues mandate careful review, including interpretation of the contract. The impact on end objectives may be paramount to all observers except the contracting parties whose assets may be at stake. In government organizations, the mission may be a military capability, an infrastructure improvement, or a societal, public welfare, or medical achievement. The industrial buyer's mission may be increased market share, entry into a market, cost reduction, product abandonment, or a new product entry.

End objectives that cause interpretation problems are likely to be derived from expanded performance requirements, or complex, difficult-to-express logistical considerations. End objectives may include maintenance, mobility, training, and spares support standards. The performance and logistical objectives are diverse and often difficult to assess in relation to contract specifications. Whether issues arise during pre- or post-award operations, the first objective of analysis is clear: decisions concerning the technical data package should be consistent with project end objectives. The second objective is to assess resource implications, which, although secondary, can be critical. Primarily a post-award issue, the third objective is to place responsibility for resource requirements. While third in overall importance with respect to end objectives, this is likely to be first in the perception of the parties and is the focus of negotiations between contract managers of both buyer and seller.

CONTRACTUAL ISSUES CONCERNING TECHNICAL DOCUMENTS

Operational or Production Requirements

Programs are placed under contract for the purpose of meeting operational or production requirements as determined by the strategic planning processes of the sponsor. Strategic planning can be understood by examining the approach of the United States government. A government contract specification should be derived from approved operational statements that provide background information for interpreting contract requirements. These statements are not designed to become a part of the official contract document. Nevertheless, they govern the preparation of contractual data packages. The documentation of recent major acquisitions contains mission element needs statements (MENS) which are derived by an analytical process in which the agency examines its mission, capabilities, and resources. These analyses reveal any deficiencies and produce lists of requirements needed to fill gaps in capabilities.

They are instrumental in establishing needs in the form of a MENS.

The mission element needs statement is the basis for awarding contracts for early phases of major systems acquisitions programs. This approach to documentation of contracts was developed under the Office of Management and Budget Circular A-109 entitled "Major System Acquisitions" to encourage a systematic and controlled approach for developing new major systems by government agencies. Principal applications of this approach have been those of military departments in connection with developing new weapons systems.

Using a mission statement instead of a data package in preparing a contract document provides a broader base for interpreting each party's contract responsibilities. This approach must be accompanied by a comprehensive statement of the required operating capabilities of the new system. Thus, even with the mission element needs statement, a contract also contains a fairly comprehensive set of constraints for use in guiding and managing the undertaking. Regardless of its content, the contract is carefully scrutinized for a correct interpretation during its executory phases.

Compiling Technical Statements for Contract Application

Depending on the nature of the contract, preparing the data package can be a major undertaking for any buying organization. The data package should be complete and its content reviewed for adequacy prior to issuing a solicitation for proposals. Formal authority for preparing technical data packages of government contracts is contained in MIL-STD-885 "Military Standard Procurement Data Packages." Originally prepared by the United States Air Force, this standard established the concept of the technical data package. It is defined in the following section, along with a description of its preparation. The preparation of data packages is often contracted out. Regardless of how it is prepared or the extent of technical input and review, the entire package should be examined for clarity in establishing the responsibilities of the proposed contractor vis-a-vis those of the buyer and/or other contractors whose work may interface with the work of the immediate contractor.

Although nearly all responsibility for compiling and approving technical data is vested in government technical codes, a review by procurement experts is desirable. In assembling the technical data package and releasing it for contractual application, the most critical issue is coordination among the buyer's organizations, including the contracting office, which is responsible for the integrity of the contractual agreement. The greatest problem with technical data packages is their tendency to be unclear in defining the responsibilities of each party. Coordination normally should precede release of the documentation for contract action.

When the package, together with the purchase requisition, is released, it should be forwarded to a contracting office, asking that the work be placed under contract.

Technical Data Packages

Technical data packages are made up of three broad groups of documents. These groupings may be loosely described as specifications, work statements, and related technical data including drawings, data lists, and reference documentation. For purposes of interpreting contract obligations, none of these groups may be ignored. Specifications fall into four general classifications, each carrying definite implications for responsibilities to be imposed on the parties to the contract. In selecting or writing a specification, the buyer is driven primarily by his or her procurement objectives. These objectives are derived from analysis of the buyer's needs or those of the potential user of the end product. However, the general classification of contract specifications is governed by the nature of the task, the stage of development of the end item, and the degree of responsibility and level of risk that the buyer wishes to pass to the supplier.

There are several bases upon which a contract may be written:

1. Preliminary conceptual statements of a perceived need
2. Functional statements of intended use
3. Fully developed statements of required functions and performance
4. A complete technical data package including drawings, specifications, and related data
5. A work statement
6. A cited part number or named item
7. A combination of two or more bases

The range of satisfactory technical statements is unlimited, but the magnitude of the data preparation job has significant implications for the buying organization. The buyer is dependent upon his mission and staffing realities. As a minimum, the buyer's internal capabilities and staff must generate program objectives, a profile of existing capabilities (inventory), and an identification of voids (needs) that must be fulfilled to meet objectives. The rest can be contracted. This requires personnel with mission knowledge, technical expertise, and judgment. Small numbers of personnel may be adequate, but internal work force needs expand as a direct function of the technical basis for contracting out. A complete statement of performance (item 3) demands more effort than a statement of intended use (item 2). A complete design package (item 4) demands far more effort than a statement of performance. Previously produced, fully defined items may require the minimum effort of buying organizations--they can procure the item by citing the part number and its existing technical data package (as in item 6). Preliminary conceptual statements (item 1) are useful only for major new undertakings for which system solutions have not been decided but relative to total resource requirements may be prepared with skeletal internal staff. Work statements (item 5) have special utility for service and research efforts and may require substantial effort and expertise prior to contract award. Technical data comprised of several types (item 7) is often used to cover all intended contract objectives but may complicate subsequent interpretation negotiation.

Specifications

   Design specification. Probably the simplest type of specification is the design specification. Here, the procuring organization attempts to buy quantities of an item which has been fully defined and designed. The design specification is a product of research and development and, ideally, will have been proven through prior use. A design specification describes the end item in terms of its physical and functional characteristics in such a manner that a complete description of the item is obtained by examining the technical data package. Design specifications frequently cite supporting data such as design drawings, lists of parts or materials, and standards or specifications essential to production of the item. The technical data package, in support of a fully designed product, is intended for use by a supplier in producing replicas of an item that is already acceptable and meets the buyer's requirements. The design specification imposes a responsibility upon the supplier for workmanlike production, using quality standards normal to the particular trade and type of end item. This level of obligation does not include responsibility for the design or acceptability of the product (when properly built) as meeting the requirements of the user. The design document should be a complete statement of what the contractor must deliver in order to meet the buyer's acceptance standards. Failure of the end product to meet the specification in precise detail will constitute grounds for rejection. Because of the possibility of rejection, design specifications may be the subject of controversy whenever the contractor encounters difficulty in producing the desired item. When this situation arises, controversy is resolved through interpretation procedures to discover the intent of the contractual parties.

   Performance specification. This type of document does not establish the design detail of the end item. Instead, it precisely states the performance requirements expected of the end item when delivered and tested under the conditions set forth in the specification. Verification of compliance with performance standards forms the basis for accepting or rejecting the product. Depending on the nature of the product, examples of performance standards include criterion such as life of the product under specified conditions of use, speed of a vehicle, rate of climb of an aircraft, range of a missile, ability to operate in a specific environment, and precision of measurement for an instrument. These and many other performance features may be measured during an acceptance test procedure. The important element of a performance specification in terms of contractual relationships is the high level of responsibility for design that it imposes upon the supplier in order to meet performance objectives. However, specification writers seldom turn out a pure performance specification. Project sponsors and users generally incorporate design concepts or design constraints intended to ensure compatibility of the end product with existing structures or system elements. When contracts are based on performance specifications, the contractor's primary obligation is to create a detailed design that functions in accordance with the specified performance. The contractor is also required to comply with imposed design constraints.

The performance specification appeals to buyers because it transfers responsibility for definition to the contractor. Its value is related partly to the staffing requirements imposed by the large amount of detail work necessary to define an item in its full physical configuration. Responsibility for end results, though largely assigned to the contractor, may not be fully transferable if the sponsoring organization constrains the design discretion of the supplier.

Functional specification. In government contract circles, the functional specification is a recently defined subset of performance specifications with a specific and unique application--the acquisition of commercial goods and services for the government. The functional specification is a statement of intended use or application of the end product. It is similar to a performance specification, but it differs primarily because it does not define, in the same fashion, specific levels of performance. Instead, it describes the user's application and the conditions under which the user is applying the product. To describe an end product in this manner enhances competition under circumstances where commercial products already exist that will meet the government's requirement. The basic purpose of the functional specification is to make it possible for commercial products of unique, proprietary design, which perform comparable tasks, to meet the demands of the government agency. By avoiding specific performance parameters and specific design in the product, the agency enhances the ability of competitors to offer their products for government use. The government, however, must specify the essential characteristics of the items. In many cases, it has found that functional descriptions can be written that meet its objectives.

Process specification. The purpose of a process specification is to describe a specific production technique, procedure, and/or sequence of steps that, together, constitute a process necessary to produce the end product. A process specification differs significantly from the other classifications because it describes the method of attaining the acceptable end product, whereas the design or performance specification describes the end product itself, and the functional specification describes the user application. Under most procurement circumstances, a process specification is not used, even though it may be applicable. A buyer chooses a supplier on the basis of his or her ability to produce the end product. The buyer assumes that the supplier is knowledgeable of the standard production processes associated with manufacturing the product. Only when the standard process will not be sufficient to create an acceptable end product should the buyer intercede by specifying the process. Process specifications may be used for producing critical end items when more than one standard process is available, but the buyer is aware that only one process will be successful. They are also used to control unique processes, those generally unknown to sources of supply. When applicable, process specifications are used as one part of the technical data package.

Work Statements

Work statements are widely used to control contract effort. They may be used alone or as a part of the data package and fit particularly well the needs of contracts requiring services or research and development. R&D contracts employ work statements because full definition of the end item's characteristics may not be feasible at the time of entering into the contract. While the objective sought in R&D work normally is governed by performance specifications, the work is frequently described in a work statement which is a part of the data package. The purpose of the work statement is to hold the contractor responsible for performing the kind of work that the buyer desires. It can be a very detailed statement of all tasks to be performed, but as a general rule, it differs from specifications because it does not attempt to describe the end product either in terms of physical or performance characteristics. The work statement is a direct method of describing the work required by the purchaser. While specifications should state clear, measurable standards for the end product, the work statement ensures that specific work will be performed, even though its performance may not be entirely controlled by the measurement or testing of the end product. The work statement is particularly useful when some level of study or research must be performed in association with the preparation of the end item.

For contracts that call for performance of services, the work statement is the only means of describing what the parties have agreed will be done. Although considerable effort is made to define the service in terms of end results, such as operation of a facility for a specified period, the discharge of contractual obligations is generally measurable only in terms of the work effort itself. Frequency and timeliness of services may be specified. Quantity of completed service units could be the basis for payments. Absence of a tangible product to which the buyer is able to apply a testing procedure causes the work statement to serve as the standard against which contract performance is rated.

BASIC QUESTIONS IN POST-AWARD INTERPRETATION

Work Plan Development by the Contractor

Upon award of a contract, the first major undertaking of the performing party is to reanalyze the specifications and other documents contained in the technical data package. It is in the contractor's interest, and a part of his obligation, to subdivide the total work effort into tasks for efficient and economical performance. This is done before resources are applied. The contractor must establish an appropriate management structure, one that is derived from his existing system but tailored, as needed, based upon the data package. By analyzing the specification, the contractor creates an internal work statement to which the various groups and departments within the company respond.

The internal work statement communicates all essential technical content needed by assigned managers for direction and control consistent with the contract. It usually omits contractual terms and provisions unnecessary for task performance. It forms the basis for negotiation between individual managers who perform segments of work and the contractor's project manager. The managers negotiate issues such as cost and schedule implications for each element of the job to which the subordinate manager has been assigned. In turn, each subordinate manager must analyze and interpret that portion of the work statement to which he or she is committed. This analysis of the work plan proceeds throughout the early stages of performance and is a vital part of effective management. If errors or misinterpretations of the work statement or specification are initiated at this stage, subsequent issues are certain to arise when customer representatives discover weaknesses in the end product. During the early stages of developing a work plan, the buyer and seller should coordinate to overcome any doubt concerning contract interpretation. The importance of coordination is directly related to the magnitude of commitments and resources involved. At this early stage, interpretation questions may be resolved with minimum (but not necessarily insignificant) costs to either party. Issues at this stage deal with the

problems of properly defining work to be performed and selecting personnel, facilities, and other resources.

Implied Warranty of Technical Data

When a contract is issued for production of an item designed or
developed by or for the buyer, the buyer is also responsible for the
content of the technical data package. Although contracts do not contain
a specific clause warranting the adequacy of the technical data package,
a warranty is imposed by the legal concept of implied warranty. Under
the concept, the purchaser assures the supplier that the technical description is capable of being fulfilled in a manner satisfactory to the
purchaser, if the performing party follows the description in a responsible
manner. Knowledge of the essential technology and production processes
is chargeable to the contractor. Because of this warranty, the performer
cannot categorically be held responsible for inadequate or unacceptable
performance of a contract. Conformity with and sufficiency of the technical data package are issues which must be negotiated between the
parties on the basis of proper interpretation of the data package. If
negotiations fail, it will become a matter for litigation.

Impracticability and Impossibility

The assumption that performance is feasible is violated when, after
entering into a contract, it is discovered that performance is literally
impossible or impracticable. This condition relieves any further effort to
perform. For practical purposes, contract managers find that impracticability and impossibility may be treated as the same problem. Issues
associated with them are similar to those raised by implied warranty of
technical data. In either situation, performance in accordance with
specified requirements is infeasible. However, claims based on the buyer's
implied warranty arise in connection with contracts controlled by design
specifications, as previously discussed.

Impracticability questions arise principally under contracts controlled
by performance specifications. The question usually results from a
specific performance requirement that is beyond the state of the art or is
so extraordinarily expensive that performance would force the contractor
into unconscionable losses. These issues may arise in manufacturing
contracts, but only when it turns out that research and development
effort or other unanticipated major expense is required to complete the
contract successfully.

Literal impossibility is rare and usually is based upon a supervening
event (one that occurred after the contract was established). Issues

raised in the case of supervening events are relatively simple to negotiate assuming that the event is not the fault of, or beyond the control of, either party. Negotiation is concerned principally with distribution of costs incurred before the occurrence of the supervening event.

The most difficult issues arise in connection with existing impracticability in which the barrier to performance existed but was not recognized at the time of contract formation. When a problem surfaces that appears to be of this type, the contractor will seek relief causing the parties to examine the contractual objectives and conditions under which the agreement was established. Relief in these circumstances is principally related to expenses accumulated in the effort to perform. If costs are substantial, litigation is likely. Whether agreed upon or decided by litigation, the conclusion that performance is impracticable or impossible relieves further cost incurrence. Review and interpretation of the contract and its surrounding circumstances may be essential to resolve the issues and questions.

In general, the contractor can secure relief for impracticability only by showing that performance is substantially more difficult and expensive than contemplated (commercially senseless, imposing losses that a reasonable business person would not risk), and that all contractors would have experienced similar difficulties. (Impracticability must be inherent in the nature of the task, not because of the inability of a particular party.) Finally, it must be shown that, when entering into the contract, the contractor did not assume responsibility for the added difficulties. The key to the issues may depend upon representations implied or expressed at the time of entering into the contract, including the factor that one party may have superior knowledge of the technology. Further cost is incurred only if it is concluded that no impracticability exists.

THE INTERPRETATION PROCESS

Performance Deficiency vs. Document Deficiency

Reconciliation of gaps between the buyer's and seller's perceptions of required performance regularly challenges contract managers. This conflict generally requires the parties to agree that either performance is deficient, or the technical data package is deficient or ambiguous. Major interpretation problems and controversies usually arise during later phases of contract performance when achievement of contractual objectives appears to be jeopardized. The likelihood of such issues increases in direct relationship to project size, complexity, and duration. The need to reinterpret contract requirements arises when contract managers become dissatisfied with progress or raise issues suggesting that end products will not be acceptable. Questions of this kind may be raised by buyer or seller, by technical or administrative personnel, or others. Regardless of who raises the question, any responsible challenge of a product's conformity with the specification (or other data contained in the contract data package) should cause a thorough review of contract documents, work performed, and progress to date. These issues frequently occur and result in either a change in the contractor's method of performance or agreement that a conforming product is being produced. If the method of performance is changed, the parties must resolve whether the performer is responsible for overcoming the difficulty, or the purchaser is responsible for modifying the contractual data package.

This issue is immediately perceived in terms of the burden of cost and time impacts. If, after analysis and examination, it is agreed that current performance does not jeopardize achievement of contractual objectives, work may proceed with no adverse impact upon either schedule or cost. When these conflicts surface, however, resolution of the situation usually requires rework or adjustment of the method of performance, or both. The course of action depends on interpretation of the contract and may involve waivers, deviations, change orders, delays, property directives, or even termination of the effort. Much depends on the extent of the differences, the likelihood of closing the gap, and the alternatives (financial and technical capabilities) of the parties. Correctable, deficient performance against a contract specification can be overcome by a change order revising or waiving the requirement, or by re-analyzing and restructuring the contractor's effort. The exact course of action and its impact on either contractor or purchaser depends on the proper interpretation of the technical data package vis-a-vis the methods used by the contractor to meet that specification.

To illustrate, let us assume that two parties interpret a specification differently in such a way that the method of performance is substantially affected. How would the parties proceed? Conflicts in government programs are ordinarily resolved by performing work as required by the contracting officer. Issues associated with responsibility for cost and time effects are negotiated subsequently. When this happens, the contracting officer should issue directions in the form of a formal change order.[1] Informal orders or technical directions have often been used but tend to create controversy over the status of the work--whether it is required by the unchanged contract or is added work for which cost and schedule adjustment may be claimed. Formal change orders are issued with the understanding that the contractor will proceed accordingly, while retain-

---

[1]Chapter 12 explains the changes process and associated issues. Chapter 13 discusses equitable adjustments, many of which are negotiated pursuant to change orders.

ing the right to submit a proposal for modification of the contractual cost, profit, and schedule agreement as well as other possible conditions that may be affected. Negotiation of an agreement may proceed concurrently with performance of the work, but work must be performed pursuant to the direction of the contracting officer.

The government's procedure cannot be applied to contracts between private parties unless pursuant to subcontract changes under government prime contracts. If private parties are unable to negotiate their differences, work is stopped, while arbitration or litigation are initiated. Resolution of issues by an objective third party is useful but may involve substantial expense and delay and, in all cases, is less beneficial than negotiation between competent contract managers.

Objective of Contract Interpretation

Correct interpretation of contract provisions ordinarily begins by examining the overt manifestation, that is, the writing signed by both parties documenting their agreement and commonly referred to as the contract. However, interpretation may involve examining matters either not covered or not adequately covered by that writing. It should be clear to the contract manager that the contract document, though predominantly important in determining the meaning of the agreement, cannot ordinarily be relied upon as an exhaustive statement of what the parties have agreed to do. The principal objective of any person who examines a contract with the purpose of interpreting its provisions should be to discover the intent of the parties at the time of entering into the contract. This is what a board or a court would seek to discover by examining the same document.

General and Technical Sources of the Meaning of Words

The wording of a contract document provides the primary source of information for discovering the parties' intent. This may include a complex set of terms some of which may be of a general character such as words commonly used by reasonably intelligent people. The contract is also likely to contain technical words that are unique to the particular undertaking or, in government contracts, unique to a government regulation or policy document.[1] The person who is interpreting the contract must be willing to examine general sources of information such as a current dictionary and, at the same time, be prepared to examine more

---

[1]The glossary defines numerous terms.

specialized sources of definitions of words such as trade publications, specialized dictionaries unique to a field of technology, or government regulations and documents uniquely pertinent to the contract. Some effort is made in every contract interpretation to give meaning to all terms and symbols contained in the documents. When these elements are of a general nature and have been accorded a generally prevailing meaning, they should be given that meaning for purposes of interpreting the contract. Conversely, when the terms or symbols are of a technical nature--viewed as terms of art with respect to a particular field of technology--they should be accorded their technical meaning.

The terms of a contract must be accorded an interpretation that is consistent with the context in which the word is used in the contract. For example, a contract using the term "sand" obligated a contractor to fill sandbags with material provided by the government. The contractor found that the cost of performance was substantially greater than estimated because the material included large stones and debris as well as small granules of sand. In light of the objective of the contract--filling sand bags--providing this material was considered to be an imposition of a greater burden on the contractor than that for which he had contracted. Therefore, an equitable adjustment of the contract price was allowed.

Similarly, the meaning of a technical term must be consistent with its use in the field of activity to which it is technically applicable. An example is the meaning of the term "equitable adjustment" as it is used in the context of federal procurement. This term has achieved the status of a term of art in government contracting and is accorded a specific technical meaning in the context of that type of undertaking. Thus, an effort by one party to the contract to add to or detract from the scope of that which constitutes an equitable adjustment is likely to fail.

Circumstances arise in which the parties to a contract disagree on the meaning of its terms, even though the terms appear to be perfectly understandable to an outsider. Assuming acceptance of the concept that the purpose of interpretation is to discover the intent of the parties as it existed at the time of entering into the agreement, some objectively supportable basis for construing that intent should be sought through negotiation. If litigated, the board or court will impose this objective and require supporting evidence. In this context, an objective test of the meaning of terms is to discover the meaning which would have been ascribed by a reasonable contractor in the field of activity contemplated by the contract. This objective test should exclude from consideration any subjective, unexpressed intention of one party regarding the meaning of the contract.

Implications of Integrated Agreements

Evidence to support proper contract interpretation is not limited to the contract language. In fact, when litigation arises over contract interpretation, a substantial part of the process of discovery is finding evidence of representations and statements of the parties associated with the award of the contract. This does not alter the overall objective of interpretation: to discover the original intent of the parties.

Correct interpretation of a contract is seldom achieved by simply reading the written document (also referred to as the integration of the agreement). Determining whether that document is a complete statement of the agreement is often a key issue. Interpretation frequently requires examining material not covered in the integration. This type of material (external to the integration) may constitute evidence with respect to the agreement. However, the writing itself is also no more than evidence with respect to what constitutes the agreement. As a result, interpreters must deal with intrinsic evidence (evidence addressed in the written document) and extrinsic evidence (matters which may not have been recorded in the writing). The term "integrated agreement" is generally applied to the writings which are represented to constitute the final expression of the agreement between the parties. In most cases, the writing will be treated as a partially integrated agreement, that is, an agreement which reflects some part of the terms of the agreement. It is not often viewed as a <u>complete</u> and final expression of the agreement. In some very rare cases, a contract document may be so complete in its drafting that it will be treated as a complete and exhaustive statement of the agreement. This is referred to as a completely integrated agreement, and it bars the introduction of extrinsic evidence for interpreting the meaning of the agreement. Ambiguity of contract language, however, may require use of extrinsic evidence in order to determine whether the agreement actually is completely integrated. Consequently, a contract document rarely stands alone as an exhaustive statement of the agreement between the parties, and extrinsic evidence of various kinds is important to the interpretation of most agreements. This subject is examined in greater detail later in the chapter.

Rules of Interpretation

It is important for contract managers to be familiar with the rules for examining and interpreting (intrinsic) contract documents. We have examined the issue of understanding the meaning of words. In interpreting a contract document, however, the parties must keep a particular set of objectives (or rules) in mind. One rule is to give the entire writing some weight, treating it as a single entity or, as this has been characterized, the contract should be read as a whole. An interpreter must look for harmony in the provisions of the document and try to give some effect to all portions in order to avoid rendering some parts meaning-less. In an illustrative case, a government contractor incurred additional cost in finishing louvers in a penthouse construction project. The louvers were concealed behind a parapet and could not be seen from most loca-tions outside the immediate area. The contractor won his claim for addi-tional funds based on the decision that the contract did not require finishing louvers which were "otherwise concealed." The common meaning of the term "concealed" was given effect in the contract because any other interpretation would render the particular words meaningless.

The interpretation process may seem to favor either party, but it must consider all of the rules of interpretation. Language should be constructed so that the principal purposes of the parties when they entered into the contract are carried out. An example of this is a case in which a contract required installation of a complete operating fire sprinkler system. The contract drawings showed only external connec-tions for a sprinkler system and omitted any reference to detailed con-struction of the system itself. Nevertheless, in litigation the contractor was required to install an entire operating fire system because that was the stated overall objective of the contract.

In summary, the interpretation of language in a contract document requires attention to four objectives or rules.

1.   View the contract as an entity. Rather than interpreting individual sections or clauses, the parties must consider all sections and terms in the context of the overall writing.
2.   Avoid reading specific terms out of the contract. This can occur if a reading is adopted that leaves portions or even individual terms useless, meaningless, or ineffective.
3.   Avoid creating a conflict internally between the terms in the document.
4.   Interpret the contract to fulfill the principal purposes of the parties.

Contract language often includes specific lists of items or work to be done by the contractor. A list may enumerate jobs requiring extreme care, things that should not be done, or items that must not be disturbed. These listings are used extensively because they simplify the reading of a contract and establish specific requirements in explicit and noticeable format. The rule states that a contractor may consider a listing to be a valid, accurate representation of work to be accomplished.

An illustration of this rule is provided by a case involving a con-struction contractor who had a contract to demolish and remove a build-ing. While doing this, he also removed a valuable fuel tank which was buried on the premises. The purchaser's representative complained, stating that there was never any intent that the tank be removed. The contract, however, contained specific listings of items on the premises which were to be protected from removal, demolition, or injury. The particular tank was not contained on these listings. The purchaser's position was overturned, and the contractor was absolved of responsibility for the losses.

The general rule states that items omitted from a list will be ignored. The rule is altered when use of a list is qualified by words specifically indicating that it is not an exhaustive one. In such cases, interpretation of the list is subject to the context in which it is used and is impacted by the meaning of those associated words.

Order of Precedence of Contract Documents

While the foregoing rules imply that the parties can discover the correct meaning of a contract through interpretation, it is frequently difficult in practice. Long and complex provisions and clauses of a contract are often conflicting, and reconciliation of contract segments requires giving precedence to one section of the total document. Since a contract is ordinarily composed of several major sections--schedule, specifications, general provisions, sets of representations or instructions, and other documents or exhibits--some order of precedence must be given. This is often difficult to determine unless it has been clearly stated in the contract. In the absence of such a statement, the rule of law prevails: Specific provisions of the contract will take precedence over more general provisions, and any typewritten articles or paragraphs will take precedence over pre-printed, general provisions. This rather broad set of rules does not apply in most government contracts when either an order of precedence is stated in the contract or certain clauses are incorporated by statute or regulation. In a government contract, whenever there is a legally mandated clause, even if it is omitted from the actual contract writing, the clause must be read into the contract and will take precedence over more specific statements.

The order of precedence in a government contract is ordinarily set forth by the contract, and the provisions used are drawn from the Federal Acquisition Regulation 52.214-11 and 52.215-18. This part of the FAR establishes an order of precedence which provides that any inconsistency in the solicitation will be resolved by giving precedence in the following order:

1. Schedule of the contract (excluding specifications even when incorporated into the contract)
2. Representations and/or instructions by the offeror or the buyer at the time of entering into the contract

3. Clauses generally referred to as business conditions or boiler-plate provisions
4. Other exhibits or attachments to the contract or documents which may be cited as applicable to the work
5. The specifications

This order of precedence is fairly standard for government contracts and is incorporated into the standard solicitation instructions, Standard Form 33A. To carry the order of precedence rules one step further, the FAR 52.236-21 provides a rule for construction contracts: "In the case of difference between drawings and specifications, the specifications shall govern."

A matter of policy in government contracts, this order of precedence is clearly evident to both buyer and seller. In many cases, however, this simplified ranking of contract parts for purposes of interpreting its meaning will lead to a decision in interpretation controversies that does not fulfill the intent of the parties. This can be expected whenever a conflict or ambiguity arises which must be resolved on the basis of predetermined rules. Precedence rules are like this; they displace the concept of discovering the original intent of the parties. The contractual order of precedence provides a practical and relatively simple solution when no superior basis for decision is recognizable.

At all stages in their work, contract managers should be alert to the fact that general rules are not consistently fulfilled when cases are litigated. The detailed examination of facts and law during a formal hearing regularly raises specific circumstances that may not fit a situation as contemplated by a general rule. Furthermore, independent third parties involved in litigation, such as administrative law judges, may have perceptions and reach conclusions that seemingly vary from the general rule.

Use of Extrinsic Evidence

Oral statements and concurrent actions. The parties to a contract exchange information and viewpoints during different time phases and in different types of situations as they approach their agreement. Exchanges occur during pre-solicitation, pre-bid (or offer), pre-award, and post-award phases and continue until a conflict or dispute has been discovered. During each of these time frames, the parties may communicate on a formal or informal basis. Competitors may make direct inquiries during pre-solicitation, pre-bid, or pre-award conferences. The two parties who ultimately enter into the contract will often negotiate on a bilateral basis. They will be in contact again on many issues when performance begins after contract award. During all of these phases and types of communications, discussions may occur or actions may be taken that will determine or indicate the true understanding and intent of the parties. These discussions and concurrent actions provide valid insight into the intent of the parties at the time they enter into the contractual relationship. In resolving conflict or disagreement arising later in performance, the interpreter may look back at the earlier indicators for evidence. Such evidence is extrinsic to the contractual writing and, consequently, its use must be consistent with the rules of law governing extrinsic evidence.

It is in this context that the meaning of an integrated (written) agreement becomes very important. Litigation rules which limit the use of parol (oral) evidence in interpreting a contractual understanding also limit to some extent the applicability of extrinsic evidence. Parol evidence rules prevent admission of evidence that contradicts the language of an integrated agreement. In addition, the rules prevent the use of extrinsic evidence to add to agreement language which is considered completely integrated. These rules are difficult to apply. Nevertheless, parol evidence may be essential in reconciling differences between possible interpretations. Furthermore, parol evidence rules do not bar admission of extrinsic evidence to resolve ambiguity. In most circumstances, evidence developed that is extrinsic to the writing is admitted by the boards and courts and is an extremely important element in the overall interpretation of the contract.

Previous actions and understandings. Dealings of the parties prior to initiation of the contract is a second major source of evidence extrinsic to the integration. This factor is important when the parties have repeated contact concerning the same general production or construction process. Furthermore, the parties frequently use terms and conditions and specifications in the instant contract that have been used many times. Even a buyer's prior dealings with suppliers other than the current supplier may influence interpretation of a current contract. During performance of prior undertakings, understandings and perceptions often develop regarding the method of administering particular contract provisions. As a result, during the course of contractual work spanning more than one project, it is common for the parties to develop an interpretation in practice that is not totally consistent with the terminology used in the contractual documents. When this occurs in a new bidding situation, the competitors may make assumptions regarding the proper interpretation of the new contract. These assumptions may govern analysis of cost and preparation of bid prices. If prior dealings and understandings have influenced the agreement, it would seem unreasonable to ignore the precedent in later interpretations. Therefore, prior dealings of the parties count heavily in interpreting the current meaning of a contract. There are many rules associated with this type of interpretation issue. A fundamental rule states that the performer who is asserting an interpretation different from the current writing of the contract must show that he actually had knowledge of the earlier interpretation and relied upon it in bidding for the current contract. This issue arises when a buyer modifies language in a solicitation without giving explicit notice of the change to the potential competitors at the time of solicitation and award. The issue also arises in connection with changes in personnel administering contracts. When personnel change, the interpretation of language may also change, resulting in controversy over a contract provision although no change in the actual wording has occurred. Consequently, prior dealings of the parties may overcome explicit words of the current contract in interpreting its meaning.

Customary practice and uses of the trade. Since contracts are repeatedly awarded that make use of specific construction trades and industrial processes, the understanding of contract language within such a trade or industrial segment becomes fairly standardized. The trades develop practices and usages that become well understood and provide insight into the meaning of contractual language governing the practical application of effort. A problem in trade usages and customs frequently arises because contract language often appears to be clear in its ordinary meaning, yet within the trade, it has developed a meaning unique to the particular situation. It is the unique meaning within the trade situation that is given effect in interpreting the contract. Applying trade usages and practices can create difficult problems because they may overturn apparently clear language. Conversely, it is well established that clear language which expressly departs from a trade practice may be used to require substitution of a unique or special method of performance, but it must be demonstrable that the contractor knew or should have known of the departure.

An illustration of this is provided by a contract that specified the use of rigid insulation material in construction. The contractor used a flexible product. When challenged on this apparent departure from the contract specification, he pointed out that the contract allowed the use of "equally suitable material." Viewed in the abstract, it appears that the flexible product might not have been as equally suitable as the rigid product. Nevertheless, the contractor was able to demonstrate that an established, regularly applied industrial practice had developed in which the flexible product was substituted for the rigid product. Consequently, the contractor's interpretation prevailed.

RESOLUTION OF AMBIGUITY

Contract language that appears to be ambiguous may be fully interpreted by applying the rules for interpreting the writing. Clarification may also require examination of extrinsic evidence. However, from time to time the interpretation process proceeds through all appropriate steps without resolving the ambiguity. The parties must then turn to a set of arbitrary rules for determining the course of action mandated by the contract. In this undesirable situation, the basic rule of contract inter-pretation--the central objective of determining the intent of the parties-- must be abandoned. Having exhausted all intrinsic and extrinsic sources of evidence, the parties must decide who is responsible for the problems raised by the ambiguity. In this narrow situation, two key rules arise. The first is that an ambiguous contract will be interpreted against the party who drafted the document, the logic being that the only evidence of intent was created by the drafting party. Consequently, it would be unfair to favor the party who created the ambiguity. This rule often operates against the buyer and frequently arises in government contracts with the effect of frustrating the position of the government's represen-tatives. This results from the fact that the government ordinarily drafts, or has drafted by a third party, the specifications and drawings or other technical documents pertinent to its contracts. However, there is an offsetting rule--patent ambiguity--which generally operates to the disad-vantage of the performing party. Patent ambiguity places a special burden on the party who offers to perform work in response to a con-tract solicitation. The presumptions behind the patent ambiguity rule follow:

1. Offerors in a bid situation are expected to be knowledgeable of the normal and ordinary industrial or construction practices pertinent to their work.
2. It is presumed that the offeror has made a reasonably complete review of the contract documents before preparing his bid and submitting it to the purchaser.

Based on these presumptions, the offeror must bring to the buyer's attention any ambiguity or deficiency in the specification which was, or should have been, discovered in the normal review of solicitation docu-mentation during the bidding process. If it can be shown that the con-tractor failed to carry out this implied duty, the burden of losses result-ing from the pertinent ambiguity will be placed upon the contractor.

SUMMARY

The objective of this chapter has been to formulate a model of the contract interpretation process as it should be carried out by contract managers.

● The basis for the model is established at the outset by reviewing

several important presumptions, the violation of which generates the
need to interpret the contract.

- The role played by technical documentation in management and control
of contract operations is studied in some detail.
- Time, changing conditions, and related factors are reviewed to highlight pressures that cause conflict between buyer and seller during
contract performance.
- The creation and release of technical data packages and their characteristics are reviewed as a means of introducing the interpretation
problems likely to arise subsequent to contract award.
- Basic questions requiring post-award resolution are identified to
introduce a model of post-award interpretation processes. The model
addresses the effort of contractors to initiate contract work and the
reinterpretation necessary when problems surface that jeopardize
performance.

TOPICS FOR DISCUSSION

1. Comment on this statement: Program or product success is ensured
   by a contract technical data package which is free of defects and
   fully complied with by the supplier.
2. Summarize the principal arguments in support of this statement: All
   contracts contain a list of deliverables, a schedule, a boiler plate,
   the price arrangement, and other parts, but the heart of the
   arrangement is the technical data package.
3. What is the difference between a performance specification and a
   design specification? A functional specification and a process
   specification? Between a work statement and a specification? Are
   these differences always reflected in contractual applications?
4. Explain the concept of implied warranty of specifications.
5. As a contract administrator, you discover that you cannot meet a
   contract requirement with your available resources and capabilities.
   Discuss the issues that will arise and explain how you will approach
   your customer and your CEO.
6. Explain the principal objective in interpreting a contract and discuss
   how that objective changes when resolution of an ambiguity is
   necessary.
7. Summarize the principal categories of extrinsic evidence pertinent to
   interpreting a contract.

CASE 5-1

Saved by the Contracting Officer

Newt Simpson, production manager for Massachusetts Signal Corporation (MSC), has encountered several problems while working on a contract for manufacture of a subminiature electronic rescue radio beacon, URT/27. MSC is a successful electronics manufacturer with a superior reputation in the design and production of security equipment. The URT/27 production had been won on a competitive bid, but from Newt's point of view it appeared to be a questionable victory. Newt's current problems arose partly because this was his first experience with a government sale. Ross Jansen, MSC contract administrator, is in close contract with Newt concerning the contract because its success appears to be jeopardized by the lack of progress.

Under its contract MSC is obligated to deliver 10 pre-production models and 31,471 production units of the radio beacon in accordance with Specification MIL-B-38401. The unit price for production units is $49. The total pre-production quantity is priced at $44,255. The company's investment in the cost of performance has been increased by delays due to Newt's problems but minimized by progress payments.

The beacon is a current version of parachute pack rescue equipment. The specification requires it to be compact--slightly larger in size than a pack of cigarettes. It is self contained in an aluminum case sealed against water, dust, and weather and includes a dry-cell battery, transistorized components, and a telescopic antenna. The unit automatically transmits a tone signal when activated by a lanyard and pin upon opening the parachute.

Central to many of Newt's problems with this production is the specification for battery life which requires a minimum of 24 hours life at $0^\circ C$ with the unit in continuous operation at rated r-f output (200 mw average). Only a few days ago, Newt discovered that previous production of these units had achieved only 55 mw average for 24 hours continuous.

After substantial effort to achieve the required life, Newt concluded it could not be done. However, in conversation with the government's project manager, he learned that the government would relax the specification to a requirement of 15 hours continuous, an achievable level. Newt had overcome other problems: quality deficiencies causing leakage of the case, and a design that required a screwdriver to replace the battery. (The specification did not permit the use of tools.)

Ross was pleased to learn that the contracting officer would sign a no-cost supplementary agreement relaxing the battery life requirement to an achievable level. Most of MSC's expenditures and commitments of $1,600,000 have been financed through progress payments, and Newt advised Ross that he expected to complete the work within his revised cost to complete of $1,270,000. Ross wondered if the contracting officer's offer was the most desirable solution.

*   *   *   *   *

What is Ross Jansen's best course of action and why?

CASE 5-2

MultiElectro[1]

In December, 1983, Mr. Byron Johnson, Manager of U.S. Government Contracts for MultiElectro in Palo Alto, California, faced what appeared to be a financial disaster for the company. In September, MultiElectro had been awarded a firm-fixed-price contract by the government which, with options, totalled $12 million. The award was based on a competitive source selection. Now company engineers claimed the government's performance specification was much more stringent than had been thought--a fact that would almost certainly increase costs by 30 percent. Byron Johnson wondered what action he could take to help MultiElectro avert a multimillion dollar loss.

General Company Background

MultiElectro was a leading developer and producer of electronic countermeasure (ECM) components and systems for the U.S. government and other prime contractors. Annual sales totaled approximately $85 million, with internal forecasts of significant future growth. The company was engaged in a modernization program which it believed would secure its place as a leader in the industry for the foreseeable future. The program required expenditure of a substantial amount of capital, part of which was supplied by the government under a separate agreement.

The Contract Management Function

Mr. Johnson was responsible for negotiation and administration of contracts with the U.S. government. He supervised two contract managers and reported to the vice president for contracts at corporate level. The contract pricing function was carried out by a separate branch, while engineering and manufacturing expertise was provided by functional

---

[1]Research and the original draft of this case were performed by Curtis Cook while a student at George Washington University.

specialists located in other departments. MultiElectro was organized along traditional functional lines, rather than in a matrixed, project management form.

The Electronic Systems Contract

The contract in question, which required development and production of a state-of-the-art ECM system that included MultiElectro's unique memory core, had been awarded in September, 1983 after a competitive source selection process. Because of the need to award a contract prior to the end of the fiscal year, the government had released an urgent Request for Proposal (RFP) and, on short notice, had invited all prospective offerors to a pre-proposal conference. At the meeting, the subject of a critical performance parameter in the specifications (the amount of time delay required in processing a "hostile" incoming signal to ensure effectiveness of the ECM system) had been discussed at length. All attenders had apparently understood the importance of this parameter in calculating the cost of the job.

A few days after the meeting, shortly before the RFP due date, the government issued an amendment to the RFP that changed numerous aspects of the specification. No mention was made in the cover letter of any substantive change to the specification. Upon receiving the amendment, MultiElectro engineers made informal inquiries to their government counterparts in an attempt to ascertain what the change "really" entailed. The government project engineers assured MultiElectro that the amendment contained nothing that would substantially affect the cost of performance.

Based on these discussions and the time factor involved, MultiElectro submitted its proposal essentially unchanged. After a quick evaluation by the government source selection team, MultiElectro was awarded a three-year contract to develop three prototype systems at a total price of $300,000. The contract also included three one-year, unilateral options (on the government's part) for production of 220 units a year, at a price of $17,500 each. Price was the basis of award of the contract.

Three months later, MultiElectro was preparing for a preliminary design review with the government when the problem surfaced. In reviewing the contract specification, company engineers discovered that the critical parameter discussed at the pre-proposal conference had, in fact, been tightened considerably by the RFP amendment. While technically feasible, development and production of the system and taking advantage of the unique memory technology while meeting the specified performance requirement would cost MultiElectro an estimated 30 percent more per production unit. The engineers immediately called Byron with the news.

With preliminary design review imminent, Mr. Johnson searched for a way out of this dilemma. He knew the issue would surface at the design review. He also knew that once the system design was established, given the capabilities of the MultiElectro engineering organization, qualification of the prototypes was a function of time. Thereupon the production options would be exercised. Time was of the essence. It was Byron's job to satisfy the contract requirements while avoiding the potential loss. The design review was less than a week away.

* * * * *

Develop a course of action for Byron Johnson, consider the possible issues to be raised, and formulate the probable outcome.

6

Post-Award Contract Management Functions

The required duties or expected activities normally assigned to post-award contract managers can best be examined by looking at the federal contract systems. Government agencies have accumulated vast experience in administering contracted programs worldwide. They have documented their experiences, reflecting work with every industrial group in the economy under a wide array of contract types. Although the work is properly characterized as administrative, it embraces effort by expert personnel in diverse fields, including the engineering and/or scientific disciplines associated with the contractual end objectives. The work calls for managers who can make judgments that properly integrate technical events, interests of the parties, behavior of workers employed by either party, and the specific provisions of the agreement. These judgments must be consistent with the established (but always changing) legal and accounting principles that govern contracts.

Contract management responsibilities in the government are split between centralized procurement offices and decentralized field contract administration offices. The work is also subdivided into several independently organized disciplines, which include audit, investigative, and contract administration offices, plus project management offices or other types of units that are staffed with personnel expert in the technology pertinent to the contract. This chapter highlights the required work activities of the offices rather than the organizational structure under which those activities must be carried out.

CATEGORIES OF CONTRACT MANAGEMENT FUNCTIONS

A comprehensive list of contract administration functions is provided in the Federal Acquisition Regulations (FAR) 42.3. (See appendix 1.) The regulation identifies over sixty normal contract administration functions, but it provides relatively little information regarding actual performance of work. In this chapter, we will identify six broad categories of contract administration functions. Under each category, the functions are grouped according to the principal management objectives. References are made to the fact that some functions are normally performed by field contract administration offices, while others are normally retained by the procuring activity awarding the contract. This break out is not entirely consistent. For example, adequately staffed government procuring offices awarding contracts which are performed locally or which are highly specialized may not assign any contract administration functions. To the extent that administrative action is required, the entire list of functions is handled by the procuring office. Conversely, procuring offices with limited staff and a location remote from contract performance and administration may assign even their key program-sensitive functions, if the staff of existing field contract management offices has the requisite skills and resources.

The six broad categories of contract management responsibilities are as follows:

1. Monitoring and surveillance functions
2. Reports and services to procuring office and contractor
3. Reviews and audits of contractor internal management systems
4. Formal decisions and actions affecting contractors
5. Direction, negotiations, and agreements
6. Program-sensitive contract management functions

Monitoring and surveillance functions. This work touches all contact administration tasks. Taken as a group, the functions are those of an informed observer--one who watches over selected activities and behavior. The contract manager's objective is to secure information concerning the contractor's compliance with contract provisions. These functions may not focus on particular decisions, but they lead to actions or decisions intended to advance contract performance or to correct and adjust the relationship (e.g., to change the contract).

Reports and services to procuring office and contractor. This area includes numerous supportive administrative tasks performed to benefit the procuring contracting office. The service orientation of functions in this category is activated by ad hoc requests or regular needs of procuring activities or contractors. The work is characterized by analyses, evaluations, recommendations, reports, and preparation or delivery of services or documents.

Reviews and audits of contractor internal management systems. Work performed under this category may be characterized as consultation. It requires a high degree of expertise in management systems and is the government's way of verifying that efficient and effective contractor systems will be used to manage its programs. The systems reviewed have an impact on government costs, the likelihood of timely delivery, and the adequacy of contractor performance. The government believes that the audits are effective; however, a contractor's view may differ. Regardless, effective contract managers for either party seek to make the reviews a superior and effective source of ideas for improving performance of their work.

Formal decisions and actions affecting contractors. Many, but not all, actions in this category adversely affect contractors. Decisions are based upon, or stimulated by, information gathered while monitoring or providing services or reviewing contractor systems. The contract manager acts to approve, disapprove, accept, reject, allow, disallow, direct, or otherwise exercise his power of discretion to alter or correct the course of contract operations or the contract relationship itself.

Directions, negotiations, and agreements. This category requires negotiating skills to resolve controversy, redirect work, make cost and price adjustments, and settle claims. The contract manager is challenged to interact with the other party--to argue, to persuade, to concede--to resolve any differences between them and to bring the contract to a successful, or at least acceptable, conclusion.

Program-sensitive contract management functions. This category of functions may include any of those listed in the other five categories. Sensitivity varies with circumstances and program management concerns. The functions most likely to be sensitive are those affecting the agreement on price, schedule, or performance. Change orders, technical directions, negotiation of price increases, changes in the rate of funding, and termination and default actions may head the list of program-sensitive matters. Any administrative action or decision can become a critical issue and vitally important to affected managers.

Staffing Requirements for Contract Management Offices

Both procuring offices and field contract management offices require staff with knowledge of business relationships, but it is in the contract management offices that in-depth knowledge of operating systems and practical understanding of the work and behavioral implications of contract requirements become vital. Central procuring activities employ negotiators and buyers who are supported by price analysts, technical experts, financial management experts, and numerous policy level functional groups such as quality assurance, property, and transportation. They are also staffed with engineers, scientists, and other specialists who have requirements for work to be contracted out.

Field administration offices have a similar complement in general but also include a very different group of operating experts. In the field administration office, a direct, daily, and continuing interaction with contractor personnel is evident. Specific work assignments tend to be ministerial in nature, requiring a skilled manager with excellent judgment. Staffing requirements for this work are derived from a need for practical, hands-on assurance that progress toward fulfillment of contract objectives is unimpeded by technical or administrative issues.

Field offices are staffed, in part, with administrative contracting officers (ACOs) who should have (but are not always afforded an opportunity to have) a comprehensive knowledge of both contractual issues and project objectives. They are in regular contact with contractor representatives and seek to accumulate and organize information relating to delivery, price, quality, reporting, and costing issues. ACOs usually report to contract operations supervisors but seldom are afforded supervisory control over more than a few, if any, lower level employees. ACOs, however, are supported by several functional specialists, including engineering personnel and industrial specialists, who regularly visit contractor plants to gather data and monitor the contractor's production and engineering operations. Functional specialists usually report to a supervisor of production and industrial resources. When available, an engineering supervisor oversees the engineering functions.

Quality assurance personnel also support the ACO, although this functional group, often comprising more than half of the field office staff, has been structured to operate in an independent manner. Many quality assurance personnel are physically located at contractors' plants, while others make regular visits to contractor installations. Their purpose is to observe and verify effective operation of the contractor's quality assurance and inspection systems.

Contract administration offices (CAOs) employ a substantial staff of financial and price analysts who can review cost and pricing detail in contractor proposals. This capability is intended to support ACOs and procurement contracting officers (PCOs) in negotiating contract prices for both modifications and initial contract awards. ACOs and PCOs draw upon the services of the Defense Contract Audit agency to secure reviews of contractors' internal data.

Property management specialists are essential to field offices. This group is concerned principally with government-owned property in the possession of contractors and is responsible for verifying the adequacy of contractors' property management systems. Their work is discussed in chapter 7.

Transportation specialists also are essential at CAOs. This group is responsible for issuing--or authorizing contractors to issue--government bills of lading when applicable. The group aids in verifying that the packing and packaging of items shipped pursuant to government contracts fully complies with specifications and standards. The transportation officer has overall responsibility for ensuring proper compliance with the shipping requirements of contracts and carriers.

In the following discussion, the major categories of contract management functions are further broken down to help clarify the types of issues that arise and the contractual objectives of the manager. These subgroups include the following:

1. Overall management
2. Financial and price management
3. Technical and quality management
4. Property and transportation management
5. Social and economic policy administration

In the monitoring and surveillance category, for example, the contract administration office performs many duties to achieve effective overall management. In this chapter, these overall management activities are grouped separately from the financial and price, technical and quality, property and transportation, and social or economic policy activities. In practice, administrative problems and issues may not be easily categorized into these groups and are likely to overlap.

The intention is that this chapter be consistent with the FAR treatment of contract administration functions. The chapter reflects the governmental concept of what should be done, much of which is clearly essential. Although the government's comprehensive list of functions performed by its contract and audit personnel is based upon extensive experience, an important perspective is found by recognizing the viewpoint of leaders in private industry. Sandford McDonnell, Chairman and CEO of McDonnell Douglas Corporation, offered his view in a recent article: "Over the years we've gotten wrapped up in a cocoon of red tape, indiscriminate application of controls, and contract compliance requirements. The innocent get penalized, punished along with the guilty . . . They [defense] will have three or four people spend millions on technical and cost proposals; they'll conduct their own exhaustive shakeout, pick a winner--and then tell him how to do the job."[1]

Mr. McDonnell's frustration may come from many possible sources, but the heart of the issue is the contract management system. The question is, has the government gone so far in its demands for information

---

[1]"One Way to Strengthen Defense: Trust the Contractors--and Save $40 Billion a Year," *Government Executive*, May, 1986, p. 18.

and its penchant for review, analysis, questioning, and direction of contractor approaches that it defeats its own objectives of encouraging initiative and innovation as well as economy and efficiency?

Monitoring and Surveillance Functions

Overall management. Contract managers at field installations are called upon to perform a variety of monitoring and surveillance functions. The essence of the field administration job is to ensure that a contractor is performing his duties in accordance with the contract. Much of this activity is accomplished through the presence of the field person at a contractor's plant. For smaller contractor organizations, field administration is accomplished on a visiting basis; larger installations are more likely to have resident government personnel. The activities of contract management personnel are very specific. Upon award of new contracts, they assess the need for, organize, and conduct an orientation conference with the contractor. Such conferences may require attendance by numerous personnel and normally are conducted by the administrative contracting officer (ACO). Many objectives of this conference are related to subsequent monitoring and surveillance activities.

Administrative oversight of a contractor's maintenance programs (e.g., condition and calibration of facilities and equipment) and his overall support of logistics matters (such as care and protection of government property) is of major importance in ensuring effective performance of government contracts. Contract management personnel are expected to observe and review these facets of contractor management. Since standards for these operations are difficult to define and verify, and since the adverse effects of poor maintenance operations are gradual, oversight in this area is a challenging issue. Similarly, overseeing a contractor's compliance with safety standards and contract requirements can be frustratingly difficult. The area of safety in operations has grown in importance with increased recognition of the adverse effects created by hazardous materials and operations related to them. Although the contract administrator is concerned principally with meeting contract requirements, the overall problem of industrial waste disposal merits special precautions by government personnel.

A strike or other labor relations breakdown can affect overall performance. While government administrators must avoid becoming involved in industrial relations issues, their duty is to ensure that they are informed and, in turn, inform other agency offices about prospective adverse situations that could impact expected deliveries.

The Contractor Data Requirements List (CDRL) used in many DOD contracts imposes on contractors numerous requirements for submitting data and reports during contract performance. The contract administrator may need to give special attention to these deliveries and should directly oversee and encourage timely submission of all items on the CDRL. Since failures in this area often foretell the emergence of more basic problems in contract work, verifying data submission progress and ensuring that reports receive appropriate attention when submitted are central issues in the contract administration process. Data submissions should be reviewed and the information used. If the information is not useful, action should be taken to remove the requirement or to revise and improve the submissions. Substantial resource expenditures are associated with the data requirements.

Restrictive markings are often applied to data by contractors. While the government recognizes the necessity for restrictive markings when data is proprietary to the supplier, its rules for determining whether a mark is proper and the exact wording of authorized markings are a source of problems. The CAO must review contractor practices in this area to ensure that restrictive markings are not placed on data when the contractor does not have rights to the data. Conversely, though of less immediate concern to the government representative, failure to properly mark data that should be marked can result in significant losses to the provider of the data. From the contract manager's viewpoint, the objective is to ensure that markings are used only when necessary and authorized. Additional discussion of this subject is found in chapter 7.

A major objective of government contract policy is to encourage value engineering (VE) operations by contractors. Value engineering serves the public interest, since it tries to achieve required functional performances at reduced costs. Because VE results in specification changes and can result in highly profitable awards to contractors, government managers are somewhat reluctant to approve them without thorough technical and administrative review. Consequently, administration of VE has proven to be difficult. Contract administration offices are charged with oversight of VE activities and the contract clauses which support them. Because contractor obligations and monetary rewards vary with the clause used, controversy arises and mixed reactions regarding the overall effectiveness of VE have continued.

Contract work frequently is distributed by contractors to remote locations. The ACO at a prime contractor's facility must ensure that CAOs located at or near remote sites are assigned responsibility for providing supporting contract administration. This service is not provided for subcontracts unless special surveillance is required in connection with major systems acquisition or other high-risk work. When the contract administration office delegates a portion of its responsibility to sister organizations, it must ensure that any unique circumstances associated with the required support are fully understood.

Financial and price management. Twenty-four (39 percent) of the functions identified in FAR 42.3 deal with financial and price issues.

These areas should be highlighted in post-award conferences and subsequently checked by government representatives. Two of the functions call for monitoring and surveillance and are treated in this section. One calls for ensuring compliance with cost contract provisions and requires notification of the contracting officer when cost incurrence reaches a specified percentage of total contract obligations. These notifications should not be necessary for fully funded firm-fixed-price contracts, but they represent a vital part of the government's information system which enables timely funding of cost reimbursement and incrementally funded contract arrangements.

The second monitoring activity in this area is verifying the financial condition of specific contracts and of the contractor. This duty may be a minor concern for large, well established and well financed contracting organizations but may affect decisionmaking within any organization and can be critical to understanding the behavior of smaller contractors. Weakened financial circumstances often jeopardize a contractor's timely performance. The astute field contract manager will search for indications that financial pressures may be causing difficulties for the supplier. Financial issues are discussed more fully in chapter 11.

Technical and quality management. A principal duty of a contract manager is to observe and systematically check the status of production and progress toward delivery being made by a contractor. Central procuring activities exercise overall jurisdiction over technical issues, but the field administrator verifies that progress is adequate and deliveries will be made on time. Since interferences with delivery can come from unexpected sources, the contract manager should be searching for new developments that may intervene. The emergence of design and development deficiencies when required by a contract can be even more subtle. The CAO engineering staff within the field office has the primary responsibility for vigilance over possible deficiencies of this kind. The basic objective of government personnel responsible for administration in this area is to develop a close relationship with the contractor's technical management team so that problems and indicated technical deficiencies will surface in a timely fashion. Although reporting systems, such as technical progress reports and related engineering reports, should reveal design and development problems, personnel cognizance of the nature of the work and of any history of associated problems is prerequisite to proper actions for working around any deficiencies that may emerge.

In many ways, the most important activity of contract managers is verifying that the contractor's quality assurance operations comply with contract requirements. The importance of this activity is highlighted in chapter 10 and may be emphasized by pointing out that quality assurance and/or inspection systems are the buyer's most reliable protection against inferior, noncomplying, or unsafe products.

Property and transportation management. The aggregate value of government property in the possession of contractors, including furnished property, work in process, and finished goods, is substantial. As a result its management is a vital oversight activity of CAOs. Property operations are particularly important when the contract type requires cost reimbursements to the contractor, which is the case with most contracts other than firm-fixed-price ones. Title and the principal risks associated with ownership are transferred to the government as reimbursements occur. Sufficient personnel with expertise in administering property issues is essential to CAO operations. Chapter 7 treats property issues more fully.

Because a large volume of property is shipped via for-hire carriers, and since the function is highly specialized, the government's transportation management activities must be adequately staffed at contract management offices. The government usually obtains favorable rates when traffic moves on a government bill of lading, and, even if the contractor pays for freight directly, the government funds it through the contract. The rules for government bills of lading, the unique characteristics of carrier organizations, complex freight tariffs, and the complex and changing regulation of transportation industries give this area its specialized character. Integrated with traffic management responsibilities should be careful consideration of the contractor's practices with respect to the preservation, packaging, and packing of materials being shipped to government destinations. Proper oversight of property movement requires coordination to ensure that the terms of the shipment comply with the contract and that the product has been released for shipment. This activity is important to the overall economy and efficiency of government contract performance. Chapter 7 treats property issues more fully.

Social and economic policy administration. Field contract administrators carry a substantial responsibility for overseeing contractor compliance with government social and economic policy and, in particular, must ensure that small business firms and small disadvantaged business firms secure subcontract opportunities under government prime contracts. As an example, CAOs have been assigned the primary role of evaluating contractors' subcontracting plans, pursuant to Public Law 95-507. Observations of contractor effort by the CAO must be documented, and the contract manager should offer advice and assistance to facilitate the subcontracting program. Administration of several aspects of government social and economic policies is performed by other agencies. For example, affirmative action is a responsibility of the Office of Federal Contract Compliance Programs (OFCCP) in the Department of Labor.

Reports and Services to Procuring Offices and Contractors

Overall management. Contract administration offices are chartered to perform a number of services to support procurement activities and contractors. A principal duty is to conduct pre-award surveys at the facilities of contractors who are being considered for award of a government prime contract. Full-scale pre-award surveys require on-site visits at the prospective contractor's plant or offices. An on-site visit may not be required if the contractor has recently been surveyed in connection with prior award competitions. The main purpose of this activity is to verify that the contractor has the necessary management, technical expertise, requisite facilities, and financial strength to perform the contract. Survey data is recorded on Standard Forms 1403 through 1408, which deal with general information about the contractor's capabilities in areas of technical work, production, quality assurance, finance, and accounting. If a pre-award survey deals with all of these subjects, it will be comprised of at least thirteen pages of specific information about the prospective source. A significant proportion of total field office capabilities is devoted to conducting these surveys.

Although the administration of the Defense Industrial Security Program is a responsibility of the Defense Investigative Service, contracting managers are responsible for proper administration of the security requirements clause contained in all contracts requiring access to classified information. Since the contract clause requires the contractor to comply with the *Defense Industrial Security Manual for Safeguarding Classified Information*, proper compliance is a contractual matter. In the event that security requirements are altered during the contract's performance period, the CAO will be required to coordinate and facilitate any required changes to the contract. The CAO is also obligated to obtain, in the case of educational institutions, a mutually satisfactory agreement for compliance with the revised security program. Negotiations in this area may become difficult because of policies at some institutions.

In accordance with the Defense Materials System and the Defense Priorities System, contracting managers may be called upon to assist contractors whose work is rated or requires use of an authorized controlled material. Administration of priorities, allocations, and allotments is a responsibility of the Office of Industrial Resource Administration in the Department of Commerce. This office has established the systems necessary for rating orders and allocating materials to an authorized program for which a priority or allocation has been established. Although these contract needs should be decided before soliciting work sources, support in obtaining requisite materials may require action by the contract manager during the performance of such contracts.

Contract managers have a responsibility to be generally current and informed regarding contractor industrial relations developments. This knowledge becomes critical if a breakdown of collective bargaining or other developments are likely to cause a strike or other work interferences. This need for awareness does not include any authority of contract

managers to intervene in industrial relations activities. Government
policy is to avoid involvement that might be interpreted as favoring
particular outcomes of a collective bargaining process. Nevertheless, the
interests of government programs may be substantially affected if the
bargaining process breaks down and a strike occurs. For this reason,
contract managers must be prepared to remove government property or
take other action to minimize adverse effects on government programs in
the event of unsatisfactory developments. Under these conditions, the
field administrator should act to ensure that full coordination with the
procuring office has been accomplished prior to taking steps that would
alter the contractual commitments of the parties involved.

Financial and price management. The principal regular duty of field
administrative offices in this area is to administer payments. Administrative procedures for making payments will vary depending upon the
location of the payment office and the type of contract involved. The
roles of the CAO and the contract auditor should be coordinated and
efficient because actual payment depends upon their verification and
authorization. The basis for payments (and, therefore, the applicable
procedures) could be progress payments under fixed-price contracts,
interim payments on cost-reimbursable contracts, payment of a contractual
fixed rate in time-and-material and labor-hour contracts, liquidation of
progress payments upon receipt of contract deliveries, final payments on
fixed-price or cost-reimbursable contracts, and others. Expertise in these
processes is essential. A substantial part of the contract manager's
responsibility in the payments process is to withhold or reject a payment
request if necessary. For instance, if no progress is made as time passes,
it becomes necessary to examine the reasons for lack of progress. Force-
ful action may be needed to capture the contractor's attention. An
effective means of achieving this is to withhold payments. Doing so,
however, exposes the government to claims that it has breached its
contract. For these reasons, contract mangers must be fully aware of the
significance of payment actions.

Government contract managers must be prepared to deal with tax
questions. In general, the government is immune from state or local
taxation. Taxes may be levied against government contractors, however,
and the issue of their reimbursement or payment by the government is
not easily resolved. The government may have a substantial financial
interest in individual cases, and it is the contract manager's responsibility
to ensure that tax exemptions are obtained whenever pertinent. Since
this area is legally complex, counsel should be consulted whenever doubt
exists. The contract manager must collect the evidence to support the
correct procedure. A U.S. Tax Exemption Certificate (Standard Form
1094) may be issued by the contracting officer to enable the contractor
to avoid taxation. The certificate would be issued only if the taxes had
not been included in the contract price, or if the contractor agrees to a

reduction in the contract price to reflect the exemption from tax. The contract manager must also issue duty-free entry certificates to cover the importation of goods for government use which would otherwise be subject to customs duties. Exemptions from customs duties are available to government agencies provided the anticipated savings to an appropriated fund exceeds the administrative costs associated with processing the necessary documentation. Administration of this responsibility should be conducted in accordance with a contract clause entitled "Duty Free Entry."

Whenever advance payments have been authorized under a government contract, the contract manager must establish a special bank account for administering the advance payments program. Rules for establishing an agreement with the bank, rules for control of the special bank account, and government rights regarding any credit balance in the account must be clearly established to ensure protection of the government's interest. Requests for advance payments may be received from a contractor either before or after contract award and must be given appropriate consideration regardless of the timing of the request. Since government policy is, in general, to refuse to make advance payments except to advance the public interest or to facilitate national defense, relatively few instances of advance payments are experienced in the contracting operations of most agencies. However, advance payments and special bank accounts are usual aspects of research and development contracts with educational or research institutions and of contracts for managing and operating government-owned plants. Authorization for advance payments may be provided in other justifiable circumstances when it complies with statutory requirements and is approved by the agency head or designee.

One of the most active areas of financial and price management work of CAOs is the evaluation of contractor proposals. Many proposals are processed by field administration offices to support new procurement actions as well as for pricing contract modifications. This work requires both technical and price evaluation and may involve intensive review of contractor documents and systems to determine methods of performance and to verify cost estimates for proposed contract actions. To complete an analysis of price proposals, the contract manager must obtain all necessary information from audit and technical evaluation sources, as well as from the contractor. This work may require securing cost and pricing data from other sources in order to perform a comprehensive assessment of the proposed contract prices.

Technical and quality management. The level of technical review activity demanded of CAOs varies according to the needs of program management personnel at the procuring activity. If a program office is staffed with adequate technical management personnel who can visit contractors' facilities, there is a tendency for the program manager to assume technical review responsibilities. In the reverse situation, a program management office may rely substantially on the field administration office for technical review work. There are, however, a number of areas in which the field administration office is asked regularly to contribute to the technical management and quality assurance needs of the program. One of these areas is the engineering review of contractor proposals in support of pricing and progress evaluation. The CAO's field engineering capability often is relied upon for these purposes. It is particularly helpful if the field engineer can visit and observe the contractor's operations regularly and develop a rapport with contractor engineering personnel. A CAO's engineering staff is expected to observe and report any deficiencies contained in government contract specifications or related technical documentation. This can substantially reduce government costs for unnecessary or nonproductive effort.

Recommendations by a contractor for engineering or design studies, engineering change proposals, and other technical suggestions call for CAO office evaluation and comments. Because of its proximity to the contractor's work place, the CAO may be positioned to provide key information to support a decision by the procuring activity whether to adopt a proposal. When contracts involve large manufacturing programs, many requests for deviations or waivers from contract specifications may be generated. These requests require evaluation and a decision regarding acceptance or rejection. The CAO engineer can provide an independent evaluation of all such requests along with recommendations for appropriate actions.

Accurate progress reporting is one of the principal services that can be provided to a procuring office. These reports are based on the field office's surveillance activities and are generated by the preparation and delivery of activity, potential delay, and actual delivery delinquency reports. These services may be expanded substantially to provide comments regarding the contractor's revised estimates of cost to complete, revisions of work plans, and so forth.

Property and transportation management. The importance of property management in the context of monitoring contractor activities has been discussed earlier in the chapter. In addition to monitoring or surveillance, the government property administrator is responsible for screening and redistributing or otherwise disposing of residual contract inventory as appropriate. The property administrator is the principal contact point for managing facilities contracts established at major contractor plants at which a large number of government facilities are used. Administration of these items requires regular review of contractor property accounting systems, processing requests for needed property, and screening property records for available facilities which could be transferred to another contractor with a recognized need. Because there are policy restraints against providing fixed assets to contractors, the administrator must be aware of the proper justifications for making facilities available for a contractor's use. The property administrator authorizes any non-contractual use of property already in the contractor's possession and collects appropriate rental fees when nongovernmental use has been authorized.

Social and economic policy administration. Contract administration offices are called upon regularly to review and evaluate prime contractor's proposed subcontracting plans for small businesses and small disadvantaged businesses. Reviews of this kind are necessary to support award competitions. The requirement for subcontracting plans for small businesses and small disadvantaged businesses is incorporated into prime contract solicitations in accordance with Public Law 95-507, and the appropriateness and acceptability of the contractor's plans must be determined on a case-by-case basis. Review of plans for their adequacy can be accomplished best by personnel familiar with the local situation.

Reviews and Audits of Contractor Internal Management Systems

Overall management. The purchasing system is one of several important internal management systems of contractors. This system is subject to a Contractor Purchasing System Review (CPSR) by a team of government experts in the field of purchasing who are usually personnel from the field CAO. The objective of the CPSR is to verify the purchasing capabilities of the contractor's personnel, the reliability and efficiency of the company's organizational structure and policies governing the purchasing function, and the contractor's consistency in following the purchasing systems practices to which he is committed. If a contractor's purchasing system is approved, the requirements for prior consent to subcontract award are reduced.

Pursuant to DOD's Cost/Schedule Control Systems Criteria, demonstration audits of contractors' internal management systems for budgeting, scheduling, and accounting are conducted. These audits are conducted to ensure the effectiveness of a contractor's management processes and the contractor's ability to create an audit record of those processes. This type of audit is discussed more fully in chapter 9 where the government's approach to progress measurement is fully treated.

Financial and price management. In coordination with the Defense Contract Audit agency, contract managers review the contractor's compensation structure or plan. During 1984 and 1985, the government adopted the stance that it could save considerable money through auditing and overseeing contractor compensation systems. Previously, contractor compensation systems, although periodically reviewed by the government, had not been significantly challenged if practiced in a consistent manner. They had not been challenged on the sole basis of seeking reduced government costs. Current compensation systems reviews attempt to ensure that a contractor does not overpay his personnel. Unfortunately, this type of systems review means that the government's processes and viewpoints are becoming a factor in the contractor's system for motivating and compensating personnel.

As with any independent source of supply, government contractors have been left to their own devices to acquire insurance and similar means of protecting their organizations against losses. Government policy, however, has tended to discourage any purchase of insurance to cover areas where the government's self-insurance practices and cost-reimbursement processes would be an adequate basis for protecting the contractor's major interests. As an aid to the contractor, the government conducts periodic reviews and audits of contractor insurance practices and planning systems. A few major contractors have established self-insurance, but smaller organizations procure insurance from external sources.

Technical and quality management. Under a government contract, the CAO conducts engineering management systems studies to verify the effectiveness of a contractor's systems of design and production, engineering release, change control, data management, and configuration management. In addition, the overall inspection and quality assurance system may be subjected to review for acceptability consistent with current contract work.

Property and transportation management. Contractors who acquire or are furnished government property are expected to develop a system of property management that can account for, and maintain control over, all government property in their possession. Property systems reviews are conducted to verify that the contractor's system can be relied upon to act as the government's system for its property. The CAO property specialist performs these systems reviews.

Formal Decisions and Actions Affecting Contractors

Up to this point, the review of functions to be performed by contract management offices has fallen more or less into the categories of data gathering and processing, service, and audit. These kinds of activities often lead to formal decisionmaking at the PCO or ACO level. Administrative decisions carry out prerogatives of the government. They affect financial, technical, and contractual obligations and rights of both parties and may affect program progress. It is in the area of formal decisions--in deliberations and negotiations leading to them as well as subsequent actions--that vital questions concerning fault or responsibility for technical problems, delays, and cost increases are defined.

Overall management. The most important contract administration action affecting the rights of the parties is the contract change notice. There are two classifications of changes. The administrative change is employed to bring about contractual updates or corrections which have no substantial impact on the contractual rights of the parties. Administrative changes may be issued by the field CAO or the PCO. However, one application of the administrative change--funding and appropriation data modifications--should be accomplished by the procuring office. Ordinary formal change orders are different. They have an impact on the contractor's technical performance plus other elements of the contract such as pricing and usually are not issued by field contract offices, unless a special arrangement or authorization has been established. However, change actions--specification and drawing changes, property changes, and schedule changes--are regular occurrences for which both PCO and ACO action may be needed and for which full coordination is vital.

Contract administration offices have a regular workload pursuant to the notice and consent provisions of the subcontracts clause. Under this clause (as in most large, prime contracts), the contractor is required to provide notice to the contracting officer when award of a subcontract is planned. In addition to notice, when the prime contract involves cost determination by the government, review of and consent to the subcontract are needed prior to award. The consent decision must be timely to avoid delaying the contractor's progress. The CAO review, however, cannot be cursory or non-substantial but must consider the numerous elements of subcontracts which could operate to waste or misuse government funding.

When disputes arise, internal coordination of PCOs, ACOs, program managers, and any other affected persons is essential. If the indicated action is a final decision of the contracting officer, the CAO must support making timely findings of fact and convey the decision to the contractor for acceptance or appeal at the contractor's discretion. Since the final decision of a contracting officer is treated as a formal, final decision of the government respecting the issue under discussion, great significance is attached to the steps leading up to that final decision and to effective management of all related contract activity. The contracting officer is expected to assume heavy responsibility for personal but impartial involvement in making such decisions. Although findings of fact and final decisions are perceived as the last step in negotiations and the first step toward litigation, relatively few contractual controversies enter into this phase of action.

The ACO is responsible for releasing shipments from contractor plants to government customers. For the purposes of shipment, two elements are vital. First, the quality assurance experts in the CAO should have concurred in releasing the product for shipment. Secondly, the terms of the contract in regard to delivery of the goods and associated payment processes should be carried out in full.

Financial and price management. Establishing billing rates and final rates for indirect costs is a requisite part of the administration of all contracts requiring determination of costs. Similarly, agreement on forward pricing rates for overhead is necessary for pricing agreements on all types of contracts. Until the fall of 1985, negotiation of these agreements had been a principal responsibility of the ACO, who traditionally secured the support of the Defense Contract Audit Agency in developing his position. Beginning in 1985, specific authority for direct determination of final overhead rates by the Defense Contract Audit Agency was inaugurated by the Department of Defense. The CAO is still responsible for the agreement on interim billing rates and pricing rates but does not enter into the negotiation of final overhead rates unless the audit agency's determination is appealed to the contracting officer by the contractor. This is an area in which a contracting officer's final decision could be appealed under the Disputes Clause to a Board of Contract Appeals. Since the rate determination process has been altered, disputes may be generated because contracting officers are unable to objectively evaluate and act upon the determinations of the audit agency.

Under FAR 42.8, the contracting officer is authorized to disallow specific costs incurred or planned by a contractor. Prior to taking such action, the contracting officer should negotiate or coordinate with the contractor in an effort to bring about a satisfactory settlement. Actions in this area result directly from the CAO's monitoring of a contractor's cost of performance. Disallowance of direct costs may result. With respect to indirect costs, however, full coordination between the auditor and the contracting officer should be accomplished prior to issuance of the disallowance action. As a means of minimizing controversy and litigation, a contract clause entitled "Notice of Intent to Disallow Costs" has been incorporated into contracts involving cost determination procedures. The notice should be issued as early as possible during contract performance whenever it is observed that costs are being charged to the contract which the contracting officer considers to be unallowable.

Contract administration offices have been delegated responsibility for implementing certain aspects of the government's cost accounting standards policy. First, the CAO determines the adequacy the contractor's disclosure statements with emphasis on whether the accounting system is in compliance with the statement. Secondly, the CAO determines whether the statement is in compliance with the cost accounting policy.

The most active decisionmaking area in the financial and price management role of a CAO is probably approval or disapproval of progress payment requests. This action occurs regularly and is important to the contractor's working capital position and to the appropriate administration of the most prevalent form of contract, the fixed-price contract. Under fixed-price incentive and redeterminable contracts, the CAO is obligated to periodically review the mandatory quarterly statement of the status of progress payments. The purpose of the quarterly statement is to provide a balance mechanism for the propriety of payments made against the current expected final price of the contract, after considering the likely price revisions which may be negotiated. The government's objective is to avoid overpayment to contractors and, if overpayment has been made, to recover the funds, pending final price determination of the particular contract.

Technical and quality management. The contract administration action of greatest significance to the contractual responsibilities of the parties is inspection and acceptance of end items. This work usually is carried out by the field CAO. Quality assurance representatives have the major responsibility of verifying that the contractor's system is producing a conforming product. Verifying product quality prior to acceptance is essential to the integrity of contract and program success. Quality issues may arise in which the quality assurance representative suspends the authority for shipment of goods. Such action is a drastic measure taken only when substantial quality assurance problems have arisen in the contractor's plant.

Property and transportation management. Special test equipment is an important property responsibility of the contract manager. It often includes general purpose equipment incorporated into an integrated test unit designed for a special testing objective. The government's special test equipment clause provides for contractors to acquire or fabricate special test equipment at the government's expense, even though the equipment is not itemized as a deliverable end item in the contract. Under the rules of the clause, the contractor is obligated to provide thirty days advance notice of his intent to purchase or fabricate special testing equipment. The responsibility for review and approval of that request falls on the contract manager. Proper accounting for the property must be established by the contractor to preserve the government's option to take title when the contract is completed.

Social and economic policy administration. The responsibility of contract administrators to review and assist contractors concerning their subcontracting plans for small businesses and small disadvantaged businesses includes master subcontracting plans--plans that govern the subcontracting program for an entire plant or division of a company.

Directions, Negotiations, and Agreements

In many ways the most interesting and challenging aspects of contract management work are found in the negotiations processes carried on in field or procuring offices. They focus on the major issues that tend to divide buyers and sellers. In long-term government contracts, extensive negotiation processes proceed subsequent to the award of

contracts. Negotiations affect the overall management of contracts;
technical and quality questions; the financial and price relationship
between the parties; acceptance and closeout of contract agreements;
disposition of property, including excess government property; and numerous other large and small issues.

Overall management. Contract changes ordinarily are issued by
procuring offices but can be issued by CAOs with prior agreement and
authorization from the procuring office. Issuing a change notice is, in
many ways, the most significant action of a government contract manager. Such notices alter agreements in a substantial manner and may
involve sizable cost changes and schedule adjustments. Consequently,
research and approval processes leading to the issuance of changes are
extensive and should involve senior management levels. The exact
processes vary with individual agencies as a function of their internal
management systems. At the contract management level, however, full
coordination among field and central procuring offices and contractor and
program management personnel is necessary to avoid unexpected effects
of directing the change. Other forms of unilateral orders, including
termination actions, stop work orders, and government property changes,
are equally significant but occur far less frequently. The overall management impact of the changes process takes on special significance at the
ACO level because it is in the field that informal changes--commonly
referred to as constructive changes--occur regularly. Although by
definition technical directions should not amount to change orders, the
incidence of inappropriate change through these processes is frequent.
Managing and controlling that process is a significant challenge to
contract managers.

Financial and price management. One purpose of post-award negotiations is to reach agreement on contract price adjustments. Other
post-award negotiation objectives include forward pricing rate agreements,
rate of expenditure and funding issues, and final pricing of incentives.
Negotiations toward these objectives require receipt and use of cost and
pricing data developed by the supplier. Preparation for post-award
negotiations is extensive and is a major workload factor at field contracting offices. Preparation includes reviewing proposals; gathering
technical, audit, and pricing data; and coordinating activities. CAOs have
a variety of additional negotiation responsibilities such as negotiating
price adjustments and executing supplemental agreements in support of
the cost accounting standards program. Similarly, negotiations of advance
agreements (these agreements cover costing areas subject to challenge as
to reasonableness) are a part of the CAO workload and have been an
important means of developing understandings with contractors. Spare
parts pricing, a major area of price negotiations in field contracting
offices, has received considerable criticism during the first half of the
1980s. Revised practices are being developed to cover the negotiation of

spare parts pricing, but it remains a major factor in the workload of CAOs.

Field administration offices usually are charged with negotiating settlements of terminations for convenience. Under the DOD system, termination contracting officers (TCOs) are designated and have become specialists in this work. When assigned the responsibility for negotiation of a settlement, the TCO prepares the negotiation plan and negotiates the supplemental agreement. Similar to convenience terminations but authorized under special cancellation clauses is the negotiation of settlements under multi-year contracts when subsequent year quantities of the products purchased are not funded by the government.

Technical and quality management. Engineering managers and quality assurance representatives have not been delegated official negotiation responsibility or authority affecting contractual relationships. However, their work in interacting with contractor personnel could be characterized as a continuous and critical negotiations process. The development of technical understandings with respect to method of performance, approaches to design verification, appropriateness of inspection and quality assurance arrangements, and procedures for acceptance testing and decisionmaking, all constitute key elements in the overall management and successful performance of contracts.

Property and transportation management. Property specialists at the contract management office are responsible for moving excess government property and for reaching settlements with the contractor concerning the necessary packing, crating, and handling services. A similar responsibility is imposed upon transportation officers to obtain proposals and to reach agreements on adjustments associated with revised shipping instructions in the event such instructions impact contractor responsibilities. If contract prices are affected by these matters, the ACO enters into this negotiation process.

Program-Sensitive Contract Management Actions

Although each area within this category has been discussed under the first five categories of contract management functions, special attention must be given to those aspects of post-award management which impact program progress, cost, and success. The areas of greatest significance are change orders, schedule adjustments, termination actions, authority to ship and acceptance of products, adjustment of price or cost, and, in some cases, modifications of contract terms and conditions. Management at all organizational levels of both purchaser and supplier is affected when contract managers initiate action, or negotiations leading toward action, in any of these areas. All unilateral directions are sensitive, and negotiation of settlements, though less urgent, often becomes controversial. Special sensitivity is attached to the negotiation of supplemental agreements. These agreements may define unilateral orders; letter contracts; other unpriced orders, such as those based on spares ordering agreements; changes to overhead rates for final pricing purposes; and negotiation of price adjustments pursuant to economic price adjustment provisions. Control of these processes remains with the procuring offices but may be delegated to CAOs, as capabilities and needs indicate.

SUMMARY

This chapter provides an overview of the functions of post-award contract administration offices (CAOs). (A more detailed treatment of post-award functions is found in other chapters of this book.) The following points are covered:

- Six major categories of functions are identified and defined as follows:
    1. Monitoring and surveillance functions
    2. Reports and services to procuring office and contractor
    3. Contractor internal management systems reviews and audits
    4. Formal decisions and actions affecting contractors
    5. Direction, negotiations, and agreements
    6. Program-sensitive contract management functions
- The work of government CAOs is referred to for two reasons:
    1. The government has documented its systems fully and made the information available.
    2. Government work in contract management includes all industrial segments and types of issues.
- Staffing requirements to adequately handle the many post-award functions are discussed.
- Five subgroups of categories of contract management functions are given:
    1. Overall management
    2. Financial and price management
    3. Technical and quality management
    4. Property and transportation management
    5. Social and economic policy administration
- Capturing the full scope of post-award action is difficult because the issues are diverse and can change, depending on personalities, the attitudes of contractor and government personnel, the financial status of the job, and the complexity of the undertaking. The work tends to lack glamour, yet it is vital to the well-being of the individual company or agency and to the entire nation.

TOPICS FOR DISCUSSION

1. What distinguishes a program-sensitive contract management action from other less sensitive actions?
2. Which is the more important decision: to make a progress payment to a contractor whose progress is marginal, or to issue a change notice to remove a production bottleneck?
3. Discuss the amount of control a field contract administration office manager has over his office's workload.
4. What actual work activities fall under the heading of monitoring and surveillance functions?
5. Assess the reasons why the government system for contract management is overly complex. How would you restructure the system to reduce complexity?
6. Explain the role of ACOs in labor relations matters.
7. Explain the administrative change procedure and how it differs from change order practices.

CASE 6-1

Simplex "A"

The energy crisis resulted from the Arab oil boycott in 1973 and generated innumerable initiatives to discover or to create alternative fuels and conserve the use of energy, particularly oil. Simplex "A" was one of the projects contracted for by the Department of Energy's (DOE) predecessor, the Energy Research and Development Administration (ERDA). Under ERDA, certain procedures were developed to encourage private sector research in energy technologies. One of ERDA's actions was the adoption of the Program Opportunity Notice (PON) as a means of soliciting proposals to perform research and development work in energy production and to demonstrate the feasibility of new concepts.

ERDA PON FE-3 was issued early in 1976. Precipitated by the emergence of perceived critical energy shortages and cost increases, FE-3 invited proposals for research and development in combustion energy, including work in coal slurry combustion as a source of energy for industrial steam generators. In general, the objectives of the PON were to prove feasibility and economic viability and to demonstrate an operating system. However, a problem was caused by the agency's policy that all such projects should be cost shared by the contractor, preferably at a rate of 50 percent. The reason for this policy concerned the overall objective of ERDA--to commercialize the new energy technology with the direct benefit of successful development accruing to the developer through commercial sales. During this period, a plan evolved to consolidate governmental energy promotion and development activities under DOE.

Company Background

Simplex is headquartered in Palo Alto, California. Since its origin in 1965, it has grown into a diversified engineering and manufacturing company providing high-technology products and services. Simplex's Aerospace Division has grown in three major markets: strategic and tactical missile systems, defense electronics and software, and composite material systems. Through its Electronics Division, advanced data acquisition systems have been developed for use by industry and utilities to monitor and control industrial processes. The Power & Environmental Division develops technologies and provides products and services that enable customers to obtain maximum energy from fuels with minimum environmental impact. The company seeks better and safer ways to use coal, oil, natural gas, synthetic fuels, and solar energy. At the time ERDA's PON FE-3 was issued, the Simplex Corporation balance sheet showed total assets of $8,152,000 and a net worth of $2,748,000. The annual net profit of Simplex at this stage in its development had not reached the $500,000 level.

In April of 1976, the Aerospace Division of Simplex Corporation responded to PON FE-3 with a proposal as a prime contractor to perform engineering and design work; install equipment; and check out, operate, and maintain a subscale coal-oil slurry combustion system at its existing subscale multi-fuel combustion facility. Their proposed system was based on developing a method of using a coal-oil mixture (COM) as the fuel for powering industrial steam generators. The Simplex proposal included a team of four subcontractors, each with substantial expertise in the field. However, Simplex did not submit a proposal with cost sharing because the company president, Gene Stanton, felt it unwise to put such a high proportion of corporate assets on the line--even though he was very interested in the technology. The company's position reflected the concern that it could not take the risk of underwriting 50 percent of the total $1,390,493 proposal.

Simplex's proposal was highly regarded by ERDA program personnel in the Division of Coal Conversion and Utilization, including ERDA Program Manager, Alfred Sims. As a result, the agency's contract specialist, Joe Rogers, contacted Simplex's director of contracts, Harold Singleton, to advise him that discussions leading toward award of a contract were in order. During negotiations, it became clear that the agency would not consider abandoning its cost sharing policy. Consequently, Simplex management was faced with a difficult business decision at the outset. How far should the company go in meeting the ERDA

requirement in order to capture the project? Some flexibility was
indicated by ERDA in two areas. Since Simplex's proposal called for two
phases, an adjustment might be negotiated regarding timing of the
Simplex share. Also, some flexibility regarding the share ratio was
discernable in early discussions with ERDA's contracting officer.

After much debate, Simplex submitted a revised proposal on February
14, 1977 which provided for two phases of the project--design and
development and boiler modification/construction and operation (demonstration). The proposal still did not offer cost sharing; in fact, it
proposed payment of a fee for the project. The revised proposal amounts
were: phase I, $1,165,821; phase II, $877,046. The proposal furnished the
basis for further negotiations. The key decision before Simplex remained
this: What level of risk could the company shoulder in order to proceed
with this project?

* * * * *

1. Consider the situation in 1977. Develop a strategy for Simplex.
    Specifically, what should be their going-in and break-off position?
2. Assume that Simplex accepted a 50 percent share. Estimate their
    change in net worth due to the project in 1982 and 1986.

7

Property Issues in Contracting

Contract managers are involved with all forms of property and the diverse issues associated with property. While most contracts require fabrication or delivery of property (or both), even those that require only performance of a service involve contractor employees working with, in, and on property. In the simplest form of contractual relationship, the supplier's personnel work only with, in, and on property owned by the supplier. In these cases, the purchaser is not involved with the property and has little interest in any aspect of it until delivery and acceptance of the end product. This relationship prevails when noncritical and noncomplex products are being sold from stock or from strictly supplier controlled designs.

Property relationships are much less clear in contracts involving critical applications (especially safety-related ones) or buyer-controlled design coupled with complex qualification requirements. Property management issues are most likely to arise if the sources of property are mixed, with some acquired by the supplier and some supplied by the purchaser. If the form of contracting involves cost reimbursement, ownership becomes a variable, and the whole property scene becomes a surprisingly versatile and dynamic subject.

Contract property under production is constantly changing in form. Value and wealth are accumulated in property, title to it may change even without delivery, and its possession may change routinely. For large contracts, the quantity of property often becomes huge, and its quality, suitability, and timeliness become variable and difficult to trace. Because of these factors, property management takes on highly specialized and technical characteristics. Finely tuned clauses have been created for government contracts to account for these technicalities, and policy covering the subject is voluminous and detailed. In this chapter we will examine property issues and use government policy and practice as a model for the principal issues. Property issues will arise under any complex contractual relationship, but the government's approach to managing the relationships is systematic and documented and, therefore, useful in developing an understanding of the subject.

MIXED OWNERSHIP OF PROPERTY

Various types of property fall under the purview of a contract for one of four purposes: (1) to perform work (e.g., in the case of equipment and facilities); (2) to have work performed on it; (3) to be consumed by the production process (as with fuel); or (4) to be incorporated into the end product (as in the case of material). It is usually the supplier's responsibility to provide or acquire the needed property. However, the purchaser may supply part of the property when it is in his interest to do so. This occurs when the material or equipment already exists in the buyer's inventory, when there is a need to control quality or finish variables in a specific manner, when more than one supplier is engaged in producing products that must be joined together in such a way that the output of one supplier must be delivered to another, when the purchaser is in a better position than the supplier to obtain needed property, or for other reasons specific to a particular undertaking.

The most readily observed reason for contract property to be of mixed ownership is the purchaser's decision to provide some part of it. The use of contract types other than firm-fixed-price is an equally important factor especially in government contracting. A large number of non-firm-fixed-price contracts are used by the government, and when they are used, title to property acquired by the contractor specifically for the contract transfers to the government upon its delivery to the contractor. In addition, cost reimbursement rules require title to material taken from contractor stores to transfer immediately upon identification with the contract. When this is done, ownership becomes mixed (partly supplier and partly purchaser owned). Moreover, when property title shifts during contract operations, it may be difficult to track. When both actions apply in the same contract (buyer-furnished property plus use of contracts with reimbursement provisions), the contractual effect is complexity in inventory and accounting procedures.

Government policy toward providing property and the intricacies of accounting for it are related to the type of property. For that reason, it is useful to examine the major property classifications. It is readily apparent that buyers would not furnish property to their suppliers in the absence of substantial benefits.   In general, reasons for providing property vary with the characteristics of the property in question.

CLASSIFICATIONS OF PROPERTY FOR CONTRACT PURPOSES

Tangible property having distinct characteristics significant to contractual relationships falls into five categories: (1) facilities (real property, and other equipment of a capital nature); (2) material; (3) special tooling; (4) special test equipment; and (5) "agency-peculiar" equipment.   While property may be classified in other ways, most important contractual implications are associated with these five categories. (Intellectual property is discussed later in this chapter.)   Exactly how do these characteristics affect contract relationships and policy?

The first category, facilities, covers real property, rights in land, ground improvements, utility distribution systems, buildings, and other structures.   Purchasers, including the government, normally do not expect to provide such property to contractors.   Within this category, real property is ordinarily conceived to be part of the supplier's fixed assets and to constitute a necessary part of the capital on which the business has been organized.   Such property, however, may be provided by purchasers when they possess real property that is essential to the needed production, yet unavailable to the supplier community; when a contract requires construction on a specified piece of land; or when a contract calls for testing operations requiring large, open, remote, or specially equipped areas, as is the case for many military testing operations. Contractual issues associated with furnishing real property include authorization for use, access to premises, scheduling and coordinating work of all users, and sufficiency of the facilities for the intended use.

Facilities other than real property generally include plant equipment or other fixed assets characterized as personal property.   This includes any property used in manufacturing, in performing services, or for administrative or general plant operations.   Some examples are machine tools, test equipment, furniture, vehicles, and other equipment.   Included are accessory items (those desired but not essential to using a piece of equipment) and auxiliary items (those essential to but separable from an item of equipment).   As with real property, purchasers do not ordinarily expect to provide facilities for their suppliers.

Regardless of the normal perceptions, both real property and plant equipment may be furnished to suppliers when sound reasons justify such a decision.   Furnishing these assets is probably far more likely if the purchaser is the government rather than a private corporation.   This conclusion is based on the nature of the items or services for which the government issues contracts, not on policy. By policy, the government is strongly opposed to providing capital items to industrial organizations (government-owned, contractor-operated facilities are a general exception). However, the reality of government acquisitions frequently overcomes policy restraints. This is particularly true for military purchases and research and development, or when production is sponsored by an agency and the end product is not useful to consumers, and the facilities are not needed or easily converted to commercial end use. Under these circumstances, private investors often cannot justify the substantial capital requirements needed to facilitate the government project. This is not always the case. If government production is of sufficient magnitude, private sources may capitalize the facilities. If the facilities can be easily converted to commercial production, and there is a need for the capacity, private capital can be attracted. These conditions frequently are not present. Contract issues associated with these forms of property relate to identifying and accounting for property, its maintenance and protection, loss and damage, timeliness, suitability, and use for purposes other than those for which the property is provided.

The second category of property, material, has a policy environment quite different from real property and plant equipment. Purchasers still would prefer not to supply it because doing so confuses responsibility for the quality and delivery of end products. However, material consists of items incorporated into the end product or consumed in the production process. Material is not capital in nature and does not survive the performance of the contract (except in the form of inventory). If economy, convenience, use of accumulated inventory, buying power, consistency of the end product, or other purchaser advantages call for providing material to the supplier, it will be done as an ordinary business decision. Timeliness, suitability for intended use, and accounting for material are important issues associated with material being furnished by the purchaser.

The third category of property, special tooling, generally includes items such as jigs, dies, fixtures, molds, patterns, taps, gauges, and other manufacturing aids. All of these items are specialized in the sense that they are useful only for the limited purpose for which they are fabricated and acquired--usually for producing a specific end item or for performing a particular service. In some cases, special tooling may require building special foundations or related improvements which have the characteristics of capital facilities, but if usefulness is limited to a particular production, the cost is a part of the special tooling. For this reason, extra care is taken when evaluating special tooling. The cost of special tooling is usually viewed as directly chargeable to the immediate production contract. If continued long-term production is expected, however, the cost may be amortized over a substantial quantity of production. In late 1985, a new policy initiative by the Navy placed the responsibility on Navy contractors for purchasing special tooling. Under that initiative, the contractor's right to recover the costs was limited to amortization over the life of expected production contracts. Controversy over that policy resulted in two actions: Congress enacted the 1987 Defense Appropriation Act, and the DOD issued a new policy which states that contractors may be directly reimbursed for no more than 50 percent of the cost of producing special tooling or test equipment. The balance of the cost may be amortized over the production contract, but the policy does not apply to single-year production, and it established exceptions which allow greater reimbursement when this is in the government's best interest. This policy was made effective on January 16, 1987.

Special tooling may survive the initial production contract and, therefore, may be used for future production. This is a particularly sensitive matter for the government because government production normally is purchased on a year-by-year basis, yet it is competitively contracted for each year's quantity. The existence of previously used, but still useful, special tooling funded by the government under prior contracts complicates the competitive process and motivates the government to exercise its right to take title to and possession of the tooling. This creates an inventory and storage expense and raises potential issues over suitability if the items are transferred for use by a second contractor. Alternatively, if tooling is not carefully accounted for, concern arises over the possibility of duplicate payment pursuant to follow-on contracts with the original contractor.

The fourth category of property includes special test equipment which is even more difficult to manage than special tooling. Special test equipment includes integrated testing units designed and fabricated or assembled specifically to accomplish a specialized testing objective associated with the contract in question. Equipment in this category may be single-purpose or multipurpose, but its value is as an interconnected and interdependent assemblage useful for the defined purpose. Its cost is generally considered chargeable to the instant contract. Because special test equipment is made up of parts and subassemblies that may have value independently when disassembled, questions of ownership and equity in distribution of costs are difficult. Like tooling, such equipment may include foundations or other improvements needed for the specialized testing objective, but unlike special tooling, recoveries that have general purpose utility may be substantial. If costs are paid as an expense under the contract, the purchaser's interest in title or disposal must be recognized.

The fifth category of property, agency-peculiar equipment, is pertinent primarily to the government. It includes special purpose property entered into agency property accounts, such as space vehicles, weapons, and other equipment which is acquired by agencies for special applications. It is often supplied to a contractor so that he or she can perform specific work with or on the property. Preserving, protecting, and properly accounting for such property are key elements associated with the contractual relationship.

Contractual implications of these five types of property are important and may be a source of conflict both before and after contract award. The principal issue prior to contract award may be whether the property should be furnished. Purchasers such as government agencies do not want to finance the supplier's capital items, yet they are forced to recognize the necessity of financing specialized assemblages as part of their project. If a capital item can be shown to have application to long-term production or service requirements, the supplier may be willing to make the investment. This is a particularly difficult negotiation issue for the government. The government's disadvantages in such negotiations are partly a function of its own policies and partly a function of the items and services it buys. Two government policies are critical: the right to terminate contracts for convenience, even during peacetime; and its determination to seek independent competition for every production purchase. These policies give the supplier little incentive to make long-term investments or to amortize costs of specialized expenditures since there may be no subsequent contract against which to amortize, and even the current contract is not an assured vehicle for amortization. When this set of problems is weighed along with the nature of the end items being purchased, the supplier's conclusion regarding investment is often negative, particularly if the end items have no commercial value.

Post-award tangible property issues relate principally to suitability and timeliness questions as well as proper accounting, preservation, protection, maintenance, and use of property that is furnished or owned by the purchaser. This chapter illustrates these issues by describing the government's property system.

PROPERTY ACCOUNTING AND MANAGEMENT

For contract managers, one of the implications of property is the task of accounting. Each category and individual piece of property needs to be identified properly and accounted for in terms of value and quantity. This is a specialized, complex, and detailed process that extends throughout the life of the contract and beyond. It is a relatively simple process only if there is no mixing of customer-owned and supplier-owned property. Unfortunately, this seldom will be the case with large-scale, technologically complex, or long-term contracts, and it is seldom the case for major contract projects of the government. It is valuable to study government policies in this area for a comprehensive treatment of the various circumstances and problems associated with property identification, location, control, maintenance, and protection. Part 45 of the Federal Acquisition Regulation covers this subject in detail. We will summarize only the overall dimensions of a comprehensive property management program.

Accounting for contract property is complicated when large numbers of items are involved; when there is mixed ownership of property in the contractor's possession; and when possession is transferred among customer, prime contractor, subcontractors, and co-contractors (independent prime contractors who work on segments of a program to generate products and information that must interface or are otherwise interdependent). Informal working environments, borrowing between responsible persons, and sheer inattention to the problems of accountability are other complicating factors. Well-defined systems for handling property which are staffed with adequate numbers of skilled personnel are essential in dealing with the complexities and issues associated with property management.

Government Standards for a Property System

When large quantities of customer-owned property are in the hands of a contractor, the hiring of a property specialist is indicated. This becomes essential if the customer is a government agency. There are two vital objectives in establishing a good property system: to protect and reduce confusion relative to property accounts, and to obtain an approval of the system from the government's property administration officer. Requirements for an approved system may seem burdensome, but only when viewed from the perspective of one who has not established a system. The government seeks a documented system that will identify, locate, value, protect, preserve, maintain, and control all government-owned property in the contractor's possession. The government prefers to do this on a contract-by-contract basis but will accept a consolidated property record system, provided information needs are met. Standards for an acceptable property control system include the contractor's ability to accomplish the following:

1. Create a record and assume responsibility for control of property when
   a. government-furnished property is delivered
   b. contractor-purchased property is delivered when purchased under a cost-reimbursement contract
   c. property is withdrawn from contractor-owned stores and charged to a cost-reimbursement contract or, alternatively, upon approval of a claim for reimbursement
   d. the government accepts title of property under the operation of a specific contract clause (for example, pursuant to a change order or termination procedure)

2. Ensure that subcontractors who use government property have a system of property control that complies with government property system requirements

3. Generate reports upon discovery of any property in excess of that required

4. Upon discovery of unrecorded government property, record the property, determine the circumstances, take steps to prevent recurrence, and report the situation to the government property administrator

5. Generate financial accounts for government-owned property in possession or control of the contractor

6. Generate a complete, current, and auditable record of all transactions--one that is protected from tampering and accessible to authorized government personnel

7. Capture and record the status of special test equipment and special tooling when fabricated from government-owned property (either government-furnished or contractor-acquired)

8. Recover and record as government property (or as property to which the government has a right to assert title) components removed from government property, such as special test equipment

9. Locate any government property in a reasonable time period

10. Generate the following elements of information regarding government property:
    a. name, description, and national stock number
    b. quantity received, fabricated, issued, and on hand
    c. unit price and unit of measure
    d. contract number or equivalent
    e. location of property
    f. date of transaction and posting reference

11. Design a system adequate to serve as the sole official government property record

12. Provide for maintenance, care, and proper use of government property. Such a system provides for the following:
    a. disclosure, performance, and report of maintenance and scheduling of maintenance
    b. inspections, lubrication, and adjustments
    c. proper storage and preservation as needed to prevent corrosion and contamination of the specific items held

13. Ensure that government property is used only for those purposes authorized in the contract and ensure that any required approvals are obtained

Although this is not an exhaustive list of requirements specific to the several types of property, it indicates associated areas of sensitivity.

Scope of Government Property Clause

The FAR contains nineteen clauses dealing with tangible government property. (Intellectual property is treated separately.) The clauses cover furnished and contractor-acquired property and reflect the particular needs of supply, research, and demolition contracts. They deal with contracts concerning facilities, special tooling, and special test equipment. They accommodate other variations in property such as furnishing it "as is." The clauses reflect differences between types of contracts and differences between awards based on price competition and those based on negotiations for which cost and pricing data submission is required.

As a general rule, the government assumes a greater level of responsibility for its property in the possession of contractors when the agreement is based on negotiation and when the contract involves cost determination. This is clearly expressed in the risk-of-loss area: For competitively awarded firm-fixed-price contracts, the contractor is liable for losses or damage to government property, whereas his risk is limited in other contracts. This is consistent with the philosophy that competitive producers operating for their own account and providing a guarantee of their product (as in firm-fixed-price contracts) should carry full responsibility for their operation, including property owned by others but in their possession.

The principal clauses for supply and service contracts have similar general coverage but differ in detail. They contain twelve subdivisions that deal with eight topics important to the rights and obligations of the contractual parties. The topics are summarized below.

Furnished property. When the government furnishes property, it warrants that the property will meet two criteria: it must be suitable for the use implied by the contract, and it must be provided in a timely manner according to the agreed-upon schedule or at the time needed by the contractor in his ordinary course of production. Contract managers oversee this aspect of the property relationship. Because substantial losses can be associated with failure in either of these two areas, care in observing and recording events is important. The equitable adjustment provisions of the clause are accessed when needed in respect to these issues.

The clause expressly reserves the government's right to decrease or substitute any property it has agreed to furnish and to substitute government property for property that was supposed to have been furnished by the contractor. This can be done at any time by written notice to the contractor. Access to the equitable adjustment provisions of the clause is provided if the contractor requests an adjustment due to decrease, substitution, or withdrawal of government property.

Title. Title to furnished property remains with the government regardless of its attachment to or incorporation as part of other property.

The property clause requires preservation of its identity. In cost-reimbursable contracts, title to contractor-acquired property passes to the government at the time of its delivery to the contractor, except for property purchased as part of normal contractor stores. In that case, title passes when the property is identified for the government project. Title to property always passes to the government when it has been paid for by the government. In firm-fixed-price contracts, contractor-acquired property remains contractor-owned until delivery of the end item. However, if progress payments have been made that reimburse the cost of the property, the government can assert its title if necessary to protect its interest.

Use. Government property in the possession of contractors is restricted to use for the contract under which it was furnished or acquired, unless there is specific authority for other uses granted by the contracting officer. Charges are collected when applicable (as when commercial use is appropriate).

Administration. The exacting requirements for managing and accounting for government property have been covered in the preceding section. The contract clause states the government's right to require that an effective system be established.

Risk of loss. Under the standard clause for fixed-price contracts, the contractor assumes responsibility for the risk of loss, destruction, or damage to government property in the contractor's possession. This liability is substantially limited when negotiating contracts with nonprofit educational or research organizations; for cost reimbursable, time and material, and labor hour contracts; or for conditions that are not price competitive.

Equitable adjustments. Equitable adjustments made when government-furnished property proves to be unsuitable or untimely are specifically tied to the procedures of the Changes clause and are the contractor's exclusive remedy under the government property clause. When necessary, the contracting officer may institute the procedure for adjustments which is favorable to the government.

Final accounting and disposition. The contracting officer retains the authority to direct the disposition of government property. The clause requires the contractor to prepare any needed inventory schedules and to carry out the disposition instructions. Any proceeds from the disposition are credited to the government.

Abandonment and restoration. The clause gives the government full power to abandon its property in place without obligation. Furthermore, restoration of the contractor's premises is specifically excluded from government responsibilities unless, in accordance with a decrease, substitution, or unsuitability situation, an equitable adjustment for such costs may be agreed upon.

INTELLECTUAL PROPERTY

The issues and management challenges associated with intellectual property differ substantially from those associated with tangible property, yet they have much in common. Both may be created by contract or provided for use under a contract, and both may be subject to quality problems, delay, and specific restrictions on use. Both may be subject to claims and counterclaims concerning title and other issues. On balance it is likely that intellectual property issues have greater long-term impact on the parties because possession, rights of ownership and use, and disclosure directly affect future economic values.

Overview of Contractual Uses of Intellectual Property

Four categories of intellectual property are important to contract managers: technical data, patents, copyrights, and computer software. Issues arising in this field include possession or delivery of the property, ownership, specific rights to use or have it used, and management (including protection, currency and retrievability) once it is in inventory. In the normal course of commerce, purchasers of all kinds of property expect, when the property is delivered, that the right to make use of it is included. Violations of this expectation may occur whether or not the property is tangible but are most likely to arise concerning intellectual property. Violations can result in litigation when owners or others who assert rights in the property attempt to bar its unauthorized use. The right to use intellectual property may be very specific: Use for certain purposes may be authorized, while use for other purposes is restricted.

The subject of intellectual property is a specialized and complex field of law, and an in-depth study may be made by consulting appropriate legal authority. The overview given here is designed to facilitate inquiry by contract managers, most of whom can expect to encounter questions in this field regularly. The broad parameters of the subject should be studied and sources of answers to specific questions identified. When challenges arise, counsel should be brought into the discussion.

Protecting a proprietary interest in intellectual property may be accomplished in different ways. Perhaps the most effective method is through secrecy, which is the method most applicable to technical data and is the subject of trade secret law. Complete secrecy is nearly impossible and prevents use by all parties other than the owner. For practical purposes technical data is transferred in confidence for specific uses by those whom the owner authorizes. Transfers are made regularly by contractual arrangements and through submissions to potential buyers when the owner seeks to make a sale. Violations of confidence and failures to properly establish confidentiality are key problems.

Patent law may provide an effective method of protecting proprietary interests in inventions. Patents differ from trade secrets because the technical data associated with the invention is disclosed as a part of the patent application procedure. The patent is a grant by the government made for a seventeen-year period upon approval of the application. Patents are essential to protect inventions that might be easily duplicated by reverse engineering as soon as the product is sold to the public. Patents are difficult to enforce in the United States, and it is even difficult to secure them in other countries, some of which do not have effective patent laws.

Copyright law establishes protection against unauthorized reproduction and sale of published works. Contractual controversies concerning published works, such as books and works of art, do not appear to be predominant in purchasing and contracting activities.

Computer software has become a difficult area for many contract transactions. It has some characteristics of technical data, and its documentation has characteristics of other published works. It also has unique complexities concerning copying and use beyond that authorized by the owner. Special rules are evolving from attempts to protect computer software. One approach has been to grant licenses for a specified limited use, such as use on one particular machine or at one particular site. Licenses may be enforceable, but violations are difficult to discover.

Contract managers should develop sensitivity to these several types of property. They are associated with all purchase and sale activities. Special rules in government contracting have evolved and warrant study by those involved.

Government Policy Concerning Intellectual Property

The government has developed a complex set of rules and policies governing intellectual property. These rules affect its contractors, and there is significant controversy over the need for some requirements. While there are substantial reasons for the rules, several inconsistencies in the policy structure have caused continuing debate for many years.

Part 27 of the FAR provides the general set of rules covering the government's policy regarding rights in patents, data, and copyrights. The most complete coverage deals with patents. This policy establishes how rights are to be determined when the government fully or partly finances the development of new technology. The general rule has been that any *subject invention* (an invention the contractor conceived or first reduced to practice in the perfromance of work under a government contract) entitles the government to assert, as a minimum, a nonexclusive, nontransferable, irrevocable paid-up license to practice the technology, or have it practiced for or on its behalf, throughout the world. When the technology is deliverable on a contract, the government may assert title to it. Procedures for waiver of title rights and protection of private investments have been developed and constitute an important aspect of contract law. Policy concerning patents for inventions discovered or reduced to practice partly or completely with government funding achieved a degree of consensus by issuance of presidential statements of patent policy. These statements are reflected in the FAR Part 27. The statements appear to balance the interests of private inventors who have an established position in a field of technology, the interests of the government in securing application of new technology and in its role as an investor in specific inventions, and the interest of the public in obtaining access to the new technology on a reasonable basis.

The policy concerning acquisition of technical data has continued as a controversial aspect of government buying activity. Technical data deliverable under a contract has been classified as either *limited rights* or *unlimited rights* data. If unlimited rights flowed to the government, it acquired unrestricted use of the data. If limited rights flowed to the government, only the right to make specified uses was acquired, and the contractor's proprietary interest remained protected. Since 1964 the key to the policy has been whether a private expense test showed that the data was developed without funding by the government. Some progress toward resolution of conflict about these policies may have emerged from the report of the President's Blue Ribbon Commission on Defense Management (The Packard Commission). The commission studied the technical data and computer software issues and made recommendations. Some of the recommendations were incorporated into the DOD FAR Supplement as part of the department's response to congressional direction in the 1987 DOD appropriations Act (PL 99-500). The act directed the department to redefine certain terms used in its regulations. The following are three aspects of the policy:

1. A new classification of rights is created: *government purpose rights.* This is in addition to the two previously established classifications: unlimited rights and limited rights. The new classification permits recognition of mixed private and public funding of the technical data, allowing ownership (and commercial use) of the data to remain with the contractor who created it, but retaining government rights to use the data for its purposes, including competitive procurement.
2. Certain key definitions are modified to be less restrictive when determining whether private funds sponsored the data.
3. A formal procedure is established that requires contracting officers to conduct a review when challenging a contractor's assertion of a proprietary interest in data delivered to the government. The procedures require responses between the parties and provide for appeals of administrative decisions.

These changes are important to participants in government contracting because government sales constitute a major source of revenue for suppliers, including innovators whose new technology may be partly or completely financed by government funds. Government policy requires delivery of technical data for which it contracts, together with specified rights for government use. The specific rights acquired are a source of concern because the government nearly always wants the right to use deliverable property, including intellectual property, for general purposes, which may include reprocurement on a competitive basis. Suppliers who possess a proprietary interest in the property usually object to that specific use since it eliminates or reduces the economic value of having the rights. Tension over these positions has existed for many years and has been fought regularly in policy controversies and in the judicial arena. Because the government is the largest sponsor of new technology, it partially or fully underwrites new developments that have commercial value. The new technology may be patentable or have economic value as technical data if held in confidence. Conflict arises because commercialization may require significant additional investment, but investors are reluctant to sponsor such effort unless their proprietary rights can be asserted.

SUMMARY

Property is a multifaceted subject in contracting. Several aspects of property are discussed, and the management of property is covered in detail. Points covered are as follows:

- Property questions arise that relate to suitability, ownership, classification, possession, accounting, protection, and usage rights. The principal issues arising in post-award management are identified.
- Contractual issues concerning property stem from the fact that property changes in location, value, form, ownership, and condition as a function of time and use. These elements are difficult to track, and at times, ownership and responsibility for proper handling may be unclear.
- Five significant categories of tangible property (facilities, material, special tooling, special test equipment, and "agency-peculiar" equipment) are discussed, along with their implications for the contractual parties.
- Principal standards for an adequate property management system are examined.
- The multifaceted character of government property clauses is explained. For supply and service contracts, several topics important to the rights and obligations of the contractual parties are examined:

furnished property, title, use, administration, risk of loss, equitable adjustments, final accounting and disposition, and abandonment and restoration.
● An overview is presented of issues associated with rights in intellectual property, i.e., patents, technical data, copyrights, and computer software rights.

TOPICS FOR DISCUSSION

1. Explain the principal mechanisms whereby ownership of contract property becomes "mixed." Is this an undesirable condition?
2. Considering the contractual relationship, what are the important similarities of, and distinctions between, facilities and special tooling? Special tooling and special test equipment? Material and special tooling?
3. Of the several standards for an effective property accounting system, identify three that you consider the most important and explain why.
4. Discuss the relationship between the property clause and the changes clause when both are contained in the government contract.
5. Technical data and inventions may need protection in order to stimulate investments that enable wider use of new technology. Explain the principal methods of protecting these investments against unauthorized use. Explain how the methods of protection differ.
6. For what reasons has computer software become a difficult and important aspect of innovators' efforts to protect their property rights?
7. Comment on the government practice of granting waivers to its rights in new technology.

CASE 7-1

Dyna-Math Disclosure Dilemma

John Ransom is contract manager and member of an ad hoc team responsible for evaluating flight test results on a missile guidance system developed by Dyna-Math Corporation. His team has a separate contract with the Navy to perform the evaluation. The contract contains "Rights in Technical Data" (DAR 7-104.9). Paragraph (d) of that clause reads:

Removal of Unauthorized Markings. Notwithstanding any provision of this contract concerning inspection and acceptance, the Government may correct or cancel any marking not authorized by the terms of this contract on any technical data furnished hereunder, if--

(i) the Contractor fails to respond within sixty (60) days to a written inquiry by the Government concerning the propriety of the markings, or
(ii) the Contractor's response fails to substantiate within 60 days after written notice the propriety of the markings by clear and convincing evidence.

The Dyna-Math contract also contains the following simple definition of limited rights:

(i) technical data, listed or described in an agreement incorporated into the Schedule of this contract, which the parties have agreed will be furnished with limited rights; and
(ii) technical data pertaining to items, components or processes developed at private expense . . .

John submitted the first of several evaluation reports to the contracting officer twelve weeks ago. On his report he marked certain data with the restrictive legend specified in the "Rights in Technical Data Clause," to indicate that certain components and processes disclosed therein were developed at private expense. Two weeks after John's report was submitted, the contracting officer notified him that he must either remove the markings, since the government had unlimited rights in the marked data, or substantiate the claim that the government's rights were limited. Believing his position to be correct, John visited the contracting officer the following week to persuade him to see his point of view. However, he failed. During the meeting, John noted that the contracting officer offered little comment. Instead, the spokesman for the government was the cognizant engineer. It was evident that he had conceived the government's position and was asserting it.

Subsequently, by letters transmitting a follow-on report (on which John also marked certain data), John advised the contracting officer that he intended to continue restricting the data in issue. He received no response to that letter but continued to submit the required reports with the particular data consistently marked.

John later learned from one of his team members that the government was obliterating his markings from the previously submitted reports. Although aware that new definitions of "private expense" have been proposed that complicate interpretation of the company's right to mark its data submissions, John was upset by this development.

*   *   *   *   *

Review the current versions of the "Rights In Technical Data" clause in both FAR and DOD FAR Supplement. Propose an action plan for John.

CASE 7-2

ProServe, Inc.[1]

Three months before the conclusion of a two-year program entitled Military Analysis Planning, or MAP, ProServe, Inc. experienced damage and destruction of two experimental disk drive systems. The equipment had been purchased by ProServe under a cost reimbursement contract from the Naval Sea Systems Command (NAVSEA). The incident occurred when a ProServe employee, Jack Smith, hand carried several pieces of equipment to an overseas installation. Jack had obtained the free services of an airline-owned forklift when he persuaded a forklift driver to carry the boxed equipment to another airline's loading area. This informally arranged transfer was not under any agreement with any airline. One disk drive was repairable at nominal cost; a second drive, however, valued at $2500, was dropped, run over, and completely destroyed. Although not a large loss in dollars, the incident highlighted some weaknesses in ProServe's operating procedures. Jack, a senior engineer with ProServe, was not particularly concerned about it. He advised his contracts administrator, Sharon Wamboldt, to take care of the details.

Background

ProServe, Inc. is a systems house engaged primarily in defense-related research and development. In 1960 ProServe was founded in southern California by three scientists who perceived the existence of a growing and open market for performing scientific studies for the government. The original owners had extensive technical expertise, enabling them to capture a part of this market. ProServe became a significant contributor within several Department of Defense agencies.

The initial staff of ProServe was comprised of ten employees--eight engineers and physicists and two secretaries. Management responsibilities were assumed by the three principals until about 1964. At that time a

[1]The research and initial draft of this case was done by Susan Edwards while a student at George Washington University.

president was promoted from within ProServe to assume the management responsibilities, allowing the principals the freedom to pursue their technical interests. The president, an engineer by profession, was selected because of his ability to address management issues from the perspective of an engineer.

By 1980 ProServe reached $83 million in annual sales and had a personnel staff of eighteen hundred. Its largest growth spurt occurred in the 1975-1980 period. The company's status changed during that time from privately owned (three-fourths of total equity held by the original owners) to publicly held; however, 51 percent of the stock continued to be owned or controlled by the three founders. This majority share enabled the founders to control all key management issues. Their management philosophy resulted in a highly centralized ProServe organization. A small executive management committee continued to exercise almost total control. The committee delegated no important decision authority below the level of vice-president.

ProServe's business continues to be 100 percent job- or project-oriented. With each new contract award, the company assigns a technical program manager to monitor expenditures, meet staffing requirements and, in general, to direct performance of the work. Typically, this program manager is the person who is most instrumental in successfully marketing and capturing the contract. Program managers report directly to a vice-president. Project staffing is negotiated among the project manager, the vice-president, and functional department heads. In contractual matters, each project is supported by a contract administrator designated by the contract administration department head. All contractual issues are the responsibility of the administrator who acts as the ProServe contractual interface with the customer.

The MAP Contract

The MAP contract, awarded by NAVSEA and valued at $2.5 million, was captured as a direct result of the marketing efforts of one of the three original owners, Dr. Black. Even though ProServe's policy was to assign technical program management responsibility to the successful marketeer, exceptions were made in cases where the three founders were involved. In this case, program management responsibility was assigned to Jack Smith, a subordinate of Dr. Black. Nevertheless, Dr. Black controlled the performance of the contract because of his rank as a principal owner. This situation left Jack the job of monitoring performance, generally after-the-fact. Jack did not possess much authority to run all phases of the program.

The MAP program required ProServe to acquire substantial quantities of minicomputers and peripheral equipment for the government. The equipment and its software was part of a system to be used in supporting NAVSEA in the analysis and planning of strategic military actions.

Until award of the MAP contract, ProServe had infrequently purchased equipment for which title vested immediately in the government. Being labor intensive, ProServe had avoided entering the equipment business. MAP confronted the company with government property regulations for which company officials were not prepared. Internal documents, such as ProServe's "Property Accountability Manual" and "Procedure for Inventory Control of Government-Furnished Property (GFP) in Possession of ProServe," had been issued by ProServe in 1971 as a result of winning a contract involving some GFP and because a government property administrator had suggested the need for policy coverage. However, the procedures established by these documents had not been implemented company-wide, had not been updated, and had received little management attention or priority.

The following general procedures were extracted from the previously mentioned documents. They constitute the principal overall system for purchasing and controlling government property while in the possession of ProServe.

A. Purchase of property for government account
    1. Authorization to purchase shall be provided for under terms of the contract. Requisitions shall be approved by the program manager, and all purchases shall be made against a completed and approved requisition form.
    2. Purchase orders shall be prepared indicating all essential details peculiar to each individual purchase such as serial number and unit cost. Maintenance of a Purchase Order Log is required.
B. Receiving and inspection of government property
    1. Deliveries of purchased items shall be compared against the corresponding purchase order and inspected immediately to ensure that suppliers correctly fill the orders.
    2. Receiving Department shall notify the Purchasing Department of completed orders.
    3. Receiving Department shall maintain a Receiving Log to provide a summary record of all items received, utilizing the Material Inspection and Receiving Report (MIRR).
    4. Receiving Department shall notify the ProServe Property Administration Manager (PAM) of the receipt of items and hold them for his inspection, completion of MIRR, and tagging.
    5. Receiving Department shall deliver items to requestor, who shall sign MIRR as having received items.
    6. Copies of MIRR shall be distributed to all cognizant departments.
C. Inventories of government property
    1. Inventory shall be taken, at a minimum, in June of each year or

as specified in contract.
2. Inventory shall be taken upon termination or completion of contract.
3. Scrap and salvage records for government property shall be maintained.

When established, these procedures were believed to be in conformity with Appendix B of the Armed Services Procurement Regulation (ASPR), "Government Property in Possession of Contractors," and were assumed to be consistent with DAR clause 7-203.21, "Government Property (Cost-Reimbursement)," a clause that appeared in all of ProServe's cost-reimbursement type contracts. Paragraph (G) of that clause provided the following exception to the general rule that the contractor is not liable for losses of property when there is

1. willful misconduct or lack of good faith on the part of any one of the contractor's directors or officers;
2. a failure on the part of the contractor due to willful misconduct or lack of good faith on the part of any of his directors, officers, . . . to establish, maintain and administer . . . a system for control of government property . . .

Sharon Wamboldt, the contract administrator, became aware of these matters as a result of her effort to take care of the details of the disk drive loss. She encountered some difficulty because there was no designated property administration manager at ProServe, and she had to acquire on her own initiative a knowledge of the ProServe property control system and pertinent government policy. She discovered that the procedural requirements, as described above, had not been fully carried out during the two-year MAP program. Implementation fell short of the requirements in a number of areas.

Modification number 1 of the MAP contract contained a clause entitled "Acquisition, Reporting, Control, and Disposition of Equipment." The clause stated that the contractor could not purchase or lease any item of automatic data processing (ADP) equipment under the contract without specific approval of the contracting officer (CO). No approvals to purchase ADP equipment had been requested, however, and none were received from the CO. The contract also required that reports were to be made to the contracting officer's representative (COR) and the NAVSEA senior ADP policy official within thirty days after purchase of each item acquired with contract funds. None of these contractual reports had been prepared.

There were two areas in which ProServe actions had differed from the company's policy and procedure documents: tagging of property and taking annual inventories. No property other than that owned by

ProServe was tagged. Instead, government property was identified by recording the manufacturer's serial number. Inventories of government property under MAP had not been taken. Sharon had some doubt as to whether all government-owned items of ADP equipment could be accounted for. Sharon was surprised that Sam Rizzo, her boss and the head of the Contract Administration Department, while quite concerned about the disk drive incident, expressed doubt concerning how the loss should be handled and any related management changes that might be needed.

* * * * *

Outline the actions Sharon should initiate at this time.

CASE 7-3

Electronic Systems, Inc.[1]

Mr. Bob Williams, Manager of Tactical Systems Contracts for Electronic Systems, Inc. in Sunnyvale, California, reviewed the letter he had received that day, July 12, 1985, from the Army contracting officer. The Army had denied ESI's claim that defective government-furnished property (GFP) had caused cost growth in its fixed price contract by $1 million. The contracting officer had implied in his final decision that a "good contractor" would have known the property was either "good or bad" much earlier than ESI had discovered the problem. The Army alleged it could have replaced any defective GFP soon after contract award thus minimizing the cost impact, if any. Mr. Williams was now faced with a tough decision--should he appeal to the Armed Services Board of Contract Appeals, or was there another way to end this dispute?

General Company Background

Electronic Systems, Inc. was founded in 1964 as an independent employee-owned corporation. Four top-notch engineers and the Director of Corporate Finance from a well known electronics firm founded the original company. ESI's expertise was in designing and developing specialized electronic reconnaissance systems for the government. Over the years, the company expanded into systems engineering services;

---

[1]Research and the original draft of this case were performed by Curtis Cook while a student at George Washington University.

direction finding systems; major research and development studies; data processing systems, including software; communications; imagery processing; and a variety of other high-tech areas. With 1983 sales of almost $200 million, ESI management expected vigorous future growth. Its business strategy was to concentrate on systems engineering, design, and production of major electronic systems for the government.

The Heliborne Direction Finding System Contract

ESI pioneered the development of aircraft-mounted 360 degree direction finding (DF) systems. In 1973 ESI successfully tested the first helicopter-based DF system capable of 360 degree coverage. In 1981 ESI delivered a heliborne DF system to the U.S. Army that represented evolution of the first such system eight years earlier. As a result of its satisfactory past performance and experience in software-controlled DF systems, ESI was awarded a follow-on contract for a number of advanced heliborne DF systems. Under the terms of the contract, the Army would supply the helicopters to ESI, and ESI would then install the necessary hardware and software, test the complete system under auspices of the Army, and deliver the overall DF system ready for operational use.

After contract award, ESI developed the system, satisfactorily bench-tested it, and prepared to install the pre-production model on the first helicopter. At about this time, the program manager, with whom ESI engineers and Mr. Williams had excellent rapport, was reassigned to another army job. His replacement was anxious to see the first system demonstrated on schedule and made that point on several occasions to ESI management. The critical test was conducted as called for in the contract, but the DF system failed. ESI engineers were baffled--the system had worked perfectly on the bench in the plant, yet when mounted in the helicopter, it produced intermittent failures. The DF system was taken out of the helicopter and returned to the plant for diagnosis and testing. Amazingly, when mounted on the ESI test bed in the plant, the system once again worked flawlessly.

These results were communicated immediately to the Army. Mr. Williams spoke candidly with his army counterpart in telling him that ESI suspected the Army's helicopters were in some way responsible for the failure of the system when airborne. Army project engineers, however, felt the fault was in the DF system itself. The helicopter had been thoroughly checked out and found to be in excellent condition. After several months of repeated tests and the same intermittent faults in the system when airborne, ESI engineers were convinced nothing was wrong with the DF system. At about this time, Mr. Williams learned that the helicopters being furnished under the contract had seen extensive duty in Vietnam. In fact, the helicopters used in the tests had all been rebuilt

"Hueys" with the tail section from one helicopter and the fuselage from another. In what can only be described as a flash of insight, ESI engineers, with passive consent from the Army, decided to test the electrical characteristics of the entire aircraft, as opposed to testing the integrity of individual circuits which had all checked out perfectly. The results of the initial test confirmed ESI's suspicions--as the temperature and pressure on the helicopter changed at different altitudes and conditions, the electrical characteristics of the helicopter as a whole changed. This, in turn, affected the operation of the DF system which used the helicopter as its electrical reference point for detecting and processing signals.

ESI's Dilemma

Mr. Williams called his team together to assess the impact on the program caused by the defective government-furnished helicopters. The cost to the company was $1 million. The program had been delayed a full year. Armed with these facts, Mr. Williams wrote a letter to the contracting officer, asking for reimbursement of all costs in accordance with the Government Property Clause of the contract. To his surprise, the Army's position was that, while the helicopters may have been defective in some way, ESI should have realized that fact at the time of the first test. The Army's position was partially based on the reasoning that the contractor, as the expert in the system being built, is responsible for detecting any obvious deficiencies in GFP and notifying the contracting officer early enough to minimize any cost or schedule impact.

After consulting with senior management, Mr. Williams formally requested a final decision from the contracting officer in order to pursue the case under the disputes clause of the contract. After a few weeks, the government's reply came by certified mail: The Army was not accepting responsibility for any part of the $1 million claimed. Mr. Williams now considered the options. Should ESI stop work on its production contract until the dispute was settled? Should the company appeal the decision to the Armed Services Board of Contract Appeals? Could they "take it to court?" Or should ESI just swallow hard, learn by its "mistakes," and perform the contract with the new helicopters which the Army was now prepared to provide? None of the alternatives seemed satisfactory to Bob Williams.

8

Subcontracting, Teaming, and Pooling

An excellent purchasing system greatly contributes to organizational effectiveness. This fact has been recognized for many years but was reinforced as a result of the 1973 Arab oil boycott. The boycott highlighted the realization that shortages and insecure supply lines seriously jeopardize an organization's ability to produce and deliver end products. Coupled with the problems of natural resource availability, the boycott initiated extreme upward pressure on the cost of purchasing materials and services for industrial production and, in turn, caused inflation of prices for end products. Although the inflationary trend during the 1970s may have resulted from a multitude of sources in addition to the boycott, the overall impact upon many corporate purchasing systems has been positive. This is because top management has given increased recognition to the significance of the purchasing function.

Independent of this general trend, the federal government has taken a major role in the further development of purchasing technology through the influence of its large-scale contracting operations. Consequently, purchasing systems have been subjected to intensive increased surveillance and oversight by both corporate and government managers throughout the last fifteen years. The importance of purchasing systems to the government is best understood in the context of a cost-type contract. Under this form of contract, the government is obligated to reimburse a contractor's expenditures. Government managers, therefore, believe that they must thoroughly examine and reach concurrence on contractor purchasing practices and policies. This applies primarily to contracts of substantial magnitude that include cost determination provisions.

PURCHASING SYSTEMS OVERVIEW

The responsibilities of industrial purchasing departments include finding and qualifying supply sources, soliciting and selecting contractors, conducting pricing evaluations and negotiations, and administering purchase orders. These operations are influenced by customers such as the federal government who have a direct economic interest in the efficiency and effectiveness of the purchase function. Because of these economic interests, a substantial body of policy and practice has developed in the federal contracting system by which the government attempts to oversee and influence contractors' methods. These practices are used for cost reimbursement and incentive contracts for which the government's payment obligation is not fixed in advance but, instead, is based on reimbursement for all allowable, reasonable, and allocable expenses incurred in pursuit of government contract work.

Several practices have emerged from this concern and are summarized in the next section dealing with government policy and the flow-down of contract clauses. Our objective is to identify the key factors that contribute to an effective purchasing system, regardless of who the buying organization may be. Government purchasing systems are as vulnerable to poor practices and ineffective personnel operations as are industrial purchasing organizations. Government policy and review standards, however, provide an excellent insight into the practices and policies that constitute effective and efficient buying. Unfortunately, the government also mixes a number of noneconomic factors into the surveillance of its contractors with the consequence that some of its standards are irrelevant to purchasing efficiency and effectiveness. On balance, however, a thorough knowledge of the government's contractor purchasing systems review program is valuable to a purchasing manager.

SUBCONTRACTING POLICY

The government's method of influencing its suppliers' purchasing practices is based on the subcontracts clauses. These clauses are part of FAR 52.244-1 through 52.244-4. Policy covering their use is found in Part 44 "Subcontracting Policies and Procedures" and in agency supplements, which may expand upon the FAR procedures. Three elements of the clauses activate the overall policy structure. They are as follows:

1. A requirement to notify contracting officers of the contractor's intent to award a subcontract
2. A requirement for written justification of the contractor's decision to award a subcontract applicable to large-dollar subcontracts and to those that authorize reimbursable costs

3. A requirement for prior consent by the contracting officer to award certain types of key subcontracts

Prior consent is normally waived if the contractor's purchasing system has been approved through the government's Contractor Procurement System Review (CPSR) program. The CPSR program is discussed at length later in this chapter. The above constraints on contractor action are viewed as necessary for adequate control over the use of public funds. The government places such importance on subcontracting policy because subcontracting dollars often exceed 50 percent of total contract value. The system of notice and consent also helps the government implement its social and economic policies.

The three requirements listed above provide the government with the basic tools for asserting and enforcing its policies regarding the adequacy of a contractor's purchasing system. The requirements are backstopped by the CPSR program. Under the review system, government teams of purchasing experts conduct extensive audits of contractors' purchasing systems. The audits are viewed as useful to both parties because they identify poor practices and stimulate improvement in contractor systems. The most immediate benefit of the CPSR, assuming approval, is removal or reduced application of the prior consent requirements. This action greatly reduces administrative lead time and cost for both parties.

Related to but independent of the subcontract notification and consent requirements is the government's policy concerning contractor make-or-buy programs. The policy's requirements are contained in FAR Subpart 15.7 and are expressed contractually by the contract clause in FAR 52.215-21. Under these provisions, the government is afforded an opportunity to review and negotiate with the contractor on his make-or-buy decisions associated with the government procurement. The provisions are pertinent only with respect to prime contracts estimated to exceed $2 million. Under the policy, make-or-buy programs are incorporated into the prime contract as an agreed upon program, and the contract clause is inserted into the contract to give the government a degree of control over changes to the make-or-buy program.

An additional dimension of government policy toward subcontracting is the encouragement of contractor teaming arrangements. This subject is covered in FAR Subpart 9.6. A teaming arrangement is a special prime contractor/subcontractor relationship, generally one which is established prior to the award of a government prime contract. The general concept of teaming is that two contractors agree to pursue jointly (write the proposal for) and undertake a government program. The team might form a joint venture, or one of the contractors could assume the role of prime contractor, the other of subcontractor. The arrangement is a unique combination because the contributions of each party to the team are worked out through negotiation. In some cases, the government has fostered these arrangements with the objective of subsequently splitting future procurement between the team participants. This has been done in complex development programs for weapon systems to create future competition and increase the production base for the system. Aside from these specialized situations, government policy toward teaming arrangements is one of support and encouragement, although the normal requirements of the subcontracts clause are not waived to encourage team arrangements.

A somewhat similar arrangement has been encouraged by the Department of Defense and is covered under FAR Subpart 9.7. The arrangement is a type of joint venture formed by independent contractors and referred to as a defense production pool. The pooling agreement sets forth the responsibility of each party in the pool. The pool itself constitutes the entity with which the government will do business. The formation of a pool and the competition for a government program by a pool are supported and encouraged by government policy. An additional dimension of the pooling arrangement policy is its orientation toward encouraging small business firms to form pools so that together they can seek projects of a magnitude which any one of the firms may be unable to undertake alone. Regardless of the government's favorable attitude, agreement on such arrangements is complicated, and efforts to form pools have not proven successful.

The government favors using small businesses, small disadvantaged businesses,[1] and women-owned businesses as contractors and subcontractors. While this directly affects its award of prime contracts, it also has the effect of encouraging or requiring prime contractors to develop programs giving preference to these special types of businesses in awarding subcontracts. The preferences are best expressed by the government's set-aside programs for small businesses and by the minority and disadvantaged business policy under Section 8(a) of the Small Business Act. The preference for small business firms was strengthened by Public Law 95-507, which mandates the development of specific subcontracting plans by major government contractors.

CONTRACT CLAUSE FLOW-DOWN

The final area in which government policy impacts industrial purchasing and subcontracting activities is in the flow-down of government clauses and policy to subcontractors. A large number of government contract clauses are applicable to subcontractors and are mandatory; some

---

[1]The Small and Disadvantaged Business Utilization (SADBU) program is an important ingredient of this policy.

are applicable at all tiers of subcontracting and are of considerable significance in the subcontracting and purchasing business. In most cases, the flow-down of a government contract clause requires slight modification in language of the clause to avoid creating any direct relationship between subcontractors and the government. The policy of government is to hold its prime contractor responsible for all work under contract, including that being performed by subcontractors, and it steadfastly avoids any direct relationship with the subcontractors. Consequently, there is no privity of contract between the government and subcontractors. Prime contractors are obligated to reflect that policy in their subcontract terms and conditions.

Chart 8-1, included in exercise 8-1 at the end of this chapter, provides a structured summary of the flow-down policy as well as an excellent overview of the varied nature of government policy implemented through its systems of contracting. Clauses are categorized into two major and four subordinate groups of clauses. Group A clauses are mandatory in subcontracts when included in the prime contract; group B clauses are not mandated by government for subcontracts but, if included in the prime contract, they must flow down in some particular way to protect the interests of the prime contractor. Under groups A and B, the subordinate groups are as follows:

1. A1 and B1: Clauses intended to control improper or excessive use of public funds, obtain access to information, or discourage unethical behavior
2. A2 and B2: Clauses intended to preserve national security and/or facilitate mobilization
3. A3 and B3: Clauses intended to establish government control over its programs and property
4. A4 and B4: Clauses intended to advance social, economic, or environmental objectives (public policy matters)

PURCHASING SYSTEMS: AUDIT AND REVIEW

The audit and evaluation of purchasing department operations have been a concern of well managed companies for many years. Managers have encountered problems as they attempted to identify appropriate points for extracting meaningful purchasing and performance data, to develop criteria for assessing effectiveness, and to determine the appropriate management technique for assessing performance records and making critical purchasing decisions. Much of the difficulty in assessing the overall productivity and effectiveness of purchasing operations is rooted in the judgmental nature of most actions and the variety of factors entering into purchasing decisions. We will address this subject by describing the government program for review of its contractors' systems, the Contractor Procurement Systems Review. CPSR is widely practiced and is carried out primarily under the direction of field organizations of the Defense Contract Administration Services (DCAS).

CONTRACTOR PROCUREMENT SYSTEMS REVIEW (CPSR)

An overall effort to assess the performance of purchasing organizations has been developed by the government as a consequence of its general policy on review of and consent to the subcontracting activities of prime contractors. The government's specific mechanism is the CPSR program. We will examine that program in detail without attempting to reflect the specialized approaches and administrative arrangements that have been developed by individual government agencies. In general, the government's purpose in reviewing contractor purchasing systems is to verify two business matters: the contractor's efficiency in expending government funds, and compliance with government policy unrelated solely to efficiency and effectiveness. One objective of the CPSR is to eliminate or reduce the number of purchasing and subcontracting actions to which a contracting officer must give prior consent (in accordance with the subcontracts clause) without reducing compliance with the purposes of the clause. In addition, when a contractor's purchasing system has been approved, the government requirement for advance notification and written justification of purchasing decisions is reduced. Because of these reduced administrative requirements, companies try to achieve and maintain an approved purchasing system. The process by which the audit and review is conducted is governed by the FAR Subpart 44.3 and by implementing regulations and practices of government agencies conducting the reviews. At one typical DCASMA in fiscal year 1985, the office conducted and completed ninety-five contractor procurement systems reviews. These reviews resulted in several types of decisions, the preferred decision being an approval of the purchasing system. When a contracting system is inadequate, approval is withheld (or withdrawn in the case of previously approved systems), and a subsequent review is scheduled after a period of time has been allowed for correcting the deficient areas. As a planning objective, subsequent reviews are conducted approximately every two years. Staffing levels may alter that frequency, but special reviews can be initiated at any time when the government's contracting officer discerns that deficiencies have arisen which call for further examination. In the event of withdrawal or withholding of approval, follow-up reviews are made to determine whether the deficiencies have been corrected.

Students of contract management will find that studying the objectives and techniques of the CPSR program enables them to discern the elements and features associated with an effective purchasing system. The scope of the CPSR is similar to that of a broadly based management audit, such as might be conducted under the overall internal audit program of any corporate or government organization.

The review program begins with an assessment of the company's organization for purchasing, including the relationships between top management and purchasing and between the ordinary purchasing operations and management of major subcontracts. Through the organizational phase of the study, an assessment is made of management's attitude toward the role of the purchasing operation. At the level of overall management, the CPSR team searches for historical material and other information that reveals the approaches and criteria used by the company in staffing and directing its buying operations.

During the organizational phase of a CPSR, other important issues include the degree of independence with which purchasing decisions are made and the openness of communications concerning product requirements, source selections, and price decisions. These questions are critical to assessing the influence and integrity of the purchasing organization in expending government funds. Overall, the quality of relationships between contracting and purchasing managers and other functional groups assumes special importance in assessing the adequacy of the buying function in all of its phases.

Another part of the CPSR is devoted to the internal organization of the buying operation. Principal questions relate to qualification of personnel at each level within the purchasing department and the methods of establishing consistent practices throughout the organization. The study team assesses the sensitivity of personnel to ethical concerns and standards pertinent to the expenditure of significant sums of money. In these areas, verification is sought concerning knowledge and awareness of corporate management regarding the capabilities and behavior of its purchasing and subcontracting personnel throughout the scope of their operations.

Closely correlated with the overall organizational concerns of the CPSR team are issues associated with corporate policy and procedure, including the documentation and dissemination of the corporate policy position to all affected parties. The government review is focused particularly on written policy and procedure. If the review discloses an absence of written policy or procedure in sensitive areas, the likelihood of approval of the purchasing system is diminished. An assessment is made of the administrative level at which a company issues its policy and the degree of control over operating practices exercised by that authority. Of the many issues that may be important to effective operations, the items summarized below have surfaced as critical during CPSR.

1.   *Review of technical documentation.* Has the contractor established

procedures and policies for review of technical documentation (such as specifications and drawings) by or for the purchasing organization, for purposes of confirming that the documents are adequate for subcontracts and purchase orders? Issues associated with this kind of review go beyond the technical content and accuracy of the documents. They reach into the question of whether the contractor has adequately defined both the subcontractor's and the prime contractor's responsibilities in such a way that the contractual obligations of the two parties are interpretable. This area of judgment is critical to maintaining adequate control over and integrity of subcontract documents.

2. *The make-or-buy decision process.* Questions arise whether the contractor's purchasing policy provides adequate coverage of the make-or-buy decision process. Coupled with this, and of particular importance to the government, is adequacy of the contractor's procedure when the contractor is requested to prepare a make-or-buy plan for incorporation into a prime contract proposal. In addition, a question arises as to whether the make-or-buy procedure provides control over changes to contractual make-or-buy plans and the submission of such changes to the contracting officer for concurrence.

3. *Development of sources.* A third area for review, one in which the government itself may not be particularly effective, is whether the contractor has a positive approach to finding and qualifying enough sources of supply to create a competitive environment for subcontracts funded by the government. Reviews cover such issues as whether purchasing personnel are knowledgeable about the markets from which they buy and whether the organization uses adequate market search tools (such as research, solicitation, public announcements, and government listings), and whether procurement is planned in a coordinated way to ensure finding potential sources.

4. *Control over source selection decisionmaking.* Procurement systems are examined for adequacy in evaluating competitive proposals from sources submitting offers. While price may be the key factor in many selections, criteria for considering other factors, such as quality and competence, remains important to the CPSR results.

5. *System for maintaining records of suppliers' performance.* The CPSR team attempts to determine whether the contractor has developed an adequate supplier performance record system. If records are adequate, does the contractor's policy mandate appropriate consideration of performance history in evaluating possible sources for new contract awards? Again, this is an area in which the government itself has not had a good track record and, in fact, is constrained from acting on the basis of performance history by its own policy maze.

6. *System for advance planning of purchase requirements.* Verification

that the contractor has an adequate planning system is sought. Many issues may arise, such as scheduling the release of purchase requisitions, whether the purchasing organization participates in advance planning, whether the generation of requirements supports the documentation and scheduling essential to effective purchase actions, and whether requirements are consolidated to take advantage of economic purchase quantities and minimum transportation costs.

7. *Contract clause flow-down to subcontractors and suppliers.* The CPSR teams verify whether the contractor's purchasing policies correctly reflect unique aspects of government policy including the need to insert specific contract clauses in subcontracts. These clause flow-down requirements, summarized in chart 8-1, may be mandated by government or necessary as a result of government policy.

8. *Purchasing from intracompany sources.* Government policy is sensitive to intracompany transactions. Any purchase made within the corporate structure of the contractor, including its affiliates or subsidiaries, may be challenged if it is not clearly equivalent to an arms-length bargain. Review teams for CPSR are concerned with the possibility of degraded quality or excessive costs because of any special relationships between buyer and seller at any tier in a subcontracting system. While it is recognized by government policy that some transactions within the corporate family are appropriate and sometimes essential, the adequacy of contractor policy and practice covering those particular circumstances and conditions is a matter of general concern.

9. *Techniques and procedures for evaluating competitive prices.* Pricing is a principal concern in all government systems reviews. Specific aspects examined include (1) the method of evaluating competitive quotations; (2) estimating systems used internally when initiating a purchasing process; (3) the approach to evaluating cost elements when a purchase is based on decision criteria other than the lowest available price; (4) the approach to decisions on single source procurement; and (5) the approach to related aspects of subcontract negotiations, such as technical competence, schedule, and key personnel.

10. *Communications control.* Interaction between suppliers' organizations and the contractor's internal engineering, production, and other functional elements may be challenged during CPSR. Questions are raised to determine whether the contractor's purchasing organization is able to monitor and control all levels of communications between counterparts within the contractor and subcontractor organizations. While the need for communication is recognized, a strong orientation toward participation in such communications by the purchasing and

subcontracting personnel is sought. In the absence of adequate control in this area, procurement systems reviewers will question with increased intensity the bases for competition and pricing decisions.

11. *Distribution of risk.* Risk inherent in purchasing and subcontracting programs varies with the nature of the undertaking and the stability of both the purpose and the funding of the undertaking. Concerns of the CPSR program in this area relate to the contractor's selection of contract types and payment practices. The government intends that prime contractors should impose reasonable risks upon suppliers, not inordinate ones. Nor should risks associated with prime contractor work be transferred to subcontractors. Members of CPSR teams recognize that the norm for contract or purchase actions and most subcontracting activity is the firm-fixed-price contract. However, purchasing and subcontracting operations under government programs should be flexible enough to adjust the type of contract to reflect the nature of a purchase action.

SUMMARY

Purchasing systems of many private companies have been strongly influenced by government practices expressed through its subcontract notice, review and consent policies. The focus of this chapter is subcontracting under government prime contracts. Highlights are as follows:

- The importance of cost reimbursement provisions under government cost and incentive types of contracts as mechanisms for imposing government practices on private purchasing and subcontracting activities
- A review of the principal provisions of the Subcontracts clause
- A summary of the influences exerted under make-or-buy review practices based on make-or-buy program requirements
- A summary of teaming arrangements and contractor pooling arrangements as encouraged by government contract policy
- Reference to subcontract plans and the general policies of government in favoring subcontracting with small, disadvantaged, and women-owned businesses
- Discussion of contract policy barring privity of contract between the government and subcontractors
- A summary and comprehensive table listing and categorizing government contract clauses that must or should be included in subcontracts under government primes
- An analysis of the Contractor Procurement Systems Review (CPSR) as conducted by contract administration offices, including a listing of the

principal issues of concern to the reviewing offices

TOPIC FOR DISCUSSION

1. Discuss the types of contracts and subcontracts for which subcontract consent is most likely to be required and explain the reasons for this practice.
2. Distinguish between notice of intent to award a subcontract and justification for such an action.
3. Analyze the idea of forming contractor teams for competing to win a government contract. What problems or issues are likely to arise?
4. Under what conditions is it mandatory to include a prime contract clause (usually with certain modifications) in a subcontract? Conversely, under what conditions is this essential although not mandatory?
5. Explain the broad purposes and the specific objectives of conducting a CPSR.
6. What pricing techniques and procedures might a CPSR team expect to observe?
7. What aspects of a contractor's purchasing practices have greatest sensitivity with respect to the distribution of risk associated with prime contract performance?

CASE 8-1

The Management Circus

As manager of the electrical subcontract under a government prime contract for building military barracks, you are expected to schedule and manage your work effectively. In fact, you are bound contractually to use the critical path method for your planning and scheduling effort. Your contract also provides for an extension of your performance schedules in the event that your work is delayed by acts of the prime contractor. Unfortunately, in performing your obligations you repeatedly encounter congestion and disruption as a result of interference by other subcontractors and by work of the prime contractor. Your work is substantially delayed by these occurrences, and you are also faced with demands by the prime contractor's manager to accelerate the pace of your work in order to meet delivery schedules. You perform accordingly, although overtime and other unplanned costs associated with the effort are approaching $1 million.

In reviewing your contract, you find another provision: you may recover an additional sum (contract price increase) or damages for delays caused by the prime contractor, provided the government is also liable and pays for the delays, but not otherwise.

You complete your work but are now faced with a difficult situation. The government is not liable to the prime contractor for the delays encountered, and the prime contractor refuses to pay your claim (which now exceeds $1 million). You are aware that the prime contractor's obligations under his contract with the government respecting management of the job are identical with those imposed on you under the subcontract.

*　*　*　*　*

Although this situation is now history, what could you have done differently at the time you encountered the conflicts and confusion? What can you do now?

CASE 8-2

DPG, Inc.[1]

The Falkland Island war had revealed the deficiency. Responsibility for ensuring timely delivery to the British Royal Air Force (RAF) of a high quality electronic countermeasure (ECM) system that could defeat the new threat now rested squarely on the shoulders of Guy Mankevich. As manager of subcontracts for DPG, Inc., Department of Radiation, located in San Jose, California, Mr. Mankevich had competitively awarded a subcontract for the classified "black box" to Electrotarget, Inc. shortly after DPG had received the prime contract from the RAF. Now, in the spring of 1984, Electrotarget was far behind schedule, their prototype system had failed acceptance tests, and Electrotarget management refused to allow a DPG on-site quality assurance representative in their plant. Mr. Mankevich knew that the RAF was intensely interested in closing the "window of vulnerability" discovered in the Falklands war as soon as possible. Surely there was something that could be done to satisfy the RAF's need . . . but what?

Background of DPG's Radiation Department

DPG, Inc. was a major developer and producer of a wide range of electronic and communications systems. The Radiation Department was

---

[1]Research and the original draft of this case were performed by Curtis Cook while a student at George Washington University.

involved primarily in electronic defense systems, such as electronic reconnaissance systems and active countermeasures systems. Total annual sales were in the hundreds of millions of dollars--over 90 percent of which was government business.

International sales comprised approximately 5 percent of total Radiation Department sales. DPG's business strategy was to pursue quality opportunities as opposed to volume business in the international arena. As a result, the company had established a worldwide reputation as a high quality, dependable developer and producer of critical electronic warfare and communication systems.

The Materiel Organization

DPG Radiation Department was organized into five subgroups: Integrated Logistics Support, Technical Data and Controls, Manufacturing, Operations Programs and Controls, and Materiel. The function of Materiel was to ensure that all materials and services needed by DPG Radiation Department were obtained on time, at the right price, from the appropriate source and, perhaps most importantly, were of the required quality. As manager of subcontracts with a staff of eighteen subcontract managers and price/cost analysts, Mr. Mankevich was responsible for the largest, most difficult and critical subcontracts placed by the division.

The Electrotarget Systems Contract

During the Falkland Islands conflict, Great Britain, as well as other nations, learned a great deal about air, land, and naval combat. As a result of post-conflict analyses, the RAF identified a critical need for enhancing its ECM capability. Due to its reputation and unique knowledge in the ECM area, DPG was selected by the RAF to develop and produce a classified ECM system (a so-called "black box") that could overcome the threat identified in the war. After conducting a make-or-buy analysis, DPG decided to subcontract out one of the system components. Competitive proposals were solicited, received, and evaluated, and in July, 1983, a subcontract was awarded to Electrotarget, Inc. for twenty-one subassemblies at a total fixed-price of approximately $1,700,000. Initial delivery was scheduled for July, 1984. The terms and conditions of the subcontract follow this case.

The Quality Problem

The policy of DPG's Radiation Department was to physically assign a quality assurance representative (QAR) to subcontractor plants with a history of problems in quality. Electrotarget Systems did have such a history, yet the Electrotarget proposal was not only the lowest priced of those submitting technically acceptable proposals but also the highest ranked technical proposal. In addition, Electrotarget management strongly resisted what it considered outside interference in its internal affairs. Senior Electrotarget management assured Mr. Mankevich that steps had been taken to improve its performance on this and future contracts.

Initially, everything appeared to be going well. Work was progressing on schedule, and DPG made customary progress payments in accordance with its normal practice. With the date for initial testing of the first unit approaching, Mr. Mankevich was surprised to learn from his Electrotarget Systems subcontract manager that Electrotarget was experiencing difficulty in meeting the performance criteria set forth in the specifications. Over the next few days, the severity of the problem became clear. The first unit failed essentially every test to which it was subjected. Electrotarget management repeatedly promised to correct the problems but, in practice, did little to cure the defects. Mr. Mankevich personally met with the Electrotarget Systems president on numerous occasions during the following weeks, with no results. It now appeared that delivery of the needed subassemblies would be delayed at least a full year, assuming that the quality and performance problems could be corrected at all. To make matters worse, nearly two-thirds of the funds on the contract already had been paid to Electrotarget as progress payments, yet not one operational unit had passed acceptance tests.

When told of the dismal prognosis, the RAF, which initially had been very understanding, expressed its concern in the strongest terms. DPG could not bear a termination for default. The company's reputation so painstakingly established over the years as a quality, timely supplier, would be severely impacted by a termination for default. Future international business, which DPG hoped to increase, would suffer.

Mr. Mankevich was out of patience. He knew he needed to take definitive action now to resolve the Electrotarget, Inc. problem one way or another. He pondered the alternatives.

* * * * *

1. Summarize what actions could be taken by Mr. Mankevich, considering the specific "General Terms and Conditions" listed below as well as the normal clauses expected in government-funded subcontracts (e.g., progress payments, quality assurance, etc.).
2. Outline the course of actions you would take if you were in Mr. Mankevich's position.

DPG SYSTEMS INCORPORATED, RADIATION DEPARTMENT
TERMS AND CONDITIONS OF PURCHASE, FIXED-PRICE CONTRACTS

The term FAR, when used in the following clauses, means the cited portion of the Federal Acquisition Regulation including, when appropriate, the DOD FAR Supplement (DFARS), as in effect on the date of the Order. Where appropriate to accomplish the purpose of the FAR or to protect the Buyer's interest, the word *Buyer* shall be substituted for the word *Government* or *Contracting Officer* and the word *Seller* shall be considered the *Contractor* hereunder in the reading of these regulations, thereby creating a legal relationship between the Buyer and the Seller identical to, but not dependent upon, the legal relationship intended to be created by said regulations between the Government and a contractor. The word Buyer as it appears in the Order means DPG Incorporated acting through the duly authorized Procurement representative of its Radiation Department. No other persons may make commitments or changes under the Order on behalf of the Buyer.

1.   SHIPPING AND DELIVERY.

(a) Shipment by Seller shall be strictly in accordance with the schedules set forth or referenced in the Order unless earlier or later deliveries are authorized in writing by the Buyer. Seller shall not, without Buyer's prior written approval, manufacture or procure materials in advance of Seller's normal flow time or deliver in advance of schedule. In the event of termination or change, no claim will be allowed for any such manufacture or procurement in advance of Seller's normal flow time unless there has been written approval from the Buyer. Further, unless advance shipment has been authorized in writing by Buyer, Buyer may return, shipping charges collect, all items received in advance of schedule.

(b) Shipping instructions will be furnished by the Buyer. If such instructions are not received in time for shipment, the Seller will ship in accordance with customs and practices prevailing in the industry, following, wherever applicable, the precedents of previous shipments to the Buyer.

(c) FAR 52.246-16 shall govern title and risk of loss. Do not insure for transportation where terms are F.O.B. origin or risk of loss has transferred to Buyer.

(d) Time is of the essence in the Order. Whenever Seller knows or has reason to believe that timely performance of the Order may be delayed for any reason, including an actual or potential labor dispute, Seller shall immediately give notice thereof, including all relevant information with respect thereto, to the Buyer. The Seller agrees to add this clause to each subcontract or purchase order issued hereunder.

2.   INSPECTION AND ACCEPTANCE. Seller shall provide an inspection system acceptable to Buyer and the Government (if the Order is placed pursuant to a higher tier Government contract) which is adequate to ensure that work being performed and supplies delivered conform to the requirements of the Order and will comply with the provisions of FAR 52.246-2. All items to be delivered under this order shall be subject to final inspection and acceptance by Buyer at destination notwithstanding any inspection at source or payments. Unless otherwise specified in the Order, Buyer shall accept or give notice of rejection within sixty (60) days after receipt. Buyer's failure to give notice of rejection within sixty (60) days after receipt shall constitute acceptance.

3.   FACILITIES, TOOLS, ETC. Unless otherwise specified in the Order, all necessary services, facilities, materials, equipment, drawings, or other items, including those purchased as line items of the Order, which may be furnished or otherwise made available by Buyer for use in connection with the Order, shall remain the property of the Buyer or the Government, as the case may be, and shall be returned in as good condition as when received, except for reasonable wear and tear or for the utilization of the property in accordance with the provisions of the Order. Seller agrees to pay for all such property spoiled or not otherwise satisfactorily accounted for, to keep the property adequately insured, and to abide by the provisions of Part 45 of the FAR with respect to Buyer's and the Government's property, special tools and test equipment.

4.   TERMINATION.
      (a) The Order shall be subject to cancellation for default in accordance with the provisions set forth in FAR 52.249-8. Furthermore, the Buyer may cancel the Order in accordance with said FAR 52.249-8 if Seller ceases to conduct its operation in the normal course of business (including inability to meet its obligations as they mature), or if any proceeding under bankruptcy or insolvency laws is brought by or against the Seller, or if a receiver or seller is appointed or applied for, or if an assignment for the benefit of creditors is made by Seller.
      (b) Buyer may, for its convenience, terminate work under the Order, in whole or in part, at any time, by written or telegraphic notice stating the extent and effective date of such termination, and the rights and obligations of the parties shall in such event be governed by the provisions set forth in FAR 52.249-2.

5.   WARRANTIES, GUARANTEES, INDEMNIFICATIONS, ETC.
      (a) Material and Work: Seller warrants to Buyer and its customers that all material and work will be in conformity with the requirements of the Order and free from defects in design (except to extent of Buyer design), material and workmanship, and suitable for the use made known

to Seller. Buyer shall not be deemed to waive any defects or noncon-formity by reason of inspection, approval of samples, or receipt of, or payment for items. Without prejudice to other remedies available to Buyer, any items found through inspection and testing or through use and service to be other than as warranted above, may be returned (F.O.B. Carrier), at Seller's expense at any time within one year after delivery, or such longer period of time as the Seller may warrant similar items for his most favored customer, for credit or for replacement or correction, or they may be retained with an equitable reduction in price which shall include cost of additional work performed by Buyer, if any such work is performed to make such item(s) acceptable. All repaired or replacement items shall be pre-shipped F.O.B. destination provided the original items were defective. In the event deliveries are made earlier than the order schedule, the one year period of the warranty shall commence on the date of delivery scheduled in the order.

(b) Price, etc.: Seller warrants that the prices, terms of payment, warranties and services extended under the Order are no less favorable to buyer than those extended to any other customer as in effect on the date of the order for substantially similar items and quantities.

6. CHANGES. Buyer may at any time by written notice make changes in the drawings, designs, specifications, quantity, method of shipping or packing, time or place of inspection, delivery or acceptance of the items or services to be furnished under the order. If any such change affects the cost or delivery schedules of the order, an equitable adjustment shall be made in price and/or delivery schedule. Any claim by Seller for an equitable adjustment must be in writing and asserted within twenty (20) days from the date of buyer's written notification or such further time as Buyer may allow. The Seller shall not be entitled to any equitable adjustment of price or delivery schedule under this article except for effort which is specifically authorized in writing by Buyer. Seller shall proceed immediately to perform the order as changed. Nothing in the clause shall excuse Seller from so proceeding, including failure of the parties to agree upon any adjustment to be made under this clause.

CASE 8-3

TAK Technology[1]

On April 19, 1985, Rich Alan, Director of Finance and Administration

---

[1]Research and the original draft of this case were performed by Curtis Cook while a student at George Washington University.

for TAK Technology of San Jose, California, received a call from Jim Ross, a vice president of Microtechnologies, Inc. (MTI). Ross told him MTI's teaming partner had just pulled out of a $7 million Air Force project, with proposals due May 3, 1985, just two weeks away. According to Ross, this created an opportunity for Jim to offer TAK Technology a chance to team with MTI. It was agreed that TAK Technology would receive $25,000 "up front" for a technical proposal for design of array processors and $2 million for TAK Technology's work under the follow-on contract. Mr. Alan knew TAK Technology had specialized technical knowledge MTI didn't possess and could see the advantage to MTI of this arrangement, but he also knew that TAK Technology needed new business. Mr. Alan delivered to Ross a teaming agreement including a nondisclosure statement. The deal would require TAK Technology engineers to start immediately and to work around the clock with MTI engineers to meet the Air Force deadline. The time-consuming details of the teaming agreement would be worked out after-the-fact through MTI's corporate lawyers, but work had to start immediately. Mr. Alan pondered his choices over a cup of coffee late in the evening of April 19. He could not delay his decision. Jim Ross was a known quantity and TAK Technology badly needed the business. Should he commit TAK Technology resources to this deal?

General Company Background

TAK Technology was founded in January, 1984, by four entrepreneurs, one of whom was Rich Alan. TAK Technology provided high quality, advanced electronic systems and services with a staff of nineteen engineers and other professionals. The company's business could be categorized into six areas of specialization: signal and imagery exploitation; artificial intelligence; command, control and communications; countermeasures; developmental and operational test and evaluation; and operational and intelligence analysis. Its business strategy was to initially seek subcontract opportunities and teaming agreements with government prime contractors while simultaneously preparing proposals on its own for long lead time government projects. First year sales totaled only $1 million, but company officials were optimistic about future growth. Long term survival of the company was tied directly to securing a number of contracts with other companies and the U.S. government, then performing in an outstanding manner.

Competition and Technology Transfer

Silicon Valley in California was marked by fierce competition in high-technology industries in the 1984-1985 time period. New companies like TAK Technology were formed by especially bright, risk-taking entrepreneurs. Typically, no more than a handful of engineers and a business manager would break away from a larger company and market their unique blend of skills culminating in a "better idea." Such small companies had to be especially careful to protect their fresh ideas from other companies seeking to gain a larger market share by reducing competition. Nondisclosure statements came into widespread use because they offered some protection to a company originating a particular product, service, or process. They were seen to be particularly important as a way of allowing disclosure but prohibiting use or release of company proprietary information. For example, engineering drawings or technical specifications developed by TAK Technology would be protected under the terms of a nondisclosure statement.

The TAK Technology-MTI Dilemma

TAK Technology needed as many new projects as possible to survive. At the same time, it depended on its unique products and services for its very existence. To join with MTI would give TAK Technology the opportunity to design a new array processor for the Air Force's latest phased-array radar system that could detect ballistic missile launches "over the horizon." To do so, Mr. Alan would need to pull five key personnel off long lead time proposal efforts and dedicate them for two weeks. The opportunity to team with MTI, a company with sales of $200 million annually, was attractive. If successful in winning the Air Force contract, the work (and the potential $2 million in revenue) was fully consistent with TAK Technology's business strategy and would provide a genuine boost to TAK Technology's business base in the immediate future.

Rich Alan was bothered by the lack of an up-front written teaming agreement with MTI, despite Jim's assurances. The standard teaming agreement delivered to MTI had been used and accepted by others many times before. Even considering that Jim Ross would have to obtain approval from MTI's corporate headquarters in Los Angeles, it should only be a matter of a few days before the agreement could be reviewed and executed. Besides, MTI was willing to pay TAK Technology $25,000 for the efforts of the technical proposal team "up front." Even if the Air Force awarded the contract to another company, TAK Technology would not be out of pocket any direct costs.

CASE 8-4

Harrington Industries

Under a cost-plus-fixed-fee contract with an estimated cost of $42,054 and fixed fee of $1,682, Harrington was given a modification directing that it move the government's Seismic Data Laboratory (SDL) from one point to another in Alexandria, Virginia, provide environmental standards for operation of computers and peripheral equipment for SDL at its new location, and provide similar standards for the Seismic Array Analysis Center (SAAC) at another Alexandria location. As part of its responsibilities under the contract and in connection with the modification, Harrington entered into three subcontracts with Environmental Contractors under which the subcontractor was to make air conditioning changes in preparation for the SDL and install air conditioning for SAAC. The subcontracts totalled $16,025. One of the subcontracts began on October 12, and two commenced on November 13.

Substantial controversy arose between the prime contractor and the subcontractor over poor, unprofessional, and delinquent work by the subcontractor. As a result, after completing two of the subcontracts, the prime contractor contracted with a third party to correct installation errors, repair damages resulting from incorrectly sealed roof openings, and complete certain omitted items (although the subcontractor indicated that he would correct these deficiencies). Also, the prime contractor issued a notice on December 18 that the subcontractor would not be allowed to proceed with the installation of air conditioning equipment, as specified for SAAC under one of the subcontracts. The prime contractor issued debit memoranda against two of the subcontracts for $2,150, effectively reducing the agreed upon price for the subcontracts to cover its correction expenses. After stopping the subcontractor's right to proceed with the third subcontract, the prime contractor separately contracted for the work to be done.

Throughout this period, time pressure was substantial as Harrington's delivery obligation was December 1 for SDL and December 15 for SAAC, and potentially severe winter weather was approaching. The subcontractor and the prime contractor had genuine differences over the quality of work and other matters. The subcontractor sought payment in full for the completed subcontracts and payment for one-half the value of the contract on which his work was terminated. This sum included $540 for the breach and $310 for preparatory work. The subcontractor also threatened litigation if the prime contractor did not pay.

After protracted discussion and negotiation, the matter was settled by compromise on January 28. The subcontractor's total claim of $4110.50 was settled for $1400. However, the contracting officer refused to pay the settlement costs to the prime contractor based on the following:

1. The settlement of the breach (the terminated subcontract) was not in accordance with sound business practice, and the prime should have terminated sooner and prevented the preparatory costs.
2. The rework costs (for the completed subcontracts) incurred by the prime contractor were reimbursed by the government, yet the subcontractor had agreed to correct the deficiencies, and, therefore, the amount associated with these claims ($550 of the total) was inappropriate. In effect, he held that the whole settlement was unreasonable as a cost to the government and therefore unallowable.

* * * * *

Comment on the excellence of the subcontract management and on the contracting officer's position.

Exercise 8-1

Contract Clause Flow-Down Analysis

Chart 8-1 is discussed in chapter 8. It is a comprehensive summary of government contract clauses that must or should be made a part of subcontracts under government prime contracts. It is organized into groups and subgroups of clauses with similar overall objectives, although each clause is unique with respect to its specific requirements and objectives. Review this chart and select one clause from each subgroup for further review and analysis. Obtain a copy of the FAR. Review the text of each clause you have selected. Locate the FAR section that guides contracting personnel concerning application and use of each selected clause. Prepare to answer the following questions respecting two of the clauses you reviewed:

1. What is the purpose of the clause?
2. How and when was this clause introduced into the contracting system?
3. What criteria govern the applicability of the clause?
4. Assess your reactions to the clause. Why is it an essential requirement at both prime and subcontract levels? Might it be eliminated or simplified?
5. What costs or other burdens does implementation of this clause impose on: a) the government, b) the prime contractor, c) the subcontractor?

Summarize your response for the two clauses in a brief report.

CHART 8-1

Flow-Down Clauses Prescribed by FAR[1]
(grouped as to purpose and whether mandatory)

General rule regarding flow-down clauses: All clauses inserted in subcontracts must be worded (reworded) to reflect the relationship between prime and subcontractor, avoiding any language implying privity of contract between the government and the subcontractor.

GROUP A: Clauses in this group, when part of a prime contract, are included in subcontracts by operation of law, regulation, and/or prime contract clause.

SUBGROUP A1: Clauses intended to control improper or excessive use of public funds, obtain access to information, or discourage unethical behavior.

Clause Title	Citation	Notations
Audit--Formal Advertising	52.214-26	If this clause is in the prime, it must be included in all subcontracts over $10,000. Self deleting if the sub is not cost reimbursable or he/she is not otherwise subject to truth in negotiation.
Subcontractor Cost or Pricing Data--Modifica- tions--Formal Advertising	52.214-28	If the prime contains this clause, it is applicable to subcontracts over $500,000 unless subcontract price was based on: adequate competition, established catalog or market prices, or prices set by law or regulation.
Examination of Records by Comp- troller General	52.215-1	If the prime contains this clause, it must be included in first-tier subcontracts.
Audit--Negotia- tion	52.215-2	If this clause is in the prime, it must be included in subcontracts over $10,000. The clause is self deleting if the sub is not cost reimbursable or not otherwise subject to truth in negotiation.
Subcontractor Cost and Pricing Data	52.215-24	If prime contains this clause, its substance must be included in all subcontracts <u>expected</u> to exceed $500,000.
Subcontractor Cost and Pricing Data--Modifi- cations	52.215-25	If prime contains this clause, it must be included in each subcontract that exceeds $500,000 at time of its award.
Price Redeterm- ination--Prospec- tive	52.216-5	If prime contains this clause, flow-down is required for the substance of portions of this clause relating to quarterly submissions of cost data in each price redetermination or incentive price revision subcontract.
Price Redeterm- ination--Retroac- tive (APR 1984)	52.216-6	Same as 52.216-5 above.

[1]This table includes 87 clauses selected from 496 clauses listed in the April 1984 edition of the FAR. Eighty-six of the clauses were identified by the Procurement Committee of the NSIA in "A Study of the Applicability of FAR Clauses to Subcontracts Under Prime Defense Contracts," (NSIA, January 1985). One clause was added by the author. Other regulations, such as the DOD FAR Supplement, contain additional flow-down clauses.

CHART 8-1, Continued

Clause Title	Citation	Notations
Incentive Price Revision-- Firm Target	52.216-16	Same as 52.216-5.
Refund of Royalties	52.227-9	Same as 52.216-5.
North Carolina State and Local Sales and Use Tax	52.229-2	A provision similar to this clause must be included in any subcontract at any tier that involves an amount in excess of $50,000.
Cost Accounting Standards	52.230-3	The substance of this clause must be included in any subcontract in which the amount of royalties reported during negotiation of the subcontract exceeds $250.
Administration of Cost Account- ing Standards	52.230-4	If prime contains this clause, flow-down is necessary because certified statements from subs similar to the prime's certifications must be provided.
Progress Payments	52.232-16	If this clause is in the prime contract, it must be included in all negotiated subcontracts (but without the disputes provision) in excess of $100,000, unless sub's price is based on established catalog or market prices or prices set by law or regulation. Subcontractor must flow down the clause to lower tier subs over $100,000.
Subcontracts Under Cost-Reimbursement and Letter Contracts	52.244-2	Same as 52.230-3.
Incentive Price Revision--Succes- sive Targets	52.216-17	If included in prime, clause is required in subcon- tracts. Rules for small and large business differ.
Reporting of Royalties (Foreign)	52.227-8	Flow-down in substance is required if included in the prime. Requires prime to flow down to cost-reimburse- ment subcontractors certain portions of FAR clauses 52.216-5, 52.216-6, 52.216-16, or 52.216-17. The prime must agree to provide progress payments to fixed-price small business subs pursuant to 32.502-1 and 32.504(f).

SUBGROUP A2: Clauses to preserve national security and facilitate mobilization.

Clause Title	Citation	Notations
Security Require- ments	52.204-2	Required for subcontracts involving access to infor- mation classified Confidential, Secret, or Top Secret.
Required Sources for Jewel Bearings	52.208-1	Flow-down required unless the part being purchased does **not** contain jewel bearings or related items.

CHART 8-1, Continued

SUBGROUP A3: Clauses intended to establish government control over its programs and property.

Clause Title	Citation	Notations
Filing of Patent Applications-- Classified Subject Matter	52.227-10	Required in subcontracts at any tier that cover or are likely to cover classified subject matter. In the case of this clause, the terms Contracting Officer, Government and United States are not replaced.
Notice to the Government of Labor Disputes	52.222-1	If this clause is in the prime contract, it must flow down to subs.
Authorization and Consent	52.227-1	Required in supply or service subcontracts at any tier if expected to exceed $25,000.
Notice and Assistance Regarding Patent and Copyright Infringement	52.227-2	Required in supply or service subcontracts at any tier if expected to exceed $25,000.
Patent Rights-- Acquisition by the Government	52.227-13	Required in form modified to identify the parties in subcontracts at any tier for experimental, developmental or research work. Bars prime from obtaining rights in subcontractor's inventions for awarding subcontract.
Special Tooling	52.245-17	If this clause is in the prime contract and if the subcontractor's price includes the full cost of special tooling, the subcontract must contain this clause or one which gives the government comparable rights to those contained in its standard clause, unless the prime and the government agree that such rights are not of substantial interest to the government.
Special Test Equipment	52.245-18	If this clause is in the prime contract and the subcontract contains provisions permitting the sub to acquire or fabricate special tooling for government account, this clause flows down. It restricts sub from buying or making special tooling without first obtaining the prime's consent. The prime, in turn, must first obtain the government's consent.
Limitation of Liability	52.246-23	When part of the prime this clause flows down.
Limitation of Liability--High Value Items	52.246-24	If the prime is over $25,000, this clause must flow down _after_ obtaining the contracting officer's advance written approval.
Limitation of Liability--Services	52.246-25	This clause must be flowed down to each subcontrct over $25,000.
Value Engineering	52.248-1	This clause must flow down to subcontracts of $100,000 or more, but is optional for smaller subcontracts.

CHART 8-1, Continued

SUBGROUP A4: Clauses intended to advance social, economic, or environmental objectives (public policy matters).

Clause Title	Citation	Notations
Utilization of Small Business Concerns & Small Disadvantaged Business Concerns	52.219-8	Required if 52.219-9 is in the prime. Should flow down under all primes over $10,000.
Small Business and Small Disadvantaged Business Subcontracting Plan	52.219-9	Required if prime is over $500,000 for subcontracts over $500,000.
Utilization of Labor Surplus Area Cos.	52.220-3	Required for subcontracts in excess of $500,000.
Labor Surplus Area Subcontract Progm.	52.220-4	Required for subcontracts in excess of $500,000.
Contract Work Hours and Safety Standards Act--Overtime Compensation--General	52.222-4	If prime contract requires or involves the employment of laborers, mechanics, helpers, apprentices, trainees, watchmen, guards, firefighters or fireguards, it must contain this clause and must flow down to all subcontractors.
Equal Opportunity	52.222-26	Required in all subcontracts and purchase orders.
Affirmative Action for Special Disabled and Vietnam Era Vets	52.222-35	Required in all subcontracts and purchase orders of $10,000 or more.
Affirmative Action for Handicapped Workers	52.222-36	Required in all subcontracts and purchase orders in excess of $2500.
Service Contract Act of 1965	52.222-41	If prime contains this clause, it must flow down to all subcontracts.
Clean Air and Water Certification	52.223-1	If prime contract is greater than $100,000, this clause must flow down, and certifications must be obtained from subs.
Clean Air and Water	52.223-2	If prime contract is greater than $100,000, this clause must flow down, and certifications must be obtained from subs.
Hazardous Material Identification and Material Safety Data	52.223-3	If prime contains this clause, it must be flowed down to all tiers of subcontracts and purchase orders.
Privacy Act	52.224-2	If included in prime clause, it is required in all subcontracts.

CHART 8-1, Continued

Clause Title	Citation	Notations
Duty-Free Entry	52.225-10	Flow down to subs is required only if, under the subcontract, there will be imported into the customs territory of the U.S.: (1) supplies identified in the schedule which are to be accorded duty free entry or (2) other foreign supplies in excess of $10,000.
Certain Communist Areas	52.225-11	If included in prime, flow-down to subcontract is required for protection against use of materials acquired from the prohibited Communist areas.
Patent Rights-- Retention by the Contractor (Short Form)	52.227-11	Required, in form modified to identify the parties, in subcontracts at any tier for experimental, developmental or research work to be performed by a small business firm or nonprofit organization. Bars prime from obtaining rights in subcontractor's inventions as a consideration for awarding the subcontract.
Patent Rights-- Retention by the Contractor (Long Form)	52.227-12	Required, in form modified to identify the parties, in subcontracts at any tier for experimental, developmental or research work if the subcontract is being awarded to other than a small business firm or nonprofit organization. The prime is barred from obtaining rights in subcontractor's inventions as a consideration for awarding the subcontract.
Workers' Compensation Insurance (Defense Base Act)	52.228-3	If prime contains this clause, it must flow down to all subs at all tiers.
Insurance--Work on a Government Installation	52.228-5	If in prime, the clause must be flowed down. It requires subcontractors to provide and maintain insurance if their presence on a government installation is required.

GROUP B: Clauses in this group are not explicitly required (by the text of the clause) in subcontracts. However, for prime contractors to protect their interests and fulfill their obligations to government, they must be included in subcontracts, if applicable.

SUBGROUP B1: Clauses intended to control improper or excessive use of public funds and/or obtain access to information and/or discourage unethical behavior.

Clause Title	Citation	Notations
Gratuities	52.203-3	Needed to secure the right to terminate the subcontract and recover damages should the sub be guilty of offering or providing gratuities.
Covenant Against Contingent Fees	52.203-5	Needed to protect against improper solicitation of a contract by a subcontractor on behalf of prime. The penalty is annulment and complete forfeiture.
Price Reduction for Defective Cost or Pricing Data-- Mods.--Formal Adv.	52.214-27	States the government's right to audit records of subcontractor modifications to determine if the subcontract price was defective. Government can proceed against prime to recover any excess amount.

CHART 8-1, Continued

Clause Title	Citation	Notations
Price Reduction for Defective Cost or Pricing Data	52.215-22	Needed because government has the right to audit subcontractor records to determine if the subcontract price was defective. The government will proceed against the prime to recover if defective data is discovered.
Price Reduction for Defective Cost or Pricing Data-- Modifications	52.215-23	Same as 52.215-22.
Allowable Cost and Payment	52.216-7	If both prime and subcontract are cost reimbursement, flow-down of the substance is needed to put subs under the same reimbursement request constraints as for progress payments.

SUBGROUP B2: Clauses intended to preserve national security and facilitate mobilization.

Clause Title	Citation	Notations
Priorities, Allocations, and Allotments	52.212-8	Obligates subcontractor to place orders on the same priority system as the prime.

SUBGROUP B3: Clauses intended to establish government control over its programs and property.

Clause Title	Citation	Notations
New Material	52.210-5	Bars incorporation of used materials. Needed to protect against a subcontractor's possible violation.
Stop-Work Order	52.212-13	Flow-down is needed to prevent continuation of work by subcontractor and his subs during the stop-work period.
Stop-Work Order-- Facilities	52.212-14	Same as 52.212-13.
Patent Indemnity	52.227-3	A similar clause is needed to cover the indemnification. Negotiation is needed to reflect substitutions and any deliveries of commercial items.
Changes--Fixed Price	52.243-1	Flow-down is need to protect against refusal of a subcontractor to comply in response to a change order issued by the government to the prime.

CHART 8-1, Continued

Clause Title	Citation	Notations
Changes--Cost Reimbursement	52.243-2	Same as 52.243-1.
Changes--Time-and-Materials or Labor Hours	52.243-3	Same as 52.243-1.
Changes	52.243-4	Same as 52.243-1.
Changes and Changed Conditions	52.243-5	Same as 52.243-1.
Government Property (Fixed Price Contracts)	52.245-2	Clause necessary for transfer of government property to subcontractor. Risk of loss must be assumed by sub in accordance with basic subparagraph (g). With contracting officer's permission, risk of loss of GFE in sub's possession can be assumed by the government in accordance with alternate subparagraph (g).
Govt. Property (Cost-Reimb. Time-&-Material, or Labor-Hour Contr.)	52.245-5	Clause necessary for transfer of government property to subcontractor. With contracting officer's permission, risk of loss can be assumed by government.
Inspection of Supplies-Fixed-Price	52.246-2	Portions of this clause needed to ensure government rights to inspect or test on subcontractor's premises.
Inspection of Supplies-- Cost Reimbursement	52.246-3	Same as 52.246-2.
Inspection-- Time-and-Material and Labor-Hour	52.246-6	Same as 52.246-2.
Termination for Convenience of the Government (Fixed Price) (Short Form)	52.249-1	Clause necessary to protect against refusal of sub to accept government termination of contract.
Term. for Conv. of the Government (Fixed-Price)	52.249-2	Same as 52.249.2.
Term. for Conv. of the Government (Dismantle, Dem. or Remove Improvements)	52.249-3	Same as 52.249.2.
Termination for Convenience of the Government (Services) (Short Form)	52.249-4	Clause necessary to protect against refusal of sub to accept government termination of contract.

CHART 8-1, Continued

Clause Title	Citation	Notations
Termination for Convenienceof the Government (Educational and Other Nonprofit Institutions)	52.249-5	Same as 52.249-4.
Termination (Cost-Reimbursement)	52.249-6	Same as 52.249-4.
Term. (Fixed Price A & E)	52.249-7	Same as 52.249-4.
Term. of Work (Consol. Facilities or Facil. Acquisition)	52.249-11	Same as 52.249-4.
Termination (Pers. Servs.)	52.249-12	Same as 52.249-4.
Indemnification Under P. L. 85-804	52.250-1	If included in prime, with contracting officer's prior written approval, it can be flowed down to sub.

SUBGROUP B4: Clauses intended to advance social, economic, or environmental objectives (public policy matters).

Clause Title	Citation	Notations
Walsh-Healey Public Contracts Act	52.222-20	Needed to carry out the basic principles of the act.
Service Contract Act of 1965--$2,500 or less	52.222-40	If clause is in prime, flow-down to all subcontracts is needed to ensure subcontractor pays minimum wages specified in the act.
Fair Labor Standards Act	52.222-43	If clause is in prime, it should be flowed-down to protect certification to the government regarding rates.
Service Contract Act--Price Adj.	52.222-44	Same as 52.222-43.
Buy American Act --Supplies	52.225-3	If contained in prime, clause is needed in subcontracts as protection of certification of the source of supplies or services.
Balance of Payments Program	52.225-7	Same as 52.225-3.
Preference for U.S. Flag Air Carriers	52.247.63	If clause is in prime, flow down to carry out Section 5 of Fly America Act (49 U.S.C. 1517) requiring use of U.S. Flag Carriers for government-financed international air transportation.

9

Progress and Status Monitoring

MANAGEMENT SYSTEMS OBJECTIVES FOR BUYERS AND SELLERS

Monitoring progress--determining whether a job will fulfill expectations on time--has proven difficult for many post-award managers. Successful progress monitoring requires careful planning, keen observation during performance, and adequate data collecting and reporting systems. It demands the analysis of events and results as they emerge, comparing them with planned status and projecting revised expectations while maintaining a record of baseline plans.

Planning and control systems have dramatically increased in comprehensiveness and overall effectiveness since the 1950s. This development has been driven by the introduction of automatic data processing along with an intense interest of executives in obtaining improved status information and enhancing their ability to assess and predict future operations. The principal reason for executive interest in improvement is the promise of increased ability to make timely adjustments in productive effort, raising effectiveness and efficiency. By applying new techniques, they have improved their products and advanced productivity.

Improving management systems has been largely achieved within the bounds of individual enterprises. However, it has also increased the quality and volume of information flowing across the contractual interface, impacting relationships between organizations. Today, sponsors of contractual undertakings are able to participate more fully with their suppliers in making the decisions necessary for project adjustments. These developments have not eliminated the sensitivities and complexities inherent in transferring status information from one organization to another. Problems in information flow between the government and its suppliers surfaced in the early 1960s when the Department of Defense (DOD) undertook massive and complex projects, and the National Aeronautics and Space Administration (NASA) initiated its space programs. The development of the Polaris submarine was representative of these efforts and illustrated the planning and control challenges of contract-based major systems developments. Polaris was followed by even more ambitious and expensive projects such as NASA's Apollo project. In the private sector, challenges in contract planning and control matured with the introduction of nuclear power plant construction. The magnitude of the sponsor's investment and risk expanded his need to participate in the decisionmaking processes necessary to fulfill project objectives.

During the early 1960s, the program evaluation and review technique (PERT) became established as a system far more capable of supporting management information needs than any prior system. PERT was developed to manage the Polaris project, and its adoption and refinement as a project management tool was founded on the availability of electronic computers. In reality, the development of advanced scheduling and costing techniques was a direct result of this electronic computing capability and could not have been achieved without it.

Although the computer is vital to sophisticated information generating systems, its use does not guarantee or replace the need for adequate summarization and for presentation techniques that convey concise and accurate information on the status of programs to management. The objective is to support management's needs for information on which decisions can be based. Consequently, older techniques for presenting information, such as Gantt charts, have not disappeared from the manager's inventory of tools for decisionmaking, but they have been refined and improved.

In contract management, both customer and producer must consider the information level that is essential to management analysis and decisionmaking. The practitioner can more easily address the challenges associated with delivering information by determining the following factors:

1.   Amount of information to be drawn
2.   Frequency and timeliness of information delivery
3.   Method of summarizing and presenting information
4.   Magnitude of the information base
5.   Depth of penetration into the performer's organizational structure
6.   Sensitivity of data to be extracted from both parties
7.   Need for verifying or cross checking information and conclusions
8.   Cost of the system

Our intent here is to examine the emerging need for sophisticated contract planning and control systems from the perspective of both performers (contractors) and buyers (sponsors). The techniques discussed are treated in greater detail in other studies that examine project management, production, and logistics systems. Our focus is the impact of contract commitments on the effectiveness of management systems. Because the parties have independent as well as common interests, conflicts may arise. The government's experience in managing contracts provides a substantial part of the basis for this study.

The buyer's overall objective in monitoring contract status is to gain assurance that a satisfactory delivery will occur in accordance with cost and schedule projections. Management systems that enhance project planning and control aid in accomplishing that objective.

BUYER INTEREST IN SUPPLIER SYSTEMS AND OPERATIONS

Since the Industrial Revolution, improved management planning and control systems have been sought to help create efficient and reliable production processes. Most systems have been developed by manufacturers to improve control of their internal operations. Refinements of their systems can be used to control non-manufacturing processes and to meet the needs of externally managed programs, such as those of procuring organizations. PERT and similar innovations represented the effort of large buyers (the government, in the case of PERT) to tailor management systems concepts to meet special needs.

Managing continuous process production requires unique methods which generally would not be subjected to refinement because of the influence of individual customers. In fact, the customer normally buys only part of a product turned out by continuous process production and has relatively little interest in production methods. This is also true for repetitive manufacture of common commercial items such as light bulbs, automobiles, and fabrics. The customer, however, may take a significant interest in the manufacturing processes of large-scale end items such as aircraft. This is most likely if the customer orders a product made to his own design specifications. The customer becomes even more involved if he or she participates in the research and development of the end item, for example, products manufactured for defense purposes.

There are three levels of buyer involvement in management systems. The first level is associated with small-scale jobs or job lot projects for which management planning and control is largely left to the discretion of the supplier. Progress reports and periodic management reviews may be used. At this level, the supplier usually controls the design, and post-award administrators expect relatively little direct involvement.

The second level of buyer involvement is characterized by procurement of large-scale, but limited quantity, production or construction projects using a design description supplied by the customer. In this situation, purchasers may impose or expect extensive data collection and reporting, but managing systems and techniques are well known and are generally based on suppliers' management systems.

The third level of buyer involvement is stimulated by contracts for large projects involving research and development or acquisition of major systems. Many projects of this type are sponsored (externally to the producer) by government or industry. These contracts generate extreme concern for timeliness and quality of performance. Suppliers' internal management systems may not be fully acceptable, and purchasers may impose systems or standards for adequate systems. This has become the practice of government agencies procuring unique or major systems.

Interest in superior management systems of suppliers is not limited to large projects or government contracts. Contract work is nearly always time-critical, regardless of project size or buyer. Nevertheless, progress monitored through ordinary expediting systems is sufficient for most procurement. In especially significant undertakings, whether public or private, the buyer may want to ask suppliers for authority to review, or less frequently, to audit their systems. There is less pressure to become deeply involved in private sector procurement because the cost and time required to conduct intensive review may not be supportable in competitive commercial undertakings. Private sector buyers strengthen their negotiating position by developing review capabilities but, as a practical matter, may benefit more by obtaining authority to audit than by a detailed examination of their suppliers' management processes.

GROWTH OF GOVERNMENT INTEREST IN CONTRACTOR MANAGEMENT

There are six principal reasons for expanded government interest in the management systems of its suppliers. They reflect aspects of government contracting that tend to set it apart from privately sponsored projects. They are

1. method of payment,
2. magnitude of public funds,
3. lack of firm pricing,
4. institutionalization of audit,
5. degradation of expected performance outcome,
6. contractual integrity.

Method of payment. Certain types of contracts, principally cost-reimbursement and fixed-price-incentive contracts, stimulate the government's interest in contractor management systems. Contracts of this type require government audit and cost determination and reimbursement of incurred costs to the contractor. These payment conditions are an important factor because they obligate the government to pay for contractors' reasonable (and allowable) expenses, whether or not their operations are considered economical and efficient. The government's effort to ensure economy in its operations has stimulated its involvement. Firm-fixed-price contracts normally are not subjected to management systems audits because the firm pricing agreement reduces the customer's concern with contractor efficiency, particularly if competitive pricing has determined source selection. Although the fixed-price-incentive contract has a price limitation, it is subject to systems reviews because total payments are variable, depending on actual costs incurred.[1] In reaction to substantial criticism of their procurement practices, the major procuring agencies, particularly the DOD, have adopted requirements and rules imposing government-designed concepts of effective management systems on major suppliers.

Magnitude of public funds. Public interest in economical and efficient use of taxpayer resources has been a driving factor in the government's extensive involvement in many contractors' operations. The magnitude of the government's expenses can be illustrated by its procurement of research and development. In 1984 the government sponsored the expenditure of $44 billion for research and development. Of this total, $33 billion was expended by contract or grant with industrial and other nongovernment institutions. Supplies, equipment, and construction contracts accounted for an additional $100 billion. These expenditures are sensitive to public criticism when reports of wasted resources emerge.

Lack of firm pricing. Lack of firm pricing is usually associated with research and development or other technologically advanced projects such as production of military systems. Susceptibility to cost growth and schedule delay accompanies this type of work, yet this is characteristic of large numbers of government-sponsored undertakings. Competitive firm pricing of such work may not be feasible because projects and resource requirements tend to be either unique or inadequately defined. This factor is an important stimulus to the government's imposition of management systems requirements on suppliers who perform such work.

Institutionalization of audit. Although the government is philosophically and by statute committed to securing price competition, it actually relies more on cost analysis than price competition in pricing major acquisitions. Verification of cost estimates and proposals is accomplished by detailed examination of contractors' costs. The government has established contract pricing offices and the Defense Contract Audit Agency as

---

[1] A full discussion of contract types is found in Sherman, Stanley N., *Government Procurement Management,* 2nd Edition, (Wordcrafters Publications, 1985). The subject is also treated in detail in FAR, Part 16.

principal organizations devoted to the examination and review of contractors' proposals, supporting data, procedures, and application of personnel
and facilities to government work. In effect, the government has institu-
tionalized its analytical approach to verifying the appropriateness and
efficiency of its contractors' practices. This capability for analysis
encourages increasing penetration into contractor systems for the duration
of a project.

Degradation of expected performance outcome. In addition to concerns regarding contractors' efficiency, the government has experienced a
degradation of expected performance outcome in many programs. Projects
begin with high expectations of new technological achievements which are
sometimes only partially achieved. Given repeated experiences of this
kind, generally accompanied by delays and increased expenditures, efforts
to mandate better management have appeal, even though management
weaknesses are not always the source of the deficiencies. In large
contracts, all of these factors combine to cause dissatisfaction.

Because of these problems, many public representatives have concluded that contractors are inadequately managing government programs.
In some cases this conclusion is warranted, but there is a tradeoff
between poor management and initial overoptimism. Either could cause
degradation. Whether improved management systems can actually improve
results remains questionable because degradation of intended outcomes
may result from unrealistic expectations. Regardless of the final conclusion as to the cause of deficient project outcomes, a major factor in
overcoming deficiencies has been the imposition of government approaches
in improving management systems.

Contractual integrity. The sixth major area of concern which has
stimulated government-imposed management approaches is the relationship
between the requirements in a contract solicitation document (as quoted
on by all competitors) and the final performance required of the winning
contractor. From the government's perspective, if acceptable work is less
than that which was specified in a solicitation, the reduced end result
implies lack of integrity in the contractual process. To ensure contractual integrity in this sense, the government attempts to have contractors install management systems capable of fully accounting for any
variations in requirements in a way that demonstrates responsibility for
shortcomings.

SOURCES OF MANAGEMENT INFORMATION

Evaluation of a contractor's progress requires the purchaser to draw
upon the contractor's internal sources of information. Reports of various
kinds may be required, and visits to work sites may prove invaluable.
Internal sources of data within the supplier's organization and techniques

used by the supplier for summarizing and assessing progress may be relied on for the purchaser's needs if they are accurate and reliable. The challenge of gaining needed information varies with the type of project. Four levels of complexity may be identified, ranging from the relatively predictable production process through three less predictable types: (1) research, (2) research and development, and (3) systems (projects that combine research, development, production and logistics considerations as parts of the overall contract).

Types of Projects

Production. Progress of production work is usually easier to measure than progress of research and development because production contracts include an end item design for which the requisite production processes are normally well defined. The sequencing and scheduling of those processes is usually well understood, and defined points may be identified for measuring progress in relation to schedule. Furthermore, production control is an area in which most contractors have developed considerable expertise.

Research. The status of progress in research work is difficult to assess. Achieving research milestones is qualified by the fact that setbacks may occur in subsequent testing and development. Additionally, researchers encounter the need for new knowledge which upsets the orderly progress expected under a contract. For these reasons, research work is less manageable than production or development work. Nevertheless, it creates fewer contractual problems because most research contracts are based on a level-of-effort approach which leaves most of the risk with the sponsor. Consequently, economic pressures to account for each delay and cost element in terms of fault are not required. Budgetary considerations remain as critical issues.

Research and development. In research and development, a complex mixture of experimenting, designing, testing, and evaluating leads to the development of new products. The practicability of designs may not be proven until after completing qualification testing on parts or all of the effort. Status of work in relation to the work plan is difficult to assess, and projects are difficult to manage. Consequently, substantial risk is associated with the work. This risk may be placed on the performer, since most development work is governed by a performance specification for which the performer is responsible. Risk also may be divided between purchaser and supplier through use of incentive contracts. With the parties sharing risk, these contracts heighten the need for superior management systems so that an accounting for problems in terms of fault may be obtained. When this work is based on a cost-reimbursement contract, it involves great financial risk to the sponsor. Because the government sponsors many projects of this kind, often on a cost reimbursable or incentive basis, it has become keenly interested in its contractors' management systems.

Systems. Large projects generally referred to as major systems encompass years of effort in research, development, production, deployment, operations, and support. Such projects are comprised of numerous individual yet interdependent tasks which may be contracted to several sources. They present the most difficult challenges for management systems. Designing effective approaches to progress measurement and techniques of projecting completion costs and schedules has proven extremely difficult and not fully reliable for major systems contracts. Because of the magnitude of these projects, effort to improve their management processes never ceases, and much of the effort to improve management systems has been concentrated on them.

Information Gathering

The buyer gains information for assessing contract progress by interacting with suppliers. Perhaps the most important technique for measuring progress of complex programs is personal contact through regular meetings between the buyer's project manager and technical personnel and the supplier's key technical managers. Through this direct contact, whether informal and ad hoc or scheduled, the status of contract action is reviewed and assessed. The status of a contract may be clarified by answering the following questions:

1. Has a subcontractor's progress been evaluated?
2. Is a design completed and approved for fabrication?
3. Has a test plan been released?
4. Have building foundations been installed and inspected?
5. Have material orders been placed?
6. Have unresolved problems surfaced?
7. Has a proposed design complied with constraints?
8. Have fabricated parts met all quality standards with verified records of inspections or tests?
9. Have property accounts been established and correctly administered?

These and other similar questions require positive answers which should be available whether or not direct, personal contact is feasible. Answers can be made available on demand through effective management systems monitored by post-award administrators.

To help acquire these answers and as a part of regular contract administration activity, the government employs industrial specialists to monitor contractor progress. An industrial specialist is expected to make personal observations of contractor work and to review reports submitted by contractors summarizing their progress. Much of this work may be based on relatively informal personal contact, depending on the existence of good contractor management systems. The informal processes support, but do not replace, the systems. Formal conferences and program review meetings between the contractor's managers and the buyer's management team are vital to post-award decisions. Formal meetings are scheduled periodically to evaluate the overall status of the project and make any necessary adjustments to ensure progress.

Sources of information regarding the contractor's management system are not automatically available to the buyer for review. Contractors usually establish internal control procedures including regular meetings of managers and periodic progress reports. Information from these meetings or reports flows to the buyer, often as monthly production progress reports, but ordinarily only to the extent that they are required by the contract. Interactions between technical representatives and project managers may also lead to immediate contacts between buyer and seller when problems arise during the course of performance.

Presentation Formats

Several presentation formats may be identified that aid in assessing progress. The simplest approach, and for many types of work the most practical, is the Gantt (bar) chart, which plots on a time scale the tasks and milestones necessary to complete the job. A somewhat more advanced technique is the *delivery forecast report.* This approach requires defining lead times and identifying target dates for specific contract deliveries. A delivery forecast report focuses on completion of the first end item under the contract. The delivery forecast is developed at program initiation to establish a base line for periodic review and assessment of actual production progress. Two assumptions form the basis for using the delivery forecast report: (1) a summary of lead times for all major components of the first end item is the critical element for accurate projection of the entire end item list, and (2) subsequent deliverable items identical to the first will be produced in an orderly manner. The critical issue is the achievement of each stage in the manufacture of the first item.

Another approach, the *phased planning chart,* combines process analysis with delivery forecasting. Lead times and target dates are identified by considering the major processes and steps necessary to reach intermediate delivery points requisite to delivery of end items. The phased planning chart is a useful device, but, like Gantt charts and delivery forecast reports, it does not promote analysis that identifies pacing items (steps in the work plan that may not be delayed without consequent delay in the end item delivery schedule).

A fourth presentation technique for assessing progress is the *milestone variance chart.* This chart includes a presentation of the target completion dates for major steps toward production of the end item beginning with the inception of the program and ending with actual shipment. The chart is updated when changes occur, and a revised program is prepared by the contractor. The actual performance dates are plotted on the chart for comparison purposes.

To use any of these presentation techniques, the manager relies on progress information from existing management systems and observations by key employees. The work is stimulated by review meetings scheduled between contractor and buyer. Their sufficiency depends on adequate information collection and summarization, timeliness, and the manager's assessment skills. They are unlikely to suffice for large-scale, complex, and lengthy contracts.

ADVANCED TECHNIQUES FOR PROGRESS MONITORING

Line of Balance

The sophistication of progress measurement takes a significant step forward when the line of balance technique is applied to the production process. Line of balance introduces an additional dimension to progress assessment: the use of a contractor's stock record system to measure actual performance. This is a quantitative tool used in determining production progress by counting the materials, parts, and subassemblies that have passed through specified checkpoints or control points as defined on the production plan. While this count is available from appropriate stock records, the technique employs systematic spot checking of the actual count of production inventory and is backstopped by physical inventories that are designed to ensure that the system is properly implemented.

Line of balance has gained wide recognition as a practical management tool that is useful without advanced computational and data management capabilities. It is presented here for that reason and because it handily illustrates progress measurement variables. MRP I and II systems[1] are replacing it in current production management because the widespread and inexpensive availability of computers for data management

---

[1]DCAA and DOD declarations that MRP I and II are not sufficient for government contract accounting purposes were made in 1987, but the efficacy of the systems for efficient operations is well established.

and computational routines has made the more advanced approach feasible for many companies.

Using the line of balance technique in large-scale production programs, managers can directly relate actual production progress to scheduled progress and can predict the likelihood of meeting contract delivery schedules. Line of balance provides a method of highlighting those parts of the operation requiring management attention. It is a technique for presenting three discreet aspects of a contractor's production status on a single chart: the objective, the production plan, and the progress chart. To prepare the objective portion of the chart, the contract delivery schedule is converted into cumulative delivery quantities. These cumulative delivery quantities are plotted on a time scale so that a cumulative scheduled delivery line can be drawn that increases as time elapses. Actual cumulative deliveries are also plotted on the objective graph. As a result, on any specified review date during the production program, the chart provides a direct comparison of planned deliveries and actual deliveries on a cumulative basis. The objective chart for production of product BB (on a review date of December 1) is illustrated in figure 9-1. Data on the chart is derived from the contract delivery schedule.

Product BB delivery Schedule (Units)

	Sep	Oct	Nov	Dec	Jan	Feb	Mar
Delivery Rate	5	5	20	20	10	5	5
Cumulative Schedule	5	10	30	50	60	65	70

Figure 9-1

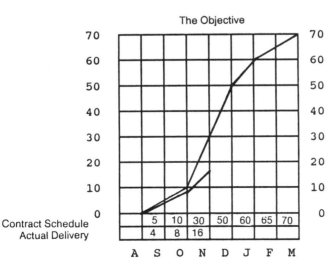

The Objective

The second element of the line of balance chart is the production plan. This plan is derived from estimates of the lead time required for each process beginning with the initiation of effort and running to the date of shipment of the completed end item. Lead time, measured in the number of work days (or weeks), is estimated for each key event. The estimate is derived by analyzing required work and considering the producer's operating methods. The estimated lead time is plotted on the production plan for each of the identified events.

Preparation of the production plan is the critical element in an effective line of balance charting process. To prepare the production plan, management must thoroughly review each part of its operations, making time estimates for each activity, identifying each event, and summarizing the total lead time to completion. The production plan is a rudimentary form of network in that it comprises an assembly tree of the major subordinate steps leading to final assembly and delivery of the end product. However, the production plan does not have the characteristics of a network such as those prepared for PERT. An accurately prepared production plan identifies all key production events necessary to the end product and assesses the facilities and capabilities of the manufacturer. The plan for product BB reveals that the production cycle from event 1 (issue purchase order for material M) through event 11 (shipment) is twenty-seven days and includes eight key events (events at which units pass through and may be tabulated or counted). Figure 9-2 illustrates the production plan for product BB.

Figure 9-2

Production Plan

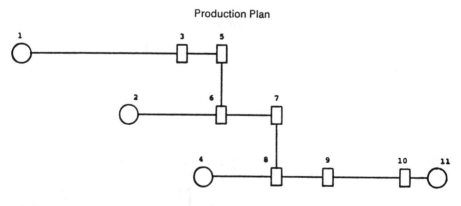

27 26 25 24 23 22 21 20 19 18 17 16 15 14 13 12 11 10 9 8 7 6 5 4 3 2 1 0

Product BB has eleven events identified in table 9-1, only eight of which are key events. The table summarizes lead times, a description of operations leading to each key event, and a calculation of the line of balance using the formula $Y_2 = Y_1 + M\,(LT/WD)$. Terms of this equation are:

Y_2 - balance quantity for the control point
Y_1 - number of units scheduled to pass the event by the review date
M - scheduled delivery rate for the production cycle that is beginning
LT - lead time for the control point (from production plan)
WD - work days per month for the production cycle just beginning

Table 9-1

Product BB Line of Balance

Event	Lead Time	Description of Operation	Calculated Line of Balance at Dec. 1
1	27	Release order for material M	$30 + (20\ 27/19) = 58$
2	20	Production release, part x	$30 + (20\ 20/19) = 51$
3	17	Receive material M	$30 + (20\ 17/19) = 48$
4	15	Release subcontract, part y	$30 + (20\ 15/19) = 46$
5	14	Complete fabrication, part z	$30 + (20\ 14/19) = 45$
6	14	Complete fabrication, part x	$30 + (20\ 14/19) = 45$
7	10	Complete subassembly A	$30 + (20\ 10/19) = 41$
8	10	Receive subcontract part y	$30 + (20\ 10/19) = 41$
9	7	Complete assembly, product BB	$30 + (20\ 07/19) = 37$
10	2	Complete finish work, test & cal.	$30 + (20\ 02/19) = 32$
11	0	Complete presv., pkg. & ship	$30 + (20\ 00/19) = 30$

As indicated on the progress chart, figure 9-3, on the review date of December 1, only 16 units had been delivered, and the required delivery rate has increased. Inventory status as of December 1 is as follows:

Key Event	3	5	6	7	8	9	10	11
Cumulative Units	70	35	16	16	30	16	16	16

The third aspect of the line of balance presentation is the progress chart, which is designed to integrate the production plan with the objectives as defined by the cumulative delivery schedule. A progress chart for product BB is illustrated by figure 9-3. On its horizontal axis, the progress chart includes a sequential listing of each of the major production events identified in the production plan. On its vertical axis, the production chart is scaled in the same way as the objective chart to facilitate comparison with cumulative deliveries as plotted thereon. Actual progress is plotted using vertical bars to plot the cumulative units of production that have passed through the specified check points (events) as derived from the production plan. To assess progress against the production plan, the vertical bars must be compared with the line of balance. However, the line of balance must be derived by projection from the objective chart. To do this, the cutoff date for a particular review is plotted on the objective chart. The analyst must then determine from the production plan the number of work days of lead time from each event to completion. The units of lead time for an event are marked off on the objective chart to the right of the study date, and a vertical line is drawn to intersect the previously plotted cumulative contract delivery schedule. This intersection is the starting point for a horizontal connection between the objective chart and the progress chart. The horizontal line is drawn through the column space for the event being plotted. If deliveries for that event are on schedule, the top of the bar coincides with the line of balance. This is done for each event. The result is an immediate visual indication of whether a sufficient quantity of production units has passed through any given event (or milestone) for the production. Wherever the vertical bar is shorter than the position of the line of balance, a potential delay is indicated. Wherever the vertical bar rises higher than the line of balance, the indication is that there is no schedule problem, but in-process inventory is greater than needed. Large gaps

Figure 9-3

Progress Chart

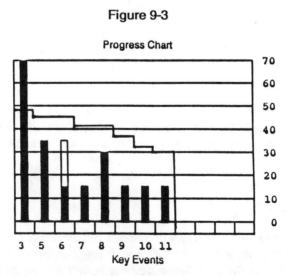

Key Events

between the line of balance and the top of the vertical bars indicate
significant delay in the overall production plan and highlight the event(s)
being directly affected. The progress chart as illustrated for product BB
in figure 9-3 highlights an unsatisfactory status of production and
reveals that a problem is impeding progress during operations leading up
to event 7. The subassembly work needs attention. Figures 9-1, 9-2, and
9-3 are assembled into the line of balance chart as shown on Figure 9-4.

Program Evaluation and Review Technique (PERT)

PERT was developed in 1958 specifically to support the planning and
control needs of the Polaris project. It was a major advance in planning
techniques for large undertakings and continues to be regarded as an excellent tool. PERT can be applied to research and development, systems
projects, or to any large undertaking in which a single major objective is
the focus of the effort. PERT has been applied in a modified form
(known as CP/M) to construction projects of all kinds. It's major contribution to the art of management is in the adoption and use of the
network as a planning tool. Graphic drawings of PERT networks are useful in visualizing the concept, but practical applications demand the use
of electronic computers for summarizing and calculating the values for
networks. Like the line of balance system, PERT is based on time estimates, but it differs from the line of balance technique in several
respects. First, it does not require summarization of cumulative deliveries
and is not based upon measurement of quantities of production units as
they move through specified production points. Instead, PERT is based
on individual time estimates associated with each identified productive
activity. The activities are derived by analyzing an entire program using
the concept of a work breakdown structure to identify all events and
activities necessary for project completion.

The first step in the application of PERT to a project is to analyze
the total effort. This requires breaking the work into discreet segments
and may result in creating a work breakdown structure with thousands of
individual activities and events. The intention is to create a structure in
which all parts are essential and none are omitted. Undertakings such as
developing and producing a weapons system are likely candidates for
application of PERT, but any complex undertaking from the construction
of a nuclear power plant to the design, construction, and installation of
an oil drilling rig can be managed effectively using the PERT technique.
Identifying the activities and events is a large effort, but defining,
sequencing, and making time estimates for an entire network is even more
challenging. Activities represent work, and they are time and resource-
consuming elements of the project. Events represent the beginning or
ending of activities, occur at points in time, do not represent work, and

Figure 9-4

Line of Balance Chart

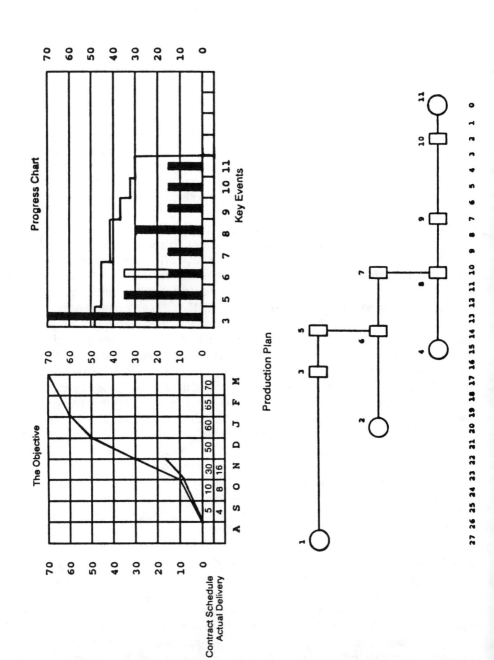

do not require time. In diagrammatic representations of the network, the events are connected by activity arrows which may be viewed as keys to the network. Since the arrow reflects work and the event reflects either a beginning point, an ending point, or both, the work activity reflected by any arrow in the system cannot begin until the preceding event at the tail of the arrow is accomplished. This is true for all events and activities and is a pivotal feature of the entire technique. Once activities are identified, defined, and fully understood, required time can be estimated in terms of days or weeks as appropriate for the application.

Time estimates are the key to the PERT system. By summing total time requirements, PERT is able to derive the expected time to complete the entire project and to identify the latest allowable starting (or completion) schedule for all events throughout the network. The time estimate for each activity is prepared as a three-time estimate, that is, estimates of the optimistic time requirement, the pessimistic time requirement, and the more likely time requirement. From these three-time estimates, the expected time is calculated as the mean of the three estimates. For major undertakings to which PERT might be applied, the number of events and activities totals in the thousands; consequently, the calculation of expected times and summation of the network are impracticable unless a computer is used.

PERT analysis provides management with a method of calculating the critical path (the path through the network that takes the longest total elapsed time from inception to completion). This critical path is the one on which management must focus major attention. Making use of the critical path requires identifying slack time associated with any and all activities comprising the entire network. Slack is the difference between the latest allowable date and the expected date for an event. If positive, some time slippage may be allowed for the activity leading to the event and possibly for the path. If slack is zero on the critical path, no slippage is allowable, and, if negative, action is needed to eliminate the slippage if delivery is to occur on time. Through the identification of slack time and critical path, management may make adjustments to a production plan and/or reallocate resources in an effort to meet required end objectives. Practical applications of PERT require both a forward and a backward pass through the lead time estimates in order to calculate the slack time, which may be viewed as the most useful management statistic derived from the PERT analysis.

Cost Schedule Control Systems Criteria (C/SCSC)

Historical notation. Some historical notes may be appropriate for placing the PERT system in perspective with the cost schedule control systems criteria or C/SCSC as it is known by the DOD. As discussed

earlier, the PERT system was the first well known development of net-
working techniques, and it reflects a very specific management system.
Since 1958 PERT has been made a requirement of many government contracts. The success of Polaris under PERT gave impetus to the government's imposition of management systems on its suppliers. Also during
that time, NASA began a major effort leading to the Apollo project and
sponsored numerous unmanned spacecraft explorations. For purposes of
NASA program management, a modification of the PERT system known as
PERT companion cost was adopted. The agency imposed this technique on
contractors selected for major research and development undertakings.

Early management systems requirements experienced mixed results at
best. Contractors frequently supported them without much enthusiasm.
In many cases, contractors already were using management systems which
they considered quite adequate for their own purposes. Consequently, the
contractor often prepared the PERT or the PERT companion cost reports
solely for delivery to the government agency while continuing to manage
the project using existing management processes. This developed into an
expensive luxury for the government. Although the government received
its mandated reports, the reports frequently did not reflect the contractors' current activities and actions. In many government projects, the
reports were unused. They were delivered--perhaps late--and were
ignored. Under these conditions, management systems were ineffective in
aiding the government to gain better control over project costs and
schedules.

These unsatisfactory experiences led to the development of a new
concept in the mid 1960s. The government experimented with establishing
criteria for adequate management systems of its large contractors. Under
this approach, the government wrote a specification for management systems and, by contract, required contractors to develop and enhance their
internal management systems to qualify them in accordance with the specification. This approach is the source of the (C/SCSC). It was intended
that C/SCSC achieve objectives identical to those desired from any management system, but the criteria were difficult to meet and required
substantial upgrading of many contractors' systems. The criteria require
accurate project status information and an adequate contractor system for
supporting decisions for future revisions. C/SCSC itself does not mandate
any specific reporting requirement, but reports are mandated by each
contract. The objective is to enable the government's contract and project monitors to assess the likelihood that the project will be completed
on time and within the current cost estimate.

C/SCSC is a part of the larger DOD selected acquisitions information management systems (SAIMS) and is designed for collecting and assessing cost, schedule, and performance data generated during contract
performance. It was adopted to provide the government with influence
over contractors' behavior without destroying the nature of contract

relationships, specifically the management obligations under which the contractor acquires control of the job.

Most authorities recognize that the contractor's project manager is in a position to control progress. The contract assigns the managerial role of assessing performance and defining the tasks for overcoming any specific problem. The contractor's manager has immediate access to information generated by his work force and is committed to managing the resources and application of effort under the contract. Nevertheless, the government mandates that government program managers and contracting officers have control over the overall undertaking. The government's ability to exercise control is based on, and limited by, the terms and conditions of the contract. Access to various types of information is required but only in accordance with the procedures in contract terms and conditions. By requiring C/SCSC in the contract, the program manager's ability to control is enhanced because it mandates sophisticated information gathering techniques. Along with adequate reporting, the government sought to overcome contractors' reluctance to facilitate government access to their information sources. Contractors were perceived as being slow to provide the government with up-to-date information on progress.

The approach of C/SCSC prevented the DOD from imposing specific management systems, but it offered the potential of using a contractor's own internal management systems to provide the government with necessary information. By using this approach, it was thought that the overall cost of management systems to the government would be minimized because redundancy would be eliminated. The DOD adopted C/SCSC as a policy and applied the requirements to all large systems contracts. Full implementation of C/SCSC for large projects requires computer based data management.

Objectives of C/SCSC. A set of four historical problems was a key motivating factor in the adoption of C/SCSC. The first was the government's concern with controlling undefinitized work. An undefinitized element of work is any part of a project which, although authorized, has not been negotiated in terms of total cost and schedule. In many larger contractual undertakings, numerous tasks were initiated by contractors that were not fully defined at the time of their initiation. Work was initiated to overcome a problem encountered in the development process, but an issue could arise as to whether the task was essential just to meet existing contract requirements. A contractor might have initiated work on the assumption that it was a change to requirements and, therefore, would have expected an increase in contract price to compensate for the extra effort. If the government held the opposite view, a controversy arose. Major projects tended to have a large number of undefinitized efforts in progress at any particular time. A key objective of C/SCSC was to regain control over all work effort under a contract so that no unauthorized work was in process, and if possible, all work would be negotiated as a fully definitized package.

A second objective of C/SCSC was to eliminate what was known as the "the rubber baseline." A rubber baseline was created when the contractor changed the numbers as a result of reassessing the basic contract obligation in order to establish a current work plan. The contractor's initial work plan, including the schedule and budget for each element of work under the contract, was lost. Under C/SCSC, the retroactive adjustment of plans to reflect actual experience was prohibited, unless a full accounting for the change in the base line was preserved. The basic objective in eliminating the rubber base line was to provide the government with the ability, through audit, to determine reasons for changes in cost and schedule.

A third area in which the government encountered significant program management problems was a tendency of contractors to borrow funds from downstream activities and apply them to current work. The danger associated with borrowing for near-term problems was that remaining funds would be inadequate for future effort. This action permitted the contractor to ignore overrun of current work and to delay reporting the funding insufficiency to the government. C/SCSC mandated that contractors cannot borrow from future tasks to finance near-term problems as a means of avoiding disclosure of current difficulties to the government.

System documentation is the fourth area in which C/SCSC overcame contractor systems deficiencies. Government contractors might have had relatively sound management systems, but they were not necessarily formalized and documented in a fashion that allowed the government to audit and review their effectiveness. In the absence of a formal system, contractors often did not develop a technique for identifying and reporting variances from plans in a current time frame. C/SCSC mandated that the systems be documented.

The earned value concept. C/SCSC is best described as the government's approach in requiring major contractors to develop an earned value system. Although the concept of earned value may not be expressly imposed by C/SCSC, its implementation creates such a system. Under an earned value system, any planned project can be evaluated to determine, in advance and in quantitative terms, cost and schedule "values" associated with achievements and milestones in the project. This quantitative measurement can then be compared with the actual "earnings" achieved by the producers as they progress through the projected work. This is exactly what the C/SCSC requires of a contractor. C/SCSC demands that a contractor analyze the total work required by his contract in terms of a work breakdown structure. The work breakdown structure (WBS) is a systematic subdivision of the tasks required for project completion, beginning with the top level of the WBS which would be the deliverable end item. The end item is analyzed to identify each essential element that must be accomplished in order for the end item to function. This breaking out of the end item into its essential components creates the second level of the WBS. Each element at the second level, in turn, is exploded into the total number of elements required for it to function. This creates the third level of the WBS for each particular element identified at the second level. This technique operates at every level, calling for complete definition of the ingredients necessary for overall program success. It is a process of exploding the end deliverable item until all of its component elements are identified, all the way to the foundation of the work breakdown structure, where work packages that do not lend themselves to further breakdown are managed.

There can be thousands of work packages in a major undertaking. Under C/SCSC, each must be identified in terms of (1) a specific defined element of work (ideally defined directly from the system specification); (2) a clear schedule of work performance necessary to the work package identifying both the elapsed time and the calendar time in which the work package must be performed; (3) projected cost of performing the work package, including direct labor, material, and overhead costs; and (4) the manager responsible for accomplishing the work package.

C/SCSC equation. The C/SCSC equation summarizes the standards for qualifying a contractor's internal management systems. When rigorously applied in evaluating these systems, C/SCSC mandates that the contractor be able to generate direct quantitative comparisons between planned and actual work. The planning objectives of the cost schedule control systems criteria are expressed by the following equation:

$$\sum IB + MR = TC + E_{ann}$$

$$\sum IB \; = \; \text{sum of internal budgets}$$

MR = management reserves

TC = target cost (the contractually agreed value)

E_{ann} = estimate of authorized but not negotiated work

The terms on the right side of the equation state contract values; terms on the left side state contractor internal planning values. At the time of contract award, the E_{ann} value should be zero because at that point, all work should be encompassed by the original target cost. The implications of the equation should become clear when one realizes that all contracts have a target cost, which is expected to be consumed by the budgeting and scheduling of work. The equation is simply saying that the target cost of any contract should be broken down into two elements by the contractor after he receives the contract award. These two elements are (1) the internal budgets (IB) allocated to subordinate managers to perform tasks under the contract, and (2) a management reserve (MR)

which is used by the project manager for use in resolving problems arising during the performance of work.[1] The equation reflects the policy
position of the government that, upon contract award, a contractor should
analyze the component parts of the total effort and establish a budget
for performing the work necessary for each part. The sum of these
internal budgets plus any management reserves should be equal to the
contract target cost. Since the fee arrangement in government contracts
requires money over and above the target cost, the fee or profit element
of the contract is not addressed in the C/SCSC planning objective.

The fourth term in the equation, E_{ann}, reflects a second objective
of the government in imposing C/SCSC: that the contractor must always
maintain a current estimate of all work proceeding under the contract,
regardless of whether the work has been negotiated into a definitive
modification of the contract. The term E_{ann} could be eliminated from
the equation if no changes or other work alterations occur subsequent to
contract award. This is an unrealistic circumstance, however, and can be
disregarded for the purposes of contract management except in rare cases
of fully defined and easily performed undertakings. Most contracts will
encounter some authorizations of work subsequent to the initial contract
award.

This equation is somewhat idealistic because it is intended to
express the state of a contract at all times. If a contractor is able to
fully meet the C/SCSC, work would never proceed that was not formally
authorized under the contract. With today's changing technologies,
however, it has been demonstrated many times that informally directed
work is almost invariably a part of large projects. When this occurs, the
effort is ultimately proposed to the government in the form of a change
request for which time and money adjustments may be needed. C/SCSC
is designed to help control that behavior.

As presented, the equation reflects the government's policy regarding the application of C/SCSC. A reasonable argument can be made that
two terms should be added to the equation: OR (overrun) and UW (unclassified work). These two terms reflect the reality that dynamic programs often involve work that is negotiable under the rules for contract
interpretation. The consequence is that contractors may perform work
which they view as additional but could be classified as work already
required by the contract without any change at all. If the work falls
into the already required category, it is authorized by the contract but
may reflect additions (overrun) to the total effort contemplated by the

---

[1]Firm-fixed-price contracts have no breakdown between cost and
profit stated in the contract. However, the supplier expects to spend a
particular amount to perform--the equivalent of target cost. Other
contract types break out cost from profit or fee.

contractor. The cost of an overrun is an addition to the required costs of performing the contract, even though an overrun is not considered a change for which additional profit or fee is paid. Work which a contractor agrees is an overrun is added to the target cost without adjustment of fee. However, a contractor may undertake work efforts believed to be over and above the contract requirement, while government representatives hold the position that the work is already required by the contract. Under these circumstances, the work is unclassified until a negotiation establishes the appropriate classification. If one were to accept this analysis of the objectives of C/SCSC, the equation would be written as:

$$\sum IB + MR = TC + E_{ann} + OR + UW$$

It should be noted that overrun could be negative (underrun). If this occurs, the OR term would have a minus value and would operate to reduce contract cost. Similarly, unclassified work could be negative and, therefore, would operate to reduce both contract cost and associated fee. These conditions are less likely to occur than upward adjustments.

C/SCSC and earned value terminology. Figure 9-5 depicts the overall concepts of earned value and the relationships of contract values when in compliance with C/SCSC. Earned value terms are useful in computations that generate quantitative indicators of contract status and projected completion. Several of the terms defined below can be observed in figure 9-5.

BAC - budget at completion. BAC should equal TC, target cost. It is the sum of all budgeted costs for scheduled work. BAC includes the budgets for all internal activities plus the management reserves (undistributed budget). At the outset, it is the contract budget base but may vary from the base because it changes only as a result of negotiations by which agreement on cost adjustments is reached.

Contract Budget Base - This quantity is the target cost negotiated for the contract plus the estimated cost of all work added but not negotiated into the target cost. The contract budget base is defined as: $TC + E_{ann}$.

ACWP - actual cost of work performed. This quantity is the actual total cost of performance as of the date of analysis. Work performed is defined as the total number of work packages completed as of that date.

BCWP - budgeted cost of work performed. This quantity reflects the earned value of work performed. It is the sum of the budgeted value of all work tasks completed as of the cutoff date.

BCWS - budgeted cost of work scheduled. This quantity reflects the cost of accomplishing the original planned effort as of the cut-off date of the report. It is the sum of the budgeted costs of scheduled work packages through that calendar date.

Cost Account - This term refers to a management control point at which actual costs can be accumulated and compared with budgeted costs. In the work breakdown structure, it is seen as an intersection with the functional organization structure. The cost account represents work assigned to a single organizational unit.

CAM - cost account manager, the individual within a performing organization who manages a cost account. This individual is accountable for schedule variances within the cost account and must generate any revisions of estimates. This manager is also the originator of the BCWS for the particular cost account and must determine the monthly budgeted

Figure 9-5, C/SCSC (example)

C/SCSC CUMULATIVE TIME COST PLOT

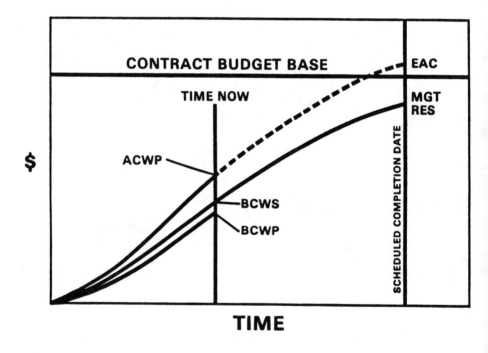

TIME

Depicts curves derived from earned value calculations when criteria mandated by C/SCSC are properly applied.

cost of work performed.

CPI - cost performance index. This term is an indicator of contract cost efficiency. As a ratio of budgeted cost of work performed divided by actual cost of work performed (BCWP/ACWP), it expresses the proportion of planned value received for dollars spent. If >1, it indicates that work has been achieved with less cost than budgeted (underrun). If <1, it indicates that an overrun condition exists as of the date of analysis.

Cost Variance - A cost variance compares budgeted cost of work performed with actual cost of work performed. It is expressed as a dollar amount derived by BCWP - ACWP or as a percentage derived by the formula BCWP - ACWP divided by BCWP. If negative, a cost variance indicates cost overrun; if positive, it indicates a cost underrun for the project as of the cutoff date.

EAC - estimate at completion. This quantity is an estimate of the final cost of scheduled work. It is derived by the formula EAC = BAC/CPI. This formulation permits an updated estimate of cost at completion, considering only the variation in actual performance reflected by the CPI. The EAC does not reflect a reestimate of the uncompleted portions of the job.

ETC - estimate to complete. This quantity is an estimate of the cost of remaining work. It is calculated by the formula ETC = BAC - BCWP/CPI. This value does not reflect a revised estimate for the work yet to be done.

LRE - latest revised estimate. This quantity is an estimate of the total cost of the planned project. It is a sum derived by reanalyzing and re-estimating the costs to complete (CTC) the project. It is the sum of CTC + ACWP, as of the date of analysis.

SPI - schedule performance index. This quantity gives an indication of schedule status. It is the ratio of budgeted cost of work performed to budgeted cost of work scheduled (BCWP/BCWS). If >1, it indicates that work is ahead of schedule. If <1, it indicates delay has occurred.

Schedule Variance - This quantity is a dollar value derived by the formula BCWP - BCWS. If negative, this value indicates a schedule slippage; if positive, it indicates the project is ahead of schedule. The schedule variance also is expressed as a percentage by the formula BCWP - BCWS/BCWS. A negative value indicates the amount of delay in proportion to the value of work undertaken through the date of analysis. In a similar manner, a positive value indicates the amount the work is ahead of schedule.

Criteria. The usefulness of the foregoing terms and formulas depends entirely on the accuracy and timeliness of the input values as generated by the contractor's management systems. The systems must be excellent, i.e., capable of reliably generating accurate, current data. Otherwise the indicators will be invalid. Under C/SCSC, high standards are set for accounting, schedule, performance, and other contractor management systems. The C/SCSC do not specify particular contractor systems for that purpose, but the criteria are demanding. Meeting the standards could require modification of those systems. One of the government post-award audit practices known as a C/SCSC demonstration audit has been used as the principal device for determining adequacy of the systems. The audit examines some 35 criteria that challenge the capabilities of any system. We will summarize them into five categories.

Organization. The criteria governing organizational qualities require the contractor to define the project in its entirety through the use of the work breakdown structure. The WBS must be interfaced with the contractor's organizational structure, so that identified levels of the WBS intersect clearly with organizational responsibility in the contractor's management structure. The organizational requirements of C/SCSC call for the work under the contract to be fully defined at the cost account and work package levels. The implication of these requirements is that managers must be responsible for the work to which they are committed. At the bottom of the work breakdown structure, the contractor is required to be able to generate work packages that, when totaled through the WBS, fully encompass the entire project. The work packages are to be made up primarily of discrete work packages, that is, ones to which a specific phase of work accomplishment can be assigned. There is provision in the criteria approach for the contractor to establish level-of-effort work packages which are not discrete in the sense of defining specific time-phased elements of work. Rather, they identify continuing work such as systems analysis. A level-of-effort task may not have any specific ending point other than the completion of the contract itself.

The organizational criteria require that responsibility for work be identified for in-house work packages, for subcontracted work, and for overhead supported by project funds. Responsibility is to be assigned to individuals. The contractor also must identify methods of allocating contract costs when costs cannot be directly charged to individual tasks.

Planning and budgeting. The second grouping of criteria applies to the contractor's approach to planning and budgeting. Under these criteria, management is expected to develop a description of each task to be staffed and managed. The description of the work should be derived from the contract specification, work statement, or both, and the analysis should result in the preparation of a work plan for the entire project. The criteria obligate the contractor to develop a schedule for all tasks that will complete the project in accordance with contract requirements. Systems should be capable of identifying all efforts and of defining performance goals for tasks and measurements of output. Planning and budgeting criteria call for the system to generate budgets for all work at the work package level. Furthermore, the budgeted work must be consistent with the description and work plan provided under this section. In addition to preparing budgets for direct costs of the work plan, the criteria call for overhead budgets related to the time required to perform the project. The contractor is obligated to identify any management reserves established as part of management's approach to the project. Also, the planning and budgeting system must be capable of reconciling revisions of contract work with original schedules and budgets, so that in all cases, the internal budgets and management reserves will equal target cost plus the estimated cost of authorized, non-negotiated work, if applicable. Coupled with this reconciling capability, the system should be able to provide traceability throughout the budget structure so that the elements of the original work breakdown structure can be identified with their respective budgets.

Accounting. Accounting is the third major sub-grouping of criteria. Under accounting criteria, the contractor must record his direct costs in a manner consistent with the budgets prepared under the planning and budgeting requirements. All records of direct costs must be subject to formal control under the general books of account. Direct and indirect costs must be recorded in a manner that permits reporting of unit or lot costs for all priced line items called for by the contract. Contractor systems should be capable of summarizing costs at the priced line item level of the WBS. The systems should enable reviewers to identify the bases upon which level-of-effort work packages are apportioned over the total effort under the contract. Finally, the system must be capable of audit so that all incurred cost records may be examined in the usual manner by government auditing staff.

Analysis. The fourth grouping of C/SCSC criteria deals with the capability of performing analyses of project results. The fundamental requirement is that the contractor's system must be designed to permit comparison of planned and actual costs. This requirement is specific in terms of the types of variances which must be generated. Specific required variances are cost and schedule. Expressed in both dollars and percentages, these variances are calculated in accordance with the formulas given earlier in the chapter. The criteria require the contractor's system to be capable of generating those variances at appropriate levels throughout the work breakdown structure. In addition to generating variances, the contractor's system must be able to further classify variances in accordance with the source of the problem. For example, variance may be caused by labor, material, overhead, or subcontract matters, and contractor systems should be able to identify these causes. The final dimension of the analysis capability is frequency. Under C/SCSC, the variance analyses should be generated monthly for both schedule and cost factors. Finally, having generated the variance analyses, the contractor's system should provide a means for identifying the management actions taken in response to the disclosed variances.

Revisions of work plans. The final group of criteria deals with the ability of the contractor's system to revise work plans on a controlled basis and without loss of historical records. Specifically, the contractor must have a method for estimating the effects of change orders and internal replanning actions on the overall contract program. This capability for estimating must be coupled with an ability to reconcile the original budgets (established at the inception of the contract) with the impacts of change orders and internal replanning actions. Furthermore, the system should be designed so that it prohibits retroactive changes to recorded costs except under carefully defined and traceable circumstances in which corrections of error are required. Through the use of management systems, the contractor must also be in a position to periodically prepare revised estimates of the cost at completion of the contract. Having prepared a revised estimate of cost at completion, the contractor should then have the capability of reconciling the estimated cost with the original performance measurement baseline, with the current operating budgets at the time of the revision, with the contract price as it may have been adjusted to the date of the revision, and with his financial reporting systems.

The C/SCSC imposes a comprehensive and detailed set of standards on a contractor's budgeting, accounting, estimating, and reporting systems. The comprehensive nature of the criteria and the detailed standards established for contractor systems have resulted in viewing the criteria as an expensive luxury. Few would argue that the standards are inappropriate or ineffective, considering the goals of improved identification and reporting of costs as well as improved capability for analysis. It is not clear to many practitioners, however, that the criteria are a cost effective set of standards for many contractual efforts. Some contractors believe that their management systems can cover all practical needs without qualifying under the criteria. Nevertheless, the establishment of the criteria by the DOD has unquestionably improved the overall quality of management systems of the larger defense contractors, and, presumably, it has enhanced the ability to manage the contracts more effectively.

One notation should be made at this point. The historical notes presented at the beginning of this chapter indicate the reasons for developing the C/SCSC approach to improved management systems. It was adopted simultaneously with the vast cost increases, schedule delays, and performance degradation that occurred during the 1960s. At that time, C/SCSC was one response to the cost growth and schedule delay problem. By the end of that decade, C/SCSC was well established as a management practice under DOD contracts. Nevertheless, major cost growth problems have persisted. It remains doubtful whether management systems can be relied on to overcome the independent pressures to increase program costs. Many pressures combine to limit achievements. They include, but are not limited to, technology advances and the tendency toward optimism by all levels of program advocates (including government agencies and managers as well as suppliers). The historical orientation of all participants toward delaying disclosure of problems associated with contract performance seems likely to result in continued growth problems.

SUMMARY

Managers have an insatiable need for current information that predicts or indicates future results. This chapter examines this need, the special problems involved, and techniques necessary to meet the need when work is under contract. The measurement and reporting of contract progress encounter some resistance because the parties have concern for their prerogatives as independent entities as well as for the information needs of the interested management groups. Factors that explain this behavior and the techniques intended to meet the needs of each party are summarized as follows:

- A set of eight factors are proposed which influence the level of information that may properly be generated in support of management analysis and decisionmaking.
- The principal objective of buyers when demanding status information is delineated.
- Factors impacting the level of information collection to be required for specific contracts have been identified.
- Three levels of buyer involvement in supplier systems are described.
- Reasons for the growing interest in supplier systems by government buyers are summarized.
- Differences in management systems requirements are found to be associated with four types of projects.
- Three presentation formats and three advanced techniques for progress monitoring are summarized.
- The features of Cost/Schedule Control Systems Criteria (C/SCSC) that make it attractive to government contract managers are summarized, including the earned value computations which the criteria facilitate.
- A sketch of the criteria for effective management systems as generated for C/SCSC demonstrations is offered.

TOPICS FOR DISCUSSION

1. Explain the manager's interest in an objective trade off-between complete information reporting and reliance on informal systems.
2. Summarize the difference between an imposed management system and the criteria approach to obtaining adequate information.
3. For what reasons would lack of firm pricing generate greater interest in a contractor's internal management systems?

4. Compare production contracts and research and development contracts in terms of the difficulties associated with management planning and control.
5. Explain the principal uses of line of balance in measuring progress.
6. Discuss and justify the terms in this equation:

$$\sum IB + MR = TC + E_{ann} + OR + UW$$

7. Discuss the computation and the validity of cost variances under the earned value concept.
8. Summarize the characteristics of each of the five categories of criteria under C/SCSC (organization, accounting, planning and budgeting, analysis, and work plan revision).

10

Product Inspection, Acceptance, and Contract Quality Assurance

CHANGING PERCEPTIONS OF QUALITY VERIFICATION RESPONSIBILITIES

Inspection prior to acceptance and acceptance are often viewed as the proper way to fulfill contract obligations. These procedures remain important, but their implementation has been modified by the concept of contract quality assurance (CQA), formerly called procurement quality assurance. This has been true especially for government contracts in which CQA is the principal tool by which purchasers ensure that delivered products conform with contract requirements. Under CQA, inspection and product verification are no longer performed primarily by purchasers but by the producer. The purchaser is concerned principally with verifying that the producer has assumed responsibility for creating an adequate inspection or quality assurance system for the product being purchased.

The traditional approach to purchasing assumed that a manufacturer was responsible for producing the product, and the purchaser was responsible for making certain that the product conform with the contract. But this approach does not work for the complex products that dominate much of today's marketplace. Complex products cannot be inspected after completion in a way that verifies that the product meets all standards of quality imposed by the contract. Internal or otherwise hidden characteristics, including the fabrication or formulation steps performed at the supplier or subcontractor level, require verification during manufacture.

Under a CQA system, inspections, tests, in-process controls, and other system features are tailored to meet the needs of each specific production requirement. With the growth of external sourcing systems, buyers for both government and industry are concerned with setting systems standards that enable acceptance of the supplier's product without subjecting it to additional inspection and test procedures. The major issue in quality assurance is how to obtain and verify the reliability of supplier systems. The CQA concept was documented as policy by the DOD in 1954. Many refinements have been introduced since that time, but today the basic presumption is that the producer is responsible for quality assurance. Chart 10-1 summarizes the philosophy that stands behind the CQA approach. An axiom underlies the assertions of chart 10-1: you can't inspect quality into a product. If this is correct, purchasers need a better approach other than to conduct post-production inspections. The philosophy expressed in chart 10-1 demands an approach for accomplishing CQA by buyer personnel through surveillance over the supplier's quality control system, including the supplier's inspection and testing procedures. This surveillance seeks reassurance that the supplier is maintaining effective controls to support contractual commitments. Although the level of surveillance activity will vary with the buyer's assessment of the supplier's control systems, some minimum level of surveillance is necessary in all cases. Surveillance is effective only when buyers have taken specific actions to ensure product quality--by fully informing suppliers of expectations for product design and performance and by stating minimum requirements for substantiating product attributes.

The effectiveness of the CQA method of oversight depends upon the buyer having clearly defined and communicated his quality expectations to his suppliers. This must be done in writing and is normally part of the contractual agreement. There are two important components used to express requirements for contract end items. The first is the description of the product using detailed design, performance, or functional specifications (section 3 of government specifications). The second is the quality assurance requirement (specification section 4) which describes specific qualification procedures (inspections, tests and examinations) to be applied to the product. Product specifications, however, are not sufficient except for the simplest procurement. Higher level government CQA is imposed through application of an inspection system or quality assurance system specification. The combination of product and CQA system specifications provides an environment in which quality should be produced.

The Federal Acquisition Regulation contains sixteen separate clauses (plus several alternate additional provisions) dealing with inspection and acceptance. The internal details of the clauses vary to reflect different kinds of contracts, such as fixed-price and cost-reimbursement, and different kinds of contract objectives, for example, providing facilities or purchasing supplies, services, research and development, or construction. The formulation of these approaches is based on the assumption and policy that manufacturers are responsible for creating and maintaining

Chart 10-1

Philosophy of A Contract Quality Assurance System

- Quality is a result of the total system in place, including planning, organizing, staffing, and independent direction of the producer's quality assurance subsystem.

- Completed product inspection cannot verify the quality of complex products.

- Product quality is ensured only when the manufacturing processes are under control.

- Control of a manufacturing process occurs only when verifiable measurement standards are consistently applied and results are recorded.

- In-process inspection and testing, together with statistical estimation, provides verifiable measurement standards.

- Manufacturing control depends on measuring and verifying incoming and in-process material, equipment calibration, cleanliness, technical data, records system, capabilities, and presence of personnel.

- Consistent performance of all quality functions can be achieved by the producer and by no one else.

- Buyers can verify that a manufacturing process is under control if the producer's system generates objective evidence that can be obtained by the buyer through consistent, random, unfiltered observation, plus review of quality records.

- A system that delivers 100 percent conforming quality is possible and is the least costly system.

those controls necessary to ensure that products conform with specifications. From the government's point of view, however, it is essential to
create proof in the form of objective evidence that products offered for
acceptance have been fabricated properly and tested by the manufacturer.
This approach is based on the recognition that many product characteristics cannot be measured and assessed after they have been completed.

GOVERNMENT IMPLEMENTATION OF QUALITY CONCEPTS

The DOD has taken the lead in establishing the policy that the
contractor is responsible for inspection of end products and, more broadly, for verifying and assuring their quality prior to offering them for
delivery. A key part of the government's approach was to develop four
levels of inspection or quality assurance systems for its contractors.
These levels are

1. contractor responsibility for adequate inspection,
2. a standard inspection system (defined by the contractor and acceptable to the government),
3. an inspection system specified by the government (MIL-I-45208A),
   and
4. a quality assurance system specified by the government
   (MIL-Q-9858A).

Contractor responsibility level of inspection means that the government will rely on the contractor to conduct all inspections and to
deliver only conforming items to the government. Under this concept,
however, the government does not set any standard for the level of inspection or the quality of the contractor's inspection system. Basically,
it relies on inspection as the contractor has set it up. This level of
reliance clearly implies that items may be accepted without having been
inspected by the government. The use of this form of reliance depends
on the likelihood that replacing or correcting defective items will occur
without a contest when nonconforming items are delivered. Used primarily for small purchases, the advantage of this level of reliance is
reducing the government's cost of inspecting large quantities of supplies
and services purchased in the small purchases category. This reliance is
based on the judgment that potential losses associated with defects are
insignificant relative to the cost of a higher level inspection requirement.

At the standard inspection level of requirement, the government
does not impose any specific inspection system specification on the contractor; instead, it requires the contractor's inspection system to be
satisfactory to the government. Under this approach, the contractor must
provide and maintain an inspection system that may be reviewed during

pre- or post-award survey processes. The contract clauses covering this level of inspection give the government the right to make any inspections and tests that it feels are necessary during the production phase. This standard inspection requirement also specifies that a contractor must keep complete and accurate inspection records and make them available to the government.

The two top levels of CQA in government practice employ a government system specification. These levels were defined by two DOD specifications issued in 1963 (both were derived from documents developed during the 1950s). They are MIL-I-45208A (which imposes an inspection system requirement) and MIL-Q-9858A (which imposes a quality assurance system requirement). These specifications remain in effect as of this writing. Although substantial challenges and reviews of inspection and quality systems have been made periodically since 1963, the basic concepts set forth in these specifications have remained intact.

Chart 10-2 provides a comparison of these higher level CQA systems concepts. Identified as quality assurance and inspection, the systems are demanding and should not be approached lightly. The MIL-I-45208A inspection system is designed for application to contracts for supplies and services that can be effectively controlled through examination and testing operations. If such operations are properly carried out, an acceptable quality level should be achieved for the products to which the specification has been applied. Where MIL-I-45208A is cited, the specification covering the product will ordinarily contain a complete and detailed set of required examinations and tests. This is not necessarily the case when MIL-Q-9858A, the quality program requirements specification, is applied. This document is usually associated with specifications for equipment that is complex and considered critical to either safety or mission. The MIL-Q-9858A requirements extend substantially beyond those for inspections and tests, extending the application of quality assurance throughout all aspects of contract performance. MIL-Q-9858A specifies that a contractor's control over his processes must be an integral part of his overall inspection system. The MIL-Q-9858A requirements cover the matters identified in chart 10-2. The key to the quality program specification is probably the word *control;* all processing and fabrication work is to be accomplished under controlled conditions. All issues associated with the quality assurance program--including planning, development of instructions, calibrations, material control, sampling, generation of records, disposition of nonconforming material, coordination of customer and source of supply inspection, in-process inspections, handling of material, storage, preservation and packaging of items, and shipping processes--are to be conducted under controlled conditions that have been described and specified by the contractor's quality assurance organization.

Although the basic requirements of MIL-Q-9858A and MIL-I-45208A are important, they do not stand alone with respect to government

Chart 10-2

Comparison of Quality Assurance and Inspection Systems[1]

Quality Assurance Under MIL-Q-9858A	Contractor Production System	Inspection System Under MIL-I-45208A
Documented quality plan, organization, & system		Documented inspection system
	Contract award	
Specification analyses; QA program instructions		
	Production engineering	
Quality planning & update: contract inspection & test		
	Production planning	
Mfg.; test equip. and tooling calibration		Mfg.; test equip. and tooling calibration
	Inventory review	
Quality review: suppliers' material control systems		
	Process development	
Select, apply statistical quality control & sampling		
	Production control	
Processes insp.; generate, control QC records		Processes insp.; generate, control QC records
	Production release	
Capture and control nonconforming material		Capture and control nonconforming material
	Fabrication processess	
Coordinate source insp. and customer oversight		
	Mechanical assembly	
In-process inspection & test; configuration mgt.		In-process inspection & test; configuration mgt.
	Electrical assembly	
Controlled handling; storage preservation; pkg.		
	Delivery	
Finished goods insp.& test		Finished goods insp. & test
	Acceptance	

---

[1]Mil-Q-9858A and Mil-I-45208A are used here to illustrate the two levels of systems requirements. Other documents that accomplish similar levels of requirements are NHB 5300.4(1B), NHB 5300.4(1C), FED-STD-368, and ANSI/ASME NQA-1.

quality assurance documentation. There are many other quality documents; one of the most important is MIL-STD-45662A, Calibration System Requirements. This specification requires a contractor to establish and maintain a defined calibration program for inspection and test equipment. Beyond that, there are numerous handbooks and standards pertinent to quality assurance management. One listing issued by the Navy contains fifty-one separate documents covering the details of quality pertinent to various commands and types of acquisition programs. None of these documents are specific product specifications; they deal with overall quality assurance or quality control requirements. If no other conclusion can be drawn from this extensive listing, it indicates deep concern with the challenge of securing acceptable quality levels from suppliers.

Many government procurement actions are based on some form of product specification. Under standard specification practices, these specifications contain section 4 that specifies standards for acceptance. It includes a responsibility for inspection statement which is similar to the one that follows:

> Unless otherwise specified in the contract or purchase order, the supplier is responsible for the performance of all inspection or test requirements as specified herein. Except as otherwise specified, the supplier may use his own facilities or any commercial laboratory acceptable to the government. The government reserves the right to perform any of the inspection and testing set forth in the specification where deemed necessary to ensure that supplies and services conform to the prescribed requirements.

The balance of section 4 contains detailed statements of specific inspection, testing, and sampling that must be performed for the particular product covered by the specification. These activities call for the contractor to demonstrate that the requirements in section 3 (which describes the product) have been met. The concept of quality assurance, however, does not limit a contractor's inspection, testing, and sampling to the items set forth in section 4. Instead, contractors are expected to carry out any additional inspections necessary for control. It is expected that compliance with section 4 will result in compliance with required quality levels. Some measurable risk may remain, but through the sampling criteria for the product, that risk can be controlled by the government. In any event, under the contractor responsibility concept, only conforming products may be offered for acceptance. This concept replaced the government's previous practice of conducting section 4 examinations. Because the product specification and the inspection system or quality program requirement are harnessed together, the government expects contractors to impose upon themselves product and process controls appropriate to the particular contract.

CRITERIA FOR APPLICATION OF
INSPECTION, QA SYSTEM LEVELS

One tool adopted by government agencies for selecting the applicable level of quality assurance is a scheme of classification. Under the FAR Subpart 46.2, end items are defined so that there are (1) categories of technical description (off-the-shelf items, commercial items, and military-federal items); (2) levels of complexity based on the nature of the end item (complex and non-complex); and (3) levels of criticality based on use of the end item (critical or noncritical). Selection of the level of inspection or quality assurance is based on these classifications. This tool is summarized here in terms of the level of contractor responsibility, standard inspection level, and higher level (which includes both systems specifications as discussed earlier in the chapter).

Two terms used in this scheme need defining. Complex items are those having quality characteristics which are not visible or discernable after completion; verification must be accomplished during the manufacturing process. Critical items are those which, if they fail in use, could jeopardize personnel or mission.

Application of the scheme can be confusing. For example, many commercial or military-federal items are built to order, but off-the-shelf items can be in either category. Critical and noncritical uses are further classified as common or peculiar. (A peculiar item is purchased only for a single application.) The contractor responsibility level (of inspection) does not apply to any critical item or any military-federal item, and neither of the higher level systems specifications applies to any off-the-shelf items. The level of inspection varies primarily with complexity, criticality, and whether the item is common or peculiar.

The idea behind this complicated system of classification is to simplify the selection of pertinent contract clauses and ensure that the level of quality assurance action prior to acceptance is consistent with (1) feasible methods that verify product conformity with the contract, and (2) risks associated with use of the products bought.

In general, the contractor responsibility level of inspection is pertinent to small purchase orders of noncritical, common-use items generally supplied off-the-shelf. While off-the-shelf items may be complex as well as non-complex, the inspection level normally remains with the contractor unless use of the item is critical. This level is also applied to the procurement of most commercial items. However, commercial items for use in critical and noncritical peculiar applications are subjected to the standard inspection level; those that are both complex and critical in application are subjected to the higher level systems requirement. Most military-federal end products are subjected to the standard inspection level, but critical items and mission-peculiar items are subjected to higher level systems requirements.

AN ALTERNATIVE VIEW OF CONTRACT QUALITY ASSURANCE

The discussion just concluded of the government-wide approach to quality assurance assumes continuation of the current reliance on contractors to perform and assume responsibility for quality assurance. This approach is based on the CQA philosophy and while unlikely to be abandoned, may need modification in light of the substantial reconsideration of quality concepts that has occurred in the United States since 1980. CQA is based on the presumption that someone already has defined a satisfactory level of quality. It is important to suggest an alternative, that is, to introduce the idea of *quality improvement*--improvement to a level without defects. The objective of a quality improvement program is to eliminate defects. Many tools of quality improvement are identical to those of CQA, but the philosophy is different. Quality improvement tells us we must continuously improve the production process and operate it to produce quality without rework. Quality improvement is also based on the concept that quality determines the level of productivity achievable by the manufacturing process. Therefore, it can be argued that a quality improvement program can be a cost-free program because eliminating rework expense and lost productivity fully compensate for the extra effort applied in designing and operating the process. Furthermore, a quality improvement program assumes that the work force can be trained and motivated to reduce carelessness. The quality improvement concept rejects the procurement of materials and incoming parts on the basis of price. It replaces the objective of obtaining the lowest price with one of defect-free quality at a price that reflects the cost of doing the job right the first time. This kind of an altered purchasing practice requires the development of a new relationship with suppliers.

The manufacturer under a quality improvement program will develop a long-term close working relationship with suppliers which includes a knowledge of a supplier's internal working capabilities and problems. Such a program requires sharing the purchaser's planning information, volume expectations, and upcoming changes in direction. It requires the purchaser to treat vendors as partners in fulfilling the needs of the purchaser's customers. A major aspect of a quality improvement program is recognizing that the supplier, contract managers, and purchaser are a team with a common objective of providing, without exception, a totally acceptable end product to the ultimate customer.

Nothing in the foregoing statement of a quality improvement program alters or reduces the need for the techniques of a quality assurance program. Expert application of statistical measurement, careful analysis of inspection needs, developing accurate and protected record systems, and maintaining control over all production process are vital elements of a quality improvement program. However, the philosophical change under quality improvement is significant--improvement does not cease short of defect-free operations. This affects both buyer and seller, requiring clear delineation of responsibilities. It emphasizes the common objectives of both and mandates close working relationships throughout the production program. It requires a modified basis for competition among suppliers such that quality achievements are recognized and operate to restrict competitive turnover of work to new suppliers in situations where substantial economic advantage without quality degradation is assured. Although this approach is being adopted by industry as part of the just-in-time revolution, its viability for public procurement is questionable because it would restrict contract-by-contract competition as currently mandated by public policy.

QUALITY ASSURANCE PRACTICES

While the philosophical approach to assuring quality is important, we should now look at the operating practices of the quality assurance function as it exists in the offices of the Defense Contract Administrative Services. The DCAS quality assurance offices are responsible for assessing contractor compliance with contract quality assurance requirements. They accomplish this through a basic program comprised of six major elements:

1. Planning for contract review
2. Review of contractor written procedures
3. Evaluation of contractor compliance with the company's written procedures
4. Product verification inspection on a sampling basis
5. Imposition of corrective actions
6. Overall evaluation of accumulated quality data

These steps reflect the overall philosophy of quality assurance indicated in chart 10-1 and embraced by the CQA policy. The intent of the first step, planning for contract review, is to ensure that planning is focused on the quality needs of the contractual effort at its beginning. This step assures that all factors relevant to the contractor's quality program and specific contract requirements will be considered in implementing the subsequent steps in the overall quality review. During this planning phase, the quality assurance representative (QAR) examines the specific requirements imposed by the contract and becomes familiar with the contractor's overall planning approach and systems design, as well as any quality intelligence furnished by the contracting activity. The QAR then makes an initial assessment of manpower requirements imposed by these factors and assesses the implications imposed by the type of contract used for the particular project. All of these elements contribute to helping the QAR decide the methods and extent of quality assurance activity acceptable for application to the new contract.

The initial planning effort leads the QAR to examine thoroughly the contractor's written quality assurance procedures which are critical to further effort in the quality area. Through the review of written procedures, the QAR becomes thoroughly knowledgeable of the contractor's intended mode of operation and receives an initial indication of the compatibility of the contractor's system with the specific requirements of the new contract award. The QAR is then in a position to report to the contractor his initial conclusions regarding the adequacy of the contractor's approach. Possible gaps in this system can develop. An example of this is the situation arising when a new contractor is acquired who has developed quality procedures independently, but who now has an award of a government contract that contains either the MIL-Q-9858A or the MIL-I-45208A systems specifications. Under these conditions, it is likely that gaps between the requirements and the contractor's system will be discovered.

Once a QAR is thoroughly familiar with the stated and required quality program, his attention is directed toward an evaluation of the actual practices encountered within the contractor's organization. The basic approach taken for this phase of the quality program is on-site observation and assessment of the contractor's actual compliance with his own procedures, the point being that stated procedures are of no value if they are not followed by the contractor's organization performing the work.

In the fourth major phase of the QAR's work, he or she selects specific products or steps in the manufacturing process for personal inspection, testing, or observation. This product verification inspection is conducted for a double purpose. The most important aspect is the opportunity to assess the effectiveness of the contractor's inspection and testing efforts. The second reason is to determine the acceptability of particular items being produced. In general, this phase of the QAR program is designed to permit the QAR to gain confidence in the effectiveness of the contractor's system. This provides the QAR with a strong indication of how much reliance to place on the contractor's tender of end products for acceptance, and what level of verification checks is needed prior to signing acceptance documents. The product verification inspections can be based on standard statistical sampling techniques or on special verification plans appropriate to the particular product and acceptable to the government.

Product verification, inspection, and testing processes provide the QAR with insight into any areas in which the contractor's system has broken down or proven inadequate. Whenever weaknesses are discovered, corrective action is indicated. At that point, it is the QAR's responsibility to take action to ensure that no compromise of product quality flows through to acceptance of products. Action indicated by the product verification process starts with advice to the contractor respecting any inadequacies, including requests to modify the system and to extract nonconforming material from the production process. Depending on the severity of quality deficiencies and the frequency or likelihood of their recurrence, corrective action, not only for the defect but also for the cause of the defect, is indicated. The objective of the QAR during this phase is to obtain the contractor's cooperation in correcting the deficiency. In the absence of effective action to correct deficiencies, this phase may lead to a recommendation by the contracting officer for contractual action, including possible contract termination.

The last of the six elements of the QAR program is an overall review of the accumulated QAR records for the purpose of reaching conclusions regarding the contractor's quality program. The QAR performs this quality data evaluation periodically based on (1) information collected from his or her observations over a period of time, (2) information and data provided by the customer or user of end items which are produced by the contractor, and (3) data gathered from the contractor concerning the contractor quality program. This evaluation process provides the basis for major reviews with the contractor concerning future operations and is a factor in developing pre-award surveys and other reports that may be significant to future government-contractor relationships.

This approach to a contractor's quality assurance program is aimed at verifying the system, rather than the individual product of the contractor. While the product verification element of the overall program provides direct insight regarding the quality of individual products, its broader objective is to build confidence in the ability of the system to create conforming products. This general approach carries out the philosophy of contractor responsibility by leaving most physical inspection and testing processes and the operation of the overall quality system in the hands of the contractor. On this basis, if a contractor's system is verified as functioning properly, acceptability of end products is ensured.

QUALITY SURVEILLANCE - ADMINISTRATIVE ISSUES

A recent study conducted by Michael F. Vezeau[1] examines a number of historical problems and issues associated with the performance of quality responsibilities by DCAS. Mr. Vezeau designed a survey of

---

[1]Vezeau, Michael, "Issues and Problems Impacting the Performance of Government Contract Administration Quality Assurance Functions," April 22, 1985. Unpublished research report prepared while a student at George Washington University.

experienced DCAS personnel in which he posed for their evaluation a number of specific topics thought to represent problems or issues facing quality assurance managers. Mr. Vezeau asked these managers to evaluate the list of issues by ranking them on a scale of 1 to 10, with the most significant issue or problem being ranked number 1. The respondents were also given an opportunity to identify other issues not on the suggested list and rank them with respect to their significance. On the basis of this survey, the issues identified by the seventy respondents as having the most significant impact on the conduct of the quality assurance function were, in the order of most to least important, as follows:

1. Recruiting individuals possessing skills to do the job
2. Manpower resources
3. Obtaining or providing technical training
4. Prime contractor control of subcontractors
5. Awards made by contracting officers to poor producers
6. Administrative procedures
7. Government quality assurance policies or procedures
8. Compensation for doing the job
9. Operational supervisors' span of control
10. Technical complexity of supplies being purchased

Mr. Vezeau's study included a cross section of persons within the DCAS organization. All were experienced and deeply involved within the system, and conclusions drawn from his study must be evaluated in that light.

It seems appropriate at this point to comment on the first five ranked issues identified in the survey. The foremost conclusion indicated is that personnel qualifications are the first concern of practitioners and are perceived as barriers or problems they must overcome to perform their work. This problem is associated with changing technology and changing product requirements that adversely impact the organization's ability to recruit and train a work force that is fully competent to evaluate the quality of products. Thirty-two percent of respondents ranked this issue number 1 of the entire set.

Since the personnel qualification issue results from increasing specialization and complexity of commodities being procured in our economy, the QAR should have expertise in the technology of supplier companies. In addition, he or she should be knowledgeable of key management functions such as materials, accounting, configuration, and other areas that influence the quality program. It is difficult to find this combination of skills in individuals and, according to the study, especially difficult in the QA field. Government pay scales and personnel practices may not be helpful in this competitive environment.

The second ranked issue, manpower resources, has been an area of complaint for many years. In fact, it is an area in which all managers in virtually every field have regular complaints. This may be a legitimate issue in quality assurance organizations of the government. Unfortunately, it is an issue requiring the exercise of judgment and one in which the problems could be associated with distributing resources rather than the overall availability of resources for carrying out the mission.

The third ranked issue, obtaining and providing technical training, is a direct corollary to issue number 1. Recognizing that it is difficult to hire fully qualified individuals, a manager may rely on training to bring new employees up to the level of job requirements. Nevertheless, substantial barriers intervene in carrying out this process. One major facet is the need to keep personnel on the job, particularly if there is a shortage of personnel. Therefore, even if a training program is available which could enhance an individual's knowledge and capabilities, it may not be feasible to train that person. As in recruitment, training needs are heightened by advances in and specialization of technology. Updating in fields such as electronics, optics, ceramics, and computer software is needed even for experienced and qualified existing staff.

The fourth ranked issue is an organizational and policy matter which may be susceptible to administrative correction. Over time, government QARs have assumed a substantial measure of responsibility for quality assurance work at subcontractors' plants. This assumption of responsibility increases the overall level of QA activity conducted by the government and creates confusion with respect to the responsibility for problems of a quality nature which may arise between the prime and the subcontractor. Although difficult to accomplish, an administrative change is feasible whereby the government turns over to its prime contractors more responsibility for managing and controlling subcontractor quality. This is, of course, already a matter of subcontractor policy on the part of the government. The issue surfaces because prime contractors find it expensive and perhaps foreign to their normal operation to set up a field work force for assuring quality within their subcontractors' plants. Since government QARs may already be present at the plants, reliance on that capability is fostered. One respondent to the survey indicated that his office had assigned twenty-two quality assurance personnel to a subcontractor's plant. In light of government subcontracting policy in which the government denies privity of contract with subcontractors and in which the government scrupulously avoids permitting subcontractors direct access to government contracting officers, it seems inconsistent that a method cannot be found to enable or require prime contractors to be fully responsible for the quality of subcontracted work. This would also relieve manpower for essential work at prime contractor plants.

The fifth issue raised in response to the survey identifies a long-standing weakness in government procurement practice--the government's inability to consider past performance information in selecting the source of supply for future procurement. A poor quality record is not well enough documented or recognized to be a relevant factor in the source selection process.

A better understanding of this subject, use of past performance information, can be gained by comparing government with industry. The industrial purchasing manager can easily make a judgment that he will no longer deal with a supplier who has delivered poor quality--and particularly one who does so repeatedly. In a comparable situation, the government contracting officer cannot freely take such action. This is a function of the government's perception that it must deal with all of its constituents, including those who are a part of companies with which it contracts, on an objective and equally fair basis. The effort to pursue this equitable and objective sourcing practice renders government procuring officers unable to act on judgments regarding performance unless voluminous, incontrovertible, objective evidence clearly indicates that the subjective decision is correct. Government bid protest procedures enforce this scrupulous behavior in the procurement process. The QAR's perception of the consequences of this "straight jacket" is clear. The QAR is forced to deal repetitively with contractors whose quality systems are not up to par, and they have relatively little leverage in the form of denial of future business in influencing such contractors to correct their internal management problems. While it is evident that quality should be considered before price in all procurement actions, it is undeniable that quality data tends to be of a subjective, non-quantitative nature, whereas price is quantitative and is immediately discernable as a basis for decisions. This issue should be recognized for what it is: the government is unable to rely upon the judgment of its working level personnel. While this may be a political reality, its consequence is reduced effectiveness in procurement and quality matters. Top levels of management and oversight functions in government seek objective, not judgmental, bases for decisions.

ORGANIZING TO OBTAIN QUALITY COMPLIANCE

The structure of government quality assurance organization was altered in 1964 as a result of the "project 60" review of defense contract administration activities. This review was conducted under the direction of then Secretary of Defense Robert McNamara. One result of that effort was the formation of the Defense Logistics Agency (DLA), known at the time as the Defense Supply Agency, and within that agency the establishment of the Defense Contract Administration Services. This new organization drew together much of the pre-existing contract administration capabilities of the Army, Navy, and Air Force. The responsibilities of DCAS included the quality assurance function. Although the consolidation reflected in the 1964 action was aimed at providing "one face to industry," it did not bring together into one organization all contract administration or quality assurance capabilities of the government. Each of the military services and some other agencies still retain important contract administration capabilities. Regardless of which agency is the parent organization, contract quality assurance is a major part of the duties of every contract administration activity.

DCAS was originally structured within the Defense Logistics Agency as an identifiable organizational entity. This has changed. At the present headquarters level, the contract administration services function of the agency is integrated into the overall DLA structure. Nevertheless, at the level of its field contract administration offices, the contract administration services operate as identifiable entities, and within each of them, the quality assurance function is organized in a manner that appears to give it equal rank with the combination of all other contract administration functions. (As a group, the other functions are organized under the heading of contract management.) Both contract management and quality assurance are headed by executive directors within the Defense Logistics Agency. Each is a directorate within the DCAS regional offices. This standing of the quality assurance function is carried out at the level of the Defense Contract Administration Services Management Areas (DCASMA) and the Defense Contract Administration Services Plant Representative Offices (DCASPRO). The overall organization of contract administration services has been discussed in chapter 6. Charts 10-3 and 10-4 give additional insight into the organization of quality assurance as a major directorate within contract administration. At each level within the DLA structure, total responsibility for quality assurance is assigned to the chief of that functional group. The charts provide insight into the overall structure at the three levels.

The DLA headquarters organization is shown in chart 10-3. At the DLA level, the programs and systems management division holds responsibility for developing quality assurance policies and procedures and for identifying programs to be used by people in the field. Technical issues and matters specific to individual commodities are the principal responsibilities of the engineering and technical management division. The DLA QA management support office is responsible for developing the agency's work force. This office conducts the quality assurance intern program and attempts to ensure that highly qualified people enter the field. The product quality assessment office is responsible for analyzing and responding when major issues and high visibility or complex quality assurance challenges arise in connection with the overall operations of the function. The other two DLA offices reporting to the executive director are responsible for matters concerning the special commodities identified by their titles, such as clothing and textiles, flight operations, and flight safety. Chart 10-4 identifies the field organization for DLA's

Chart 10-3

Defense Logistics Agency
(Partial Structure - Acquisition Management)

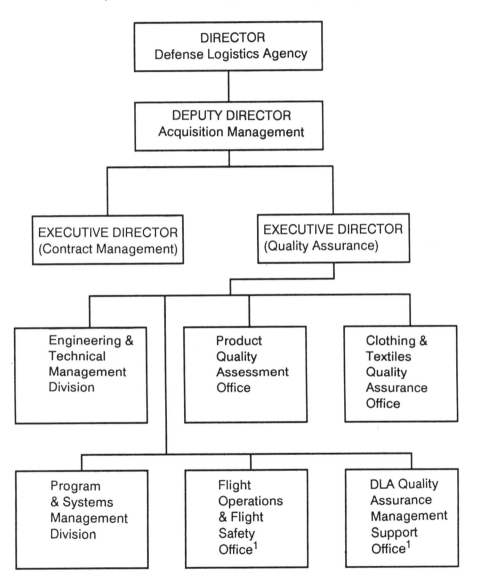

[1]Located in Atlanta, Georgia

Chart 10-4

**Defense Logistics Agency
(Partial Structure - Regional
Quality Assurance Organization)**

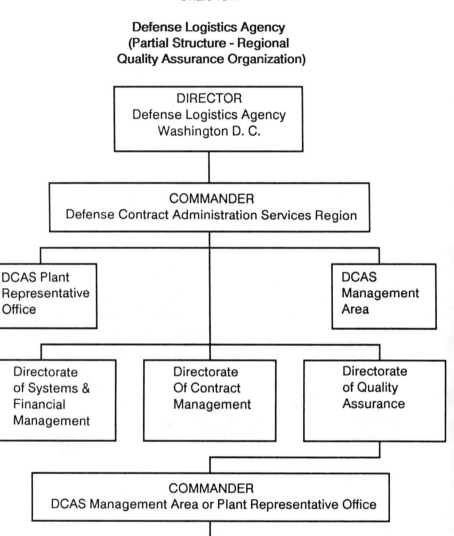

contract administration services. The chart is generic and provides a representation of the organizations at both regional and management (including plant representative) levels of the service. There are nine Defense Contract Administration Services Regions (DCASR) located in major cities of the United States--Atlanta, Boston, Chicago, Cleveland, Dallas, Los Angeles, New York, Philadelphia, and St. Louis. Within each of these regional offices, the director of quality assurance operates as the regional commander's principal advisor on quality assurance subjects. He or she also provides management and technical direction to the quality assurance personnel within the DCASR and has technical oversight at the subordinate command levels of DCASMA and DCASPRO.

The primary level at which direct contact between DCAS and suppliers occurs is found in the Defense Contract Administration Services Management Areas and the Defense Contract Administration Services Plant Representative Offices. The QA portion of those offices is depicted in figure 10-4. The offices are directed by a chief of the quality assurance division. Two types of branches exist within the division. The first type, the operations branch, employs the quality assurance representatives (QARs). The number of operations branches and QAR personnel in these offices depends on the particular region in which the office is established and the number of contractors and dispersion of the work. Quality assurance representatives carry out the procedures and practices established for them by the DCAS organizations. It is their responsibility to ensure that contractors comply with contract requirements. The plant representative offices are established at large contractor organizations where a substantial amount of quality assurance work is necessary. The management area offices are staffed with QARs who, in many cases, are assigned to major contractor plants as resident QARs. The resident QAR is responsible for surveillance of quality assurance at the particular plant. The DCASMAs employ many QARs referred to as nonresident QARs. Individuals in this group have responsibilities with respect to numerous contractor organizations and often have special expertise in particular commodities or specialty areas. They carry out their work by visiting contractor plants that have been assigned work responsibilities.

The operations support branch of local offices is staffed to provide specialized technical guidance or expertise as needed to support the quality assurance operations under the direction of the operations branches.

INSPECTION AND ACCEPTANCE OF END ITEMS

Having examined the philosophy of quality assurance as well as some of the organizational concepts and issues associated with it, we need to look at the specific government policies for controlling the acceptance of

end items. This longstanding historic policy has been to accept contract
end items after inspection conducted by or for the government. This
policy has been strongly and clearly stated in most of the government's
inspection and acceptance clauses and has been put into effect by the
following words: "Acceptance shall be conclusive, except for latent
defects, fraud, gross mistakes amounting to fraud, or as otherwise specified in the contract."

This language has the effect of cutting off implied warranties of
merchantability and fitness for use which the courts would otherwise
impose in evaluating the burdens imposed by patent defects discovered
subsequent to acceptance. Nevertheless, depending on the nature of the
items, the benefits of these warranties, if normally extended to commercial customers, may be conveyed to the government. Additionally, the
language may be expressly overcome if a specific warranty clause is
included in the contract. This has not been the normal practice for most
government contracts.

APPLICATION AND USEFULNESS OF WARRANTIES

Controversy over the subject of warranties in government contracts
has been increasing during the 1980s. Most conflicts are associated with
warranties on major items procured by the government such as weapons
systems. Similarly, the overall concept of product liability for U.S.
manufacturers has evolved over the last twenty years, increasing the
expectation that manufacturers will assume responsibility for product
deficiencies even in the absence of specific product warranties. Some
expansion seems to have occurred in the concept of a supplier's responsibility for his product under the implied warranties of merchantability
and fitness for use. It has already been noted that these warranties on
government purchases generally have been cut off by the operation of
government contract clauses. Consequently, and regardless of the historic
position of the government regarding these matters, Congress has acted
to change government warranty policy by enacting Public Law 98-525, the
Department of Defense Authorization Act of 1985. Congress specified
that prime contractors who provide weapons systems to the DOD must
issue written guarantees that the end item will conform to the design and
manufacturing requirements stated in the production contract, will be free
from defects in material and workmanship, and will conform to the essential performance requirements as specifically delineated in the production
contract. Although these requirements are applied to major systems
acquisitions, the philosophy of extending the government's requirements
for warranties has had a marked impact on the government-contractor
relationship. Chart 10-5 identifies several factors which indicate that the
imposition of government warranties may not be cost effective.

Chart 10-5

Background Factors Affecting the Use of
Special Warranties

- Warranties require additional costs associated with the warranty service that will be required. Prices of end products must reflect (1) the actual service of warranties and (2) the cost of risks that are difficult to define and may be of an insurable nature.

- The historical alternative to obtaining special warranties has been to contract for field services in a manner that ensures the presence of personnel competent to correct most defects at or near the site where products are located.

- Systems, subsystems, and components acquired by government often are unique and lack a history of the cost of warranty service adequate for accurate pricing at the time of contract award.

- Systems procured by the government are used under variable conditions, are often undocumented, and are frequently remote in distance and time from the delivery of the item to the government.

- Potential losses from the use of some government systems are great and difficult to estimate.

- Identifying and correcting defects in property and carrying out a notification procedure are extremely difficult for military items distributed worldwide.

- The history of warranty service on military items is variable at best and is complicated by the large number of military personnel at all levels who may have a role in distributing, using, and maintaining the end items.

It is evident that defective products introduced into military inventories can catastrophically impact the performance of military missions and, perhaps, the safety of its operations. Nevertheless, the requirement for extension of the government's recourse against its suppliers is challenged on several fronts. Chart 10-5 summarizes several strong arguments against the new policies but does not reflect the fact that modern communication and transportation methods facilitate conveying information and defective products to the supplier for repair. Under current conditions it may be that defects can be corrected under warranty procedures without the need for a service contract. In any case, the traditional government position (relying on its quality assurance and inspection processes to ensure that products conform with specification when delivered) has been modified, based on the concept that suppliers should carry a higher level of responsibility for the quality of end items. The general trend is toward obtaining warranties that, for a stated or specified period after acceptance, will enable the government to demand correction of patent defects contractually. Although the FAR indicates that benefits to be derived from a warranty must be commensurate with the cost of the warranty, recent legislation modifies the validity of cost trade-offs for warranties on weapons systems.

SUMMARY

Product quality has been recognized as a major factor affecting productivity and competitiveness throughout the United States. It has received intensive scrutiny since the end of the Second World War. Responsibility for product quality is a source of concern in contract relationships. This chapter treats several dimensions of the subject as they affect contract managers.

- The overall philosophy of contract quality assurance
- Four levels of quality assurance as defined by the government
- A comparison of inspection systems and quality assurance systems
- A comparison of contract quality assurance with the recently advocated alternative concept of quality improvement
- The role of the quality assurance representative (QAR) employed by the government for quality surveillance of contract operations
- A review of a recent study of issues that appear to complicate effective performance of contract quality surveillance functions
- Government organization for quality assurance
- A review of the relationship between warranties and inspection and acceptance in government contracting

TOPICS FOR DISCUSSION

1. What is the importance of the contractor responsibility concept?
2. What is meant by the statement, "The manufacturing process is under control?"
3. Compare the government's standard inspection requirement with its requirement when an inspection system specification is imposed.
4. Distinguish between complex items and critical items.
5. Defend the proposition that the proper philosophy pertinent to quality is that of *quality improvement*.
6. Explain the basic DCAS program for establishing quality surveillance of new contract awards.
7. In relation to quality assurance, explain the importance of prime contractor control over subcontractors. Why is this an issue?
8. Discuss the implications of this statement: Acceptance shall be conclusive, except for latent defects, fraud, gross mistakes amounting to fraud, or as otherwise specified in the contract.
9. Summarize the arguments for and against the use of special warranties in government contracts.

Case 10-1

Mobile Test Vans

The Naval Air Station at Patuxent River, Maryland, solicited bids for two mobile test instrumentation vehicles. The vehicles (mobile vans) were to be of standard commercial design that did not require special equipment or use of advanced technology. However, the vans were to be built to permit the Patuxent facility to equip them for field testing of strike aircraft. In response to the invitation three bids were received, and on December 10, 1982, contract N00421-83-0012 was awarded to the lowest responsible bidder, Monarch Systems, Inc. The contract required the vans to be built to best commercial practices and specifically required them to be equivalent in design and construction to the ITHASCA model 29R or Winnebago model 29R commercial mobile vehicles. In addition, the contract specified that acceptance of the mobile vans would occur after delivery at the Patuxent River naval test facility. The contractor agreed to build and deliver the vehicles within a 150 day performance period with a specified contractual delivery date of May 9, 1983.

Two months after contract award, DCASMA representatives from Indianapolis contacted the contracting officer at Patuxent River and recommended that inspection and acceptance of the end item vehicles be performed at the contractor's plant by the DCASMA quality assurance representatives. The contracting officer agreed to make that change.

In mid-February, 1983, Ellen Simpson, DCASMA contract administrator in Indianapolis reported that she encountered difficulty in communicating with Monarch regarding contract specifications, and, in a telephone conversation with NAS contracting personnel, she expressed reservations concerning the likelihood of timely delivery. These communications were the first indication that performance problems may be encountered in the manufacture and delivery of the vans. The problems and reservations concerning Monarch Systems had developed to the point that the government decided to hold a post-award orientation conference with the contractor. The conference was held on March 10, 1983, in Indianapolis and was attended by the contractor, DCASMA representatives, and NAS-Patuxent technical personnel.

Some additional problems also emerged during April, and the contracting officer issued a modification, authorizing the change in the place of inspection. On May 19, 1983, the first of the two vans was accepted by Mr. Dave Rogers, a contract quality assurance representative at DCASMA in Indianapolis. The second van was also accepted on June 7, 1983. Delivery of the two vans to Patuxent occurred on June 10 and 11, 1983.

Problems began to emerge sometime subsequent to delivery of the vans. Delamination of the sides of the vans, omission of a floor to protect batteries from road splash, problems with the engines, and loose batteries were observed. The problems became so great that numerous telephone calls were made between NAS technical personnel and the manufacturer during the fall of 1983. These communications culminated in a letter written by the NAS contract specialist on January 18, 1984, which provided the manufacturer with official notification of the various discrepancies and defects. On that date, the problems with the vans were turned over to the procurement office.

Several unsatisfactory attempts to communicate with the manufacturer by telephone were initiated by contract specialists at the NAS during January, February, and March of 1984. Lacking adequate response from the manufacturer, a show cause notice was issued on March 28, 1984, in which the Navy requested the manufacturer to show cause why the contract should not be terminated for default. This notice brought about a meeting on April 11, 1984, between representatives of Monarch Systems and the Naval Air Station. Monarch, the NAS procurement office, NAS counsel, and NAS technical codes were represented. At the meeting, a discrepancy list was provided, listing numerous defects which the government maintained were latent defects. In addition, the Naval Air Station had obtained reports on inspection of the vans by the Maryland State Inspections Office, which found that neither van was road worthy. Also during this meeting, the vans were inspected by the group. At the conclusion of the meeting, Monarch Systems' attorney, Mr. Roger

Lentil, advised the Navy that he would send a proposal regarding the remedial actions that Monarch would be willing to undertake.

On April 18, 1984, the contracting officer received a letter from Mr. Lentil in which he acknowledged receipt of the show cause notice. In another letter dated April 23, l984, Mr. Lentil offered to have Monarch repair some of the minor deficiencies of the vehicles; some repairs were to be made at no charge to the government, but other deficiencies were to be corrected on a time and material basis at government expense. However, the repairs were to be accomplished only after transporting the vehicles from Maryland back to Indianapolis at government expense.

Monarch contended that the vehicles sustained substantial use and that the defects were caused by government abuse and misuse. Conversely, the government took the position that there had been no abuse and little use of the vehicles. They had been used sparingly because of the deficiencies and, in fact, during the entire period of government ownership, the vans had accrued less than 3,000 miles, including the transport from Monarch's Indiana plant to the Naval Air Test Center at Patuxent River. The Navy, however, considered the van's defects to be so severe that they were rendered unsafe, not road worthy, and incapable of performing the missions for which they had been expressly purchased. The Navy took the position that the defects were unrelated to government usage, repairs, or custody. While the extent of the defects caused the Navy to doubt Monarch's ability to perform repairs that would bring the vans up to the best commercial standard, it was willing to have the contractor attempt the rework. The Navy felt that the performance of repairs, including the cost of transporting the vehicles, was a responsibility of Monarch, not the Navy. Therefore, in August of 1984, the NAS contracting officer decided that an inspection by recognized qualified experts in commercial van manufacture would be appropriate and issued a purchase order for two people, Mr. R.E. Busman and Mr. Sam Rukeyser, to conduct an inspection of the vans. They were selected after a comprehensive search for experts in van manufacture which included universities, trade associations, motor vehicle manufacturing associations, the Society of Automotive Engineers, an RV trade association, and the federal government. The two selectees were considered top experts in the construction of such vehicles.

Among other things, the inspectors' report stated that excessive deterioration and degradation of both vehicles were obvious despite their extremely low mileage. Additionally, major deficiencies, such as leaking propane tanks, were discovered which affected the safety and operation of the vehicles. The report indicated that the vehicles failed to meet the commercial equivalency requirements and did not reflect best commercial standards of construction or comply with standards and safety practices.

As a result of the reports and the series of events through the fall of 1984, the Navy issued an additional show cause notice to Monarch on

December 14, 1984. As in the earlier notice, it listed the numerous defects in detail. The government's position was that Monarch had delivered to the government two mobile vehicles that (1) contained numerous
latent defects, rendering the vehicles not in conformity with the contract
specifications (that is, not equivalent to ITHASCA or Winnebago models);
(2) were not equivalent to best commercial practices; and (3) were not
suitable for use due to numerous safety hazards inherent in their construction. Subsequent to delivery of these vans, it was also the government's position that Monarch used dilatory tactics in all negotiations
regarding repairs to the vans. Based on these circumstances, on January
29, 1985, the contracting officer issued an amendment of solicitation/
modification of contract, citing contract number N00421-83-C-0012. The
key statement in this modification is quoted below.

> The purpose of this modification is to issue a notice of termination:
> You are notified that acceptance of CLIN0001 and CLIN0003 pur-
> chased by Patuxent River Naval Air Station (NAS) from Monarch
> Systems Inc. (Monarch) under contract N00421-83-C-0012 ("the con-
> tract"), dated 10 December, 1982 is hereby revoked. In addition, the
> contract is hereby terminated for default, in the entirety, in accord-
> ance with the contract clause entitled, "Default," general provision
> 7-103.11, August 1969. Such termination for default will be effective
> immediately upon your receipt of this notice.

* * * * *

Please comment on this course of events and detail any alternative
actions or procedures that you think could have been followed in this
case. Set forth your judgment as to what events should now occur to
bring this situation to a conclusion.

CASE 10-2

Rejected Parts

It was a beautiful spring morning in 1984 in Silicon Valley. Joe
Rivers, contracts manager for the Armored Division of RCI Corporation,
had just received a disturbing telephone call from the division's quality
control manager, James Byers. James was upset as a result of a meeting
with John Sims, the senior DCASMA quality assurance representative
(QAR) at RCI. Sims had advised him that he was rejecting lot one of a
spares order for TDB P/M 12295623-1 and VDB P/N 12292086. These
parts were contained in a critical electronic countermeasures device
essential to operational readiness of the LPC (land/sea personnel carri-

er). Their rejection meant that RCI would be cited as being delinquent in its delivery obligations and that the army project manager would be calling to express extreme displeasure.

Company Background

RCI is a large, diversified corporation with substantial industrial sales. The Armored Division is one of its principal activities but special-izes in the manufacture of military vehicles. The division is largely devoted to government sales and holds several major government con-tracts for production of mobility systems for the Army such as the LPC.

The New Material Surprise

The QAR had told Byers to check out the contract, particularly clause 25 of the schedule entitled "New Material." Joe was thoroughly familiar with that clause and was distressed that anything other than new material would have been offered for acceptance by the government.

The following paragraph contains the text of the clause:

> Unless this contract specifies otherwise, the Contractor represents that the supplies and components, including any former Government property identified under the Used or Reconditioned Material, Resi-dual Inventory, and Former Government Surplus Property clause of this contract, are new, including recycled (not used or recondi-tioned) and are not of such age or so deteriorated as to impair their usefulness or safety. If the Contractor believes that furnishing used or reconditioned supplies or components will be in the Government's interest, the Contractor shall so notify the Contracting Officer in writing. The Contractor's notice shall include the reasons for the request along with a proposal for any consideration to the Govern-ment if the Contracting Officer authorizes the use of used or reconditioned supplies or components.

As a result of the call, Joe set up a 2 P.M. meeting with James Byers and John Sims to discuss the situation. At the meeting, Joe learned the full circumstances of the reject. The spares order was one of several that called for phased deliveries through the balance of 1984. There had been a history of problems associated with the two rejected parts. Both of them were subsystems referred to as black boxes and were essential for operational readiness. Since the delivery schedule was tight, Joe had authorized drawing these two parts from inventory for final test, checkout, and delivery earlier in April. The parts were in inventory because several months earlier (during delivery of the 1983 quantity of the LPC), they had failed acceptance testing and were removed from vehicles, thoroughly examined to identify deficiencies, and remanufactured to the extent necessary to correct defects. After retesting and qualifying the parts, they had been returned to inventory.

Joe thought the items to be deliverable, that the new material requirement didn't apply, and that this delay was unnecessary. Regardless, Joe learned at the meeting that John Sims could not be dissuaded. The rejection stood, and the parts would be returned to inventory.

Although John Sims would not alter his decision, Joe remained unconvinced. He decided to initiate action for review of the circumstances by higher authority. He wanted a reversal of this rejection.

★ ★ ★ ★ ★

1. What is the impact of rejection/acceptance under normal government contract policy?
2. Outline the steps you would now take if you were in Joe River's position. Draft any correspondence that may be needed.
3. What do you expect will be the outcome of this situation?

CASE 10-3

RCI and the Data Warranty

Several complaints about Robert Stimsonn's organizational plan for control of major government programs were highlighted by the controversy and conflicts that arose within Armored Division in connection with the Department of Defense initiative to impose warranty obligations on suppliers of technical data. The difference in the perceptions of issues associated with that initiative on the part of business managers, project managers, and proposal/contract managers was dramatic.

Warranty had become a major political issue in government during 1983 and 1984 because of published accounts of deficient products built by defense contractors. An outgrowth of this was the action taken by personnel at operating levels in government to impose warranty requirements on existing as well as new contracts. A new clause was proposed which sought to make contractors assume a greater level of responsibility and risk associated with the technical data they prepared and delivered to the government. Stimsonn found that his project managers were not greatly concerned with the new warranty requirement. They believed that technical data should be defect free, and they worked to make that happen. Similarly, his business managers didn't have any major problem with the new requirement; they noted that the company would be allowed to adjust prices to reflect the cost associated with the warranty. The contracts people were the ones that objected, complaining that the company should not accept this new requirement.

In effect, the contracts people took the viewpoint that the newly proposed clauses asked the company to accept a "pig-in-a-poke." They argued that no one, either in the company or in the government, knew or could reasonably project the costs associated with the new clauses.

James Price, Stimsonn's manager of proposals and contracts in engineering, made this point quite clear in a letter to TACOM dated September 5, 1984, in which RCI took exception to the proposed FAR clause 52.246-7001, Warranty of Data. He gave the following reasons for not accepting the clause.

A. The inclusion of a warranty clause in a cost reimbursement contract is not cost effective.

Cost reimbursement contracts are authorized by the Government when the uncertainties involved in contract performance are of such a magnitude that cost of performance cannot be estimated with sufficient reasonableness to permit use of a fixed price. These cost reimbursement programs make it cost effective for the government in that they are charged only the actual costs incurred. This is preferable to agreeing to a fixed price which would include contingencies to cover unforeseeable cost risks. In circumstances where a fixed price contract is not cost effective, for the same reasons, it is not appropriate to include a warranty in a cost reimbursement contract.

B. The inclusion of a warranty clause creates a cost effectiveness problem.

It is possible that a warranty clause could create in the contractor an incentive to incur excessive costs prior to delivery because these costs would be reimbursable. This would be in lieu of incurring guaranty costs after delivery that would not be reimbursable.

C. The scope of work exposes RCI to a risk of high liability.

This scope of work is not clearly defined and is of a developmental nature. A warranty under these conditions which could expose RCI to a high risk of liability is inappropriate.

Action by the Army's Deputy Chief of Staff for Procurement and Production on September 11, 1984, reinforced the TACOM effort to add a data warranty to its contracts and was a factor in rejecting the position of RCI. Price continued his effort to find a set of provisions acceptable to both Armored Division and TACOM, and further discussions and negotiations proceeded through the balance of 1984 and the first half of 1985. This process was strongly influenced by the position of the Deputy Chief of Staff as quoted in the following excerpt from his September 11, 1984, correspondence.

1.   The OSD Technical Data Rights Study Group recently concluded a review on acquisition of Technical Data Rights and use of Warranty of Data clauses. The group has made strong recommendations in regard to an expanded and mandatory use of the Warranties of Data clause contained in the DOD FAR Supplement 52.246-7001 as it pertains to acquisition of technical data.

2.   Based on these recommendations, it shall be the policy of this Headquarters that all Major Subordinate Command Acquisition Offices maximize use of the Warranty of Data clause as set forth in DOD FAR Supplement 52.246-7001 and prescribed in 46.770 when buying technical data in support of hardware/end items and parts. Pending formal revisions to DOD FAR Supplement, the sample clause and alternatives set forth at enclosure 1 are offered for consideration and adaptation on a specific case-by-case basis.

3.   Request addressees take the necessary steps to ensure acquisition files are documented to support rationale for not procuring warranty of data as the rule rather than the exception.

The Army's proposed clauses and alternates I and II follow:

WARRANTY OF DATA
(a) Technical data means recorded information, regardless of form or characteristic, of a scientific or technical nature. It may, for example, document research, experimental, developmental or engineering work; or be usable or used to define a design or process or to procure product support, maintain, or operate materiel. The data may be graphic or pictorial delineations in media such as drawings or photographs; text in specification or related performance or design typed documents; or computer printouts. Examples of technical data include research and engineering data, engineering drawings and associated lists, specifications, standards, process sheets, manuals, technical reports, catalog item identifications, and related information, and documentation related to computer software. Technical data does not include computer software or financial, administrative, cost and pricing, and management data, or other

information incidental to contract administration.

(b) Notwithstanding inspection and acceptance by the Government of technical data furnished under this contract and notwithstanding any provision of this contract concerning the conclusiveness thereof, the Contractor warrants that all technical data delivered under this contract will at the time of delivery conform with the specifications and all other requirements of this contract. The warranty period shall extend for three (3) years after completion of the delivery of the line item of data (as identified in DD Form 1423) of which the data forms a part; or any longer period specified in the contract.

(c) The Contractor agrees to notify the Contracting Officer in writing immediately of any breach of the above warranty which the Contractor discovers within the warranty period.

(d) The following remedies shall apply to all breaches of the above warranty provided that the Government notifies the Contractor of the breach in writing within the warranty period.

(1) Within a reasonable time after the Contracting Officer notifies the Contractor of a breach of warranty, he may:

(i) by written notice, direct the Contractor to correct or replace at his expense the nonconforming technical data promptly; or

(ii) if he determines that the Government no longer has a requirement for correction or replacement of the data, or that the data can be more reasonably corrected by the Government, inform the Contractor by written notice that the Government elects a price or fee adjustment in lieu of correction or replacement.

(2) If the Contractor refuses or fails to comply with a direction under (1)(i) above, the Contracting Officer may, within a reasonable time of such refusal or failure:

(i) by contract or otherwise, correct or replace the nonconforming technical data and charge the Contractor the cost occasioned to the Government thereby; or

(ii) elect a price or fee adjustment in lieu of correction or replacement.

(3) The remedies set forth in this clause represent the exclusive means by which the rights conferred on the Government by this clause may be enforced.

(f) The provisions of this clause apply anew to that portion of any technical data which is corrected or furnished in replacement under (d)(1)(i) above.

(End of Clause)

Alternate I (Optional for Use Under Fixed Price Incentive Contract)

(3) In addition to the remedies specified under (d)(1) and (2) above, Contractor shall be liable to the Government for all damages

sustained by the Government as a result of breach of the warranty specified in this clause; however, the additional liability under this subparagraph (3) shall not exceed 75% of the target profit. If the breach of the warranty specified in (b) of this clause is with respect to data supplied by an equipment subcontractor, the limit of the prime contractor's liability shall be 10% of the total subcontract price in the case of a firm fixed-price subcontract, 75% of the total subcontract fee in the case of a cost-plus-fixed-fee or cost-plus-award-fee subcontract, or 75% of the total subcontract target profit or fee in the case of a fixed-price or cost-plus-incentive type contract. Damages due the Government under the provisions of this warranty shall not be considered as an allowable cost. The additional liability specified in this paragraph (3) shall not apply:

(i) with respect to the requirement for data for reprocurement of spare parts, provided that the data furnished by the Contractor was current, accurate at time of submission and did not involve a significant omission of data necessary to comply with such requirements; or

(ii) with respect to specific defects as to which the Contractor discovers and gives written notice to the Government before the error is discovered by the Government.

Alternate II (Optional for Use Under Firm Fixed Price Contract)

(3) In addition to the remedies specified under (1) and (2) above, the Contractor shall be liable to the Government for all damages sustained by the Government as a result of breach of the warranty specified in this clause: however, the additional liability under this subparagraph (3) shall not exceed 10% of the total contract price. If the breach of the warranty specified in (b) of this clause is with respect to data supplied by an equipment subcontractor, the limit of the prime contractor's liability shall be 10% of the total subcontract price in the case of a firm fixed price subcontract, 75% of the total subcontract fee in the case of a cost-plus-fixed fee or cost-plus-award fee subcontract, or 75% of the total subcontract target profit or fee in the case of a fixed-price or cost-plus-incentive type contract. The additional liability specified in this paragraph (3) shall not apply:

(i) with respect to the requirement for data for reprocurement of spare parts, provided that the data furnished by the Contractor was current, accurate at time of submission and did not involve a significant omission of data necessary to comply with such requirements; or

(ii) with respect to specific defects as to which the Contractor discovers and gives written notice to the Government before the error is discovered by the Government.

* * * * *

1.   Develop a negotiation position for RCI based on the situation given
     in this case. Consider the following list of elements that may be
     pertinent to warranty obligations, and develop your position on the
     basis of what you think is reasonable for the company, yet capable
     of meeting the government's concerns.

     a.   Period of the warranty
     b.   Beginning of warranty period
     c.   Specific delineation of data to which the warranty applies
     d.   Effect of change orders that operate to reduce the contractor's
          time for producing the warranted data
     e.   Applicability of warranty to data that is dependent upon
          government-supplied data
     f.   Data generated by RCI but based on technology supplied to RCI
          by the government or a government contractor
     g.   Typographical or grammatical errors
     h.   Interim submissions of technical data
     i.   Timeliness and content of government notice when the govern-
          ment discovers a breach of the warranty
     j.   Responsibility for design or equipment changes that surface in
          connection with discovery of deficiencies in warranted data
     k.   Responsibility for consequential damages
     l.   Approach to pricing the warranty

2.   State your expectation regarding the outcome of these negotiations.

11

Funding,
Financial Administration,
and Payments

INTRODUCTION

Money factors dominate much of the administrative activity associated with contracting. Suppliers attempt to predict when they will receive payment by their customers, and they try to advance the schedule when feasible. Their special interest in the timing of payments is derived from the need to reduce their investment in working capital. Buyers have a reverse motivation; they seek slower payout to minimize investment and retain leverage over their suppliers. The payments process is vital to the interests of both parties. Government procurement regulations reveal fifteen different clauses designed for use in governing the payments process under fixed-price contracts and an additional eight clauses that are designed to govern the reimbursements and payments due under cost-reimbursable instruments. Some of these clauses are complex because they attempt to govern both the procedures and the application of policy in this vital area.

Numerous implications can be derived from payments and financial policy associated with contracts. Not the least of these is the motivational impact of payment policy. An attraction of doing business with the government is its reliable and relatively rapid reimbursement of working capital through the payments process. Reliability and timeliness are important because of the large amounts expended in the aggregate and under each contract. The receipt of payment is a strong motivational factor in the calculations of the performing party because of the working capital and profitability leverage associated with financial assets.

In addition to the usual concerns that any contractor has regarding payment, government contractors are affected by the government's historic and adamant refusal to pay interest as a cost element of contracts. The government's logic is that interest and profit are essentially similar payments for the use of capital, and that it does not want to compensate contractors differentially, according to their source of capital (debt versus equity). This position has never been fully accepted by the private sector which views interest as a cost, not as a part of profit. Even though the government will not pay interest as a cost, it employs relatively liberal policies regarding payment as work progresses. This is an important element that somewhat offsets the nonrecognition of interest as a cost and, in general, is relied on as part of the contractual environment associated with government contracts.

Payments and finance as covered in this chapter are related to the closeout procedures discussed in chapter 15, which treats completion of work, delivery of end items, and acceptance of work and products produced by a contractor. These steps are conditions precedent to final payments under contracts. The purpose of this chapter is to examine policy matters and procedural steps necessary to achieve timely payment during performance. We will also examine funding procedures which operate as a constraint on the ability of disbursing officers to make progress or partial payments and other types of interim payments. In addition, we will examine the rules applicable to cost-reimbursement contracts. These rules differ in important ways from those governing payment under firm-fixed-price contracts. They introduce issues such as the allowability of costs (specifically, their allocability to public contracts). Complex as these rules are under government contracts, the payments process is additionally influenced by the unique set of rules incorporated into government cost accounting standards (CAS). These accounting standards, which are pertinent to most major government contracts, are summarized in this chapter.

FUNDING AND PAYMENTS

A principal part of the contract award process is creating an obligation to pay a specific sum to a designated recipient, that is, to the contractor. In the government system, the authority to make obligations is delegated to contracting officers and is performed repetitively during the performance of large, long-term contracts. Obligation of money is broadly referred to as funding the contract. It is the step in the procurement process that reserves appropriations and restricts the use of funds so that they are available for dispersal only for the specific contract and only upon approval of the contractor's invoice.

Funding of a contract should be distinguished from contract pricing. The price of a contract represents an agreement between the parties with respect to the amount that must be paid to compensate the per-former for contract work. Therefore, the price is the expected total amount to be paid upon acceptance of all required work. In many gov-ernment programs, the availability of funds in appropriation accounts is not adequate at the time of contract negotiation and award, and the instrument is not funded to the full amount of the agreed upon-price. Consequently, funding is a procedure whereby the government allocates appropriations by making periodic obligations as work progresses.

The funding level of a contract operates as a legal limitation on the total obligation of the government to make payments. By means of several *anti-deficiency* statutes, Congress prohibits executive agencies from making obligations in excess of appropriations, causing the funding level to be a vital part of contract operations. The level at which a contract is funded may be less than, or equal to, the total agreed-upon price, but should not exceed it[1]. It is normal for contracts involving large sums to be funded incrementally at a level which is less than the total agreed-upon price, until the period of performance is drawing to a close, and the completion of the contract is at hand. The practices of government agencies have evolved in such a way that they take advantage of incremental funding operations to reduce total obligations. This permits agencies to pursue the maximum level of contract activity within their total authorized funding. Since Congress appropriates money annually, and appropriation accounts are released to the agencies on a quarterly basis by the Office of Management and Budget, agencies have a legal barrier to obligating funds too rapidly. Incremental funding, as opposed to full funding of agreed-upon contract prices, facilitates plan-ning and scheduling of large-dollar undertakings.

In addition to legal constraints on the funding of contracts, agencies recognize that it is an uneconomic restraint on their use of appropriation accounts to obligate funds too early in production, so that large, obliga-ted, but unexpended balances exist in contractual accounts. These funds are totally unavailable to an agency for other applications than the one covered by the specific contract. These factors lead to maximal use of incremental funding provisions by most agencies as part of their normal contracting processes.

An agency's funding operations are important from a contractor's viewpoint because they constrain the timing of anticipated payments. No payment can be made to any contractor under any contract beyond the amount funded. Consequently, both contractors and agencies have a

---

[1]It is possible for change activity to cause total contract cost to increase faster than price adjustments are negotiated. This has occurred on some cost contracts with the result that funding exceeded the formally agreed-upon price.

lively interest in the budget operations of government.

There are two important clauses that have been developed and included in the procurement regulations which, in practice, effectuate the management and legal implications of incremental funding. The Limitation of Cost (FAR 52.232-20) and Limitation of Funds (FAR 52.232-22) clauses provide a legal limitation of the government's liability to make payments under cost-reimbursement contracts. Similar clauses have been applied to fixed-price contracts.

The Limitation of Funds clause is designed to cover the government's needs when it wishes to fund a contract incrementally. The clause specifically provides and establishes a procedure for periodic allotments of funds to the contract by the contracting officer. It also obligates the contractor to notify the government within a specified number of days whenever the already-obligated funds drop below the point at which over 75 percent (variable to 85 percent) of the total amount will have been expended. This important action is the responsibility of the contractor's contract manager. In the absence of having made the notification, risk of discontinuity in the adequacy of funding is increased. A provision in the limitation of funds clause releases the contractor from continued performance of work at any point when the funds allotted to the contract have been exhausted, ensuring that contractors are not obligated to perform when there is no right to bill the government for their costs. However, under the dynamic conditions normally existing in ongoing projects, contractors are extremely reluctant to stop work at any time, as long as they expect funds to be ultimately made available for payment of expenses accrued under the contract. In association with the incremental funding practice, contractors are often in a position where they must decide whether to commit risk capital to the continuance of the effort. Once a contract has been funded, costs may be billed in accordance with normal practice.

While the Limitation of Funds clause is designed to cover incremental funding practices, the Limitation of Cost clause accomplishes almost the same objective, but it is designed only for contracts which are fully funded at the time of their issuance. The Limitation of Cost clause provides a legal constraint on the government's liability for payments in a cost-reimbursable type contract. The clause exists because of the statutory barrier prohibiting government officials from obligating the government to any payments in excess of available appropriations. The need for the clause in a cost-reimbursable contract results from the basic nature of these contracts. They provide that the government, as purchaser, becomes obligated to reimburse the contractor's allowable costs. This obligation differs from that of a fixed-price contract in which the government, as purchaser, is obligated to pay only a determined sum, the fixed price of the contract. In the absence of the Limitation of Cost clause, a cost-reimbursable contract is illegal because it would not include a fixed and determinate maximum liability of the government.

The most important management implication derived from the foregoing discussion is that the amount of funds obligated to support a contract can be managed so that the funding level is closely associated with the level of incurred costs at any particular time. This avoids funding the entire agreed-upon price of the contract in advance of actual incurrence of costs.

PAYMENT PROCEDURES

The payment of contractors is a relatively simple step in the total contracting process. Before making a payment, the disbursing officer must receive an invoice (a reimbursement voucher for cost-reimbursement contracts) and verify that the charge is correct and appropriate under the terms of the contract. A check must then be written in a timely manner and delivered to the supplier. These basic steps need not be complicated or time consuming, but, in practice, the payment process may not prove to be so simple. One factor contributing to difficulties in the handling of payments is volume. Payment offices may process thousands of invoices per day, varying from insignificant individual sums to millions of dollars. A substantial paper-checking process is associated with each payment, and a voucher, covering only payments that are authorized and appropriate in accordance with the underlying contractual arrangements, must be prepared and signed.

In addition to the clerical function of checking documentation, the payment must be consistent with financing policy that prevents early payments, as well as the prompt payment policy designed to restrict delayed payments. In the government, these policies are established by regulation or statute. Some inflexibility is introduced by the policies because of equally important rules that the basis for payment must be documented. For example, upon acceptance of end items, an acceptance document must be forwarded to the paying office. On the other hand, an acceptance document for progress payments does not exist, because payments are made without delivery of final products. Instead, a contracting officer must have authorized the payment. The invoice and associated statements of costs or other items required of the contractor must be attached. Under government financing policies, a disbursing officer may adopt the practice of holding invoices until the due date, at which time checks are issued or electronic funds transfers authorized.

Progress Payment Requests

Though data accumulation procedures have many pitfalls, they are probably the minor problems associated with payments of contractor invoices. A more significant problem concerns the appropriateness of a contractor's payment requests. This problem frequently arises when making progress payment requests under fixed-price contracts. Government rules for progress payments are explicit. Such payments should be requested only to cover costs that are consistent with authorized methods of computing the proper amount of the payment. The authorized methods are somewhat restrictive. For example, submission of a contractor's progress payment requests for purchase of supplies and services are authorized only after the contractor has paid the source of supply. This restricts contractors from invoicing the government for known incurred costs of suppliers that are currently recognized and payable but not paid. The effect of the rule is to increase working capital requirements. Many contractors have encountered problems as a consequence of attempting to reduce the effect of this rule. However, for costs such as the application of direct labor, travel, or other direct in-house costs, invoices may be presented upon incurrence of the cost. This minimizes working capital investments. It also facilitates recovery of costs for materials issued from contractor stores for production purposes. Progress payments also permit recovery of a contractor's indirect costs by allowing them to be billed upon incurrence at an agreed-upon billing rate, provided they are properly allocated and allowable under the prime contract.

The payment rules make it necessary for the contractor's manager to review billings carefully to avoid violations. Some categories of contractor expenses are specifically restricted because the timing of the contractor's actual payment cannot be determined. This situation arises in connection with contractor contributions to employee pension plans, profit sharing, and stock ownership plans. In addition to restraints on the amount of costs that a contractor can bill to the government under the normal progress payment rules, contractors cannot submit payment requests more frequently than monthly. This restriction may be waived for small businesses.

Payment of Cost-Reimbursement Contracts

Rules similar to those for progress payments apply to invoicing the government for allowable costs under the cost-reimbursement type of contract. The principal contractual coverage of this subject for government procurement is the Allowable Cost and Payment clause (FAR 52.216-7). Under the rules, the government is obligated to make payments in response to contractor requests only if the request is in accordance with the restrictions of the clause. Rules of the Allowable Cost and Payment clause authorize a contractor to submit billings every two weeks, thereby allowing him to recover costs on a more rapid basis than permitted by the progress payment. To obtain cost reimbursement, the contractor must submit an invoice or voucher along with a statement of the claimed allowable costs applied in performance of the contract. In a manner similar to fixed-price contract progress payments, the allowable costs for reimbursement during performance of the contract are defined as only those costs that the contractor has paid out in cash, or in some other form of actual payment, for purchased services or material. However, again, when a contractor has incurred costs for in-house expenses, such as issuance of material from his inventory or the application of direct labor, travel, and other in-house direct costs, the contractor is permitted to bill the government upon recording the incurred costs. Similarly, he may bill for allowable indirect costs at an agreed-upon billing rate.

In summary, under the payment rules for periodic payments during the performance of a contract, contractors can request their internal costs on a cost-incurred basis but must not request reimbursement for amounts incurred by other parties until those payments have actually been made.

Payment of Fixed-Price Construction Contracts

Payment during performance of construction contracts is made by progress payments, but the amounts payable are determined by using the percent of completion method instead of the cost incurred method as already discussed. For government contracts, the rules are provided by the Payments Under Fixed-Price Construction Contracts clause (FAR 52.232-5). The rules are simpler than those for supply and service contracts because cost incurrence need not be addressed directly. But the amount of payment can become an issue since a judgment must be made regarding the percent of completion achieved. The contractor initially makes this estimate and must support the estimate with a breakdown of the total price by the principal categories of work. Materials for the project that are delivered to the construction site or owned by the contractor may be considered a part of the estimate of completion percentage. Payment is reduced by retaining 10 percent of the estimated percent of completion unless a smaller retention is deemed appropriate by the contracting officer. Material and work covered by these progress payments become the property of the government, but this does not relieve the contractor of responsibility for the property or satisfactory completion of the contract. Final payment is not made until completion and acceptance of all work and delivery of a release from all claims (except specified ones).

CONTRACT FINANCE POLICIES AND PRACTICES

Procurement managers expect their source of supply to provide all facilities, manpower, and expertise to carry on the work under contract. Ordinarily, they also assume that the source of supply will provide whatever capital is necessary to perform the work. It is widely recognized, however, that providing large sums of working capital may be burdensome, perhaps impossible, if the project is large relative to that of the supplier organization. This is frequently the case when small businesses compete for the contract. Nevertheless, contract managers expect suppliers to obtain capital from private sources to cover not only their fixed asset needs but also necessary working capital. This preference toward the provision of capital to contractors is implicitly expressed in government policy. The listing that follows ranks advance payments as the least preferred method of providing capital to contractors because it provides the purchaser's capital to the supplier in advance of the performance of work. In contrast, the buyer's preferred method of financing--private sources--is probably least preferred by most contractors.

Buyers in each sector, public and private, recognize that payment practices are vital to suppliers because they determine the amounts suppliers can invest to carry out required work. Government policy is described in this section because it reflects the numerous possible situations and is fully documented. Government policy in regard to payments is similar to that of any purchaser in a competitive economy. There are, however, several structural arrangements under which the government operates. Government approaches to contract payments can be categorized in terms of preferences and authorizations. The following list consists of the principal mechanisms for making payments under contracts.

Approaches to Payments and Contract Finance Methods as Preferred and/or Authorized by the Government (Listed in Order of Preference)

1. *Private sources* independently acquired: preferred method of financing contractor working capital needs
2. *Assignment of claims* with no set-off: preferred method of facilitating contractor access to debt capital
3. *Partial payments* for completed increments of work: preferred method of minimizing working capital
4. *Customary progress payments:* preferred method of financing work in progress prior to acceptance
5. *Guaranteed loans:* authorized as a principal method of ensuring contractor access to debt capital under conditions of necessity such as mobilization

6. *Payment of interim cost vouchers* on cost-reimbursement contracts and incentive or redeterminable contracts: authorized as a normal method of financing work in process under contracts in which payment is based on cost determination
7. *Unusual progress payments:* an authorized but exceptional method of financing work in progress prior to acceptance
8. *Advance payments:* authorized only under specific circumstances, such as for government-owned-contractor-operated (GOCO) contracts, for university research contracts, and for special circumstances. This method provides capital in advance of work so that contractor working capital requirements are eliminated.

Private sources. Regardless of the sources of capital, equity, or debt, from the buyer's viewpoint, the desirable situation is for the contractor to provide all needed capital. This method of financing prevails in the procurement of most common items, certainly those items which are manufactured for inventory and sold from stock. Under these conditions, purchasers do not provide capital. Instead, upon delivery and acceptance of end products, the seller's invoice is honored, and payment is made, so that in one step the supplier recovers both the costs of performance and the earnings from the transaction.

This preferable method of financing work unfortunately is not acceptable or viable for many larger transactions. Whenever significant increments of time are needed to perform the work subsequent to the award of the contract, the contractor expects to receive reimbursement of his working capital as work proceeds. Several methods of financing that are indicated in the foregoing list reflect these perceptions. Instead of advancing funds, a buyer is often able to help the contractor to acquire capital by facilitating borrowing processes.

Assignment of claims. In government procurement, facilitating access to debt capital is achieved by allowing the contractor to assign claims under the contract to a financial institution as security for repayment of debt. This method has been authorized by the Congress through the Assignment of Claims Act, which gives contracting officers the authority to allow assignment of claims. (Under an assignment, payments are made directly to the financial institution.) This policy protects the financial institution from the government's exercising powers of set-off against the financial institution. The financial institution is protected against the possibility that payments due--based on the assigned contract and payable to the financial institution to reduce the amount of its loan to the contractor--will be interrupted because of government action to collect separate debts of the contractor. Set-off protection does not protect the financial institution if the contractor fails to perform under the contract for which the assignment is made. Under that circumstance (a default), there is no obligation to pay.

Partial payments. Providing working capital to contractors by authorizing partial payments for partial deliveries of acceptable work is a natural and relatively risk-free method of financing for buyers. Partial payments, however, are viable only on the condition that work has been delivered and accepted. It is a useful method of payment when there are interim deliveries of completed end products that can be accepted by the purchaser, or when milestones have been identified that represent the completion of significant phases of work. The milestone approach to authorizing partial payments is often used when the work rendered by the contractor is in the form of service or reports, instead of tangible end items capable of being tested and qualified for acceptance purposes. The partial payment reflects the conclusion that a part of the total contract work has been completed, and it is a preferred method of financing. Even in the event that subsequent phases or deliveries are rejected, the contractor will have discharged at least a part of his total obligation.

Customary progress payments. Customary progress payments have been defined by the government in great detail through clauses that identify the methods and procedures for the request and payment for progress. A progress payment is made periodically during performance of the contract prior to acceptance of end items, but it is made in recognition that the contractor is progressing toward fulfillment of the contract obligation. An important dimension of progress payment practices is the nature of the debt created when they are made. Contract managers should be aware that the receipt of a progress payment creates a liability for the contractor back to the purchaser. This liability is for the total amount of the progress payments. The debt is extinguished by the delivery and acceptance of end items called for by the contract. If some event intervenes during performance of work so that the contractor is unable to proceed and, therefore, is unable to complete and make delivery of an acceptable end product, the contractor is liable for reimbursement of the progress payments received. Progress payments are a method of financing; they are not final payments. They apply to fixed-price contracts, and the purchaser is not obligated to pay for incomplete or unaccepted end items. Therefore, the risk of default or failure to perform is measurable and is quantifiable as an unliquidated progress payment. In order to extinguish the unliquidated liability, a liquidation rate will be established by the parties to the contract. Once this is agreed upon, as deliveries occur, there will be a reduction of the accrued progress payment liability in accordance with the liquidation rate. The rate of liquidation of progress payments is frequently the same rate at which the progress payments are made. However, other liquidation rates may be negotiated according to the circumstances of the particular project. To illustrate, when partial product deliveries are accepted, the contractor's contingent liability is reduced by the unit price of the accepted items. However, progress payments are a percentage of cost incurred, not of unit price, and further payment should reflect the full price of the accepted items but should not operate to increase or decrease the proportion of costs paid for undelivered end items.

As an example, the calculation of amount to be paid may be as follows: Assume that a contract specifies five deliverable items at a total price of $20,000, and the cost of producing each is $17,000. If the progress payment rate is 80 percent, the reimbursement rate on total price is 68 percent, or $13,600 maximum per unit if all costs have been incurred. When the first item is accepted, its full costs have been incurred. At the time of first-item delivery, if $50,000 of incurred cost has been properly paid, how much more should be paid? Since 68 percent of the $20,000 price for the first item has already been paid, the remainder, or 32 percent ($6,400), would ordinarily be the correct sum. As a result, $56,400 in total could be paid, made up of $20,000 for the delivered item and $36,400 for progress payments on the remaining four items. At that point, total costs are $45,500 for the undelivered items ($36,400.80), and 67 percent ($45,500/$68,000) is the indicated percent of completion of the undelivered items based on cost incurrence. The reimbursement rate (68 percent of the price until the item is accepted) leaves 32 percent to be paid at time of delivery.

Guaranteed loans. The fifth-ranked method of reducing contractor working capital needs, the authorization of guaranteed loans, is substantially different from all other methods of financing. A guaranteed loan is a loan in which the government guarantees to the financial institution that the institution's loan to the contractor will be repaid. This approach differs from authorizing the assignment of claims with no set-off. The distinction is that, with a guaranteed loan, the financial institution is assured of repayment of the loan regardless of whether the contractor who receives the loan is successful in performing the project. For example, a contractor who defaults upon his contract would not be entitled to payment for uncompleted (unaccepted) work; therefore, he may be unable to reimburse a bank for working capital advanced to him. With a guaranteed loan, however, the government assumes the liability and will repay the loan, thereby making the financial institution whole with respect to its loan. At the present time, guaranteed loans are not used in government contracting to any significant degree. During periods of mobilization, however, the guaranteed loan program may be augmented in order to facilitate the mobilization effort. A fee is charged for guaranteed loans, and the loans are established through the offices of the Federal Reserve System.

Interim cost vouchers. The sixth method of reducing the contractor's working capital needs is the method authorized for cost-reimbursable contracts. This approach differs from the customary progress payment made on fixed-price contracts only in its legal effect. The payment of interim vouchers on cost-reimbursable contracts does not create any unliquidated liability. By the nature of a cost-reimbursement contract, the government is obligated pay the contractor's allowable incurred costs regardless of final acceptance of products. This alters the basis upon which the work is performed. The government carries the risk of performance to the extent that it must reimburse allowable costs. Furthermore, payments under cost reimbursable contracts are made at 100 percent of the costs incurred, instead of the (current) percent as with fixed-price progress payments. Since these payments are authorized every two weeks, the cost-reimbursable contract is a very attractive financing instrument from a contractor's viewpoint.

Unusual progress payments. Unusual progress payments differ from customary progress payments only in the amount of the reimbursement authorized and in a slight liberalization of the circumstances under which the progress payments will be allowed. An unusual progress payment made under the government payment structure calls for reimbursement at a rate higher than the standard rate authorized for usual and customary progress payments. Currently, for large contractors, these are rates in excess of 80 percent of cost incurred or for small contractors, 85 percent of cost incurred (75 and 80 percent for DOD). In addition, customary progress payments are not generally authorized for projects in which the work is performed over a short period. The authorization of unusual progress payments, however, may permit payments to be made even though the contract does not have large accumulated sums of working capital.

RULES FOR ALLOWABILITY OF COSTS

Buyers should try to avoid examining in detail the internal operating practices of their suppliers. Whenever this is not feasible, significant costs, time delays, and frustrations are generated. Examinations may involve many supplier systems, such as accounting, estimating, budgeting, and management control. In this area, however, government contracting differs substantially from that done by industrial buyers. The government regularly employs thousands of persons for the express purpose of examining the internal systems and practices of its suppliers. Whether this capability should exist at its current level is debatable. Aggregate governmental expenses for this effort are substantial, and the process creates frustration and delays that may not justify the cost. Industrial purchasing organizations, even those of multi-billion dollar companies, have no analogous system. Nevertheless, in an effort to protect the public from paying excessive prices or inappropriate expenses, the government has developed comprehensive methods and rules for obtaining access to contractors' internal management systems and actually conducts in-depth reviews. Part of this capability is devoted to examining costs incurred by contractors in light of government rules as to whether the costs are payable by the government (allowable). Government-initiated rules for determining what costs are allowable under its contracts are, in many ways, the most complex aspects of the government's procurement regulations. Because of the cost rules, administration of contracts by the United States requires government representatives to project themselves into the accounting practices and systems of government suppliers.

In this section, we will address a portion of the special rules developed by the government for the purpose of gaining insight into the cost and management systems areas of suppliers' organizations. On a more limited scale and under specialized conditions, many corporate organizations obtain audit rights and review authority regarding their suppliers' internal operations. This authority is generally associated with purchases made when no history of prior cost exists, and when the nature of the work being procured is such that the generation of cost data is of particular interest to the buyer. The projection of industrial buyers into the internal operations of suppliers is generally limited to a narrow scope of review and is carried out only when a clear benefit to the purchaser is evident. Such action is also rare because most supplier organizations are reluctant to permit access by other private firms to their accounting, estimating, and other internal management systems. Nevertheless, it is done on a limited scale.

When the government is involved in procurement, the circumstances may be unique. Many government agencies engage in contractual efforts for which neither competitive price data nor historical cost and management information pertinent to the specific procurement objectives are available. Whenever purchases involve services and products that are so specialized or unique that they are not competitive with the economy, the need for cost data increases. For many years this situation has prevailed for a broad assortment of government acquisitions and has led to the development of today's comprehensive disclosure rules and large audit and review staffs. Their purpose is to verify that public expenditures are justified.

A brief historical sketch of the development of these comprehensive rules may be of value. The beginning probably can be marked as the year 1934 when the Vinson-Trammel Act was passed, which called for profit limitations to be imposed on the purchase of naval vessels and aircraft by the government. This enactment made it essential for profit levels to be determinable and brought about the necessity of breaking down contract prices into cost and profit components. To accomplish this on a uniform basis, it was necessary to develop cost principles (or rules). This need was first addressed by the Treasury Department which issued a series of regulations or guidelines culminating in the issuance of Treasury Decision 5000 in 1940. Treasury Decision 5000 was the first widely used set of cost principles for government contracts. Experience with T.D. 5000 led to a shift of emphasis from the measurement of profit to the measurement of costs pertinent to government contracts. In 1942 the War and Navy Departments published a pamphlet known as the *Green Book* which was applied as an alternative set of cost principles. Both publications were used during the Second World War as tools for the measurement of contractor costs. The development of cost principles was further advanced when the Contract Settlement Act of 1944 was enacted and presented a need for rules providing for settlement of contract terminations. The Joint Contract Termination Board placed a statement of rules into effect in August, 1944. These rules were developed more fully by 1952 and were incorporated into the Armed Services Procurement Regulation (ASPR), Section VIII. Section XV had been a part of ASPR when issued in 1949 but at that time was required only for cost-reimbursement contracts as the basis for determination of allowable costs. The approach was modified by the 1959 revision of the ASPR in which section XV, Cost Principles, was established as a guide for nego-tiating prices of fixed-price contracts, modifications of contracts, and settlements of fixed-price contract terminations. Section XV continued as the basis for determination of costs under existing cost contracts, but its use was expanded into the arena of pricing by the 1959 revision. By 1970, after considerable debate and expressions of concern, the ASPR cost principles were made mandatory for the negotiation of price agreements for all types of government contracts. Subsequent to that action, the cost principles have continued to be revised and expanded regularly.

With the adoption of the Federal Acquisition Regulations on April 1, 1984, the contract cost principles were published as Part 31 of the new regulation. The major portion of Part 31 is Subpart 31.2, which covers contracts with commercial organizations. The regulation also applies (primarily by reference to other source publications) to contracts with educational institutions, with state, local, and federally recognized Indian tribal governments, and with nonprofit organizations.

An excellent understanding of the scope and complexity of cost principles is obtained by examining table 11-1 which lists all major sub-divisions of the FAR cost principles as they apply to commercial organi-zations. The table provides a rating of the relative complexity of the rules for each cost category and classifies the fifty categories into seven groups according to the degree of allowability and unallowability. The length and detail of these cost principles is indicated by the thirty-six typeset pages which they occupy. (The number of pages is growing on a regular and continuing basis.) Table 11-1 was based on Part 31 of the FAR as published and current through June 27, 1984. Since then the number of cost principles has increased and, as of the end of 1985, pursuant to the direction of Title IX of the fiscal year 1986 Defense Authorization Act, numerous additions and revisions to the cost principles have been proposed and are under consideration. The clear trend of all

Table 11-1

Selected Cost Categories with Estimated Complexity and Classification in Terms of Allowability, Based on Analysis of FAR 3.205

FAR Subsection (31.205#)	Cost Category	Complexity Rating*	Allowability Group**	FAR Subsection (31.205#)	Cost Category	Complexity Rating*	Allowability Group**
1	Advertising	2	UX	25	Mfg. & Prod. Eng.	2	AQD
2	ADPE	6	AQD	26	Material	3	AQD
3	Bad Debt	1	U	27	Organization Costs	1	UX
4	Bonding	1	AQD	28	Other Bus. Exp.	1	AQD
5	Civil Defense	1	AQD	29	Plant Protection	1	A
6	Comp. Pers. Serv.	10	AQD	30	Patent	1	AQD
7	Contingencies	2	UX	31	Plant Reconversion	1	UX
8	Contrib. & Donate	1	U	32	Precontract Costs	1	AQD
10	Cost of Money	5	ALQ	33	Prof., Cons. Serv.	3	AQD
11	Depreciation	7	AQD	34	Recruitment	2	AQD
12	Economic Planning	1	AQD	35	Relocation	6	AQD
13	Empl. Morale	3	AQD	36	Rental	2	AQD
14	Entertainment	1	U	37	Royalties	2	AQD
15	Fines & Penalties	1	UX	38	Selling	2	AQD
16	Gain/L Cap. Asset	3	GLR	39	Service & Warranty	1	AQD
17	Idle Facilities	2	UX	40	Sp. Tool, & Sp. Test Equip.	1	AQD
17	Idle Capacity	1	AQD	41	Taxes	4	AQX
18	IR&D plus B&P	9	ALQ	42	Termination	6	AQD
18	Defrd. IR&D, B&P	2	UX	43	Trade & Prof. Act.	1	AQD
19	Ins. & Indemnifi.	5	AQX	44	Tng & Education	4	ALQ
20	Interest	1	UX	45	Trans. of Goods	1	A
21	Labor Relations	1	A	46	Travel	4	AQD
22	Lobbying	2	UX	47	Defense of Fraud	2	UX
23	Loss on Contracts	1	U	48	Deferred R&D	1	UX
24	Maint. & Repair	1	AQD	49	Goodwill	1	U

Code	Allowability Group	#
A	Allowable as defined or understood; no explicit qualifications	3
AQD	Allowable with qualifications or subject to specific definitions	25
ALQ	Allowable with specific limitations as well as qualifications	3
AQX	Allowable with qualifications and exceptions	2
U	Categorically unallowable as defined or understood	5
UX	Categorically unallowable with specified exceptions	11
GLR	Gains and losses, recognition mandatory, appropriate credit or charge	1

*These complexity ratings were developed by the author based on the number and proportion of text column inches devoted to each cost category in subpart 31.205 of the Federal Acquisition Regulation (FAR). Other indicators of complexity such as board or court decisions and other policy documents are not considered. An assumption is implicit in the rating that a cost category that can be described in a few (1-5) lines of text is less complex (more easily comprehended) than a cost category requiring many lines of text to describe, e.g., category number six requires 650 typeset lines of text.

**The allowability groups and codes were developed by the author on the basis of cost category content, i.e., definitions, qualifications, restrictions, limitations, and exceptions as set forth in FAR 31.205.

of these proposed modifications is to increase the level of definition, the limitations imposed, and the qualifications pursuant to the charging of cost categories to government contracts.

This aspect of the contract administration process generates frustration on the part of contractor personnel as well as government managers whose concern is accomplishment of the end objectives of contractual programs. The trend reflected in the expansion of cost principles is a result of a mind set that is keynoted by the publicity and negative implications associated with news reports critical of cost practices associated with government contracts. This mind set holds that the correction of errors and the control over apparently unreasonable practices can best be achieved by detailing and explicitly restricting costing practices that are perceived as unreasonable or unfair. The unfortunate consequence of this approach has been expanded complexity, increased paperwork, increased contractor staffing for purposes of tracing and justifying cost proposals and cost recording processes, and increased staffing on the part of government agencies charged with verifying the appropriateness of contractor costing.

When the cost principles are carefully read, it is evident that most of the rules are reasonably consistent with good business practice and appear to be reasonably consistent with perceptions of public policy and public interest. From a practical viewpoint, however, the sheer number of rules and the interrelationships among rules delineating government policy toward the allowability of costs render the subject an abstruse field, requiring increasingly specialized personnel for staffing both government and contractor offices. Of all the ways in which private and public sector contracting activities differ, these costing rules are probably the most important. In normal, private, industrial relationships, avoiding these amplified administrative processes is absolutely critical to competitive costing and practicing. In fact, even in government procurement, avoiding involvement in detailed review of cost activity is preferred, at least in theory, to engaging in actual audit and investigative oversight. Government policy, however, does not permit the avoidance of these expensive practices under those types of contracts for which cost and pricing data are required of contractors or for which cost determination is an essential part of the administrative steps necessary to meet regulatory requirements associated with payments and completion of contractual obligations.

The cost principles are applicable to all forms of contracts, including cost-reimbursable and fixed-price contracts written on an incentive or redeterminable basis, whenever cost determination is necessary. Furthermore, every negotiated government contract that exceeds $100,000 in total cost is subject to the cost and pricing data submission requirements imposed by statute. Whenever these requirements are imposed, the allowable cost rules restrict the basis for pricing of the contract, regardless of its type.

From the viewpoint of contractor organizations, avoiding the special complexities associated with government contracts is a reasonable business objective, since it allows a lower overall cost operation. However, actual avoidance of the rules is extremely difficult for any contractor who engages in a substantial amount of government contracting. It should be noted that the costing rules are not applicable to contracts entered into on a competitive basis if the type of contract is firm-fixed-price. Such contracts can be entered into without subjecting the contractor to contract audit for either pricing or cost determination purposes. Unfortunately, if the market conditions pertinent to a given contract award are not competitive, avoiding direct involvement in the cost principles and procedures is extremely difficult. Contractors should also be fully aware that even with competitively awarded firm-fixed-price contracts, the possibility of changes or other noncompetitive modifications of existing contracts will subject any proposals for a price change greater than $100,000 to the cost and pricing data and certification requirements and, potentially, to cost determination reviews by government audit agencies.

COST ACCOUNTING STANDARDS

Although the cost principles are comprehensive, they do not prescribe accounting rules for contractors. The cost principles delineate only whether a cost, as developed by a contractor, is allowable as a charge against the government. However, in 1970 under Public Law 91-379, the Congress determined that cost accounting by defense contractors should be subject to standards to be developed and prescribed by a government Cost Accounting Standards Board (CASB). Accordingly, the statute authorized establishment of the CASB which, over a period of years, proceeded to develop nineteen cost accounting standards pertinent to defense contracts.

Chart 11-1 lists the standards promulgated by CASB. Although Congress discontinued funding for the board, and it was disestablished, the standards remain in effect. The absence of a board has created administrative difficulties because there is no substitute organization with authority to interpret or modify the standards. The Department of Defense has asserted that it has authority to maintain the standards, but a final resolution of this matter has not been decided as of this writing. The policies and regulations associated with cost accounting standards have been extended by administrative action to certain non-defense government contracts. Throughout their existence, the standards have been controversial, and the need for CASB has been hotly debated. Regardless of the debate, the standards are firmly established and are defended as a mechanism for requiring government contractors to adopt

Chart 11-1

Cost Accounting Standards

A.   STANDARDS RELEVANT TO BASIC COST ACCOUNTING PRACTICES

Standard 401:   Consistency in Estimating, Accumulating and Report-
                ing Costs
Standard 402:   Consistency in Allocating Costs Incurred for the
                Same Purpose
Standard 405:   Accounting for Unallowable Costs
Standard 406:   Cost Accounting Period

B.   STANDARDS PERTINENT TO CAPITALIZATION AND CAPITAL
     ASSETS

Standard 404:   Capitalization of Tangible Assets
Standard 409:   Depreciation of Tangible Capital Assets
Standard 414:   Cost of Money as an Element of the Cost of Facili-
                ties Capital
Standard 417:   Cost of Money as an Element of Cost of Facilities
                Under Construction

C.   STANDARDS RELEVANT TO PERSONNEL COMPENSATION

Standard 408:   Compensated Personal Absence
Standard 412:   Compensation and Measurement of Pension Costs
Standard 413:   Adjustment and Allocation of Pension Costs
Standard 415:   Accounting for Deferred Compensation Costs

D.   STANDARDS PERTINENT TO ACCUMULATING AND ALLOCATING
     INDIRECT COSTS

Standard 403:   Allocation of Home Office Expense to Segments
Standard 410:   Allocation of G&A Expense
Standard 416:   Accounting for Insurance Costs
Standard 418:   Allocation of Direct and Indirect Costs
Standard 420:   Accounting for IR&D and B&P Costs

E.   STANDARDS RELEVANT TO DIRECT COSTS

Standard 407:   Use of Standard Costs for Direct Material and Direct
                Labor
Standard 411:   Accounting for Material Acquisition Costs

cost accounting system practices and policies that, in the government's view, are appropriate to the costing of public contracts. Cost accounting standards are not applicable to all contracts, however. There are approximately fifteen categories of contracts and subcontracts that are exempt from all CAS requirements. These are delineated in FAR Subpart 30.301.

As a general statement, the cost accounting standards are applied to contracts with a value in excess of $100,000 which are not entered into as a result of sealed bidding. Individual contract awards up to $500,000 are also not subject to CAS unless other CAS-covered defense contracts are held by the contractor. In addition, firm-fixed-price contracts and subcontracts, if awarded without required submission of cost and pricing data, would be exempt from CAS.

Coverage of CAS is defined in two ways. Full coverage requires that the contractor's business comply with all of the cost accounting standards. Modified coverage requires only that the business unit comply with Standard 401, Consistency in Estimating Accumulating and Reporting Costs, and Standard 402, Consistency in Allocating Costs Incurred for the Same Purpose. The modified form of CAS coverage is allowed only for covered contracts less than $10 million and only when the business unit to which the contract is awarded has received a total of less than $10 million in national defense CAS-covered contracts.

In addition to the applicability of the cost accounting standards themselves, the cost accounting standards policy requires submission of disclosure statements by contractors who receive national defense awards amounting to $10 million or more. Disclosure statements must be submitted by a contractor to the administrative contracting officer cognizant of his plant. In reviewing the statement, the ACO draws upon the services of the Defense Contract Audit Agency to initially determine the currency, accuracy, and completeness of the statement. In the case of subcontractors, when the subcontractor views his disclosure statement as privileged or confidential information, he is authorized to submit it directly to the ACO and audit office. These provisions are designed to permit subcontractor organizations to avoid providing their confidential internal information to other contractor organizations who may, under some circumstances, become competitors. Each of the rules associated with the cost accounting standards program is supported by an appropriate contract clause. The clauses vary according to whether cost accounting standards are applicable in full or in modified form and whether the requirement for a disclosure statement is pertinent to the contract.

SUMMARY

Contacting parties discuss and agree on monetary and related issues that routinely impact their financial results. There are several important monetary factors that operate to constrain or to motivate progress. The following highlights are discussed or identified in this chapter:

- Funding as a constraint on payments
- Clauses to provide for incremental funding and firm limits on government obligations when cost type reimbursement rules apply to contracts
- Procedures and limitations on payments during performance of contract work
- Eight methods of financing work in progress, including a summary of the preferred methods
- A brief history of the development of rules for allowability when cost-reimbursement provisions govern payments
- Forty-nine cost categories classified into seven groups based on the rules pertinent to their allowability under government contracts
- A summary of the nineteen cost accounting standards promulgated by the government and mandated for most major defense contracts

TOPICS FOR DISCUSSION

1. Differentiate between partial payments and progress payments.
2. Explain the differences between limitation of funds and limitation of cost in government contracts. In terms of management discretion, which lends greater flexibility to agency managers?
3. Discuss the rules for making payment requests (1) when progress payments are authorized, and (2) when working under a cost-reimbursement contract.
4. Compare guaranteed loans with the assignment of claims under government contracts.
5. Interest is categorized as an unallowable cost with specified exceptions. Evaluate this policy decision.

CASE 11-1

Cajun Company Pricing Defense

The Cajun Company was established as one of the leaders in CAD/CAM (computer aided design/computer aided manufacture). Its sales were primarily commercial--95 percent to nongovernment customers. Cajun's president, Steve Roberts, liked it that way. As he put it, "The administrative gaff associated with government sales is painful, and the cost of documentation would make us noncompetitive in our principal markets." Nevertheless, government-sponsored projects constituted potentially profitable business, and Cajun found that some of its systems fit government requirements admirably. A number of their sales to government prime contractors had been obtained during the late 1970s and early 1980s.

During 1981 Cajun was acquired by General Supplies Corporation, one of the nation's Fortune 500 companies and a large government contractor in several business lines. One customer that Cajun had developed whose work was government funded was the Arbuckle Co. Arbuckle was established at the Hanford, Washington, facility of the Department of Energy and was responsible for several aspects of the agency's nuclear material disposal processing activities at that facility.

Arbuckle had bought several CAD/CAM systems from Cajun and was very pleased with their overall performance. These past sales had been handled in the normal manner with which Cajun was familiar (firm-priced and based on some degree of competition). In making those sales, Cajun had not been asked for cost and pricing data, and the prices paid had been consistent with Cajun's normal pricing policies, which afforded the customer an opportunity to examine price information but not cost data.

Cajun prepared price manuals covering all of their standard products. The manuals were developed in-house and reflected Cajun's methods of doing business, including their special expertise in cost estimating and price projection in the field of computer software creation and related work in knowledge-dependent systems. The company believed its price manuals to be proprietary and extremely important to its competitive position. The manuals were not made available outside the company except to established customers and then only for examination at Cajun's offices.

In January, 1985, Arbuckle asked Cajun for a proposal to design and supply a new system for nuclear material disposal. At first the sale appeared to be a simple addition to Cajun's earlier sales to Arbuckle. However, shortly after hearing that the Cajun system was selected by Arbuckle, Cajun's contract manager, John Simpson, learned that Arbuckle had requested delivery of cost and pricing data as part of the Cajun proposal. This request brought John up short. He was thoroughly familiar with the cost and pricing data requirements imposed on government contractors by statute and regulation. Furthermore, the particular contract was one in which Cajun had a great interest. It was estimated to involve technology in which Cajun had developed a commanding lead over its competitors and would provide $3 million in sales over an eighteen-month period.

The particular system desired by Hanford was intended to support architectural design and engineering for special nuclear processing facilities. It involved use of a number of proprietary and widely marketed software packages that Cajun had created, but it also required special work efforts by Cajun to specifically fit the applications at Hanford.

Furthermore, adoption of Cajun's system could prove valuable in preserving their lead in providing CAD/CAM at the facility.

Cajun's historic mode of operations reflected the peculiarities of the knowledge business in which product life cycles are short, products must be customized, decisions must be made quickly, and the firm must be free to deal with the marketplace. Coupled with these characteristics, Cajun also strongly felt that its true assets were not its fixed ones. Instead, their chief asset was talent--the unique qualities associated with the creative genius necessary for success in high-tech. That type of asset unfortunately has legs capable of immediate movement. Variable, seemingly indefensible pay rates and cost incurrences were a consequence of this situation. Furthermore, Cajun did not develop costs on a job basis and could not identify specific contract costs without modifying its accounting system. These factors led John Simpson and his boss, Steve Roberts, to resist providing cost data to customers, even those of the stature of the U.S. government and its prime contractors.

As a consequence of these perceptions, immediately upon hearing of the Arbuckle request, John began to devise a strategy for convincing Arbuckle (and as it shortly became evident, a very smart but unsympathetic government auditor) that the CAD/CAM sale should not be subject to the requirement for submission of cost and pricing data.

* * * * *

1. Use available FAR, DOD Far supplement, and other information to devise the appropriate basis and strategy for John Simpson to use in persuading the auditor to support his request for a catalog or market price exemption (or any other applicable type of exemption) from the cost and pricing data request.
2. Assume that you are John Simpson. Prepare a one-page report for Steve Roberts detailing the options available to Cajun in the event that your initial attempts to obtain an exemption are not successful. Be prepared to justify your options.

CASE 11-2

The Able System Development Proposal

Seymour Houseman, known by his employees as Sy, was nearing his thirty-fifth year managing research and development projects and manufacturing programs involving advance technology. As president of the Aerospace Division at Able, he had led the company into a period of expanding defense sales and had initiated the volume production operation at the Armplaza facility. The Armplaza facility represented a true micro-cosm of large-scale, high-technology production. It was designed to effi-ciently produce either volume or limited quantities of products, such as the Mark 81 tactical display and the AN/AYQ-21 imaging system. In May, 1984, questions surfaced concerning Able's pricing of the products assembled at Armplaza, presenting Sy with a set of conflicts over the structure and equity of costing systems that had been generally accepted and followed for several years by Able management.

Robert Johns, the Manager of Planning and Administration for volume production, found his program jeopardized by pressures from outside the corporation. Robert's background as an MBA and computer analyst had provided him with a keen perception of the competitive impact of seemingly small elements in building the cost basis for pricing products of the division's volume production program. He was dismayed by what he called the broad brush approach taken by some of his con-temporaries involved in management of R&D programs--the dominant work of the Aerospace Division.

Volume production had built its business base on a different prem-ise. It sought production subcontracts for small and medium quantities of high-technology devices from major systems producers of Department of Defense weapons. In fact, none of the work at the Armplaza facility involved R&D. Its contracts were firm-fixed-price and were acquired as a result of competitive solicitations. Nevertheless, Armplaza's special expertise in devising methods and procedures for critical high-technology assembly and qualification testing gave it an edge that sometimes helped win contracts, even at prices above the competitive floor. As Robert assessed this type of success, certain weaknesses seemed important. In his opinion, Armplaza prices were too high to ensure repeat business. His view was strongly supported during early 1984 when several events focussed attention on the issue of price.

The first event was loss of a competitive contract for the produc-tion of printed circuit boards for Solarwick Corporation. This loss was directly caused by Able's high price, even though Able was superbly equipped and suited for the job. The second event was loss of the Mark 81 Tactical Display contract in a competition for production of 200 units. In debriefing, the loss was attributed to price alone--Able was rated technically superior, but its proposal was criticized for being excessively expensive in G&A and overhead rates, labor hours per unit, and profit. Although for technical reasons the contract was subsequently negotiated and awarded to Able, the original loss contributed to the understanding that competitive price had become vital to future expanded business. The third event, loss of a production contract for the AN-62 mapping spec-trometer, was similar to the second, only the briefing official complained that indirect costs were too high and that some of Able's direct labor should have been provided under overhead. Robert reacted strongly to these complaints. He believed in the long-run profitability of building substantial repeat business for fabricate-to-print contracts, and he immediately conveyed his concern to Ray Solomon, Business Manager for Volume Production. He and Ray took up the matter with Kevin Markley, the Director of Contracts for Aerospace Division. Robert's enthusiasm for building the fabricate-to-print business was shared by all, but his approach to reducing Able's price through reallocations caused great dismay. Kevin raised the point that Able's government customers accounted for sales approaching $300 million (of which volume production accounted for less than 10 percent), and reallocations of indirect expenses, regardless of internal validity, might encourage government audit agency action to suspend payments. Kevin pointed out that government regulations demand that only allowable costs be reimbursed and that reallocation of overhead that increases the burden on cost-reimbursable business may raise challenges.

As a result of this discussion, Robert developed the following cost adjustment program proposal:

Memorandum For: President, Aerospace Division
From: Robert Johns
Subject: Competitive Pricing for Volume Production

Recent instances of lost contracts and customer complaints that our prices for fabricate-to-print production are excessive have prompted a thorough review of contract costing and pricing practices at our Armplaza facility. As a result of that review, I propose that Able management authorize certain changes in our costing and pricing practices. My purposes in proposing these changes are as follows:

1. To create a pricing structure for competitive costing of fabricate-to-print contracts
2. To redistribute overhead and G&A to better reflect beneficiaries of the costs included therein
3. To increase the basic level of work in volume production to meet three objectives:
    a. To capture repeat sales of fabricate-to-print production in place of our current tendency to lose the repeat business on a price basis
    b. To gain spinoff benefits accruing from an increased level of fabricate-to-print work (e.g., our experience in using our automated production equipment developed for the Solarwick job was the key factor in capturing the mast-mounted sight camera production)
    c. To advance our operational techniques in volume production, creating a recognizable "Able system" manufacturing and pricing

plan with superior cost and delivery capabilities

To accomplish these goals, I propose these actions:

1. To remove from overhead allocated to volume production, specialized labor categories essential to the support of R&D operations
2. To exclude charges for specialized facilities costs, such as V-T chambers and solar radiation equipment, from overhead allocated to volume production
3. To exclude independent research and development from G&A allocated to volume production
4. To quote fabrication-to-print job prices at a lower profit rate than R&D jobs because the production effort is inherently in a lower risk category

Sy was disturbed by this proposal because it contained some sound logic combined with a large element of skeleton-rattling change.

CASE 11-3

Stock Options

ASPR 15-205.6(a) states, "The cost of options to employees to purchase stock of the contractor or of an affiliate is unallowable."

However, ASPR 15-205.6(a) also states, "Compensation for personal services includes all remuneration paid currently or accrued, in whatever form and whether paid immediately or deferred, for services rendered by employees to the contractor during the period of contract performance. It includes . . . employee stock options . . . *and* such costs are allowable . . ."

Although the first quote is an exception to the second, it appears that some form of employee stock options must be allowable, or else the general language needn't include "employee stock options" as an allowable cost.

It has been held that the regulation writers had in mind rendering unallowable stock options that

1. limit eligibility to a small group of key employees,
2. state the number of shares in the option,
3. involve a formally signed contract between the employee and contractor,
4. cover a significant number of years,
5. bar the shareholder from acquiring any rights until the option is exercised, or

6.   provide that the option remain in effect, even if the plan is terminated.

The WBS-ADP Co. developed a stock option plan that differs from the above in that

1.   all employees are eligible,
2.   the number of shares are limited to a percentage of the employees' compensation,
3.   no individual contract is signed with any employee,
4.   the period for stock acquisition is relatively short,
5.   the shareholders' rights accrue as soon as the first share of stock is acquired, and
6.   the contractor can terminate the plan at any time.

* * * * *

1.   Should the cost of this option plan to WBS-ADP Co. be allowable? (The cost is the difference between what its employees paid for stock and the fair market value of that stock.)
2.   Evaluate these concepts as management tools.

CASE 11-4

Security Services, Inc.

Security Services, Inc. provided security guard and fire protection services as a subcontractor to NASA under a cost-reimbursement base support services prime contract. A part of the NASA PR (15.205-39) provides for reimbursement of severance pay costs to the extent that they are required

1.   by law,
2.   by employer-employee agreement (collective bargaining),
3.   by established policy (creating an implied agreement between the contractor and his employees), or
4.   by circumstances of the particular employment.

As a result of a class action suit, a state court ordered Security Services, Inc. to make severance payments to a number of its nonunion supervisory and administrative employees. However, Security Services had no established policy or implied agreement with these employees, or any historical practice of making such payments. The payments were made in accordance with the court order.

The contracting officer now refuses to reimburse the prime contractor, and the prime refuses to reimburse Security Services for its costs in making the required payments. Security Services is appealing its claim to the NASA Board of Contract Appeals (in the prime's name).

* * * * *

Should these costs be paid? If not, how could Security Services have managed this affair more effectively?

CASE 11-5

Space Center Communications

The cost of advertising has been prohibited by DOD appropriation acts (exceptions delineated) since 1962. AG Corporation operated under contracts with the government and was subject to the following definition of advertising costs:

> Advertising costs mean the costs of advertising media and corollary administrative costs. Advertising media include magazines, newspapers, radio and television programs, direct mail, trade papers, outdoor advertising, dealer cards and window displays, conventions, exhibits, free goods and samples, and so forth.

AG Corporation incurred costs of the following items:

1. Magazine: issues printed and distributed monthly as a report of contractors' technological developments, progress on programs, and personnel changes
2. Brochures: one containing factual information about the company; one containing a speech of the corporate president; and one designed to enhance employee political knowledge
3. News release materials
4. Liaison activity (press desk at agency launch facilities, fact sheets, press kits, membership in an industry association, preparation of articles on its cost reduction program)

* * * * *

Are these costs allowable?

CASE 11-6

Who Pays?

The contractor was a small business. He provided engineering services in support of the Space communications program (error analysis studies). His contract was cost-reimbursable and was the fifth consecutive contract awarded to him for this work. He was notified on September 25, 1986 that he would not be awarded another contract, although the first Space communications launch had not occurred, and the work was not finished. The contract contained a limitation of cost clause that required the contractor to notify the contracting officer when he had reason to believe a cost overrun would occur. It also contained a negotiated overhead rate clause that provided provisional overhead rates and required negotiation of final rates based on the contractor's actual cost experience. The contract was completed on October 31, 1986. The contractor's fiscal year ended on December 31, 1986. The team of engineers employed by the contractor was retained during November and December, 1986, while the contractor sought new business unsuccessfully, and the salary cost of this team was transferred from direct to overhead for that period. This caused the overhead cost for the fiscal year to overrun the provisional rates.

* * * * *

What are the issues raised by the facts, and who should fund the overrun costs, the contractor or the government?

12

Change,
Update,
Proposals,
and Orders

Changes in a contract ordinarily are made only with the agreement of both parties. The need for agreement endows the parties with a form of equality; both participate in decisionmaking. This notion is fundamental in private party agreements, and if one party acts to change the relationship without concurrence of the other party, a breach of the contract occurs, permitting sanctions to be imposed by the injured party through legal action. In government contracts, this relationship is modified in a significant manner.

PRINCIPAL ELEMENTS OF CONTRACTUAL CHANGES AUTHORITY

The best known and most actively used standard clause in government contracts is the Changes clause. There are several versions corresponding to the specific type of contract, but all have certain common characteristics. The clause, mandatory for most government contracts, provides a contractual grant of authority to the government by its supplier. It gives the government the right to alter unilaterally specific matters affecting the performance of the contract. Such authority is seldom a part of private sector contracts except subcontracts under government primes. The clause specifies a procedure for issuing unilateral orders and vests the power to use the procedure in the government's contracting officer. Furthermore, it obligates the contractor to perform the altered contract in accordance with the direction of the contracting officer. The clause declares that nothing contained therein excuses the contractor from proceeding with the work as changed. Consequently, a contractor who fails to comply with a change order properly issued by the contracting officer may be subjected to default action.

While this grant of authority is significant, a major element of the Changes clause is its limitation that unilateral orders may be issued only for changes that are within the general scope of the contract. This limitation prevents use of the Changes clause as a general authority for the government to procure new work or new products. In addition, the standard Changes clause does not provide unilateral authority to alter terms and conditions or delivery schedules. The unilateral authority applies to changes in the following areas: (1) specifications, drawings or designs; (2) method of shipment or packing; and (3) place of delivery. In cost-plus types of contracts, the unilateral authority also covers changes in the amount of government property provided under the contract.

An important procedural aspect of the Changes clauses requires change orders to be in written form and signed by the contracting officer. The clauses afford a degree of balance in the contractual relationship by specifying the method by which contractors may seek compensatory adjustments of their contracts. The method is to submit a request for equitable adjustment as compensation for the change. The recognized areas for which compensation is given include cost, profit or fee, delivery schedule, and, if affected, adjustment of other terms and conditions of the agreement. The government's policy regarding equitable adjustments is to permit adjustment of the contractor's price, including profit or fee, only to the extent justified by the amount of change in the contractor's costs of performance caused by the altered work effort.

As a further requirement of the Changes clause, a contractor is obligated to assert his claim for a contract adjustment within a specific number of days (usually 30 days) after issuance of the change order. Claims submitted after the specified number of days may be acted on at the discretion of the contracting officer, but not if they are submitted subsequent to final payment of the contract price.

These bare elements of the Changes clause hardly begin to address its true impact on the relationship between the buyer and the seller in government contracts. The interactions and subtleties of this clause have major implications for the management process associated with acquisitions by means of a contract. Several specific factors must be recognized to gain full insight into the contractual impact of the Changes clause. A major factor is non-enforcement of the specific rules for issuances of changes and for presentation of claims. When changes occur, the use or non-use of a written order signed by the contracting officer has not greatly affected whether boards and courts will review and make decisions on disputes brought before them. Furthermore, on their own initiative, contracting officers may ratify actions taken by other agents or officers of the government. Time limits on submission of claims have not generally barred recovery for changes, since contracting officers are enabled by the clause to recognize claims presented later than the authorized period. Under normal circumstances, it is unlikely that a contracting officer will refuse to act upon a claim provided it is submitted prior to final payment under the contract. A second important factor in the administration of changes is the lack of any specific requirement that a change order include, or be accompanied by, a proportionate adjustment of funds under the government contract. Although a contracting officer is not empowered to make change orders without requisitions adequate to cover the cost of the change (as it is estimated by the government), the actual obligation of the money is not a prerequisite to the issuance of the change order.

Change action can be initiated in many ways. For example, the manufacturer of a pump (already under contract to a specified design) may identify a simplified, less expensive, but nonconforming way to machine hydraulic cylinders that meet quality standards of the contract. Consequently, the manufacturer submits a value engineering change proposal (VECP). Similarly, a bridge construction contractor identifies a marginal aspect of a specified structural requirement. He submits a change proposal. The initiative may start with the customer who revises design or test level requirements after contract award and requests an engineering change proposal (ECP) from the contractor. The source of changes and their causes have few limits, and the associated cost can range from insignificant to gigantic, sometimes exceeding the original cost of the contract.

A contract proposal from the supplier is normally required before a change is put into effect, regardless of the source of the need. If the buyer identifies the need, he or she will initiate action, usually by requesting an ECP. Similarly, if the supplier identifies the need, he or she initiates action by preparing an ECP. Of course, personal contacts and discussions may precede the ECP process.

Contractual action to order changes is ordinarily based on a requisition or procurement request that cites funds available for the action and provides a specification or other appropriate technical documentation of the requirement. The action to initiate work on a change to a government contract may be unilateral or bilateral and is based on the authority of the Changes clause. Action ordering the change should not be taken without having fully considered technical, logistics, schedule, and cost implications. In many government agencies, the pre-action process is based on a configuration management system.

CONFIGURATION MANAGEMENT

The issuance and negotiation processes of a contractual change are frequently carried out without specific reference to the engineering management processes that generate the need for contractual action. The two processes, however, are closely interrelated and should be placed in perspective by examining the objectives and basic procedures associated with each. The initiation of contractual change orders follows identification of a need for design or other engineering change. In fact, for many years engineering change proposals (ECPs) have been a standard method for initiating a technical review of design and for verifying the need for contractual action. The use of ECPs alone, however, is an inadequate method of securing and maintaining control over the configuration of complex end items. The ECP provides a method of systematically documenting the need for, and impacts of, a proposed change in specification or design. There are several other dimensions of the overall configuration management problem. The four principal elements of configuration management are

1. change control,
2. identification and documentation of configuration,
3. accounting for the status of configuration actions, and
4. an audit system to verify that the technical documentation of a configuration item is an accurate and current representation of the actual physical product.

Each of these major elements is made up of a substantial set of procedures, documents, and verification methods. Each step in the entire configuration management process needs to be fully coordinated with users of the end product--logisticians concerned with post-delivery support of the product and others, such as financial and contracting authorities, who are interested in and affected by the design. This ensures that the action taken will reflect the nature of the product under management and will be consistent with the overall application of the product in use. Similarly, it ensures preservation of the contractual system for initiation and negotiation of the cost and time effects.

Some objectives of a well designed configuration management system are as follows:

1. To secure prompt action on essential changes for production contracts to minimize retrofit expenses on work in progress
2. To clarify the authority to make change decisions and to assign responsibility for developing the modifying configuration
3. To recognize the differences in levels of control required in managing configuration of development projects and production programs
4. To create a method for positively identifying documentation associated with and essential to the support of field operations
5. To ensure that items in the field and records pertaining to them have been updated to conform with current approved configuration

6.   To minimize the cost and collateral effects of ECPs through timely and comprehensive evaluation of their total impact

The level of detail to which configuration management extends depends on the stage of development or production that the end product has reached. Most authorities would assert that during the early development phases of a new product, the control of product configuration should be limited to functional (not detailed design) characteristics. Once a product has moved beyond development and into production or preproduction stages, the engineering documentation should comprehensively cover the physical and functional characteristics of the end item.

Change control is the aspect of configuration management most directly pertinent to the contract changes process. This activity is a visible part of the work of configuration managers; it is a vital effort, because the change control process results in approval or disapproval of engineering change proposals. It is the process by which decisions are made on requests for deviation or waiver of technical requirements for a particular product. The change control module of configuration management is designed to ensure that only necessary changes are approved. An objective of configuration managers is to limit the approval of ECPs to those which will

1.   correct deficiencies in the product under study,
2.   significantly improve the operational effectiveness of the end product,
3.   reduce the support requirements for the end product,
4.   achieve significant life cycle cost savings, or
5.   prevent slippage in an approved production program.

Whether a specific end item is to be subjected to configuration management depends on the need of the owner to control the inherent characteristics of the item. Some level of configuration control should be applied in all programs, but a large and complex system requires a much greater depth of control over its configuration than may be required for simpler systems. This is accomplished using configuration management. The following definitions may be helpful in clarifying the objectives and techniques of configuration management:

1.   **Configuration** - the functional and physical characteristics of hardware or software. Configuration should be delineated in technical documentation in a manner identical to its fulfillment in the product.
2.   **Configuration management** - a management system designed to
     a)   ensure correct identification and documentation of the physical and functional characteristics of a configuration item,

b) control changes in the defined characteristics,
c) establish a record and provide appropriate reporting of change
    actions in process, and
d) implement changes in the configuration item.

3. **Configuration items** - a discreet aggregation of hardware or software
    that satisfies an end use function. Such items are designated by the
    owner for configuration management. For operation and maintenance
    purposes, a configuration item will include any repairable item to be
    separately procured and supported. For purposes of development and
    production, configuration items are identified as contract end items.

From the viewpoint of configuration managers, all contractual
change actions should be preceded by following the steps of the configuration management system. Time requirements for coordination, evaluation, funding, and approval have not always been consistent with program
needs, however.

THE NEED FOR INFORMAL CHANGE AND UPDATE OF CONTRACTS

Project managers, technical directors, contracting officers, and other
managers who administer large contracts usually experience pressure
generated by shortage of time. Much of this pressure is created by
persistent change external to the contract effort, such as advances in
technology and altered requirements. Changes emerging after award of a
contract generate a demand to alter the course of work. While certain
types of changes, such as discovery of design deficiency or incompatibility, arise directly from work pursued under a contract, independent
activities are a greater source of urgent changes. Change is a function
of society. It is driven by scientific and technological achievements and
by political and economic developments. Since World War II change has
occurred so rapidly that, even within the time frame of a single large
contract, alterations in work become imperative. The need for alterations
arises from numerous sources which can be grouped into six general
categories:

1. Changes in requirements emanating from the intended user of the
    product
2. Discovery of incompatible specifications or designs, necessitating a
    modification of product design
3. Production incompatibilities recognized only after work has been
    initiated and necessitating modification in order to prepare a work-
    able end item
4. Discovery of opportunities for cost savings through redesign (for
    example, as a result of a value engineering examination)

5. Funding shortages necessitating cost reduction by eliminating originally required features of the end product
6. Discovery during performance that an improved product is possible and desirable

By examining these sources of change, the reasons for urgent action can be recognized immediately. Incompatibilities, funding cuts, design deficiencies, and other sources are unpredictable yet when discovered, demand immediate correction or adjustment of work. For instance, when a production incompatibility surfaces, continued production under the old design will result in creating obsolescent or unserviceable end products. Urgency may be complemented by other factors inherent in contracting, including the tendency to incorporate overly optimistic performance, schedule, and funding expectations into the original agreement. Once established as commitments, these expectations cause managers to act cautiously lest some rights or entitlement be lost to the other party. Regardless of the reason for time pressures, they create a strong impetus for immediate action when the need for a change has been recognized.

POLICY BASIS FOR CHANGES AUTHORITY

Justification for vesting in government managers the authority to issue unilateral, binding changes rests on the government's perception that it must maintain control of work that is being performed in the public interest. As sovereign, the government could do this regardless of the presence of a clause but, under the United States' system of law, would be subject to breach of contract claims. The Changes clause provides specific contractual recognition that the government can change its mind and redirect work even though it has made a valid contract for pursuing the work in a particular way. This preservation of the government's options for altering a course of action is viewed as reasonable because the Changes clause provides for *equitable adjustment* as compensation to contractors for having responded to the government's change order. The equitable adjustment includes cost and profit, and schedule adjustments (upward or downward) to reflect the nature of the change and may alter other terms and conditions of the contract.

The Changes clause is the principal mechanism (but not the only one) by which the government overcomes the fact that its contracts, like those of other buyers, are normally viewed as completed actions when issued, i.e., fully defined at the time of issuance. This perception may be inconsistent with the nature of the major undertakings for which contracts are issued. A key objective of procurement action is to define projects fully, thereby enabling the parties to formulate a stable and properly funded contractual charter. Contractual parties do not expect their agreement to be altered without positive action even though the nature of the project may be such that change--substantial and regular dynamic activity--is also expected.

Change orders have been used for unilateral changes of delivery schedules when the specifications have been drafted to include schedule data. This is feasible only if the schedule information is made part of the specification. To be successful, such orders must call for a feasible schedule. The contractor's effort to comply with such an order would be compensable under the Changes clause, regardless of actual delivery.

MANAGEMENT OF INFORMAL AND CONSTRUCTIVE CHANGES

Urgency underlies the reality that many changes have been initiated on an informal basis in advance of formal contract action. One consequence of informal action is conflict, both internally (within the buyer's organization) and between the buyer and the seller. For example, the internal conflicts within a government agency are rooted in the frustration of senior managers or contracting officers who discover that their budget authority and their prerogatives for evaluating and making decisions have been diminished by the passage of time and the initiation of work that was not formally authorized through appropriate procedures. The magnitude of change activity of this type has been so great that drastic management steps have been taken by agencies to try to prevent recurrence of such behavior.

One of the realities of government contracting that lends impetus to the initiation of informal changes is the very existence of the Changes clause. The clause is important because it authorizes unilateral direction of changes and provides a procedure for making cost and time adjustments (including profit) after work is initiated (and even after it is completed). This, coupled with general nonenforcement of specific procedural requirements of the clause, encourages informality and has established the concept of the *constructive change.* The term constructive change arose from a series of decisions made by boards of contract appeals[1] that examined contractors' claims for price and schedule adjustments which contracting officers had refused to grant through normal negotiation procedures. Literally thousands of constructive changes cases have been decided by the boards. In these cases, the contractor claimed that the government contract was changed, even though no formal, writ-

---

[1]There are eleven Boards of Contract Appeals. They were established by agency heads to handle administrative appeals from decisions of contracting officers. Their existence, jurisdiction, and staffing have been given a statutory basis by the Contract Disputes Act of 1978.

ten change order signed by the contracting officer had been issued. The boards of contract appeals construed these controversies as being within their jurisdiction by evaluating the cases on the basis of their authority to decide appeals arising under a remedy granting clause (such as the Changes clause). The appeals procedure is defined by the Disputes clause which, like the Changes clause, is a standard part of government contracts. The boards found that they could accept jurisdiction if a change had occurred and had been authorized in an informal manner by the government. Once jurisdiction was established, the board could make a decision on the claim in accordance with the remedies authorized by the Changes clause.

In the absence of this interpretation by the boards of contract appeals, unauthorized change action initiated by government representatives would have constituted a breach of contract, an issue not within the jurisdiction of the boards prior to enactment of the Contract Disputes Act of 1978. In effect, the boards found that a change order could be recognized, even if not directed by a contracting officer's formal written order. This broad interpretation of the Changes clause as an authority for the boards' action was reduced to only historical importance after passage of the Contract Disputes Act of 1978. Nevertheless, it has important explanatory significance and is the source of the term constructive change which is still relevant in the administration of government contracts. Regardless of procedural questions the problem of control over contract change activity persists. It is a problem of management control brought into focus by the operation of a contract, rather than a problem unique to the existence of the contract.

While the constructive change may be the best known form of informal change, many changes and alleged changes occur a result of informal communications between government representatives and contractors. Many are subsequently ratified by contracting officer action. The power of a contracting officer to ratify changes initiated by other personnel is an important though limited power. It is a limited power largely because agency managers are concerned that possible excessive use of ratification within their agencies will cause senior managers to lose control over resources and personnel. Whenever a contracting officer ratifies actions initiated informally by others, associated cost and schedule adjustments must be contractually recognized and appropriate modifications of the contracts issued. Ratification of a change permits, but does not quantify, the amount of cost or schedule effects. The amounts must be agreed on through negotiation and generally require additional funding by the agency. Contracting officers tend to be reluctant to ratify informal changes and will take such action only when persuaded that the government's interest and equity in the contractual relationship clearly demand it.

The term constructive change has become well established in government contracting but should be understood as no more than a legal term to describe informal change. There are five broad categories of situations that result in informal (or constructive) changes. Actions in each category are heavily influenced in practice by the government's technical director. The role of technical directors has been highlighted in case 4-1 "Technical Direction Policy for the Strategic Defense Initiative" and is further examined in this chapter under the heading "Techniques of Altering Contract Work." In the case of technical directives, the contracting officer's technical representative (COTR) may inappropriately impose work on the contractor that is beyond the contract requirement. The categories of action or inaction that result in such changes are Inspection and Acceptance, Knowledge and Acquiescence, Defective Specifications, Acceleration, and Noncooperation or Interference.

Inspection and Acceptance

Acceptance of contract end items is an action for which authority is vested in the buyer's agent. Under government contracts, a contracting officer holds this authority, but for practical reasons (location and technical expertise are principal ones), the authority usually is delegated to a COTR or to a quality assurance office near the point of acceptance. Acceptance is preceded by inspection or review of quality assurance records to determine whether the end product conforms with contract requirements. This duty requires an interpretation of the contract to determine the proper inspection procedure and standards for acceptance. The process may generate informal changes when the inspecting official imposes a higher standard of performance than that called for by the contract specification. In such cases, the inspecting officer requires the contractor to perform extra work or rework in order to gain acceptance of the end item. Under government contracting procedures, the contractor has no other option than to perform accordingly. A contractor placed in this position will often assert a claim for the extra work based on the constructive change concept.

Knowledge and Acquiescence

The second major source of informal change has been referred to as knowledge and acquiescence. Under this general category, a contractor will seek relief when he finds that his performance exceeded that required by the specification of the contract; that it cost him more to perform than he should have expended; and that, at the time he was expending effort to achieve the higher level of performance, the government knew that the approach had been changed and was benefiting from

the improved method of performance but said nothing. Knowledge and
acquiescence occurs when a government representative knows, or should
know, that a contractor is performing work in good faith beyond that
required by the contract but says nothing, thereby permitting the contractor to incur excessive costs against his own interest. If the work is
accepted by the government, and the contractor asserts a claim, it is
likely that he would recover under the constructive changes concept.

Defective Specifications

This type of informal change occurs because purchasers are held responsible for the efficacy of their contractual specifications. This notion
is rooted in the implied warranty that the specification is adequate as the
basis for performing the job when used by a qualified contractor. If the
specification proves defective for any reason, such as omitted information,
conflicting provisions, or imprecise or erroneous wording, the purchaser
will be held responsible for the cost of excessive work expended by the
contractor in attempting to comply with the defective documents. If not
handled by negotiation and ratification, the constructive changes theory
applies to this situation. After review, if a board or court determines
that a change should have been issued at the start of performance or
before the contractor had uselessly expended energy and cost pursuing
the defective specification, compensation will be awarded.

Acceleration

Acceleration claims occur regularly as a result of contract operations. They are based on acceleration of the pace of work mandated by
the government but seldom on an order to deliver the product earlier
than called for by the contract schedule. Instead, the principal source of
acceleration claims is requiring adherence to the existing contractual
schedule when the contractor has experienced delays in performance that
are excusable under the contract's excusable delays provisions. When a
contractor experiences excusable delays and is refused a request for an
extension of the contract delivery schedule, the basis for acceleration is
established. Acceleration can be compensated through negotiation and
ratification of the cost and time effects, but claims are likely to be
litigated. If so, and if the board or court finds that an acceleration in
performance has been required just to maintain the original contract
schedule, and if such a speed-up imposes additional costs on the contractor, an equitable adjustment to compensate for the extra costs is likely.

Noncooperation or Interference

Constructive changes are found in cases where the government fails to cooperate with the contractor in a timely manner during performance or interferes in any material way with the contractor's work. Failures of this kind can arise under various circumstances. One circumstance is government delay in furnishing a contractor with necessary information. If the contractor is thereby forced to perform extra work, or perform work out of sequence that would not have been necessary had the government cooperated more fully, compensation may be justified. A similar situation arises if a government officer is dilatory in rendering an approval necessary for the contractor to proceed. This could occur, for example, under the consent provisions of the subcontracts clause. A failure to cooperate will also arise if the government holds technical data needed by a contractor and fails to deliver the information in a manner timely to the contractor's performance of work. Another form of interference occurs when the government insists that the contractor use a specific method of performance when he could have chosen other valid methods. If restricting the contractor's options results in forcing him to perform in a more expensive manner, he will have a valid claim for equitable adjustment.

TECHNIQUES OF ALTERING CONTRACT WORK

One method of altering work under contract is by technical direction (TD). Such directives are authorized under many government contracts, but they are somewhat difficult to define and very difficult to manage and control. The general concept is that technical directions are instructions and information or suggestions emerging from technical discussions between the government's technical monitor of the contract and the contractor's program or project management personnel. The technical direction is distinguished from a change order because it may be issued in an informal manner and occasionally may not even be documented at all. Under normal procedures, only a contracting officer's technical representative may issue technical directions; they must be issued in writing with copies for the contracting officer. A contractor is normally expected to acknowledge the receipt of a TD and include in his acknowledgement a recognition that the effort contemplated by the TD does not involve changes to the contract specification, extension of schedule, or expenditures that require additional funding for the overall contract work. Many agencies have developed technical direction clauses and contracting officer technical representative delegation forms that spell out these restraints. Nevertheless, technical directions frequently have proven to be the source of informally issued changes to contract requirements.

It is useful to compare technical direction with contract change notices (orders) and with contract amendments for the addition of new work. Although it may be argued that the three types of procedures are independent--each having application only for actions pertinent to the procedure--the boundaries between types of actions are frequently unclear areas subject to management judgment which may be colored by practical considerations as well as policy.

Chart 12-1, Administrative Implications of Modification and Change Under Government Contracts, summarizes the administrative effects or consequences of altering contract work using three ordinary procedures-- technical direction, change order, and new procurement amendment. These procedures are commonly used. They differ substantially in their admin- istrative impact on the work force and on the length of time required to initiate the revised effort. For example, regarding the intended effort originally contemplated by the parties (the scope of the contract), two of the methods of alteration--technical directions and change orders-- contemplate no change. The work change directed by either of these mechanisms should be within the general scope of the existing contract. The technical direction and change order differ in their intended rela- tionship to the contract specification. While both procedures affect method of performance, the technical direction should not cause or require a change in specification, whereas a change order is needed for just such a change. When additions to end objectives or to a specifica- tion change are so substantial that they alter the basic intent (scope) of the contract, a new procurement amendment should be used. Such changes are dubbed *cardinal changes.*

A new procurement modification to a contract contemplates an addi- tion to the overall objectives of the previously existing contract. This distinction (within scope or outside scope) is of great significance to the government and to proper use of the changes authority. From the view- point of most supplier organizations, the question of the scope of a contract is less important. The supplier's principal interest is whether additional work is being added to the job for which recognition of addi- tional costs and profit is accepted by the government.

The implications of these alternative procedures for administrative effort--securing funds, lead time needed to initiate work, steps needed to initiate work, and contractual follow-up--are self explanatory as presented in chart 12-1. Overall, the technical direction is administratively the least burdensome approach to altering work; but it must be approached judiciously because it short-circuits the management controls otherwise in place if inappropriately applied.

The most significant administrative consequences of each of the recognized methods of altering work under contract may be summarized in one word: time. For technical directions both administrative effort and

Chart 12-1

Administrative Implications of Modification and
Change Under Government Contracts

Administrative Factor or Procedure	Technical Direction (TD)	Contract Change Notice	New Procurement (Amendment)
Relation to contract intent (scope)	Within	Within	Outside
Relation to original performance requirement (specification)	Within requirement of spec without CCN***	New obligation is incident to change in contractual specification	New item or quantity, or cardinal change
Administration	Simple	Formal management review	Full contractual activity
Funding	None	Usually an increase	Increase
Time delay from order to starting work	None	Days or weeks	Weeks or months
Steps needed to initiate work	Discussion and letter	Discussion ECP,* PR,** CCN	Discussion, PR, solicit, neg., award
Contractual follow-up	None if properly issued	Normally two actions: CCN and two-party modification	None except when letter amendment

*ECP: Engineering Change Proposal
**PR: Procurement Request
***CCN: Contract Change Notice

time required are minimal, so work can begin immediately on the directed effort. Because of the constraints on technical direction authority, such directions should not involve additional funding of a contract. A technical direction is issued on the basis that it does not impact the terms and conditions of a contract, and a properly issued direction should have no contractual follow-up, such as the preparation of proposals, negotiations, and issuance of new contractual modifications. Thus, on all counts the technical direction is an administratively expedient way to alter the method of performance of a contract. For this reason, technical directions have appeal to the working level managers responsible for the success of a contract's contemplated effort.

In contrast to the technical direction, a contract change order can involve a large amount of time and administrative effort because it is a formal modification of a contract. It contemplates that a change in the original specification or design has been directed, and that some cost and schedule impact may flow from the existence of that change. This factor, the recognition that requirements are altered or that specified designs or performance require formal change, often initiates a full-scale review and sign-off at top echelons of management. Delay and justification processes may be incident to these factors. In addition, the issuance of a contract change order often involves the preparation of cost estimates and pricing proposals, initiation of negotiation processes, and the ultimate preparation and issuance of a modification adjusting contract funding, schedule, and other terms and conditions to compensate for the effects of the change. An additional impact of change orders is that contracting officers, as agents of the government, are not in a position to issue such orders without having received a requisition or purchase request citing adequate funds to finance the estimated cost of the change when issued. The necessity for adequate funding of the estimated cost of a change can be a major delaying factor in initiating work under the change order--a particularly difficult problem if the project is underfunded or temporarily has no funds available for change order work.

In addition to the need for funds, one other element is necessary to issue a formal change order. There must be an adequately drafted technical description of the change being ordered. Consequently, contract change orders may require a number of days (perhaps weeks) to initiate action. Such delays are difficult for program and project personnel to accept. Once a decision has been made that a different course of action is needed, no responsible manager wants to have work continued under the expired definition. One characteristic of the changes authority, the fact that an order can be issued unilaterally, is a partial response to the need for rapid action on change work. Nevertheless, under urgent conditions the change order is potentially a more cumbersome administrative procedure than a technical direction.

The change order is more expeditious than issuing a new procurement amendment. With the change order, formal preparation of estimates and negotiation of prices can be accomplished subsequent to initiation of work on the required modification. This is not the case with a new procurement amendment to a contract. With new actions, a request for proposal is needed, the contractor must be allowed time to develop a price and technical proposal, the proposal must be subjected to appropriate technical and cost analysis reviews, and a negotiation of the new work must be completed prior to issuance of the amendment authorizing the initiation of work.

The proposal and pricing requirements of new procurement amendments add to the management review and funding processes introduced by change order action. Under a procurement amendment, it may take weeks or even months for work to be initiated subsequent to the identification of the need for the addition. Such amendments do have the advantage of being issued as a complete action at the time of the amendment and thus require little follow-up effort. Nevertheless, the general tendency on the part of the managers of a contract is to avoid the full-blown processes associated with new procurement amendments. One alternative when new procurement action is indicated is the use of a letter amendment. In some cases, this can be a means of expediting the start of work. Because it allows price to be negotiated later, the letter amendment to a contract has administrative characteristics not too different from those of the change order itself.

SUMMARY

Change activity opens agreements to renewed negotiations and leads to price and schedule adjustments. Changes provide the principal mechanism for maintaining contracts as current reflections of work being performed. The government approach to changes differs from that of the private sector because it incorporates a unilateral directive authority into its contracts. The principal features of governmental post-award changes authority are summarized.

- An explicit procedure for directing changes is provided by the Changes clause, but actions are broadly interpreted as falling under the clause, even if the procedure is not followed precisely.
- Control of product configuration is generally maintained under the guidance of a configuration management system, but the contractual rules authorizing adjustment of cost and schedule for changes are recognized as the more critical contract management issue.
- The objectives of configuration management, an outline of its four principal elements, and uses of the engineering change proposal.
- Six sources of the demand for contract change action.

- Informal and constructive change activity as it relates to the Changes clause, to the demand for change, and to the formal appeals procedure that has operated to define the process.
- Five broad types of constructive changes.
- Three methods of updating contracts: technical direction, new procurement and change orders.

TOPICS FOR DISCUSSION

1. Discuss the relationship between configuration management and the contractual changes process.
2. Summarize the provisions of the government Changes clause.
3. Recognizing the existence of strong policy objections to the use of unilateral change directives, explain the reasons for imposing the Changes clause into virtually all government contracts.
4. Why don't private parties to contracts join the government in adopting a similar changes procedure?
5. What accounts for the appeal of technical direction over contract change notices within the program and project offices of contractors? Of government agencies?
6. What elements of acceleration cause it to be an important source of constructive changes?
7. To what degree could effective management practices in government agencies overcome the need for the Changes clause?

CASE 12-1

LPC Change Game

It was April 1, 1985. Joe Rivers, the Contract Manager at RCI, had found the discussion at the weekly directors' staff meeting interesting and provocative. Bill Larsen, the Manager of the Cost and Pricing Section, had kicked off the discussion with a complaint that the inclusion of not-to-exceed prices by government contracting officers when issuing change orders was inappropriate and inconsistent with the Changes clause. Bill had pointed out that most change orders issued to RCI by the government are unilateral directives, and that the not-to-exceed price constrains the company's estimating and pricing and, sometimes, even the technical response. He concluded that it was bad policy and should be changed. Bill's complaint generated a lot of comment, because every manager attending the meeting had encountered the practice repeatedly. With five major hardware projects under contract, the Armored Division had dozens, sometimes hundreds, of ECPs or change orders at various stages of initiation, performance, or negotiation.

The contract clause underlying the change activity was found in each of RCI's production contracts. It is included as appendix 1 of this case.

As part of the discussion that followed, Joe stated his view that, while it may be true there was some inconsistency between the unilateral nature of the order and the not-to-exceed price, there was also a benefit to the government in doing it that way and, perhaps, even to the company. Joe rationalized that the use of the not-to-exceed price caused both the company and the government to be more careful in developing estitmated costs for future change orders. Consequently, RCI fully analyzes its ECPs for technical content to ensure coverage of all required change work and prepares its engineering change proposals to reflect all costs that might be incurred. Furthermore, Joe argued that it didn't make much difference to the company financially because, under the incentive contract arrangements established for production contracts, the actual cost of performing work was recoverable, and the only impact of the practice was the advance limitation on target and ceiling prices.

During the meeting, Ray Milligan, the Director for Proposals, Contracts and Pricing, told the group that government practices using not-to-exceed prices had been initiated by a memorandum written on November 8, 1972, by then-Chief of Naval Materiel, Admiral L.C. Kidd. Admiral Kidd's memorandum had been directed to the systems commanders and project managers at the Naval Materiel Command (NMC). Ray, who worked at NMC at that time, had retained a copy of the memo. He asked his secretary to prepare a copy for each of the managers at the staff meeting. The text of Admiral Kidd's memorandum read as follows:

Subject: Change Orders.
1.   This is just a reminder that change orders are to be priced promptly before we sign anything directing the accomplishment of the changes in question.
2.   I believe that 30 to 45 days would be a reasonable amount of time for a contractor to price a change once we decide that the change is essential.
3.   Incidents wherein ship changes continue to plague us as building blocks for downstream claims indicate the closest adherence to this policy.
4.   No change orders will be directed unpriced without the personal approval of the CNM.

According to Ray, in the years since 1972, Admiral Kidd's memorandum had resulted in strong pressure within all agencies of the government to price change orders prior to initiating work. However, the dynamics of high priority projects, urgent completion schedules, time required for definitive pricing, and other factors had prevented final pricing for many changes until after the work had been officially directed or initiated. As a compromise solution, a new practice emerged--that of issuing not-to-exceed prices as part of the text of the change order. These prices represented a limitation on the contract price adjustment that a contractor might claim for any given change order.

At that point in the staff meeting, Ray Milligan cut off the discussion so that other more immediate issues could be covered. It was clear, however, that some dissatisfaction existed regarding change order pricing.

Upon returning to his office after the meeting, Joe Rivers found among his correspondence a transmittal letter with two contract modifications he had negotiated three months earlier. They had been sent to him by the contracting officer for signature. Joe's first reaction after examining the modifications was, "Well, it really is April Fool's Day." The coincidence of the staff discussion with Joe's receipt of the modifications seemed even more significant as he digested the new terminology inserted into the modifications by the contracting officer. The transmittal letter was essentially a request for RCI to sign both modifications. They provided for increased work on RCI's major production contract for the LPC. The modifications were referred to as P00106 and P00107 and with a value of $2,173,035, brought the LPC contract to $573,258,231. Together, the two modifications settled outstanding claims on 25 separate and independent change orders. The change orders affected several of the 30 deliverable end items identified under the prime contract. Joe was concerned with the following language contained in both of the modifications.

WHEREAS, there is now in force between the Parties hereto a contract identified as Contract DAAEO7-81-C-0046, which, together with all modifications thereto is hereinafter referred to as the "Contract;" and

WHEREAS, the Parties desire to equitably adjust the Contract as a result of the equitable adjustment of Engineering Change Proposals (ECPs) . . . which were incorporated into the contract by means of modification P00079 (P00077); and

WHEREAS, the Parties agreed, through Modification P00079 (P00077), to establish Ceiling Prices for each of the ECPs incorporated therein and the agreed to Ceiling prices are as follows:

P00079

ECP	QTY	CEILING PRICE	ECP	QTY	CEILING PRICE
H3743A	432	$ 8,963.00	H3725R2-A	340	9,026.00
J9542A	243	8,415.00	K7417A	400	50,899.00
J9559A	289	30,463.00	K7426A	400	59,945.00
J9583A	432	358,921.00	K7514A	432	19,333.00
J9661A	400	13,737.00	K7525A	432	7,449.00

P00077

ECP	QTY	CEILING PRICE	ECP	QTY	CEILING PRICE
J9804A	400	$ 17,664.00	K5885A	400	11,351.00
K1199A	432	5,011.00	K6022A	400	173,846.00
K1323A	432	40,618.00	K6040A	400	20,513.00
K1383A	400	17,014.00	K6055A	400	44,763.00
K1563A	400	661,837.00	K6191A	432	148,852.00
K1725A	400	259,699.00	K6192A	170	125,260.00
K2166A	230	17,434.00	K6193A	400	54,787.00
K5677A	400	7,235.00			

WHEREAS, the Contractor submitted costs for the following ECPs in excess of the Ceiling Price established therefore:

P00079   P00077

ECP	CEILING PRICE	CLAIMED COSTS	ECP	CEILING PRICE	CLAIMED COSTS
K7417A	$50,899.00	$67,126.00	J9804A	$ 7,664.00	$ 20,934.00
J9661A	13,737.00	45,615.00	K1199A	5,011.00	19,173.00
			K1323A	40,618.00	60,244.00
			K1563A	661,837.00	677,713.00
			K2166A	17,434.00	36,666.00
			K6022A	173,846.00	313,369.00
			K6040A	20,513.00	26,252.00
			K6055A	44,763.00	77,045.00

WHEREAS, THE Parties agree that any costs in excess of the agreed-to Ceiling Price for an individual ECP shall not otherwise be made part of any claim for adjustment; and

. . .

NOW, THEREFORE, the parties hereto do mutually agree as follows:

(End of text in proposed modifications)

Joe figured that the language for both modifications would cause RCI to lose $297,816.00 because it would prohibit the company from billing the government for the production costs of the changed work. He knew that failure of RCI to sign the modification and return it to the contracting officer would cause considerable delay in receiving any payment at all. Nevertheless, he was not particularly anxious to see 14 percent of the total cost of the change actions eliminated from RCI's right of recovery. Joe felt a keen sense of responsibility for the situation since he had negotiated the values for these changes which resulted in the modifications. Joe needed to work out a complete course of action.

* * * * *

Prepare a statement of the alternative actions RCI could take at this point and outline a complete course of action for Joe Rivers in working out the problem. Prepare any needed correspondence for him.

Appendix 1 (case 12-1)

52.243-1 Changes--Fixed-Price (April 1984)
(a)   The Contracting Officer may at any time, by written order, and without notice to the sureties, if any, make changes within the general scope of this contract in any one or more of the following:
  (1) Drawings, designs, or specifications when the supplies to be furnished are to be specially manufactured for the Government in accordance with the drawings, designs, or specifications.
  (2) Method of shipment or packing.
  (3) Place of delivery.
(b)   If any such change causes an increase or decrease in the cost of, or the time required for, performance of any part of the work under this contract, whether or not changed by the order, the Contracting Officer shall make an equitable adjustment in the contract price, the delivery schedule, or both, and shall modify the contract.
(c)   The Contractor must submit any "proposal for adjustment" (hereafter referred to as proposal) under this clause within 30 days from the date of receipt of the written order. However, if the Contracting Officer decides that the facts justify it, the Contracting

Officer may receive and act upon a proposal submitted before final payment of the contract.

(d)   If the Contractor's proposal includes the cost of property made obsolete or excess by the change, the Contracting Officer shall have the right to prescribe the manner of the disposition of the property.

(e)   Failure to agree to any adjustment shall be a dispute under the Disputes clause. However, nothing in this clause shall excuse the Contractor from proceeding with the contract as changed.

CASE 12-2

Armored Division and the Value Engineering Crisis

On June 21, 1985, Al Benton was somewhat distressed after he was called into the office of Joe Rivers, the Manager of Contracts and Proposals, Operations, to discuss a letter he had received that day from the contracting officer for the corporation's major production contract. In the letter, the contracting officer had taken a position that would reduce RCI's potential earnings from its investment in the value engineering effort which it had initiated early in the Land/Sea Personnel Carrier program. Al was familiar with this longstanding VECP program, and he, as well as others in RCI, was proud of the fact that their work in the VE area had been well recognized as an outstanding contribution to the overall defense effort. In fact, as Al understood the situation, very few other contractors had achieved truly successful value engineering programs in spite of the government's extensive and comprehensive coverage of that area in its contracts. It was quite clear from the DAR clauses contained in the RCI contracts and from the policy statements in the DAR (and the subsequent FAR) that the government's policy was to encourage contractor participation in value engineering programs.

In light of that encouragement, it was somewhat discouraging to realize that the contracting officer for RCI contracts was taking a position that, in RCI's view, would undermine the understanding established three years earlier regarding RCI's sharing in the savings from its VE efforts. That understanding was the basis for a deviation from mandatory DAR clauses so that in specified cases RCI would be compensated at a rate higher than that set forth as standard value engineering policy.

Background of RCI's Armored Division

The Armored Division of the RCI Corporation is located in Sunnyvale, California. The division is involved in major defense contracts, particularly with production of armored vehicles for overland military operations. The largest of the programs currently held by the Armored Division is the Land/Sea Personnel Carrier production program. RCI Corporation had done much of the development work for that vehicle and had been producing it since 1981 under a series of contracts for annual quantities. Each of the production contracts (fixed-price incentive contracts) contained a value engineering incentive clause. In addition, the Armored Division held a separate contract referred to as the Systems Technical Support contract (STS). The STS contract (a cost-plus-fixed-fee contract) provided a vehicle for conducting engineering studies and other necessary technical support activities associated with the large production contracts. Both RCI and its customers had found this arrangement to be quite effective. Its advantage was that it supported an organizational separation of technical support activity from production. Consequently, the technical support work was performed without being allocated the high overhead costs associated with production and was less costly to the government.

The Value Engineering Program

The following paragraphs are quoted from the contracting officer's letter of June 20, 1985.

Referenced Modification P00003 was issued under contract DAAE07-84-C-A005 to incorporate undefinitized VECP FOM-H9235 which had been submitted thereunder. A review of this action has been conducted and a determination made that the VECP should not have been submitted under contract DAAE07-84-C-A005. The VECP should have been submitted under the mandatory VE Program Clause of Systems Technical Support (STS) contract DAAE07-83-C-R053 pursuant to which it was developed and evaluated. Under prior year production and STS contracts, a DAR Deviation was obtained whereby the then concurrent production contract was designated the "instant contract." However, no such DAR Deviation has been authorized for the current STS contract.

As a result, the following is applicable to the definitization of the VECP. First, contract DAAE07-84-C-A005 will be, for this one time only, utilized as the instrument by which the implementation costs and share of future savings are paid to RCI. Second, the proper share ratio, as prescribed by the DAR for a VECP developed under a mandatory VE Clause in a cost reimbursable contract (i.e., the STS Contract) is 85/15 rather than 75/25. The definitization modification will so state and savings will be paid in accord therewith.

Al was discouraged. For three years, his understanding had been that all LPC value engineering actions taken by either RCI or the government were based on the assumption that the "instant contract" would be defined as the production contract under which the VECP is initially proposed and accepted. This assumption applied only to VECPs resulting from a specified list of value engineering projects, those that had been initiated by RCI prior to adding VE to the STS contract. This approach permitted all VE development work to be conducted under the STS contract at lower cost but without compromising the incentive earnings contemplated by RCI. The issue involved a significant dollar amount of incentive payments.

The basis for this issue is found in a February, 1982 request for a deviation for the value engineering clause incorporated into the system technical support contract at that time. The following is a quotation from that request for deviation (we are referring here to a deviation from the Defense Acquisition Regulation clause 7-104.44). This quotation clarifies the background of the current situation.

1. Deviation is sought from the general provision "Value Engineering (1980 Dec)" DAR 7-104.44(a) as modified by 7-104.44(b), Alt I, mandatory VE Program Requirement as follows: (1) Subparagraph (f)(1), the contractor's share is limited in concurrent and future savings under the Program Requirement to 25% for fixed price type contracts inclusive of incentive contracts. It is proposed to provide a greater contractor share in net acquisition savings for concurrent and future contract savings not to exceed 30% for certain agreed upon VE concepts. It is our intent to negotiate a definitive percentage(s) with such ceiling prior to contract modification for each of these concepts. (2) Subparagraph(b)(6) defines instant contract as the contract under which the VECP is submitted. It is proposed to define instant contract as that production contract under which the VECP is initially accepted (modified) by the government.

2. A full description of the deviation and the circumstances in which it will be used:

a. As background, the Land/Sea Personnel Carrier System (LPCS) program has completed development and entered into production contracts for the fabrication of a total of 500 vehicles (100 each in FY 80 and 400 each in FY 81). Negotiations are in process leading to award of an FY 82 definitive contract for the procurement of an additional 600 vehicles. Since award of the initial production contract, intensive efforts have been undertaken to reduce production costs of the IFV/CFV. As a part of this overall effort, RCI, the LPCS prime contractor, and its principal subcontractor, Samson Aircraft Company (SAC), have, at their own expense, initiated actions to preliminarily investigate a number of VE concepts which have the potential for substantial savings in production. While each of these production contracts contains the DAR7-104.44(a) Value Engineering (Voluntary) provision, the contractor is unwilling to proceed to further expend its own funds and continue to assume the sole risk in the event that the VE concepts may not prove out or may not otherwise be acceptable to the government.

There is also in existence a companion System Technical Support (STS) contract (DAAE07-82-C-4006) presently containing no VE provision. It is proposed to modify this STS contract to allow for the inclusion of the VE program clause (7-104.44(b), Alternate I) mandatory VE Program Requirement and thus provide the contractor with a government-funded means by which to more fully develop the preliminary VE concepts previously identified. Given the facts that (1) the contractor/subcontractor have voluntarily conceived the concepts, (2) that they have expended in excess of $1M to date to bring them to a preliminary phase, (3) that they are determined to be worthy of further effort, (4) that significant funds may yet be necessary to bring them to a point where they can be accepted as a VECPO, and (5) that there is yet a significant degree of risk as to their ultimate acceptability, it is the government's position that it should provide the remaining funds as may be necessary to develop the VE Proposals, and in recognition of the contractor's effort to date, provide a greater contractor sharing arrangement than that provided for in paragraph (f)(1) (i.e., from 25% to an agreed upon share in excess of 25% but not to exceed 30%) for the Program Requirement for concurrent and future savings. This greater share shall be limited to those concepts identified in Attachment I. (Attachment I, not provided in this case, listed system specific change concepts)

b. In view of a. above, it is proposed to enter into a VE program with the prime contractor, under the above identified STS contract. Under this Program Requirement, those concepts identified in Attachment I, if ultimately found acceptable, would result in the contractor sharing at a to be agreed upon ratio not to exceed 30%. It is felt that the increased contractor share ratio is advantageous to the Government in that it will provide greater motivation to the contractor and the greater share ratio to be paid him will be more than off-set by the potential savings to be realized by the Government. It is projected that overall estimated savings for the concepts identified in Attachment I will be approximately $90M.

c. For VE concepts pursued under the Program Requirement other than those shown on Attachment I, the contractor would share at the standard 25%.

    d. Notwithstanding that the VE program will be made a part of the STS contract, a CPFF undertaking, and be submitted thereunder, the instant contract shall be deemed to be the production contract under which the VECP will be initially accepted. The VE program requirement is being made a part of the STS contract as opposed to any of the production contracts to lower significantly the cost of the VE program. Due to the divisional make-up of RCI, production contracts are handled by RCI, Sunnyvale Armored Plant, whereas Engineering efforts are the responsibility of and performed by RCI, Armored Engineering Division. If a VE program requirement was added to a production contract, Sunnyvale Armored Plant would subcontract such engineering work to AED, which has traditionally been the STS contractor. This would result in the Government paying Sunnyvale Armored Plant general and administrative expenses and profit for such subcontracted work. (Current combined G&A and profit being paid Sunnyvale Armored Plant is 20%.)

3. <u>A description of the intended effect of the deviation</u>:
    a. The deviation will enable the Government to benefit from identified preliminary VECPs having significant cost reduction potential which otherwise might not be pursued.

    b. The deviation allows recognition in the form of an increased contractor share for effort in terms of funds and expertise already expended by the contractor to identify concepts which have a high probability of being successful.

4. <u>A copy of any pertinent forms or clauses and the proposed contractor's request, if any</u>:
    (The proposed clause reflected the request cited.)

5. <u>A statement of the period of time for which the deviation is needed, if any</u>:

    This will be a one-time deviation to the VE (Mandatory) general provision of the STS contract covering only those concepts identified in Attachment I. The instant contract definition as stated in 2d will apply for the duration of the STS contract.

6. <u>Detailed reasons supporting the request</u>:

    As discussed in 1a above, the Land/Sea Personnel Carrier System is intensively working on methods to reduce the cost of the

M2/M3 Vehicle.   This deviation will provide a means of reducing the vehicle price, while providing the contractor an equitable share of the savings.   It is essential we receive approval of this deviation quickly in order to ensure that VE concepts are timely pursued in order that they may be applied to the maximum number of vehicles to be produced.

*   *   *   *   *

1.   Please develop a detailed course of action for Al Benton, RCI's contract administrator, for this program.   Your response should consider DOD FAR Supplements and the FAR concerning the VE policy.   Include in your discussion the objectives Al should set for negotiating this situation to achieve a desirable outcome.

2.   Analyze this situation from the perspective of the government's contracting officer.

13

Performance Schedules and Delay

An important advantage of using external sources to acquire goods and services is the purchaser's ability to specify the delivery schedule and once the contract is established, to hold the supplier responsible for meeting that schedule. This advantage is an important element in acquisition planning. Within reasonable limits, buyers are able to view their suppliers as single purpose entities. They expect that purpose to be timely delivery of the specific contractual end items. This contrasts with work assigned for internal performance because internal sources of supply may receive higher priority work assignments from equally positioned or superior internal managers. At any time, changes in priorities may arise as issues for negotiation among the competing functions within any business or government entity. Although nominally greater control over supply may be achieved through internal sourcing, the element of changing priorities is especially difficult to manage.

Because an external source is independent and subject to contractual sanctions, a higher level of commitment to meet schedules may be expected than that secured from internal sources. Delivery schedules are most easily managed using firm-fixed-price contracts. Such contracts create an aura of reliability because the supplier may be held to the delivery obligation as a guarantor.

The Presumption of Timely Delivery

The formation of a contractual obligation creates a presumption that delivery will be timely and will happen more or less automatically without much effort on the part of the buyer. Even so, doubt concerning delivery compliance leads to extensive use of the expediting system wherein purchasers employ telephone calls, follow-up memoranda, and similar forms of reminders, inquiries, and pressure tactics to determine the status of and to advance the supplier's progress. Even the introduction of a comprehensive contract administration system is largely aimed at ensuring compliance with delivery. The basic presumption in either of these systematic approaches is that the supplier is responsible to the purchaser for timeliness.

Regardless, delay is common. Schedule problems may not be the fault of the supplier. Consequently, buyers cannot afford to take lightly the presumption of timely performance. Administrative action related to delivery is common and is complicated by the problem of determining the factual circumstances that may be causing delay. Knowing the circumstances should aid in overcoming the problem and is necessary for decisions regarding contract obligations. The reasons for delay may be unimportant to the end user since performance is the only vital question, but for the contract manager, the cause of delay and associated questions of fault and responsibility must be treated as central issues. The parties to the contract have a vested interest in the questions of fault. These interests may color their concern for programmatic success and at times may override good program decisions. Unfortunately, the effort to assign fault for delay sometimes assumes priority over end objectives.

Actions Intended to Limit or Eliminate Delivery Delays

Buyers have many options in attempting to secure compliance with the delivery schedule. Available options range from positive support actions to cancellation. They include increased pressure through the normal expediting system, involvement in supplier management actions, and threats of contractual sanctions. Aid in the form of technical expertise, use of facilities, securing financing, or influence with supply sources could, in some circumstances, relieve the delay problem. For technically difficult work, a modified specification or a waiver of specific requirements may be feasible. All of these actions and others are within the discretion of buyers.

Of the available options, threat of default is the most stringent, and assessment of damages is a close second, provided a liquidated damages clause is part of the contract. These contractual sanctions are available to the government under appropriate contract clauses. In private contracting, similar actions will be imposed through court action or, if provided for, through arbitration or other specified dispute procedures. But drastic actions have limitations. Default, in particular, defeats the contract objective or forces reprocurement action with probable time losses.

The best time to forestall occurrence of delays that affect end item delivery is at the outset of contract performance. At the beginning, a post-award conference permits assessment of the contractor's intended approach and enables the contractor to learn, in a direct and open forum, how the buyer perceives performance. Mutuality is enhanced and problems can be assessed and discussed. Overall plans of each party can be stated and a consensus reached on operating relationships and courses of action. Differences in the expectations of the parties can be explored. However, the post-award conference can hardly be expected to forestall several types of problems arising during performance. The following list enumerates causes of delay which are difficult to foresee:

1. *Technical or management failures* resulting in inability to meet a specified requirement
2. *Supervening events,* such as strikes or fires
3. *Failure of subcontractors* to comply with the requirements of their subcontracts
4. *Defects in specifications*
5. *Changes* in the specified requirements
6. *Interference* by the purchaser or by other contractors performing work in the same area

These six causes fall into three classes. Causes 1 and 3 imply weakness in the contractor's management or in that of his supplier for whom he is responsible. Number 2 represents insurable risks or ones otherwise not under the control of the supplier. Numbers 4, 5, and 6 imply fault or responsibility of the purchaser.

Occurrence of these causes may not result in end item delay, but they make it likely because they introduce a delay in work at some point during contract performance and present management with the problem of correcting deficient effort or of working to overcome the effects of the event. Overall, delay and the effort to overcome its effect on delivery obligations are pervasive challenges in the performance of contracts.

The management problem associated with delay (if it cannot be avoided or reduced by a change in the work plan) is how to cope with its consequences. Coping with consequences depends partly on whether timeliness is important. Schedule may or may not be critical to the buyer. The important initial question is, are we relying on schedule, and shall we emphasize it? The action to be initiated depends on where and how the delay is introduced--by the contractor, the purchaser, or some external source not controlled by either party to the contract. The actions necessary to cope with the delay must first consider the importance of correcting the problem. Delay often increases supplier costs, but not

always. Delay may or may not impose added costs and programmatic burdens on the purchaser. Actions taken should match the needs.

Senior executives and production and program managers may resist
the suggestion that delay is sometimes unimportant. Contracting officers
may also resist because schedule is fundamental to competition and award
of contracts. Both effort and expense are devoted to planning and
coordinating schedules. Gantt charts, Line of Balance, Critical Path and
PERT networks, and Cost/Schedule Control Systems Criteria are widely
practiced techniques for managing schedule. These techniques are addressed in chapter 9.

Regardless of which systems are in use, the question of whether
schedule is critical is still valid for individual contracts because its
importance varies with time and may depend on external events. It is for
the very programs for which sophisticated scheduling systems have been
developed that reduced importance of schedule may temporarily arise.
One reason for this is that managers of large undertakings assign work to
many independent performers. Some are in-house, some are under contract. Each performer depends upon the others for information or material, and the entire system depends on continued support of the sponsor.
Funding shortages, requirement modifications, failure of a key performer,
and unpredictable events in any part of the overall system may introduce
delay that renders timeliness less critical for other parts of the system.
While such eventualities should not be accepted with indifference, they
sometimes reduce the need to exercise contractual sanctions. Additionally, when a reduced rate of funding is the source of a slowdown, delay of
selected work elements may be a valuable tool for conserving resources.

Distribution of Burdens Imposed by Delay

There are three broad categories of delay.

1.   Delays generally chargeable to the contractor
2.   Delays for which the contractor is excused
3.   Delays generally chargeable to the purchaser

Chart 13-1 groups the various causes of delay into these categories.
It distinguishes between delays that are ordered by the buyer and those
caused by (but not ordered by) the buyer. The power to order changes
in schedule is extraordinary, but from the perspective of government
managers, it may be considered essential and is provided for in the terms
and conditions of government contracts. Ordering delays is not a responsibility to be taken lightly. Contract agreements are built around understandings of the parties regarding delivery and price, and these two elements are associated with the expected performance. In the absence of

Chart 13-1

Delay Causes and Burdens, Fixed-Price Government Contracts

Causes for Delay (Generic)	Principal Burdens of Delay Fall upon:	
	Cost	Time[1]
Causes Generally Charged to Supplier		
Commitment to unattainable schedule	K[6]	K[6]
Poor management or lack of diligence including:	K	K
Managerial or technical deficiency		
Failure to secure essential materials		
Failure to secure competent work force		
Inadequate facilities or equipment		
Technical failures, misdirection, errors	K	K
Subcontractor or supplier failures[2]	K	K
Financial incapacity or bankruptcy	K	K
Causes Generally Excusable to Supplier[3]		
Strikes, floods, fires	K	G
Unusually severe weather	K	G
Government acts, freight embargoes	K	G
Subcontractor delays, if all criteria are met[2]	K	G
Epidemics, quarantines	K	G
Acts of God or public enemy	K	G
Acts of another contractor (construction)	K	G
Causes Generally Charged to Buyer (Government)		
Ordered delays: construction suspension	G[4]	K
Ordered delays: (stop work order)	G[5]	G
Government act or omission, unreasonable delay	G[4]	K
Delays while making a decision to change	G[4]	K
Funding delay[7]	G	G
Inspection delay[7]	G	G
Property actions (GFP)[7]	G	G
Delay in granting approval[7]	G	G
Deficiency in specification[7]	G	G
Interference or noncooperation[7]	G	G
Wrongful withholding of payments[7]	G[4]	G
Delays caused by performing a change[7]	G[5]	G

[1]The time burden determines whether sanctions for failure to deliver can be imposed.

[2]Prime contractor is excused for these causes of delay only if the subcontractor's delay meets excusability tests and is not caused by fault or negligence and is beyond the control of prime and subcontractors at every tier in the subcontract chain.

[3]Delays in this category are excusable only if not caused by the fault or negligence of the contractor and if beyond his control.

[4]Cost only. [5]Cost and profit. [6]K: Contractor, G: Government

[7]Adjustments for delays in this category are normally made as part of the adjustment for changes, constructive changes, or government property actions.

special provisions, the purchaser is not in a position to change delivery schedule unilaterally without being in danger of breach of contract.   In government contracts, the possibility of breach is overcome by incorporating a contract clause that gives the contracting officer a right to direct the contractor to change his work schedule.   The problem of delay is so pervasive in government contracts that several contract clauses have been crafted to provide numerous options to the contracting officer regarding a course of action when delays occur.   The clauses pertinent to this are Suspension of Work (construction contracts), Stop Work Order, and Government Delay of Work (supply contracts).   Suspension and Stop Work Order clauses give the government's manager a unilateral right to direct the contractor to delay or slow performance of work, and they authorize adjustment of cost (in suspension cases) or cost, profit, and time (in stop work order cases).   The government Delay of Work clause provides for cost and time adjustment if the government causes delay but does not authorize ordering a delay.   Even with clauses of this kind, the government manager's unilateral authority to order a speed-up of contract performance is questionable.   Regardless of the existence of unilateral ordering authority, schedule adjustments require cooperation and replanning effort by the contractor and are likely to affect the cost of performance.   Schedules for performance can be altered in any case and in either direction by agreement between the parties.   Agreements on changes in schedule may involve adjustments of contract price and other terms and conditions of the contract.

Two issues arise when delays occur in the performance of a contract.   One is how to overcome the delay.   The other, as summarized in chart 13-1, is how to distribute between the buyer and seller the burdens imposed by the delay.   Cost increases and lost time are the principal burdens to be allocated.   When a contractor is responsible for introducing a delay, both of these burdens fall upon him in accordance with normal contractual requirements.   This is indicated in the first group of causes in chart 13-1.   If additional costs are required, the contractor must bear them; if a delay in delivery occurs, the contractor may be subject to sanctions, such as liquidated damages or default.

If a contractor encounters an externally caused delay which he cannot control or avoid, the burdens of the delay may be distributed differently.   Delays which are deemed excusable may entitle the contractor to an adjustment of the end item delivery schedule to the extent that the delivery is affected by the cause of delay.   As an example, consider the accidental flooding of a contractor's premises.   If the flood renders timely performance infeasible, the delay will be considered excusable if it can be shown that the flood was not the contractor's fault, was beyond the contractor's control, and if no reasonable way was available to fulfill the contractual obligations.   The contractor is then entitled to an extension of time to perform that is equivalent to the amount of delay imposed. (Note, in a construction contract, the contractor must demonstrate that the occurrence of the flood was unforeseeable. This condition is not imposed in supply contracts.) The fact that such a flood may increase the contractor's cost of performance has no impact on the contractual price. In general, a contractor is entitled only to time adjustments when excusable delays occur. Adjustments are agreed upon only as a result of the effective presentation of facts in negotiation between the parties.

If a contractor's performance delay results from an act of the government, it may be feasible for the contractor to claim both cost and time adjustments. Such acts frequently occur in construction work. For example, when the government or one of the government's contractors prevents another contractor from entering a work site, the overall performance of that contractor may be delayed, requiring a time extension to avoid either being declared in default or assessed liquidated damages for lateness. If this happens, a schedule adjustment should be negotiable, and if additional costs are imposed, the terms of the contract will allow payment of compensation for added costs, but not profit. Negotiation of such adjustments is authorized by certain of the causes summarized in chart 13-1 under the subheading "Causes Generally Charged to the Buyer (Government)." Negotiation of both cost adjustments and equitable adjustments (those that include profit) is the subject of chapter 14.

Government Contract Clauses Covering Delay Actions

The government has developed several contract clauses as a means of establishing positive control of its programs and to help prevent it from breaching contracts. The clauses used in construction contracts differ in certain details from those applicable to supply, service, and research and development contracts. These distinctions are summarized in chart 13-2, which groups eighteen clauses into three categories.

1. Clauses permitting the government to make adjustments for delaying a project
2. Clauses not written explicitly for the purpose of covering delay issues but which provide adjustments that may be partially based on government-caused delay
3. Clauses having no adjustment provisions at all but which are important in setting up specific government contract administration duties and obligations

The summary provided by chart 13-2 is intended as an overview of schedule adjustment clauses. It is a starting point for understanding the managerial implications of these important contractual tools. The rele-

Chart 13-2

Government Contract Clauses On Which Claims Are Based[1]

Clause Title	Applicable to: Constr.	Other	Principal Purpose of Clause
Clauses that Adjust for Delay			
Suspension of Work	x		Provides for unilateral orders to delay work; authorizes cost adjust. for unreasonable delay
Default	x	x	Establishes government discretion to declare default; provides for excusable delay
Stop Work Order		x	Provides for unilateral orders to delay work; authorizes cost, profit and time adjustments
Government Delay of Work	x		Provides cost and time adjust. for delay
Clauses Providing for Adjustment By Explicit Language			
Changes	x	x	Provides for unilateral orders to change; authorizes cost, profit and time adjustments
Notification of Changes	x	x	Requires notice of constructive changes; authorizes cost, profit, time adjustments
Differing Site Conditions	x		Authorizes cost, profit, time adjustments for hidden site conditions; requires timely notice
Value Engineering	x	x	Promotes VE work; authorizes sharing of savings
Government Property	x	x	Multipurpose property clause; authorizes cost, profit, time adjustments for deficient GP
Gov't. Property Furnished As Is	x	x	Authorizes use of government property without warranty (unless GP is not as when inspected); authorizes cost, profit and time adjustment
Commencement, Prosecution and Completion of Work	x		Ties completion date of construction to Notice to Proceed
Time Extensions	x		Re: liquidated damages; makes time adjustments independently for separable parts of constr.
Use and Possession Prior to Completion	x		Authorizes equitable adjustment if government delays or otherwise causes KTR greater expense
Termination For Convenience	x	x	Provides for unilateral termination by government specifies settlement rules for terminated work; authorizes Equitable Adjust. for continuing work on the contract
Desired & Required Time of Delivery		x	Provides definitive statement of delivery date
First Article Approval		x	Specifies rules for first article approval and authorizes equitable adjust. if government does not provide timely approval per clause
Clauses Imposing Duties For Which Claims Arise if Government Action is Wrongful			
Inspection	x	x	Specifies obligations and rules for quality and inspection
Payment clauses	x	x	Specifies obligations and rules for payments

---

[1] Clauses vary in specific provisions for construction and supply or service contracts. Several versions of clauses may be applied and alternate provisions added for specific situations. Each clause is specific as to authorized adjustments except in inspection and payment. Adjustments for improper government actions in those areas are negotiated as constructive changes.

vance of including the two clauses in the third group, which were not written for the purpose of making contract adjustments, lies in the fact that many adjustments are based on these clauses when the government fails to carry out properly its duties as buyer. The failure may be the basis for claims for equitable adjustments. Such claims are usually asserted pursuant to the changes clause.

The clause titles used in chart 13-2 are drawn from the Federal Acquisition Regulations. Several versions of each clause exist. There are variations in the content of the clauses for different kinds of projects, such as services, facilities, supplies, research and development, and others. Chart 13-2 is based on a general appraisal of the overall purpose of the clauses and of their specific provisions for adjusting the time or cost of performing the contract. In chart 13-2 the fact is ignored that many clauses that provide for equitable adjustments permit the parties to modify terms and conditions of the contracts other than price and time. Modifications of terms and conditions tend to be less immediate in their impact than price and time modifications but may have long-term effects that are equally or more important.

The four clauses in chart 13-2 written specifically to accommodate delays are grouped under the subheading "Clauses that Adjust for Delay." The content of these clauses varies substantially. As an example, the major purpose of the default clause is to establish the government's power to declare that a contractor who has breached his duties of performance is in default. This substitutes an administrative procedure for what would otherwise be a judicial one and makes such action a discretionary procedure that facilitates management of programs. The fact that a contractor is late in delivery or has otherwise breached his contract does not necessarily mean that the government would want the work to halt while the parties litigate to determine damages. However, if a default notice is issued by the government, the contractual sanctions permitted in the contract clause are similar to those that would be imposed in a court of law in private contractual relationships. A key part of the government default clause is the enumeration of several excusable causes of delay. This part of the default clause is summarized in chart 13-1 under the heading "Causes Generally Excusable to Supplier" and has been discussed earlier in the chapter.

The Suspension of Work clause is used in government construction contracts. Its purpose is to provide, under the unique circumstances of construction work, for the government to exercise its discretion in controlling progress of the construction. The clause specifically permits the government to issue unilateral orders to suspend or to delay all or any part of the overall project. The clause also provides for negotiating a cost adjustment if the suspension order unreasonably delays the contractor's work. This same adjustment provision also covers costs generated by any unreasonable delays caused by, though not ordered by, the government. In the case of suspensions caused by (but not ordered by) the government, the contractor is obligated to provide notice to the contracting officer of the cause of delay within twenty days of its occurrence.

In supply, service, and research and development contracts, the Government Delay of Work clause has been provided to cover situations in which the government acts in a way that delays progress. This clause differs from the Suspension of Work clause because it does not allow the issuance of an order to stop work. Its provisions for adjustment as a result of a government delay include adjustment of cost associated with the delay. Unlike the Suspension of Work clause, the Government Delay of Work clause authorizes time adjustments. It is similar to the Suspension of Work clause in restricting adjustment to costs (it excludes profit adjustments).

The Stop Work Order clause provides for orders to stop work for periods of ninety days or less under supply, service, and research and development contracts. The purpose of the clause is to permit the government to control progress under situations in which it is considering an important change in contract specifications or the possibility of termination. Use of the clause permits a time period for gathering facts and making decisions. The clause is more complete in its adjustment provisions than the Suspension of Work clause because it allows adjustment of cost, profit, and schedule as compensation for the stop work order. Under the rules of the clause, a contractor who receives a stop work order is obligated to cease all work and to minimize contractual expenses during the period of the order. Nevertheless, if costs of performance are increased because of the order, an equitable adjustment is provided under the clause. The period of a stop work order may be ended by termination action or by restarting the job with redefined requirements. The period of the order may be extended by agreement of the parties.

Twelve clauses are summarized in chart 13-2 under the heading "Clauses Providing for Adjustment by Explicit Language." All of these clauses provide for adjustments of contract pricing and/or schedule as well as other terms and conditions if called for by the action treated under the clause. They are not designed especially for schedule adjustments except as an appropriate part of the overall settlement. The basic purpose of each clause and its general authority for adjustment provisions are set forth in chart 13-2.

The third group of clauses in chart 13-2 includes those for inspection and payment. These clauses do not provide specific coverage for adjustment of cost and time, but timely and appropriate actions in the inspection and payment processes are critical matters to both parties of the contract. Because of this, proper administration of these processes is a specific obligation of the government requiring good judgment. If decisions are erroneous and adversely affect the contractor (for example, by increasing his cost burdens), an equitable adjustment may be required. The clauses are important as the basis for action to compensate for wrongful acts of the government. However, the pertinent equitable adjustment rules are those in the changes clause which becomes applicable through the constructive changes theory.

Practical Approaches to Managing Schedule

An interesting perspective on the management of schedule is gained by observing the operations of a field contract administration office. Chart 13-3 and the following description are drawn from the operations of a Defense Logistics Agency field organization. The specific organization represented is a Defense Contract Administration Services Management Area. At the time of the study, this office was staffed at a level of 206 personnel and had 3,100 contractors within its jurisdiction, of which 1,400 were currently working under contracts with the government. The total number of active contracts at that time was 4,700. The activities of the office with respect to delinquent contractors is of particular importance to the study of delay. As with all DLA field contract administration offices, this office regularly generates two schedule oriented reports: the Production and Administration Delinquency Report (PADR) and the Production Schedule Completion Report (PSCR). These reports provide summary information for higher headquarters levels within DLA. More germane is the management activity at the field office level that is initiated to overcome, or otherwise react to, delinquent contractor performance. Data on delivery compliance in this office is secured by quality assurance representatives and administrative contracting officers who are stationed at or visit the contractor's plant. When failure to ship occurs or is indicated, these personnel evaluate the seriousness of the situation and may present the matter at a meeting of the Contractor Improvement Program (CIP). This meeting is perhaps the most important tool relating to this subject. CIP meetings are scheduled once a month and provide an opportunity for the commander and key employees of the office to review delinquencies and to decide on actions relating to the problems. Chart 13-3 summarizes the status at one such meeting. It shows the interesting statistic that only 7 contractors out of the total of 1400 were included as subjects of the Contractor Improvement Program at the time of the study. This one-half of one percent of active contractors required application of a large portion of the total available staff time in efforts to overcome the delinquencies. When contractors are placed on the Contractor Improvement Program, they are immediately scheduled for visitation at least once a week. The increased schedule of visitation attempts to maintain current knowledge of the status of their operations.

Chart 13-3

Snapshot Study, Delinquent Contracts
Government Field Contract Administration Office

Active Contractors Under Administration:	1400
Active Contracts Under Administration:	4700
Contractors in Contractor Improvement Program (CIP):	7
Contractors with Serious Delinquency:	4

Contractor	Number Contracts Held	Number Contracts Late	Months in Trouble	Major Source of Problem	Remarks
Contractors in CIP:					
A	63	38	8	Production delay	Unpaid suppliers; shortage of parts; financial management problems
B	13	8	6	Quality	Production: unqualified, careless assembly.
C	32	18	3	Production delay	Purchasing system failure; incoming parts rejected
D	77	10	14	Quality	Machine calibration (worn equipment); tolerances missed; corrective action in progress
E	86	19	6	Quality	Defective material (castings)
F	12	12	4	Production delay	Questionable inventory, accounting, financial practices
G	14	11	5	Quality	Missed tolerances, production management problems
Contractors Considered for (or had been) CIP & Still With Serious Delinquency:					
H	27	27	12	Falsified quality records	Random sampling not random; shipments embargoed; corrective action taken
I	44	11	2	Quality	Failure of controlled clean environment
J	17	2	1	Test failure	Signal distortion, corrective action in progress
K	16	3	1	QA, insp. records deficient	QA system error, corrective action in progress
	401	159			

Because of the workload implications, decisions to add contractors to theCIP program are studied carefully to determine whether concentrated attention is necessary.

SUMMARY

Timely delivery marks the successful contract. Acceptance and payment confirm that outcome. The contract manager strives toward this conclusion and is concerned with the following:

- Work plans and coordination to ensure that effort is directed toward contractually prescribed deliveries
- Sensitivity to indications that any of the six broad categories of causes of delay may be occurring
- Maintaining a record of events and actions that may cause delay
- Familiarizing key personnel with the three types delay, including the distribution of burdens associated with each type
- Study of eighteen standard clauses plus specific contract provisions that provide for price or time adjustments

TOPICS FOR DISCUSSION

1. Discuss whether a more reliable delivery is achieved by internal or external sourcing.
2. Under what conditions are delivery delays extremely important? Under what conditions are they not?
3. Discuss the actions buyers may initiate to minimize delivery delay.
4. A contractor's facilities are lost in a fire. Under what circumstances might he be held in default because deliveries under his contracts were late due to the fire?
5. Compare the adjustment provisions of the Suspension of Work and Government Delay of Work clauses.
6. What are the reasons for not adding a delinquent contractor to the contractor improvement program?

CASE 13-1

Southwest Electronic Systems[1]

Mr. Robert Snyder is Manager of Tactical Communications Division contracts for Southwest Electronic Systems (SES), Battlefield and Sensor Systems Group, in Boston. He pondered the events of the past few weeks. When he had learned that a sole supplier of a critical component would deliver several weeks late, he had immediately notified the Army that delivery of its Battlefield Reporting System (BRS) would also necessarily slip. Now, as Mr. Snyder reviewed the Army's cure notice dated July 11, 1985, he wondered whether he had been too honest. The way Congress had been playing with program funding, and considering the strained atmosphere in defense contracting, the Army just might terminate the $260 million contract for default, unless he could somehow minimize the impact of his supplier's delinquency. But something else bothered Robert just as much--the lack of communication between SES contract management and the Army contracting officer, before the Army "fired both barrels" with its cure notice. Whether this was due to the general climate that now seemed to exist between defense industry contractors and the government or to a specific cause, he couldn't tell, but it was Robert's job to find a way out of this milieu before the ten-day cure notice deadline expired.

General Company Background

Southwest Electronic Systems is one of the nation's largest developers and producers of advanced electronics, missiles, and space systems. The company provides 12,000 different products and services and has almost 70,000 employees of which 20,000 comprise the scientific and engineering technical staff. SES is organized into six major operating groups, each with total capability to pursue business in its area of responsibility. One of these six is the Battlefield and Sensor Systems Group.

The Battlefield and Sensor Systems Group

Southwest's Battlefield and Sensor Systems Group (BSSG) specializes in command and control systems, communications, radar, electronic war-

---

[1]Research and the original draft of this case were performed by Curtis Cook while a student at George Washington University.

fare, data processing products, displays, sonar, torpedo electronics, software, and support products and services. With nearly 14,000 employees, BSSG received over $1.5 billion in contract awards in 1984 alone. The group is organized into seven major divisions, one of which is the Tactical Communications Division. Its specialties include networks that provide circuit switching capabilities, local and long-haul transmission links for voice and data, encryption, and anti-jam capabilities.

The Battlefield Reporting System. Conveying information between friendly forces on the modern battlefield was a significant technological problem. Battlefield location and direction--the ability for a unit to know its exact location and to position itself to coordinate with other friendly units--was extremely important. The use of conventional radio was vulnerable to misunderstanding, enemy jamming, and eavesdropping.

The Battlefield Reporting System (BRS) was intended to provide Army and Marine units with an automated system that would furnish jam-proof, continuous, and accurate data on the location of friendly forces. The BRS also was an integral part of a larger Southwest Electronic Systems system being designed to satisfy the Army's urgent requirement for an overall secure, real-time battlefield data communication system.

The BRS contract. Engineering development of the BRS began early in 1977. It led to concept demonstration and evaluation by the Army during 1982, and with minor exceptions, the program progressed according to schedule. SES was the system developer and won the first production contract on a sole-source basis in mid-1983. The $260 million production contract called for fifty production verification units to be delivered and tested prior to starting full scale production early in 1986.

During the first two years of the contract, SES met scheduled contract milestones, including critical testing of the first verification unit. By July 1985, however, several SES suppliers had indicated that they might have trouble keeping to promised delivery dates. In most cases, SES had alternate sources where needed subcomponents could be purchased without impacting the BRS schedule. In other cases, SES could build the parts in-house until suppliers were able to meet commitments. However, Mr. Snyder knew of two key sole-source suppliers whose work was critical to performance and delivery--any failure by either to deliver on time could cause a schedule slip.

Unfortunately, on June 20, 1985, that's exactly what happened. A letter from Beta Circuits informed Mr. Snyder that delivery of forty-four display control consoles which were promised for mid-July would be delayed at least until August 15, due to failure of the units to pass reliability demonstration tests. Mr. Snyder immediately called his BRS contract manager into his office to discuss the problem. He decided to "lay it on the line" to the Army and, after confirming the severity of the problem, signed a letter dated July 1, 1985, to the contracting officer explaining the situation.

On July 11, the Army responded with its cure notice. Three sentences were of particular concern to Mr. Snyder:

> . . . the government intends to reduce/suspend progress payments on or about 29 July 1985, pending the receipt and review of any factual SES submission, which will cure the impact of the acknowledged schedule slip.
>
> Pending a final decision in this matter, it will be necessary to determine whether your failure to perform arose out of causes beyond your control and without fault or negligence on your part. . .
>
> Your attention is invited to the respective rights of the contractor and the government under General Provision I.22 entitled "Default" and the liabilities that may be invoked in the event a decision is made to terminate.

The cure notice gave the company ten days to present to the contracting officer, in writing, any facts bearing on the question.

* * * * *

1. Comment on the procedure and practices indicated in this case after considering the overall situation and pertinent standard terms and conditions of government contracts.
2. Design an action plan for Robert Snyder to bring the situation to a satisfactory solution.
3. Under what conditions might neither Beta Circuits nor SES be held responsible for this situation? What scenario would place responsibility on SES but not on Beta Circuits? Regardless, would this affect actions Snyder must now initiate?
3. Assuming that Beta Circuits' reliability problems are ones for which Beta Circuits is responsible, how would you expect this case to be resolved?

14

Post-Award
Negotiations

Formulating agreements to modify contracts tends to dominate other post-award administrative challenges because it brings the parties into negotiation over the principal elements: product, price, and schedule. The work demands intensive preparation and normally is consummated in conference at which technical and administrative issues of all kinds are refined until an agreement is reached on work, price, and schedule. The process is important in direct proportion to the amount of change and adjustment associated with the contract.

The statistics and graphical data in chart 14-1, schedules a and b, summarize U.S. government negotiation activity. The charts reveal that a large proportion of total government contract obligations are subject to negotiations after the award of a contract. There is no comparable summary of industrial contract negotiation data (data comparing the original value of contracts with the value of modifications). A much higher proportion of the total buying activity of private organizations is concerned with firm, stabilized products, and it is probable that their contracts are subject to a smaller proportion of post-award negotiations than government contracts. Because major government acquisitions tend to involve new technologies and less than fully defined objectives, they are subject to greater variations in design and work processes and, therefore, subject to more post-award negotiation toward adjustment of the original contractual agreement.

In examining chart 14-1, schedule a, it is evident that most contract actions occur when the original contract is awarded. In the three years recorded, the proportion of original contract awards ranged from 72 to 73 percent of the total contract actions (line 11 divided by line 12, schedule

351

Chart 14-1

United States Contract Activity[1]

Schedule a, Number of Actions (1984-1986)

Line #	Kind of Contract	1986	1985	1984	Total
1.	Definitive Supersede Ltr.	816	741	776	2,333
2.	Modification	114,979	108,382	112,575	335,936
3.	Termination for Default	512	399	379	1,290
4.	Term. for Convenience	1,558	728	807	3,093
5.	Post-Award Total	117,865	110,250	114,537	342,652
6.	Initial Letter	1,098	1,385	1,269	3,752
7.	Definitive	123,776	124,070	123,071	370,919
8.	Internal Order	141,872	143,159	136,286	421,317
9.	GSA Schedule	27,580	33,198	33,118	93,896
10.	External Order	2,574	2,971	3,126	8,671
11.	Award Total	296,902	304,783	296,870	898,555
12.	TOTAL ACTIONS	414,767	415,033	411,407	1,241,207

Schedule b, Value of Actions (millions) (1984-1986)

Line #	Kind of Contract	1986	1985	1984	Total
1.	Definitive Supersede Ltr.	$ 4,821	$ 4,264	$ 4,153	$ 13,238
2.	Modification	94,246	88,452	81,659	264,360
3.	Termination for Default	(121)	(106)	(85)	(312)
4.	Term. for Convenience	(444)	(617)	(160)	(1,221)
5.	Post-Award Total	98,505	91,993	85,567	276,065
6.	Initial Letter	2752	5,603	6,335	14,690
7.	Definitive	57,626	58,611	49,624	165,861
8.	Internal Order	21,488	23,969	22,526	67,983
9.	GSA Schedule	1,901	2,085	2,465	6,451
10.	External Order	287	346	297	930
11.	Award Total	84,054	90,614	81,247	255,915
12.	TOTAL VALUE (MILLIONS)	$182,559	$182,607	$166,814	$531,980

[1]*Federal Procurement Data System Standard Report,* Fiscal Years 1984, 85, & 86 (Federal Procurement Data Center, General Services Administration). Data extracted from total federal year-to-date tables. Data excludes small purchase orders.

Chart 14-1 (continued)

Definitions Associated with Chart 14-1:

<u>Post-Award Contract Actions:</u>
Definitive Contract Superseding Letter Contract:
   An award based on a price agreement reached subsequent to
   original contract award
Modification:
   Any Modification of an existing definitive contract, letter
   contract, or order that obligates or deobligates funds
Termination for Default:
   Action cutting off right to proceed with work, implying use of
   sanctions associated with a contractor's failure
Termination for Convenience:
   Action cutting off right to proceed with work for reasons of
   convenience to the government

<u>Award Actions:</u>
Initial Letter Contract:
   New contract award without final price agreement
Definitive Contract:
   First binding document, including notice of award; an instru-
   ment containing all the terms and conditions of the agreement
Internal Order:
   An order under reporting agency's contract; creates a firm
   obligation (order) against a contract or agreement placed by
   the reporting agency
GSA Schedule:
   Requirements contracts permitting authorized agencies to place
   orders
External Order:
   An order under another agency's contract; does not include
   orders under GSA schedule or contracts placed with Small
   Business Administration pursuant to Public Law 85-536, Section
   8(a)

a). It is interesting to note that the data is nearly reversed when summarized by dollar value instead of by number of actions, as can be seen
in chart 14-1, schedule b. These statistics reveal that the proportion of
contract dollars negotiated at time of award (i.e., prices fully agreed
upon) ranged from 46 to 50 percent of the total value of actions (line 11
divided by line 12, schedule b). If the value of definitive awards is
compared with the value of modifications (line 7 divided by line 2, schedule b), it becomes clear that definitive (i.e., agreed upon) initial contract
values are only 63 percent of the value of contract modification agreements. Overall, the statistics indicate that the predominant amount of
total negotiation activity is performed under the auspices of post-award
management rather than pre-award procurement. Implications for competitiveness, risk allocation, negotiation procedure, and workload are indicated by these statistics. One consequence is the need for allocating
manpower resources to the post-award phases of the process. In this
chapter, we will examine these implications.

The relative importance of post-award negotiations indicated in the
foregoing paragraph is understated. Four of the categories of award
dollars represent orders that are priced subsequent to award or that
constitute additions to existing contracts that authorize post-award
ordering. These categories are initial letter contracts, internal orders,
GSA schedule contracts, and external orders, all of which involve additions to existing contracts or negotiations completed subsequent to the
award of the contract but are included in the statistics for the total
amount of contract awards (see the definitions associated with chart 14-
1). If the dollars for these four categories of awards were treated as
post-award administration, the proportion of dollar value established
subsequent to the original award rises to 69 percent (sum of lines 6, 8, 9,
10 and 5, divided by line 12, schedule b) for the three years under
study. These two schedules are revealing because they indicate that a
large part of post-award manpower must be devoted to preparing and
conducting price negotiation.

At this point, please refer to chart 13-1 to review the numerous
types of causes which require post-award negotiation of contract modifications. Although chart 13-1 was designed to highlight the causes for
delay, it also provides a summary listing of the principal causes for
post-award negotiation activity (causes generally charged to the buyer).

ACCUMULATION OF DATA, PERFORMANCE HISTORY

Whether working for buyer or seller, a principal responsibility of
contract managers is to accumulate a record of the events, decisions, and
participants in contract activity. To do this well, the manager must give
close attention to detail and should possess an acute sense of how

contract commitments are affected by events. Knowledge of these matters enables the presentation (or defense) of claims for adjustments based on facts and causes for action. The actual circumstances of an event and the persons involved, together with the requirements of the contract, determine which party should shoulder the burdens. Sorting out these factual background matters and interpreting contract provisions and cost issues are the vital elements of negotiations.

Negotiation of contract modifications mandates a review of the contract for purposes of interpreting the original intent of the parties. (See chapter 5) However, examining the rules of interpretation and applying them to a contract is only meaningful in relationship to a particular set of facts. This is the principal reason for contract managers to establish reliable systems that generate complete, factual records of steps taken, comments (along with the names of those who made them), and responses and actions taken during performance activity. While there is no specified format for the accumulation of such a record, it is helpful if the contract manager has developed a method plus a set of check lists as an aid in remembering important items. Records help but will not support the negotiation of price and schedule adjustments without, in addition, an accounting system that captures and retains a formal record of all costs incurred, including substantiating original entry documents. This is a necessary part of the background accumulation responsibility. It is particularly important in government contract work because of the high level of post-award modification activity and the likelihood that negotiation of cost and time effects will occur after work has been initiated. When this happens, the government expects contractor claims to be supported with actual cost information pertinent to the specific change (or other basis for the claim) for which the price adjustment is requested. Contract managers should note that actual cost information is presumed to be a reasonable indication of the total cost impact of such activities and will justify the magnitude of price adjustments unless rebutted on the basis of substantial evidence indicating that the expenditures were unreasonable.

ACCOUNTING FOR WORK AND CHANGE COSTS

The rules and principles for negotiating contract modifications pursuant to change activity are covered later in this chapter. One of the realities of contract work is that contractor accounting systems are not generally structured to automatically initiate a record of changes on a change-by-change basis. Such records are expensive to establish and are not needed for internal control purposes. When costs are sponsored by the customer, however, cost data lends credibility to claims. Change order accounting becomes vital in government contracting when the incidence of change and the nature of change work are such that their costs and costs of other work under the project are not readily segregated and are significant in amount.   In one contract for which the author was responsible, work pursuant to change orders totaled four times the original contract value.   In that contract, which was for research and development, the overall configuration of the end item (a satellite) was changed during performance, subsequent to completion of the entire design.   The change was made in order to reduce the weight of the satellite to fit within the restrictions of a satellite launching vehicle that was revised due to program necessity.   Negotiation of a definitive price for the change was difficult because no change order accounting requirement existed, and collection of viable supporting data was nearly impossible.

To ensure that a contractor's accounting system will segregate and capture the costs associated with significant changes, the government has adopted a contract clause entitled Change Order Accounting.   The clause is published in FAR 52.243-6.   It specifies the following:

> The contracting officer may require change order accounting whenever the estimated cost of a change or series of related changes exceeds $100,000.00.   The contractor, for each change or series of related changes, shall maintain separate accounts, by job order or other suitable accounting procedure, of all incurred segregatable, direct costs (less allocable credits) of work, both changed and not changed, allocable to the change.   The contractor shall maintain such accounts until the parties agree to an equitable adjustment for the changes ordered by the contracting officer or the matter is conclusively disposed of in accordance with the disputes clause.

Although this clause explicitly establishes the requirement for an accounting of changes, it is not to be used lightly because it imposes additional expenses for the accounting process and increases the complexity of allocating and attributing costs for segments of work.   When used, the clause authorizes the contracting officer to require the contractor to identify and segregate recurring and nonrecurring costs associated with changes from the cost of work not affected by the change(s).

CONTENT OF PROPOSALS

The responsibility for preparing proposals for modifications is ordinarily assigned to the supplier's contract manager who accomplishes this task by initiating and coordinating change analysis and cost estimates. The analysis of the change for technical impact is an engineering and/or production function and may be documented by a revised work statement, plus schedule, manpower, and material estimates. These estimates are subjected to review and further analysis by management in accordance with the contractor's system. Solicitation of supplier quotations, application of labor and usage rates, and application of indirect costs may be controlled by the material, estimating, and pricing functions, according to the contractor's practices. The whole process may be under the jurisdiction of the comptroller or comparable company officer.[1] The contract manager's role is to ensure full consideration of contractual directives and compliance with customer expectations and rules. His or her principal concern is to protect the rights and property of the company while providing substantiation of quantities and prices in a manner consistent with customer requirements.

In many cases, the key to success in submitting proposals is effective presentation of the basis or justification for the submission. Accomplishing this requires careful accumulation of data which must be summed and organized in a manner appropriate for the particular submission—whether of a preliminary nature, such as an engineering change proposal (ECP), or final, such as the claim (proposal) in response to a formal contract change notice (CCN).

Initiation of proposal activity pursuant to existing contracts may be viewed as an opportunity rather than an obligation, since the objective is increased sales. It is stimulated by requests for ECPs, issuance of change orders, discovery of product improvement possibilities, identification of value engineering savings, emergence of constructive changes, changes or deficiencies in government-furnished property, receipt of stop work orders, a convenience termination directive, and other actions. In construction contracts, when site conditions in an excavation have been identified that are different from those expected, proposal action should begin.

Most contractually specified factors that justify the initiation of post-award proposal activity are covered by the contract clauses summarized in chart 13-2. However, a contract manager must be sensitive to all events and activities that may fit into one of the specified bases for a claim. An area for special awareness is technical direction and specification deficiencies that may change costs and schedules, even though not documented by the issuance of a contracting officer's written order. Situations such as these are likely to be treated as constructive changes. They arise whenever an expansion of the contractor's work effort beyond that required to meet the contract obligations is imposed by acts or omissions of the customer. Compensable actions include customer orders

---

[1]Cost estimating is examined in depth in Rodney D. Stewart and Richard M. Wyskida, *Cost Estimators Reference Manual* (Wiley-Interscience, New York, 1987).

to delay, accelerate, or otherwise act in a way that interferes with progress. Causes for initiating proposals by suppliers may occur in connection with approvals or other support action if not handled properly by the customer, and proposals may be demanded by the customer whenever events occur or changes emerge that reduce contract cost. A proposal is likely to be essential in connection with delays and may have both time and cost aspects. Many proposals incorporate both downward and upward adjustments. Chart 13-1 summarizes the numerous causes of action for which proposals are needed.

NEGOTIATION STRATEGY

No aspect of contract management is more important than properly approaching the customer with proposals to alter contract price or schedule. Such claims are viewed with some level of suspicion and are likely to be challenged as to the amount requested. They may be challenged with respect to the basis for claiming any adjustment at all, particularly when the requested adjustment is upward. A major responsibility of the contract manager is to sell to the customer the legitimacy and propriety of claims. Fulfilling this responsibility mandates that the contractor carefully analyze the contract requirements, including specifications and drawings and other background information regarding the original agreement. Additionally, it mandates careful examination of the events occurring subsequent to award of the contract. The objective is to justify the reasons for cost, schedule, and/or profit adjustments. The adopted strategy must suit customer perceptions. In the case of proposals to the government, support by proper documentation is fundamental.

ORGANIZATION, CONTENT, AND BACKUP
FOR GOVERNMENT CONTRACT PRICING

The pricing section of proposals to the government must be submitted using the government's Contract Pricing Proposal Cover Sheet, Standard Form 1411, (chart 14-2). It should be completed and signed in accordance with the rules for submission. The form is important because it requires explicit representations to be made by the contractor and a breakdown of the total proposal into prices for each contract line item affected. There are eighteen categories of information required by SF 1411. All but two are self-explanatory or require no discussion relating to proposals for modifications of price. Two of the items are critically important whenever cost and pricing data are submitted in support of the proposal, which is the case for all contract modification proposals with aggregate cost changes of $100,000 or more.

Chart 14-2

Contract Pricing Proposal Cover Sheet

CONTRACT PRICING PROPOSAL COVER SHEET	1. SOLICITATION/CONTRACT/MODIFICATION NO.	FORM APPROVED OMB NO. 3090-0116
NOTE: This form is used in contract actions if submission of cost or pricing data is required. *(See FAR 15.804-6(b))*		

2. NAME AND ADDRESS OF OFFEROR *(Include ZIP Code)* | **3A. NAME AND TITLE OF OFFEROR'S POINT OF CONTACT** | **3B. TELEPHONE NO.**

4. TYPE OF CONTRACT ACTION *(Check)*

A. NEW CONTRACT	D. LETTER CONTRACT
B. CHANGE ORDER	E. UNPRICED ORDER
C. PRICE REVISION/ REDETERMINATION	F. OTHER *(Specify)*

5. TYPE OF CONTRACT *(Check)*
☐ FFP ☐ CPFF ☐ CPIF ☐ CPAF
☐ FPI ☐ OTHER *(Specify)*

6. PROPOSED COST *(A+B=C)*

A. COST	B. PROFIT/FEE	C. TOTAL
$	$	$

7. PLACE(S) AND PERIOD(S) OF PERFORMANCE

8. List and reference the identification, quantity and total price proposed for each contract line item. A line item cost breakdown supporting this recap is required unless otherwise specified by the Contracting Officer. *(Continue on reverse, and then on plain paper, if necessary. Use same headings.)*

A. LINE ITEM NO.	B. IDENTIFICATION	C. QUANTITY	D. TOTAL PRICE	E. REF.

9. PROVIDE NAME, ADDRESS, AND TELEPHONE NUMBER FOR THE FOLLOWING *(If available)*

A. CONTRACT ADMINISTRATION OFFICE	B. AUDIT OFFICE

10. WILL YOU REQUIRE THE USE OF ANY GOVERNMENT PROPERTY IN THE PERFORMANCE OF THIS WORK? *(If "Yes," identify)*
☐ YES ☐ NO

11A. DO YOU REQUIRE GOVERNMENT CONTRACT FINANCING TO PERFORM THIS PROPOSED CONTRACT? *(If "Yes," complete Item 11B)*
☐ YES ☐ NO

11B. TYPE OF FINANCING *(√ one)*
☐ ADVANCE PAYMENTS ☐ PROGRESS PAYMENTS
☐ GUARANTEED LOANS

12. HAVE YOU BEEN AWARDED ANY CONTRACTS OR SUBCONTRACTS FOR THE SAME OR SIMILAR ITEMS WITHIN THE PAST 3 YEARS? *(If "Yes," identify item(s), customer(s) and contract number(s))*
☐ YES ☐ NO

13. IS THIS PROPOSAL CONSISTENT WITH YOUR ESTABLISHED ESTIMATING AND ACCOUNTING PRACTICES AND PROCEDURES AND FAR PART 31 COST PRINCIPLES? *(If "No," explain)*
☐ YES ☐ NO

14. COST ACCOUNTING STANDARDS BOARD (CASB) DATA *(Public Law 91-379 as amended and FAR PART 30)*

A. WILL THIS CONTRACT ACTION BE SUBJECT TO CASB REGULATIONS? *(If "No," explain in proposal)*
☐ YES ☐ NO

B. HAVE YOU SUBMITTED A CASB DISCLOSURE STATEMENT (CASB DS-1 or 3)? *(If "Yes," specify in proposal the office to which submitted and if determined to be adequate)*
☐ YES ☐ NO

C. HAVE YOU BEEN NOTIFIED THAT YOU ARE OR MAY BE IN NON-COMPLIANCE WITH YOUR DISCLOSURE STATEMENT OR COST ACCOUNTING STANDARDS? *(If "Yes," explain in proposal)*
☐ YES ☐ NO

D. IS ANY ASPECT OF THIS PROPOSAL INCONSISTENT WITH YOUR DISCLOSED PRACTICES OR APPLICABLE COST ACCOUNTING STANDARDS? *(If "Yes," explain in proposal)*
☐ YES ☐ NO

This proposal is submitted in response to the RFP, contract, modification, etc. in Item 1 and reflects our best estimates and/or actual costs as of this date.

15. NAME AND TITLE *(Type)*	16. NAME OF FIRM

17. SIGNATURE	18. DATE OF SUBMISSION

NSN 7540-01-142-9845   1411-101   STANDARD FORM 1411 (10-83)
Prescribed by GSA
FAR (48 CFR) 53.215-2(c)

Item 13 of Form 1411 asks whether the proposal is consistent with the contractor's established estimating and accounting practices and procedures and with the cost principles of FAR Part 31. A negative response to this question would not be acceptable to the government. The cited cost principles have been discussed in chapter 11. They are comprehensive, complex, and subject to change. Nevertheless, consistency with FAR Part 31 is mandatory for pricing actions subject to submission of cost and pricing data. An affirmative response to item 13 results in a certification and should be made with an awareness of the statutory requirements discussed in chapter 2 and summarized in chart 2-2.

Item 14 is equally important if the contract is subject to cost accounting standards (see chapter 11) or if the contractor has submitted a CASB disclosure statement. Item 14D requires a certification of consistency with these matters, if they apply. The certification should be made with an awareness of chart 2-2.

The most useful representation of the summary data required with contract modification proposals is probably that found under the headings specified for presentation of line item summary information by the FAR Subpart 15.804-6[1]. The headings are reproduced in charts 14-3A, B, and C. They call for three types of presentation, differentiating between new procurement, change orders, and other price revision proposals. The columnar breakout indicated by these three headings is applicable for the contractor's summary of cost elements that are included as part of a proposed price. Chart 14-4 summarizes the cost element breakdown requirements. The price is developed by the contractor, but support for the price is acceptable only if both the columnar breakout and the cost element breakdown meet government expectations. A separate table of data is required for each line item affected by the proposal. In preparing the tables of data called for by these government policies, the manager gains full insight into the expected structure of the contract modification proposals.

The columnar headings for new procurement actions (chart 14-3A) are applicable to actions negotiated subsequent to the start of work, as occurs with letter contracts, but is designed for pricing items that have not previously been covered by a price agreement. For such actions, each contract line item should be supported by a summary presentation, giving a breakdown of cost elements together with a reference indicator that would identify any supporting attachments to explain the basis for the total or unit cost being proposed. Whenever the line item is to be delivered in quantities greater than one, it is likely that the unit cost

---

[1]A complete treatise on contract pricing, including detailed explanation of headings for line item cost summaries, is found in the *Armed Services Pricing Manual* (GPO, 1986).

Chart 14-3A

Headings for Submission of Line Item Cost Summaries

New Procurements

COST ELEMENTS	PROPOSED CONTRACT ESTIMATE—TOTAL COST	PROPOSED CONTRACT ESTIMATE—UNIT COST	REFERENCE
(1)	(2)	(3)	(4)

(1) Enter those necessary and reasonable costs which in the judgment of the offeror will properly be incurred in the efficient performance of the contract. When any of the costs in this column have already been incurred (e.g., letter contract or un-priced order), describe them on an attached supporting schedule. When "preproduction" or "start-up" costs are significant or when specifically requested in detail by the Contracting Officer, provide a full identification and explanation of same.

(2) Optional except where required by the Contracting Officer.

(3) Attach separate pages as necessary and identify in this column the attachment in which the information supporting the specific cost element may be found.

Chart 14-3B

Headings for Submission of Line Item Cost Summaries

Change Orders (modifications)

COST ELEMENTS	ESTIMATED COST OF ALL WORK DELETED	COST OF DELETED WORK ALREADY PERFORMED	NET COST TO BE DELETED	COST OF WORK ADDED	NET COST OF CHANGE	REFERENCE
(1)	(2)	(3)	(4)	(5)	(6)	(7)

(1) The "estimated cost of all deleted work" includes (i) current estimates of what the cost would have been to complete deleted work not yet performed, and (ii) the cost of deleted work already performed.

(2) The "cost of deleted work already performed" is the incurred cost of such work, actually computed if possible, or estimated in the contractor's accounting records. Attach a detailed inventory of work, materials, parts, components, and hardware already purchased, manufactured, or performed and deleted by the change, indicating the cost and proposed disposition of each line item. Also, if the contractor desires to retain such items or any portion thereof, indicate amount offered therefor.

(3) The "net cost to be deleted" is the "estimated cost of all deleted work" less the "cost of deleted work already performed."

(4) When nonrecurring costs are significant or when specifically requested in detail by the contracting officer, provide a full identification and explanation of same.

(5) The "net cost of change" is the "cost of work added" less the "net cost to be deleted." When this result is a negative amount, place the amount in parentheses.

(6) Refer to 7A(3) above.

Chart 14-3C
Headings For Submission of Line Item Cost Summaries

Price Revision/Redetermination

CUTOFF DATE	NUMBER OF UNITS COMPLETED	NUMBER OF UNITS TO BE COMPLETED	CONTRACT AMOUNT	REDETERMINA- TION PROPOSAL AMOUNT	DIFFERENCE
(1)	(2)	(3)	(4)	(5)	(6)

COST ELEMENTS	INCURRED COST— PREPRODUC- TION	INCURRED COST— COMPLETED UNITS	INCURRED COST— WORK IN PROCESS	TOTAL INCURRED COST	ESTIMATED COST TO COMPLETE	ESTIMATED TOTAL COST	REFERENCE
(7)	(8)	(9)	(10)	(11)	(12)	(13)	(14)

(1) Enter the cut-off date required by the contract, if applicable.

(2) Enter the number of units completed during the period for which experienced costs of production are being submitted and the number of units remaining to be completed under the contract.

(3) Enter all costs incurred under the contract prior to starting production and other nonrecurring costs (usually referred to as "start-up" costs) from your books and records as of the cut-off date. These include such costs as preproduction engineering, special plant rearrangement, training program, and any identifiable nonrecurring costs such as initial rework, spoilage, pilot runs, etc. In the event the amounts of the foregoing are not segregated in or otherwise available from your records, enter in this column your best estimates of such costs. Explain the basis for each estimate and how such costs are charged on your accounting records (e.g., included in production costs as direct engineering labor, charged to manufacturing overhead, etc.). Also show how such costs would be allocated to the units at their various stages of contract completion.

(4) Enter in column (b) the production costs from your books and records (exclusive of preproduction costs reported in column (a)) of the units completed as of the cut-off date. Enter in column (c) the costs of Work-in-Process as determined from your records or inventories at the cut-off date. When the amounts for Work-in-Process are not available in your records but reliable estimates for them can be made, enter the estimated amounts in column (c) and enter in column (b) the differences between the total incurred costs (exclusive of Preproduction Costs) as of the cut-off date and these estimates. Explain the basis for such estimates, includ-ing identification of any provision for experienced or anticipated allowances, such as shrinkage, rework, design changes, etc. Furnish experienced unit or lot costs (or labor hours) from inception of contract to the cut-off date, improvement curves, and any other available production cost history pertaining to the item(s) to which your proposal relates.

(5) Enter those necessary and reasonable costs which in your judgment will properly be incurred in completing the remaining work to be performed under the contract with respect to the item(s) to which your proposal relates.

(6) Refer to 7A(3) above.

(7) Where residual inventory exists, the final costs established under FPI and FPR arrangements should be net of the fair market value of such inventory.

(8) In support of subcontract costs, a listing shall be submitted of all subcontracts subject to repricing action, annotated as to their status.

Chart 14-4

Cost Elements Suggested by Government for
Breakdowns of Cost Data in Support
of Pricing Proposals

Materials: Provide a consolidated priced summary of individual material quantities included in the various tasks, orders or contract line items being proposed, and basis for pricing (vendor quotes, invoice prices, etc.).

Subcontracted Items: Include parts, components, assemblies and services to be produced or performed by other than you in accordance with your design, specifications or directions and applicable only to the prime contract. For each subcontract over $100,000, the support should provide a listing by source, item, quantity, price, type of subcontract, degree of competition and basis for establishing source and reasonableness of price, as well as results of review and evaluation of subcontract proposals when required by NASA PR 3.807.

Standard Commercial Items: Consists of items which you normally fabricate, in whole or in part, and are generally stocked in inventory. Provide appropriate explanation of basis for pricing. If based on cost, provide cost breakdown; if priced at other than cost, provide justification for exemption from submission of cost or pricing data as required by NASA PR 3.807.

Interorganizational Transfers (at cost): Include separate breakdown of cost by element.

Raw Material: Consists of material which is in a form or state that requires further processing. Provide priced quantities of items required for this proposal.

Purchased Parts: Includes material items not covered above. Provide priced quantities for items required for this proposal.

Direct Labor: Provide a time-phased (e.g., monthly, quarterly, etc.) breakdown of labor hours, rates, and cost by appropriate category and furnish basis for estimates.

Indirect Costs: Indicate the method of computation and application of your indirect costs, including cost breakdowns, and showing trends and budgetary data, to provide a basis for evaluation of the reasonableness of proposed rates. Indicate the rates used and provide an appropriate explanation.

Other Costs: List all other costs which are not otherwise included in the categories described above (e.g., special tooling, travel, computer and consultant services, preservation, packaging and packing, spoilage and rework, and Federal excise tax on finished articles) and provide basis for pricing.

Royalties: If amount exceeds $250, the offeror must submit a DD Form 783 Royalty Report or its equivalent. (See NASA PR 9.110 and 16.202-1)

Facilities Capital Cost of Money: The offeror must submit Form CASB-CMF and show calculation of proposed amount. (See NASA PR 16.202-3) column will be required to facilitate analysis of the costs on that basis.

In chart 14-3B, the format reflects columns pertinent to modifications pursuant to change orders and other similar actions leading to an equitable adjustment. The elements of cost are to be listed for each item on which a proposed change is applicable. For each cost element, the additional columnar breakout is called for to help establish the basis for the proposal. It specifies three categories of deleted work. One is an estimate of the cost of all work deleted by the change order. From that value, the cost of work already performed but deleted is deducted (since it must be paid for) to provide a net cost reduction associated with the deletions. The net cost reduction is then added (algebraically) to the cost of the additional work required by the change to determine the net cost. The pricing form requires this process for each cost element. The sum of all cost elements is the cost value for the line item to which a profit may be added. The sum of line items provides the price of the modification. The reference column allows, for each cost element, an identification of additional supporting schedules or statements to justify or explain the summary cost information.

Chart 14-3C is designed to support a similar contract modification negotiation, but one which proposes a price revision for an item upon which an earlier tentative agreement has been established. Actions of this type are characteristic of redeterminable contracts. In this situation two headings are indicated by the form. One heading requires the identification of units of contract work that have been completed and those that have yet to be completed as of the cutoff date for the particular proposal. This heading calls for a summary value of the original contract price, of the redetermination proposal, and the overall difference between the two numbers. This is done for each line item.

The second part of the heading requires a breakdown of the elements of cost for each line item, but it amplifies the number of columnar headings to ensure the provision of additional useful breakouts for analysis purposes. These elements are to be identified as of the cutoff date for the proposal, differentiating between costs incurred prior to that date and costs yet to be incurred. The already incurred costs are to be broken down further into those categorized as pre-production expenses, production expenses associated with the units of work that have been completed, and production expenses associated with work still in process as of the cutoff date. These three incurred cost elements are summarized in a total figure to which is added the estimated cost to completion, computed from the cutoff date to the end of the contract. An estimated total cost column is provided to combine the incurred and to-complete costs. Finally, a reference column is provided for identifying backup material associated with each cost element. Regardless of which of the three formats is applicable, contractors are expected to transfer the summary data for each line item to the Standard Form 1411 cover sheet for submitting proposals.

Contract managers who are responsible for preparing proposals to the government for contract modifications should become thoroughly familiar with these expected breakouts of costs, so that their proposals will facilitate the analysis and negotiations processes which must follow.

COST AND PRICING DATA REQUIREMENTS, GOVERNMENT CONTRACT PROPOSALS

Development of a negotiation strategy and organization of contract modification proposals for government contracting have evolved over a period of twenty-four years subsequent to the enactment in 1962 of Public Law 87-653, known as the Truth in Negotiations Act. This enactment has been subject to adjustments subsequent to 1962, including important changes by the Competition in Contracting Act (CICA) of 1984. The policy is easily summarized with respect to the cost and pricing data requirements aspects of this legislation. It requires cost and pricing data to be submitted in support of contract proposals leading to the negotiation of contracts or modifications. The enactment applies (with exceptions) not only to negotiation of prime contracts but also to subcontractor negotiations. In general, all proposals negotiated during the post-award administration phases of a contract are subject to the statute if the total amount of the claim (determined by the absolute sum of reductions and additions) exceeds $100,000. This general statement can be made because virtually all cases of modification negotiations are conducted under non-price competitive conditions. Therefore, unless either catalog price or market price exemptions can be shown to apply to the modification action, the submission of cost and pricing data will be necessary.

The basic cost and pricing data requirements are straightforward. When they apply, a contractor who makes a proposal for price adjustment to the government not only must submit the data, but also must certify that the data is current, accurate, and complete as of the date of certification. These two requirements work in tandem to ensure that the government negotiation team has the same basic information pertinent to the proposed adjustment as that known to the contractor's people. Once submission and certification of cost and pricing data are accomplished, the provisions of the contract permit the government to demand a price reduction in the event data is later shown to have been noncurrent, incomplete, or inaccurate. Price reduction will reflect the direct and indirect costs and profits associated with the overpricing. The legislation also requires that a contractor who is subject to these rules agree to permit an audit of his accounts, books, and records associated with the contract pricing proposal. This audit right exists for the period of performance of the contract plus three years. The audits are designed to verify the currency, accuracy, and completeness of the proposal cost and pricing data. These requirements flow downward to each subcontractor whose proposals meet the thresholds for applicability.

Although the Truth-in-Negotiation legislation does not impose criminal sanctions for noncurrent, incomplete, or inaccurate data submissions, contract managers should be aware of recent moves toward use of anti-fraud statutes in such cases and the imposition of penalties in some situations (see chapter 2 and chart 2-2).

POSITION DEVELOPMENT BY GOVERNMENT NEGOTIATORS

Policies governing the negotiation of prices by government contracting officers and negotiators are provided in Federal Acquisition Regulation Subpart 15.8. General guidance with respect to the analysis of proposals is provided in Subpart 15.805. Authority to reach agreements on adjustments is vested in contracting officers, but analysis of proposals and supporting data is a team effort, employing technical, audit, and pricing expertise. The work of this team is analogous to that of the contractor's estimating and pricing system. It differs in one key way: the government team starts with the contractor's proposal and proceeds by questioning and verification. In some cases, a complete independent cost estimate may be developed by a government team, but this applies only in special cases. The government team is headed by a negotiator and in addition to its normal complement, may be augmented by specialists from legal and technological disciplines who may make vital contributions toward a full analysis and understanding of contractor proposals. All members of this team are not necessarily present at a contract negotiation; however, all will have contributed to developing the contracting officer's position. A cost analysis by the contracting officer or his team members is particularly important to the negotiation of contract modifications. It is made up of a set of verifications and comparisons of the elements of costs incorporated into the offeror's proposal as it relates to the specification, work statement, or other form of work definition pertinent to the contract. This analysis begins with a technical appraisal of the contractor's work plan, and estimates for labor, material, tooling, and use of facilities. With full technical understanding achieved, verifications of quantities, types of material and labor, quotations, pricing factors, rates, and the bases for them as used by the contractor are checked by audit and cross-checked by pricing and negotiation personnel.

Analysis of costs is approached on an element-by-element basis and seeks to identify any trends characteristic of the contractor's operations. Trends that indicate rising or falling labor costs and changing overhead or material costs should be explored fully. The analysis attempts to ensure that practices projected by the contractor into future operations will not incorporate previously demonstrated inefficient or uneconomical practices. The philosophy is to arrive at a position that represents what the modification "should cost."

Comparisons that are useful in cost analysis include comparisons of current costs with (1) actual costs previously incurred for the same or similar work; (2) cost estimates previously developed by the offeror for the same or similar items; (3) cost estimates received from other respondents to the request for a specific or similar product; and (4) independent cost estimates which may be developed by a special team organized for that purpose.

In addition to these verifications, the cost analysis process addresses the question of appropriateness of the cost submission under FAR Part 31, Contract Cost Principles and Procedures. FAR Part 30, Cost Accounting Standards, is similarly a point of verification during the prenegotiation development phase. Consistency of the cost package with these rules, to the extent that they apply, is a responsibility of the contracting officer; however, the verifications are performed by other members of the pricing team, specifically the audit and field contract administration offices cognizant of the offeror's plant.

Technical analysis provides the foundation for the cost analysis process. It strengthens the understanding of any proposal and is essential for actions in which cost and pricing data are required. The purpose of technical analysis is to verify that the prime elements of cost associated with the specification or work statement are appropriate in terms of magnitude and kinds of effort applied. For example, the technical officer may be expected to provide evaluation of the

1. relevance of proposed work to requirements,
2. kinds and quantities of material needed,
3. kinds and quantities of labor needed,
4. need for application of other direct costs,
5. scrap or spoilage factors,
6. need for special tooling or test equipment,
7. need for government-furnished property.

All of these assessments are important to any project under consideration and are areas in which the assigned technical officer should be knowledgeable. In addition, the technical evaluator may be able to provide information concerning the price or rate at which each of the above estimates should be computed for pricing purposes. The technical officer's expertise should also provide insight and background for developing arguments to support the buyer's position in negotiations, vis-a-vis that of the contractor. In these areas, pricing expertise supplied by price analysts may aid in refining data and in developing the buyer's negotiation position.

In preparation for negotiations of modifications, the government team may acquire pricing reports from field administration offices. Field offices employ price analysts and quality assurance, engineering, and audit personnel who have direct exposure to a contractor's working site. They are able to provide a review of proposals, drawing on their knowledge of the contractor's operations. Furthermore, they may be sensitive to the local conditions which generate particular cost or pricing positions of a contractor. The field support should lend strength to the negotiation position of the buyer. A field pricing report may be supported by an audit review of the proposal and may be able to put into perspective the views of audit and technical personnel, because of the CAO's specific knowledge of the operations under negotiation. If proposal value exceeds $100,000, review by auditors is required, normally by the Defense Contract Audit Agency (this threshhold was increased by a regulation waiver for Defense contracts in June 1987 to $500,000 and $1,000,000 depending on contract type--further variations could occur). Regardless, the insight provided by the auditor who has direct access to the contractor's books and records is viewed as essential for major contract modifications.

All of the foregoing activities are focused on the objective of strengthening the contracting officer's ability to prepare a negotiating position and to respond to the contractor's proposal with insight and knowledge of its quality. The contracting officer summarizes all input data, integrates the effects of these informational resources, and develops a position. He or she is responsible not only for the cost analysis but also for an overall price analysis.

The price analysis is based on comparisons of prices. Its purpose is to assess the value and/or fairness and reasonableness of the price in light of known prices for comparable work. Price analysis may require comparisons between the overall price offered and

1. other quotations of price for the particular work;
2. earlier quotations and price agreements for the same or similar end items, adjusted for time and other differences;
3. prices developed through an independent cost estimate;
4. other comparisons available to the contracting officer, such as published prices or market prices as adjusted by indices, and any known discount or rebate arrangements that may be pertinent.

NEGOTIATION OBJECTIVES FOR MODIFICATION ACTIONS

The question of price is fundamental to negotiating contract modifications. Although specific negotiations may focus on calculating schedule adjustment or other issues, such as modifying a particular contract clause, these actions reflect special circumstances. The amount of price change remains central to agreements in almost all cases, even when other issues are factors leading to the agreement.

Equitable Adjustments

Effective negotiation of modifications requires appreciation by both parties of the concept of an equitable adjustment (EA). The EA includes both cost and profit as elements that may be subject to change under the negotiations. A number of rules have evolved regarding the way in which parties should approach their agreement on the amount of adjustment. They have been developed and documented through litigation but are applicable to negotiation between contract managers. Litigation over a dispute under a government contract is normally conducted before a board of contract appeals. Over the years thousands of cases have been decided by the boards (many have been appealed to the Court of Claims, now the U.S. Claims Court), and a fairly definitive pattern of adjustment rules can be discerned from the decided cases. These cases are decided in an after-the-fact mode. Under government contract procedures, work continues while litigation proceeds, but litigation is a long, drawn-out process. In almost all cases, the project under litigation is completed before the decisions of the board and/or court have been made. Nevertheless, the rules developed by these deciding bodies of record are extremely important to the negotiators dealing prospectively with the negotiation of contract modifications. Probably the central, overall rule developed in litigation but applicable to negotiation is the stated objective: to return the parties to the same relative positions they held prior to the event for which the equitable adjustment was made. This rule refers to the profitability of the contract. The government's objective is to leave the contractor with the same relative profit (or loss) he had achieved at the time the change was issued. The principal effect of this rule is to require analysis of costs specifically affected (increased or decreased) by the change. This requires isolating change costs from overall performance costs and mandates careful analysis of the costs that would have been incurred to perform work deleted by the change. The essential purpose of this rule is to avoid overall contract repricing actions, when only a portion of a contract has been altered by the change order. This objective is the genesis of the Change Order Accounting clause which was discussed earlier in this chapter.

Measure of damages. Perhaps the second most critical rule in the equitable adjustments process concerns the basis for arriving at the amount of change in the agreed-upon contract price. Cost is the measure of damages for calculating the amount of the equitable adjustment. This measure is limited so that only the change in cost incident to the change order is considered. Under this rule, an equitable adjustment may be downward or upward, according to the contractor's cost of performing the work as changed. If the cost is less than it would have been without the change, the overall contract adjustment will be downward and will include a downward adjustment of overhead and profit and vice versa.

To state that cost is the measure of damages for an equitable adjustment is not adequate. Evidence is needed regarding how much the contractor's costs have changed. To determine this factor, a set of standards based on the concept of reasonable cost has been developed through litigation. Under the standards, the courts or boards will seek evidence to indicate how much the cost should have changed, assuming the contractor is a reasonably prudent person, knowledgeable of the circumstances involved, and operating in a competitive environment. Given this assumption the question is, what would the contractor have expended to accomplish the change? Based on this concept, the court or board will try to find evidence to support an assessment of the reasonable cost. Negotiators seek similar support for their agreements.

Actual costs. Under the standards established in Bruce Construction Corporation v. United States, 163 Ct. Cl. 97,324 F.2d 516, 1963, the court was able to determine that evidence showing the actual costs incurred to perform the specific work would be presumed to be reasonable for purposes of the pricing adjustment. This ruling still stands as fundamental to litigation in this area. Importantly, the rule affects negotiations and agency procedures as well as litigation. (At the time of this writing, statutory and regulatory changes have been proposed, placing the burden of proof on contractors respecting challenged actual costs. This may alter the effect of the judicial presumption.) In the negotiation process, the government invariably attempts to determine the actual costs associated with a change, if such costs are available. If negotiation is conducted prospectively, or if change order accounting has not been practiced, actual costs will not be available, and reliance is placed principally on estimates as a fundamental part of the price negotiation.

Estimated costs. When entered into evidence in a litigation, estimated costs may also be satisfactory as the basis for determining the reasonable cost of a change. Estimates are appropriate for consideration by a board of contract appeals if supported by evidence that shows the reasonableness of claimed costs.

Historical costs. Boards of contract appeals encounter claims that have neither actual costs nor appropriate evidence of estimates of costs. In that situation a board may accept into evidence data showing historical costs of similar or identical work. Although generally less desirable as the basis for decision, historical data may be accepted. The same general statement can be made regarding assessments of fair market value for services rendered under a change. Although market value alone is seldom an acceptable basis for the pricing of a change, it could be an acceptable part of the evidence in support of a change decision if it represents an established market value for a particular part of the overall claim. As an element of prospective negotiations conducted by the negotiating parties, historical evidence and fair market value evidence may be useful in validating estimates, thereby lending support to price.

Deleted work. The cost of deleted work associated with negotiation of changes is a difficult issue. Two categories of deletions have already been identified: work already performed but deleted, and work not yet performed and deleted. The negotiation for work already performed is relatively simple. These costs should be supportable by actual cost data and should be paid because they have already been incurred in good faith. However, the work produced by the deleted elements may have value in disposal; therefore, disposal value should be credited to the government in negotiation of the changes adjustment. Evidence of credits earned should be easily gathered.

It is more difficult to determine costs for deleted items of work which have not yet been performed. Such items are often a part of the overall negotiation of contract modifications. The deleted items that have not been performed represent elements of the job which should reduce or offset the increased costs associated with additions to the work precipitated by the change action. However, calculation of the cost value to be attributed to the deleted work items is difficult and can never be substantiated by actual costs. Therefore, deleted costs must be estimated or based on historical or other evidence appropriate to the adjustment. The cost of work deleted prior to performance must be dealt with whether a modification is being decided under negotiation or under a litigation. It is with respect to these deleted costs that the government objective of returning the parties to their positions prior to the change becomes most difficult. For example, it is unacceptable merely to calculate the original cost estimate for a deleted element of work and to subtract that amount. Instead, the parties must assess what the cost of performing the deleted work would have been at the time the change was initiated. The amount of credit due the government for deleted costs could be greater than or less than the amount the contractor originally included in the proposal for the deleted item.

Subcontractor cost change. A complicating factor regarding the amount of an equitable adjustment is the method of calculating the contractor's cost of performing the change when a subcontractor or supplier is actually performing the work. This problem arises because the price agreement between the prime contractor and his subcontractor may be for an amount different from the actual cost experienced by the subcontractor in performing the work. In a case of this kind, a government change was made to replace a thermometer which was to be incorporated into the end item being prepared by the prime contractor. The true cost of the deleted thermometer was $34.67. The true value of the replacement thermometer was $8.53, leaving a reduction of $26.14, according to the government's claim. As a result of audit, however, it was found that the supplier actually had quoted a price of only $12.80 to the prime contractor. If the contract had remained unchanged, the subcontractor would have suffered a loss. When the change order was issued, the replacement thermometer was obtainable from the supplier at a cost of $8.53. The difference between the cost to the prime of the deleted and replacement thermometers was $4.27. Since this was a downward adjustment, it was clearly in the interest of the prime contractor to base the cost adjustment (credit) to the government on his actual firm subcontracted price for the originally required thermometer. The contractor's position in this case is referred to as the *subjective concept* for the price adjustment. In litigation most cases of this kind have been decided on the basis of the subjective theory, with the consequence (in the illustration given) that the contractor would have obtained the smaller price reduction. In circumstances where the quantity to be delivered is several thousand, the amount of the pricing differential may be large. It should also be noted that the illustrated benefit to the contractor of adopting the subjective theory cuts in precisely the opposite direction when the errors are reversed. For instance, if the true value of the original thermometer had been $12.80, and the price agreed upon had been $34.67, effecting the change would result in a substantial loss to the contractor. If the alternate or *objective concept* of price adjustment were to prevail in a given case, these consequences would be reversed.

Overhead. Another issue frequently raised in negotiations of modifications is the application of overhead for extended periods of performance caused by the change or delay. Overhead accounts frequently include large segments of fixed expenses, those that do not change over reasonably short periods of extended performance, and arguably they should be ignored in making price adjustments. On the other hand, ignoring overhead adjustment is inappropriate in the larger context of a contractor's operations. The fact that overhead is a period charge does not make it disappear as an expense. Several different formulas for calculating such adjustments have been adopted in individual cases. The most prevalent formula is referred to as the Eichleay formula. Under the Eichleay formula, the total amount of overhead allocated to the contract during the entire period of performance prior to the incidence of the delay must be put into evidence and is drawn from the contractor's accounting records. This total sum is divided by the number of days of performance during that active period of the contract. The result is a dollars-per-day cost for the overhead expenses during the period of performance. This dollars-per-day figure is then multiplied by the number of days of delay caused by the situation under negotiation. By this calculation, the amount of the overhead adjustment to be added to the direct costs incident to the change can be determined. While the propriety of this formula is questionable, it has been applied extensively in negotiations of modifications.

Other issues arise in the course of negotiation of contract modifications, but the foregoing discussion summarizes the most significant and is indicative of the overall problem. The rules that have been discussed are government-inspired rules and are not necessarily applicable to negotiation of modifications between private parties. Much simpler methods of negotiation may be applicable. However, the negotiation of modifications in most private contractual relationships does not proceed after the fact. The industrial buyer and seller do not rely on a unilateral changes clause, nor do they have at their discretion other unilateral ordering mechanisms. In the absence of these mechanisms, the incidence of litigation, and even the incidence of after-the-fact negotiation based on actual costs, is rare. The private parties generally will negotiate the cost of any work changes, delays, or other events that arise during performance prior to doing the work as changed. With this approach, the cost of modifications is less subject to controversial differences of opinion.

SUMMARY

The post-award negotiation process for government contracts is shown to be larger in terms of dollar values than negotiation and pricing activity prior to contract award. This is true of all post-award actions for projects subject to altered approaches and methods of performance, such as research and development and production contracts for government high-technology work, but not for less volatile types of undertakings. Challenges faced by the contract manager include the following:

- Systematic accumulation of a record of events and actions occurring during performance, together with sensitivity to cost generating activities
- Maintaining superior accounting systems with an awareness of a duty to account for costs associated with changed work
- Timely preparation of proposals, including ECPs and contract price change proposals
- Cognizance of all contractually specified bases for contract price and time adjustments
- Study of the expected pricing methodology and data requirements of customers such as government agencies
- Compliance in proposal preparation with formats, cost and pricing data requirements, certifications, and cost accounting standards as applicable to the pricing action
- Proper use of the supplier estimating and pricing capabilities and customer technical analysis, audit and pricing capabilities for proposal

preparation and evaluation purposes
- Developing proposal strategy and negotiating positions in preparation for negotiations
- Negotiating with an awareness of the factual and contractual circumstances of the modification action

TOPICS FOR DISCUSSION

1. Explain the differences between negotiation before and after contract award. Compare and explain the statistics in chart 14-1 concerning numbers of actions and value of actions.
2. Differentiate between a definitive contract and an external order.
3. What is the purpose of change order accounting? Why isn't it always used?
4. Why break out deleted work already performed from other deleted work?
5. Discuss the purpose of the reference column provided on the Headings for Submission of Line Item Cost Summaries.
6. Why are interorganizational transfers broken down separately in contract modification proposals?
7. Explain the rules for cost and pricing data submission pursuant to Public Law 87-653 (and later amendments).
8. What information would you expect to be provided by an engineering officer in support of a planned contract price modification negotiation?
9. Explain the concept of an equitable adjustment.

CASE 14-1

Simplex "B"

The Simplex Corporation won its first cost sharing contract on July 21, 1977. The contract was awarded by the Energy Research and Development Administration (ERDA) for research and demonstration of the concept of using a coal oil mixture (COM) in a retrofitted, existing industrial steam boiler plant. In addition to the formulation of a COM, the contract included design and reconstruction of the existing boiler system and operational demonstration of the combustion process using the COM as fuel.

The contract was awarded after substantial delay occasioned by the demand of the sponsoring agency that the contractor share 50 percent of the cost of the development. An agreement was worked out on that issue. The provisions of the agreement were summarized in ERDA's negotiation memorandum as follows:

Contract Type and Cost-Sharing

The proposed contract will be performed in two phases. Phase I covers the design and development of the system. This phase will be cost-reimbursement. Since this plan involves research and development work, it is recognized that the Contractor may find it necessary to perform more work than contemplated in the negotiated estimated cost. Therefore, provision is made for cost-sharing on the basis of fifty (50) percent Government and fifty (50) percent Contractor for any increase in the estimated cost agreed to by the Government (i.e. cost growth).

The provision of cost-sharing by the Contractor of any cost-growth in excess of the negotiated estimated cost was proposed by the Government as a method to control costs for the research and development efforts under this contract. Although the Program Opportunity Notice did not provide for cost-sharing of overruns on Phase I, the Contractor accepted this arrangement.

Phase II, which provides for boiler modification/construction and operation of the system at the tobacco drying facilities of Loveland Corporation in Danville, Virginia, will therefore be cost-sharing for both underrun and overrun costs. Costs incurred up to the estimated costs will be shared initially on the basis of 65 percent Government and 35 percent Contractor. Upon completion of the Demonstration Phase (Phase II) the Contractor will reimburse ERDA for an additional 15 percent of Phase II costs based upon the revenue realized by the Contractor from coal-oil slurry retrofit system sales. The reimbursement rate for the 15 percent "pay-back" arrangement will be 5 percent of each retrofit sale.

The cost-sharing contribution by Simplex is then 35 percent of the total Phase II estimated costs of $850,549 resulting in a total contribution initially of $297,692.15. This portion of the Contractor's cost-share consists of actual expenditures or costs incurred by the Contractor.

As indicated above, the balance of the targeted fifty (50) percent cost-share by the Contractor for Phase II up to a maximum of 15 percent additional of Phase II costs or $127,582.35 will be based on the actual cash pay-back arrangement specified above.

The maximum possible cost-share by the Contractor is therefore fifty (50) percent of estimated Phase II costs or $425,274.50.

Finally, costs incurred in excess of Phase II costs will be shared on a 50-50 basis.

. . .

Of the total accepted estimated costs, $1,131,645 are Phase I costs and $850,549 are Phase II costs.

Subsequently, ERDA became the Department of Energy (DOE), personnel changes at the agency occurred, the demonstration concept for the retrofitted COM boiler grew, the energy crisis matured and indicators of a potential oil glut became discernable, and the cost of the project became (by agreement of DOE and Simplex):

Phase I	$2,426,071.00
Phase II	997,500.00
	$3,423,571.00

However, the negotiations at which this revised cost estimate was agreed upon again encountered an issue that had substantially delayed the original contract: cost sharing. Simplex was not willing to proceed with up-front cost sharing, since it viewed the scope of the project to be substantially expanded and was not willing to place its net worth on the line for the effort. Consequently, the company proposed a revised sharing plan, dated April 11, 1978, in which it summarized a proposal for contract increase.

At the time of the April 1978 negotiations, both Simplex and DOE managers felt optimistic regarding the likely usefulness of the technology that would be created by the Simplex project. All who were involved at the program level were enthusiastic and supportive. However, in the contracts offices (government and contractor) feelings were running in a strongly protective mode. The DOE contracting people wanted to retain maximum protection for the DOE budget and did not want to agree to any solution that could be challenged as a give-away of government funds. Conversely, Simplex, although willing to cost share at the con-tractual level, was unwilling to absorb the risks to its corporate assets associated with concurrent sharing of the cost growth. The following statement is extracted from the company's April 11, 1978 letter.

Table 1a indicates the new total contract amount ($3,423,570) and the total increase ($1,441,375) over the existing amount ($1,982,195). Table 1b shows how the total increase is distributed over the contract phases for DOE and Simplex including the 65/35 cost sharing provision for Phase II. Note that the DOE increase is

$1,294,425 for Phase I, $95,517 for Phase II and, therefore, $1,389,942 overall. Simplex will add $51,433 to this amount to provide a total increase of $1,441,375. Table 1c defines the final post-contract reimbursements Simplex will make to DOE. The Phase I increase ($647,212) is 50% of the DOE increase shown on Table 1b. The new Phase II Simplex reimbursement ($149,625) is 15% of the new Phase II total (Table 1a). This boosts Simplex Phase II cost sharing from 35% to 50%. The total reimbursement increase over the existing contract is $669,254. (See tables in Attachment A)

The DOE contracting authority felt that Simplex's position was inappropriate. Based on the April negotiations, DOE issued a contract modification incorporating the increased cost estimate values but retaining its view that the contractor should share invoice by invoice in the increased Phase I costs.

The contractor, in response to receipt of the modification, initiated further discussion but did not sign or accept the contract amendment. Also, Simplex slowed its expenditure rate precipitously, and DOE contract representatives introduced the thought that a termination for default was under consideration.

* * * * *

1. Develop a position on the basis of which this project might have been continued.
2. Assess the likelihood that this contract may be terminated for default.
3. Specify actions that Harold Singleton, Simplex's Director of Contracts and Administration, should now initiate.

Attachment A (Simplex "B")

TABLE 1 - COST SUMMARY, DOE CONTRACT EF-77-C-01-2563

a. Revised Contract Costs

	Phase I($)	Phase II($)	Total($)
Cost through 12/31/78	455,500	0	455,500
Cost to complete from 1/1/78	1,970,570	997,500	2,968,070
Total	2,426,070	997,500	3,423,570
Existing Funding	1,131,645	850,550	1,982,195
Cost Increase	1,294,425	146,950	1,441,375

b. Cost Sharing

	DOE Cost ($)			Simplex Cost ($)		
	Existing Funding	Negot'd Funding	Increase	Existing Funding	Negot'd Funding	Increase
Phs I	1,131,645	2,426,070	1,294,425	0	0	0
Phs II	552,858	648,375	95,517	297,692	349,125	51,433
Total	1,684,503	3,074,445	1,389,942	297,692	349,125	51,433

c. Post-Contract Reimbursement by Simplex

Phase I	0	647,212	647,212
Phase II	127,583	149,625	22,042
Total	127,583	796,837	669,254

CASE 14-2

CSG Corporation[1]

Introduction

The CSG Corporation was badly in need of improvement. The three

---

[1]Case written by Professor David Lamm, United States Navy Postgraduate School. Used by permission of the author.

owners, Dave Capizzi, Chris Sager, and Frank Goral, had been comparing their sales and cost trends. Although sales had been rising steadily over the years, costs had risen faster and were eating into profits at an alarming rate. For some months the partners had been searching for methods to reduce the increasing costs. They already had initiated some "get well" projects but had continued to carefully evaluate further possibilities for becoming more cost efficient. One fact to which all three had agreed was the state of their aging equipment. Maintenance costs on most of the equipment they owned--lathes, shears, punch presses, grinders, etc.--had been one of the costs that seemed to have gotten out of hand. Furthermore, the equipment was becoming less and less efficient, which also added to the corporation's cost of sales figure. After some careful analysis, the decision was made to invest in new industrial equipment in an attempt to increase efficiency and to reduce maintenance costs. Since most of the equipment was approaching thirty years of service, it was determined that scrap value was about all the corporation would be able to realize from its disposal.

New Lathes for CSG

CSG had decided to request bids from major equipment manufacturers to replace ten of their oldest lathes. Bids were to include several specific features CSG wanted on the lathes, as well as the cost to remove the existing equipment and to install the new lathes. Fourteen proposals were received and reviewed by Chris Sager, the corporation's materials manager. Chris had been involved in just about all of the firm's capital equipment purchases.

Within a week, Sager had gotten his technical review team together to examine the proposals and to select a source. South Lake Equipment Company came out on top on the basis of CSG's rating scheme, which considered cost, delivery schedule, and technical ability. Over the next three weeks, Sager held several meetings and negotiation sessions with South Lake before concluding the deal. When it was completed, Sager was pleased with his work and with the contract between CSG and South Lake. Modifications to South Lake's standard lathe were begun almost immediately by the company, while at the same time, plans were finalized concerning the exact dates for equipment rip-out, site preparation, and installation of the ten new lathes to allow for a minimum of disruption to CSG's production schedule.

Progress Report

Two months after Sager had reported to his partners, Capizzi and

Goral, concerning the details of their new acquisition, everything was on schedule. All ten of the old lathes had been removed and disposed of, site preparation was virtually completed, and three new lathes had already been installed. It appeared that the project was going to be completed on time, perhaps even earlier than planned. Everyone involved was pleased.

It was at this time that it came to Sager's attention that the equipment industry had developed an expanded capability for the multipurpose lathe. Upon investigation Sager discovered that by substituting only one major component in the lathes produced by South Lake for CSG, their lathes could have this same expanded capability. He talked it over with his partners and decided that the additional flexibility afforded CSG would be well worth the investment. Sager asked South Lake to initiate the change for just the remaining seven lathes. Exhibit 1 is South Lake's proposal submitted to CSG as a request for equitable adjustment. Exhibit 2 contains facts and estimates which Sager obtained from South Lake's supporting data and the original contract negotiations.

Analyzing the Request for Equitable Adjustment

In discussing the data from South Lake's request for equitable adjustment, Sager learned that the new component was going to alter significantly the foundation work which South Lake had constructed in CSG's factory upon which the lathes were installed. The old foundations would have to be ripped out. To Sager's further dismay, South Lake wanted to charge CSG the costs they would incur as a result of the labor force standing idle while the new component was being obtained, particularly those workers with specialized labor skills South Lake had acquired in order to make the modifications CSG had wanted right from the start. In searching for vendors for the new component, South Lake found two sources and decided to select Vendor A with a longer delivery period (four weeks) but a lower price of $4,000 per unit. Delay costs were based on a four-week waiting period. Sager also noticed that South Lake had proposed $2,800 as the cost for installing the foundation for each lathe during the original contract negotiations but was now showing in the request for equitable adjustment actual foundation costs of $3,000 per unit ($21,000/7 units). One of the things concerning changes Sager and South Lake had agreed to in the contract was the following repricing technique:

Added Component - Deleted Component + Work Effort
+ Overhead + Profit = Total Adjustment

The original components for all ten lathes already had been purchased by

South Lake but could be used for other lathes produced by the company.

* * * * *

1. Analyze South Lake's request for equitable adjustment.
2. Develop a negotiation position for Sager to effect an equitable adjustment to the original contract.

Exhibit 1, CSG Corporation

South Lake Equipment Company
Request For Equitable Adjustment

1.	Component cost		$7,000
	Cost of new component less cost of original component ($4000 - $3000)		
2.	Foundation costs		53,300
	Original foundations	$21,000	
	Rip out	4,300	
	New foundations	28,000	
3.	Delay costs		19,100
	Labor	17,600	
	Facilities	1,500	
4.	Setup costs		<u>1,200</u>
	Subtotal		$80,600
5.	Overhead (10%)		<u>8,060</u>
	Subtotal		$88,660
6.	Profit (10%)		<u>8,866</u>
	Total contract adjustment		**$97,526**

Exhibit 2, CSG Corporation

Facts and Estimates

1. **Cost of original component**
   Estimate (original negotiation) $3,000/unit
   Vender price (firm purchase order negotiated
     by South Lake after CSG award)   2,700/unit

2. **Cost of new component**
   Vendor A (four-week delivery)   4,000/unit
   Vendor B (one-week delivery)   4,200/unit

3. **Foundation costs**
   As already installed for seven lathes   21,000
   Rip out work   4,300
   New foundations, added work   28,000

4. **Delay costs**
   Labor,   Specialized--CSG contract (2 people
              @ 40 hours/week, 4 weeks @ $15/hour)   4,800

            Regular--CSG contract (8 people @
            40 hours/week, 4 weeks @ $10.hour)   12,800

   Idle facilities   1,500

5. **Production retooling**
   Setup costs for incorporating new component   1,200

6. **Overhead**
   As agreed on during original negotiation   10%
   South Lake's actual rate through time of
     component change   9%
   South Lake's projection through performance
     of component change work   9.5%

7. **Profit**
   As used in original contract   8%
   As proposed for new component modification   10%

15

Contract
Completion

Both parties look forward to successful contract completion, attempting to reach that point by fulfilling all objectives of the agreement. Most achieve satisfactory results. The workload of the boards of contract appeals is an indication of the level of success in government contracting. During fiscal year 1985, the Armed Services Board of Contract Appeals docketed 1,638 appeals, a historic high. Viewed in relationship to the thirteen million contracts issued by the Department of Defense in that year, only 1/100th of 1 percent of the procurement workload of the department proceeds into litigation. These 1,638 cases were based on 53 different types of issues, one of which was default. Only for those cases in the default category could one conclude that a complete lack of success occurred respecting the major purposes of the contract. There were 256 default cases disposed of in 1985. While some additional cases proceed directly to the United States Claims Court, these statistics provide a strong indication that the contracting process achieves end results that satisfy the parties in nearly all cases.

Our objective in this chapter is to examine the principal methods of completing contracts: normal delivery acceptance and closeout; and completion in the absence of delivery and acceptance, including breach of contract, termination for default, and termination for convenience.

Absence of default is one measure of success in contract programs, but for individual contracts, successful completion is signified by final payment and closeout of the contract after acceptance of all line items specified for delivery. Data on these elements is available for government contracts. For example, federal payment practices have been revitalized under the Prompt Payment Act passed in 1982. Prior to passage

of the act, timely payment was achieved by the government only 70 percent of the time. Subsequent to its full implementation by 1984, 99
percent of all government payments were made on time. This remarkable
improvement strongly indicates that, today, government objectives on this
front have been met at the prime contract level. Extension of the act to
subcontractors is under consideration at the time of this writing (1987).

   In chapter 11 one of the two major categories of payments made to
contractors--those made for financing purposes periodically during performance of the contract--was discussed. The other major category
concerns payments made for completed work. These include both partial
payments made as portions of a total delivery obligation are fulfilled
(leading to a final payment upon delivery of all contract items), and
payments made on a single pay basis upon completion of a contract. Full
payment of a contract signifies that the required work was totally
completed and accepted. To facilitate this process, contractors have one
major requirement beyond performance--to submit a properly prepared
invoice. An invoice should contain (1) the date; (2) citation of the
contract and/or purchase order number; (3) name and address of the
vendor; (4) total amount of the invoice; (5) unit and total prices for
items delivered; (6) quantity of each item delivered; (7) applicable shipping and payment terms; (8) name, title, proper address and telephone
number of a person who is available to clarify any questions; and (9)
other specific information or substantiation that may be required for a
particular contract, for example, citation of appropriation data as may be
required for contracts funded by multiple appropriations. Omission of any
of this data could delay payment. The government's payments process is
diagramed in chart 15-1.

CONTRACT COMPLETION WITH NORMAL
DELIVERY, ACCEPTANCE, AND CLOSEOUT

   Contract completion is accomplished by final payment and closeout
which is contingent upon inspection, acceptance, and delivery of the
product. Of these steps toward contract completion, the one most likely
to uncover failures is inspection, more broadly defined as quality assurance of which inspection is one phase (see chapter 10). Responsibility
for in-process and final inspection has been placed on the contractor by
inspection and acceptance clauses. Nevertheless, government acceptance
means the government has taken ownership of the end item, and the act
of acceptance is final with respect to any patent defects. It signifies
that payment is due upon receipt of a proper invoice and expiration of
the terms of the invoice, or within thirty days in accordance with the
Prompt Payment Act. Regardless of the apparent simplicity of this
delivery and acceptance process, the final closeout steps for major con-

Chart 15-1

Government Payment Processes

CONTRACTOR ACTIONS	GOVERNMENT ACCEPTANCE ACTIONS

Receipt of
Contract Document

Performance of Contract

Delivery of Materials
and/or Services to
Receiving Activity

Delivery of Invoices and
Public Vouchers to
Designated Activity

Quantity and Quality
Check of Materials
or Services Received
and/or Test and
Inspection as Applicable

Acceptance of Material
and/or Services

GOVERNMENT
PAYMENT
ACTIONS

Original Invoice,
Contract or Purchase
Order, and Acceptance
Document Matched by
Receiving/Payment
Activity

Issuance of Check
to Vendor

Invoice Processed by
Payment Activity in
Accordance with
Prompt Payment Act
and Cash Management
Procedures

tracts are complex and lengthy. Only for small purchase orders and other relatively simple procurement actions is the closeout of a contract accomplished in a speedy fashion.

Sources of complexity and delay in closeout include the following:

1. Departure from the firm-fixed-price contract format. Unfortunately, this is the case in most larger contracts. Large contracts may include contract incentives or may be written on a cost-reimbursable or fixed-rate basis. When using these contract forms, administrative control over performance and cost requires the government to verify time for services rendered and/or to audit costs incurred. This extends the closeout process.

2. Verifications associated with liquidation of progress payments and other forms of contract financing, including interim payments under cost contracts. These procedures require an accumulation of data and review of all payments made prior to disposition of the final invoice upon completion of the job.

3. Events that occurred during performance, such as changes, compensable delays, or additions and deletions from the original contract requirements. These actions require negotiations to arrive at an equitable adjustment, but frequently the negotiations are not completed coincident with the delivery and acceptance of end items. Closeout cannot be accomplished without settlement of these matters.

4. Completion of audit and determination of indirect cost rates pertinent to all unsettled periods of performance, even in the absence of pending claims for equitable adjustment.

5. Extended warranty provisions or the government right to demand price reduction for defective cost and pricing data which may delay closeout.

6. Complexity existing in the accumulation of data regarding inventory and subcontract claims caused by partial or complete termination, stretching closeout over a long period.

7. Contracts over which there is litigation remain open throughout the period of the dispute.

Contract closeout procedures are covered in Part 4 of the FAR. The following checklist is based on those procedures. Examination of the checklist is valuable as a means of identifying sources of delay or pitfalls in obtaining payments and discharge.

Checklist for Contract Closeout

1. Contractor final invoice, designated as such, must be on hand and for cost reimbursable contracts, public vouchers must have certain

attachments. These include a statement of the allowable costs; assignment to the government of refunds, rebates, credits, and other amounts received by the contractor and due to the government; a release signed by the contractor discharging the government and its officers, agents, and employees from liabilities, obligations and claims arising out of or under the contract (specified exceptions may be permitted within the release).

2. Receiving report. The report provides evidence of acceptance of property and must be specific as to what has been accepted under the contract.
3. Evidence of disposition of classified material.
4. Verification of completion of any required contract audit.
5. Receipt of any required final patent report identifying inventions either discovered or reduced to practice under the contract.
6. Receipt of a final royalty report, if required, pursuant to the contract.
7. Verification that there are no outstanding value engineering change proposals.
8. Verification that all price revisions and negotiations have been completed and documented as a contract amendment.
9. Verification that all disallowed costs and adjustment of interim allowed costs have been completed.
10. Verification that all inventory has been accounted for and a plant clearance report executed.
11. Verification that the prime contractor has made settlement with all subcontractors.
12. Verification that all indirect cost rates for prior year periods have been settled.
13. Verification that no outstanding termination action is pending.
14. Verification that action to deobligate excess funds has been initiated.
15. Receipt and examination of the contractor's closing statement.
16. Execution of the contracting officer's verification that the contract has been completed.

Upon satisfaction of all of the foregoing, a contract can be considered closed out. Disposal of the contract file is subject to specified retention periods in accordance with FAR Subpart 4.805.

CONTRACT COMPLETION WITHOUT NORMAL DELIVERY, ACCEPTANCE, AND PAYMENT

The foregoing discussion has focused primarily on the normal course of events during which the contractor has performed all required duties successfully and has achieved an acceptance of the product of his work. This is not the case for a small but important subset of total contract awards for which there are several other methods of ending the contract. A contract is occasionally ended by agreement of the parties. This is likely when expended effort is minor and cessation of performance is advantageous to both parties. Their agreement would include an amicable settlement of obligations. Government contracts are sometimes cancelled by the intervention of the Comptroller General (also, under the Competition in Contracting Act, by the intervention of the General Services Board of Contract Appeals), or of a court which finds that the contract was not awarded in accordance with prescribed regulations. Cancellation prior to expenditure of resources could be effected without incurring settlement costs.

The executory portion of a contract might be ended by supervening events that render performance impossible, such as a catastrophe or imposition of public authority. In these cases, settlement for accrued expenditures to the date of impossibility may require negotiation. Government contracts might be completed simply by exhaustion of funds. This could occur, for example, in a cost contract containing a limitation of cost clause, when the government declines to add funds to the contract after existing funds have been expended. This method of completing a contract should be accompanied by discussions between the parties to ensure that no misunderstanding exists regarding any likelihood that subsequent funds could be added to the contract. In multi-year government contracts, completion of performance is also possible because of the government's failure to provide funds to finance subsequent annual periods of performance. Settlement of claims under the multi-year contract includes adjustment for unrecovered, nonrecurring costs as specified under the cancellation provisions included in such contracts. The balance of this chapter is devoted to the two most important methods of contract completion when work is not fulfilled under government contracts: default and convenience termination.

An important form of contract completion unique to government contracts is termination for convenience. Under this procedure, the government exercises its prerogatives of declaring a contract to be ended, requiring all work to cease, and entering into negotiations for settlement of claims pursuant to the Termination for Convenience clause. The special implications of this technique are discussed later in the chapter. The most important method of completing contracts in which work is not fulfilled is perhaps that associated with a material breach by one party. In a government contract, this results in exercise of the government's discretion to issue a default notice to the contractor who has failed to perform duties satisfactorily under the contract. These actions are taken under the default clause in which the government may require all work to cease and proceed to enforce the contractual sanctions provided for in the Termination for Default clause.

Breach of Contract

A breach of contract occurs when one party fails to perform duties imposed by the contract without excuse, thereby injuring the other party. This is a material breach and can be caused by either party, but most breach situations are brought about by the performing party. In private contracting, the uniform commercial code establishes basic rules and procedures for handling breach of contract. The three principal types of breach in private contracts are failure to deliver on time, demonstrated inability to perform (managerial or technical inability not based on impossibility or impracticability), and declared unwillingness to perform--in effect, a repudiation of the agreement.

These three methods of breaching a commercial relationship are equally applicable to government contracts. The government, however, uses slightly different language. A government contractor may be found in default for either failing to perform at the appointed time or failing to make progress which may endanger performance at the appointed time, even though that time had not arrived. Additionally, a government contractor could repudiate his contract. Another basis for default is failure of a contractor to conform with various material provisions of a government contract. This possibility is important to the government because of its extensive use of contract provisions aimed at social or economic objectives related to its policy positions. This type of default could also be caused by failure to maintain required records, failure to perform warranty duties, failure to provide a required certificate, and so forth.

In general, contract breach in commercial contracting and default in government contracting have similar effects; they both operate to compel performance by the threat of economic sanction for failure. An important government departure from the uniform commercial code is the default clause which makes default an administrative act that is discretionary for the contracting officer. Coupled with the Disputes clause, which creates an obligation to proceed with unterminated work while any claims are processed, the administrative control over program progress retained by the government manager is rather complete. Even though failures amounting to breach occur, work must proceed until decision by the government. Of course, inability to do the required work or repudiation of the contract would cause work to cease, but sanctions may be imposed.

The Effect of Termination for Default
on the Defaulting Contractor

The impact of a default action on the contractor is severe. Issuance of a default notice is an available sanction in all government contracts, but its principal use is for fixed-price contracts, including incentive and redeterminable versions. When these contract types are used, the contractor is conceived as a guarantor of performance. If the contractor breaches any of the fixed-price types of contracts, the sanctions available to the government are related to that guarantor position. They are designed to encourage a contractor's commitment to fulfill all terms and conditions. The following list contains some impacts of termination for default in fixed-price contracts:

1. The defaulting party is not entitled to payment for any uncompleted work. This sanction is particularly severe when the default occurs at or near the completion of performance, when the contractor has made a maximum investment in the effort to perform. The default action cuts off his right to complete performance as well as all right to payment if no part of the work has been completed (completed parts of the work are limited to parts accepted by the government). If any work has been completed, the government is obligated to make payment for that portion of the contract.
2. The contractor must return to the government all payments received for uncompleted work. Again, this sanction reaches its maximum impact if the contract is nearing completion, and substantial progress payments have been made. These become due and payable back to the government.
3. The government retains the right to claim any inventory residual to the contract. Of course, if the government does take title to any part of the inventory, it is obligated to make a payment reflecting the value (accumulated cost) of the property taken.
4. The contractor is liable for reprocurement costs. Reprocurement costs are costs associated with securing performance by an alternate source of supply. The defaulting contractor's liability is for that part of the reprocurement cost which exceeds the amount that would have been due to the defaulting contractor for successful performance.

Factors to be Considered in
Advance of Default Action

The default of a contract constitutes the ultimate sanction of a contracting officer to compel performance of the contract. It is, however, a sanction that jeopardizes program status and progress. Because of this reality, the most important aspect of the default sanction is found in the threat of default, not in its execution.

When a default appears likely, the contracting officer must consider the legal relationship between the parties, including the written agreement and related events; but default decisions may be dominated by programmatic concerns. Specifically, if the default action is taken, does it mean that the underlying government program will be delayed or lost? There are several considerations which, nominally, are concerns of the contracting officer; but since they have an agency-wide impact, the contracting officer should ensure that a consensus has been reached among program and senior executive personnel that the default action is best. The considerations are as follows:

1. The specific provisions for default action contained in the contract. Each clause varies slightly in its rules, in the nature of excusable delays, and in the effectiveness of allowed sanctions.
2. The specific failure for which a default action is being considered. The question here is whether the failure of the contractor is a material one when viewed in light of contract objectives and when viewed against the overall time frame and delinquency of the contractor.
3. Whether the supplies or services being defaulted are available from other sources. A default action does not ordinarily relieve the government's need to pursue the end objective of the contract. It would be fruitless to default a contractor who could ultimately perform if there is no alternative source who is competent and available to complete the job.
4. The issue of urgency and the trade-off of time between the existing performer and possible alternates. Performance failures invariably delay completion to some extent. The principal questions are whether the program is adversely affected, and whether the delay incident to declaring default is greater than the delay incident to remaining with the defaulting contractor. The contract manager's interest is to make the decision that will secure the most timely performance.
5. Essentiality of the contractor to the government. A contractor's capabilities may be an important factor in the planning and programming of several government undertakings. If a default action will render the contractor unavailable to an agency in need of his capabilities, the contract manager's considerations should extend to the overall impact on affected programs.
6. Effect of default on the liquidation of progress payments, guaranteed loans, or advance payments which have been made to the delinquent contractor. This issue is directly related to the company's financial

position. If the company will be unable to repay the funds already invested in the contract, the effectiveness of the default sanction may be minimal. This likelihood is probably not a valid reason for not declaring default, but it removes one of the benefits of taking such action. Default under these conditions may precipitate the contractor's bankruptcy, if it has not already been declared.

7.   Availability of funds to finance repurchase. The importance of this consideration is heightened if it is likely that the contractor will be unable to finance reprocurement costs to which the government will be entitled by taking the default action. Although the default clause establishes the government's right to recover excess costs of reprocuring the items on which the contractor has defaulted, it is an empty gesture to demand payment if the contractor is left with no assets. In some cases, the availability of funds to finance reprocurement is a factor independent of the contractor's likelihood of repayment. If the government's budget for work under an existing contract is exhausted except for funds obligated under that contract, the ability to recover funds already obligated may be essential to reprocurement. The contracting officer could deobligate unexpended funds and use them to cover the initial cost of a reprocurement action. However, deobligation is normally an action that requires agreement of the parties, and it could be a cumbersome procedure in a default termination because the contractor may seek to overturn the default and could oppose deobligation.

8.   The extent of the adverse effects of termination action on the employees of the contractor and on the community within which the contractor's business is established. These considerations, while somewhat remote from the issues associated with the procurement, sometimes assume great importance in a political environment.

Progress Failure

The right to declare a contractor in default during the period of performance is limited. Failure to make progress toward completion is more difficult to demonstrate than passing a delivery date without delivery but is, nevertheless, a valid cause for a contracting officer to declare default. To do this he must be able to demonstrate that timely performance is endangered by the contractor's lack of progress. Showing that delivery is endangered does not require showing that performance is impossible, but the contractor must be given an opportunity to prove that performance is not endangered. Therefore, in a progress failure case, the contracting officer must issue a cure notice, allowing at least ten days for the contractor to respond with a showing of adequate progress or a demonstration that an excusable delay has occurred. In the absence of such showings, the contractor could be defaulted at the end of the cure notice waiting period. The intent of the cure notice is to ensure that a contractor has an opportunity to communicate to the contracting officer the nature of any excusable delays or other circumstances which may justify a continuation of patience instead of default action. Whenever a cure notice is issued, the contractor is immediately placed in the position of having to respond because failing to do so, in itself, can be a basis for default.

Anticipatory Repudiation

Anticipatory repudiation may be found if there is a set of words or actions by a contractor indicating that he does not intend to perform the contract. The act of conveying this sentiment is itself a breach of contract under common law and gives the contracting officer a clear right to declare the contractor in default. Although the breach (the set of words or actions) actually ends the contract, it is still advisable to issue a termination for default notice to avoid any possible misunderstanding, such as a conclusion that the contracting officer has waived some part of the contractor's performance duties. Issuing a default notice also prevents retraction of the repudiation.

Anticipatory repudiation can occur as a result of an outright refusal by the contractor to perform the contract. An explicit refusal is not essential, however. Anticipatory repudiation can be found if a contractor demonstrates his intent not to perform either by an express verbal statement or by actions such as abandoning premises, disposing of or returning equipment essential to performance, etc. A contractor can be found to have repudiated if it can be shown that he has relinquished or failed to secure technical or managerial capability to perform.

Contractor's Duty to Proceed with Performance

Government contracts differ from ordinary private contracts by imposing a higher duty to proceed with work, even though some action or direction by the government appears to be erroneous, improvident, or not in accordance with the contract (a material breach). The basis for this conclusion is the Disputes Clause (FAR 22.233-1) which specifies that "the contractor shall proceed diligently with performance of this contract, pending final resolution of any request for relief, claim, appeal, or action arising under the contract, and comply with any decision of the contracting officer." The logic of this higher duty is rooted in the concepts of public interest, which do not permit interfering with government operations that may involve the public welfare or the government's political position in its worldwide commitments and responsibilities. This concept of the responsibility of contractors limits, to some degree, protection of their rights in contracts. In particular, it impacts their discretion in abandoning performance or otherwise rescinding their obligations in the face of a material breach by the government. This duty to proceed is similar to that contained in the supply contract changes clause which provides that nothing in the clause excuses the contractor from proceeding with the contract as changed. These clauses cause a contractor to use extreme caution in reaching any decision to stop performing work. The rules with respect to this duty are complex.

Infrequently, a contractor feels he should not proceed with work or seeks to abandon work for reasons he thinks are valid. Before taking that action, he should carefully consider whether the contracting officer has given any form of notice to proceed with work or whether the circumstances of the situation clearly indicate that he should proceed. The mere fact that a contractor encounters difficulty in performing, or that he encounters excessive costs in performing, and even his opinion that performance will not obtain a result that is desired by the government, will not suffice as excuses for failure to proceed with work.

Receipt of an explicit notice to proceed from the contracting officer should be followed unless the contractor is certain that an exception exists that will relieve the obligation to proceed. There are several exceptions. One is a government failure to pay valid invoices when obligated to do so. This situation might exist in a cost-reimbursement contract in which the provisions state that the contractor is entitled to payment of incurred costs (consistent with invoice rules) up to the established limitation of allocated funds. This failure is viewed as a material breach in which the government can no longer compel the contractor to continue performance. A similar material breach might occur in a fixed-price contract when the government wrongfully fails to make progress payments. The contractor's problem in assessing government fault in failing to make a payment is knowing whether the failure is wrongful or an appropriate action precipitated by the contractor's deficiencies in progressing with the work.

A material breach on the part of the government may also occur if the government directs the contractor to perform work that is beyond the scope of the contract. For example, the disputes clause specifies that a change directive amounting to a cardinal change cannot be issued for work arising under the contract. The reason for this is that a cardinal change fundamentally alters the contractual undertaking to which the parties had agreed at the outset. There is no contractual duty to proceed with work that is not under the contract. Although this and some other forms of conduct by the government may justify a refusal to proceed, it is somewhat risky for the contractor to assume that they exist. Examples of wrongful acts include unreasonable and untimely inspections and government failure to follow the procedures specified in its disputes clause.

In DOD contracts for ships, airplanes, and major weapons systems, even the existence of a cardinal change may not constitute a valid reason for a contractor to fail to proceed with work. The disputes clause in such a contract may contain the alternate disputes provision contained in FAR 52.233-1. The provision specifies that the contractor must proceed diligently with performance "pending final resolution of any request for relief, claim, appeal or action arising under *or relating to* the contract." The words "or relating to" could be interpreted as compelling the contractor to proceed with performance regardless of the existence of a material breach.

A contractor is relieved from a duty to proceed with a contract if it is impractical to proceed. An impracticability could arise when government interference delays or prevents performance. Many types of action can constitute interference, such as untimely approvals, untimely or excessive inspection, and failure to provide essential information. Impracticability can arise because work is impossible, because of defective specifications, or other possible eventualities. However, discovery of such conditions should be communicated to the government and an opportunity afforded the government to modify its actions, change the specifications, or otherwise remove its interference. In the absence of communication, the contractor's position is compromised. A special case of impracticability arises when a contractor knows that the work will result in a defective or useless end product. In such circumstances, the contractor has a duty not to proceed without advising the contracting officer of the facts. Work should be resumed only upon receipt of direction from the contracting officer.

Cases have arisen in which the government has imposed an improper inspection method, or a specified tolerance has resulted in an extremely high rate of rejection, causing the contractor to stop work while seeking a waiver from the government or a method of performing that will remove the rejections. Provided the contractor has notified the government of the problem and of the likelihood that an unacceptable end product will be created if work proceeds without a change or waiver, a temporary stoppage pending receipt of the contracting officer's direction should be acceptable. However, the contractor's duty to proceed resumes upon decision by the government.

A contractor is relieved from the duty to proceed if the government fails to provide clear direction on the method of performance. Again, it is vital that a contractor request clarification because the lack of clear direction is a factual issue. It is insufficient for a contractor only to raise questions about the method of performance; the lack of clarity in a contract is established only upon direction given by the government. The contractor must decide whether clarification is essential in order to proceed successfully. The issue, of course, is whether to stop work. Whenever a stoppage occurs, the possibility of a default action arises. There is probably no completely satisfactory way of discerning in advance whether a work stoppage is appropriate, but a contract manager must apprise himself of the issues and be prepared to support actions taken.

Managing a Default

When a contractor fails to deliver a contract on time without any excusable delay, his right to continue work depends upon actions of the government. Default actions cut off further effort. Conversely, government actions encouraging further effort, if acted on by the contractor, amount to an election to continue and normally are treated as a waiver of the government right to terminate for default. If waiver occurs, the right cannot be reinstated without first reestablishing a new, enforceable, delivery date. The facts and circumstances surrounding the situation are critical to the interests of the parties. The government does not want to lose the right to terminate for default, yet the contractor who continues to expend resources in pursuit of contract completion increases his losses if, subsequently, default is imposed.

When conditions have deteriorated to this level, managers have a responsibility to reassess the likelihood of bringing the project back to a successful delivery, even if late. Government tendency has been toward patience in most cases, provided a reasonable hope of completion exists. Much depends on the supplier's management and attitude, but the time frame for decisions is short. After the delivery failure, the government manager is afforded a limited time for fact gathering and deliberation. His or her right to default is preserved during that time, but only for a limited period while decisions are formulated. The forbearance period evaporates shortly and waiver occurs. This mechanism is monitored by the boards and courts who seek to avoid an unfair forfeiture, especially one enlarged by good faith effort of the contractor to perform. Encouraging a contractor to continue to expend resources in an effort to perform without allowing sufficient additional time to actually complete will accomplish this undesirable result.

Contracting officers must consider these issues carefully. Waiver will occur only under circumstances in which the contractor has relied upon the contracting officer's encouragement and continued to pursue completion; it will not occur if the contractor has stopped performance. The key to resolving the issue is agreement on a new delivery date. Extension of time is common but never automatic. An example of explicit forbearance without waiver normally can be found in the issuance of a show cause notice immediately upon passage of the delivery date. Since a show cause notice is not mandatory (a default notice can be issued as soon as a delivery date has been missed), its existence does not bar default action. A show cause notice ordinarily allows a ten-day period for the contractor to show a willingness and ability to perform in a reasonable period of time. An extension of the delivery date may be agreed upon if the showing is satisfactory to the contracting officer. If it is not satisfactory, default action can follow immediately. Even without a show cause notice, allowing a short period of time for fact gathering and considering impacts, does not, in and of itself, constitute a waiver of the government's right to default.

The existence of these conditions imposes an obligation on both parties to fully communicate their intentions and capabilities. If the contractor seeks to continue performance, he should communicate this intention to the contracting officer. If the contracting officer is willing to have performance continue, he should so indicate to the contractor. However, a waiver will come into existence, after which it becomes the duty of the parties to reestablish the delivery obligation. The most acceptable method for doing this is by an agreement of the parties in which a specific delivery date is freely committed. If the parties cannot agree, the contracting officer has the power to unilaterally determine a new delivery date, provided the date is communicated specifically to the contractor and allows a reasonable period consistent with the capabilities and resources of the contractor to complete and deliver the acceptable product.

Termination for Convenience of the Government

Up to this point, our discussion has dealt with a form of termination familiar to private contractual relationships. Breach of contract and default of contractors by the government have similar causes and effects resulting from the actions. Some special rules have been introduced which serve the public interest and are pertinent only to government contracts. The subject of convenience termination is based entirely on a unique characteristic of government contracting. The termination for convenience clause has been developed to provide the government with a power which does not exist for either party in the standard commercial or private contractual relationship. Termination for convenience provides the government with a unilateral power to abrogate contracts into which it has entered freely and with complete knowledge of the circumstances surrounding the agreement. This right granted to one party ordinarily is viewed as a contractual right not supported by consideration and, therefore, not enforceable in the normal course of contract law. The development of this clause by the government is related to the public interest nature of government contracting and to the unique status of the government as a sovereign. Managers should recognize that sovereign powers hold authority to terminate contracts at any time, regardless of the existence of a termination for convenience clause. This authority exists for all sovereign powers, and the United States is no exception. However, because the United States government operates under a constitution which guarantees due process of law, the government cannot terminate a contract in the absence of a termination for convenience clause without incurring the normal sanctions imposed by courts against defaulting parties in the ordinary course of contract affairs.[1] If the government takes action to terminate contracts without having established a contractual right to do so, substantial burdens will be imposed on the public in the form of damages payable to the injured party.

In private contractual relationships, a key part of court-imposed sanctions against defaulting parties includes payment of anticipatory profits by the defaulting party to the injured party. Anticipatory profits are defined as profits payable for work not performed. This payment is viewed as a reasonable sanction to be imposed upon defaulters in ordinary contractual relationships. The termination for convenience clause established for government contracts bars payment of anticipatory profit.

A substantial history exists regarding the development of the termination for convenience clauses in the United States. The basic need for them arises out of wartime procurement, especially at the time when conflict ceases, and contracts for production of war goods are no longer needed, yet are in effect. It seems evident that it is in the public interest for the government to abrogate unneeded contracts and thus avoid sponsoring useless production.

Termination for convenience clauses had not been developed to cover war contracts during the earlier periods of U.S. history. At the end of the First World War, a large number of contracts were terminated, and settlements were negotiated between the government and its suppliers pursuant to the Dent Act. However, this legislation did not provide a systematic treatment for costs and profits to be recognized in these settlements. In 1944 the Contract Settlement Act was enacted explicitly to provide for termination and settlement of war contracts awarded during the Second World War. Based on that act, termination cost principles were developed which subsequently were incorporated into the Armed Services Procurement Regulation and, in updated form, are now included in Part 31 of the FAR. Settlement of terminations for convenience are constrained by the cost principles and the provisions of the termination for convenience clause.

---

[1]Since the FAR is published pursuant to law and has been interpreted to have the force and effect of law, and because the FAR makes the termination clause mandatory, mere omission of the clause from a contract document does not remove it from the contract.

Decisions to Terminate for Convenience

The government power to terminate for its convenience under the termination for convenience clause is nearly unrestricted. Such action must be taken only when it is in the government's best interest. However, it is extremely difficult for a terminated contractor to show that a convenience termination was other than in the interest of the government. A decision to terminate under the termination for convenience clause establishes government liability for the contractor's incurred costs and profit on the work done, commits the government to compensate for the cost of drawing up a termination settlement, and commits the government to reprice, as required, any work under the contract which is not terminated. Because of its clear acceptance of responsibility for these forms of settlement, the convenience termination clause provides a definable benefit to contractors. In addition, the settlement rules for convenience termination have become mandatory for settlement, in the event that a default termination is later overturned as having been improper. Upon conversion of a default into a convenience termination, the rules for settlement contained in the convenience termination clause become applicable. While in many cases this may be viewed as a benefit to contractors, it may actually operate to their disadvantage, because through such conversions the government is protected against any significant risk of loss for having improperly defaulted a contractor. This mechanism operates to protect the government against being found in breach of contract by reason of its default actions. This insulation of the government from sanctions for a breach may enable it to use inappropriate but more favorable bases for ending contractual relationships (such as default) even when not justified.

Policy Considerations Associated
with Termination for Convenience

In a manner similar to the changes, stop work order, suspension of work, disputes and other clauses, the termination for convenience clause provides a substantial degree of control to the government in managing procurement. Since 1957 it has become a consistent policy to require these clauses, including termination for convenience, in nearly all government contracts whether awarded for wartime mobilization purposes or for normal peacetime pursuits, defense-related or otherwise. Particularly with respect to the termination for convenience clause, the public policy implications are significant. The inclusion of the clause in peacetime contracts affords the government such complete protection against recognized sanctions for breach of contract that it raises a reasonable question whether government contracts should be viewed as binding contractual commitments.

Termination for convenience effectively gives the government an unfettered right to cancel contracts without suffering any form of sanction. Although the advantages are substantial, some question remains with respect to whether it is necessary during peacetime or even good public policy. Contractors who enter into agreements with the government have no assurance that their agreements will be fulfilled. Consequently, a contractor finds that he is unable to make substantial long-term investments in facilities and equipment that have value only for government programs. This limitation on a contractor's ability to predict future events results in the well publicized failure of the private sector to make major long-term investments in production equipment suitable for military applications. While major long-term investments to secure property that is also useful for commercial production are not affected, it is a fact that major segments of military acquisitions require investment in equipment that is not well suited for the production of commodities useful to the general economy. The effect of termination for convenience rights is to deny the suppliers any ability to predict the length of a production run. This limits willingness to amortize long-term investment because the contractor cannot count on even the completion of the initial contract for such production. In addition to this limitation, the contractor is unable to count on future contract awards for the same production because government policy requires that each contract award be competed individually whenever possible. As a result, the combination of public policies operates to limit the ability of the private sector to assume risk beneficial to public sector production.

This discussion does not focus on the legal aspects of the general use of termination for convenience clauses. It does raise a question regarding the trade-off of advantages and disadvantages associated with the policy during normal peacetime activity. Under the settlement provisions of the clause, the government cannot be required to pay anticipatory profit. To obtain this advantage, the government gives up the advantage of entering into contracts on a basis that will permit the private contractor to count on retention of work until fulfillment of the end objective. This disadvantage is difficult to measure in cash terms, but it has the effect of making the government a less desirable customer than private purchasers, because the private economy's demand for production of materials for the general public is predictable. Since government-sponsored production is cancelable without penalty at the government's option, and since government programs are variable in their level of activity and can be phased down, accelerated, or prolonged at the whim of the government, the true cost of transferring the risk of complete termination rights to the supplier may be quite high. The possibility of partial termination further increases the effect of termination power on contractor risk. Termination may be exercised for the entire contract or for any part of it at the discretion of the government. A partial termination could result in eliminating the attractive portion of a total contract, leaving only a small and, conceivably, unprofitable part for continued performance.

Convenience Termination Procedures

Although the contracting officer is subject to few restrictions in exercising discretion regarding a termination for convenience, the act of termination requires a written notice to the contractor, either by hand delivery or by certified mail with return receipt. The written notice must clearly state (1) that the contract is being terminated for convenience of the government; (2) the effective date of the termination; (3) the total extent of work terminated; (4) any special instructions associated with the termination; and (5) advice to the contractor, listing specific steps he can take to minimize the impact of the termination action. Once this notice has been issued, the termination is considered to be final, and the contractor no longer has any right to proceed with work. The finality of the T for C notice bars the government from subsequently converting the convenience termination to a default termination. There have been cases where a convenience termination notice was issued by mistake when it was the intent of the contracting officer to terminate for default, in which case the termination notice was retracted and replaced with a default notice. Although the termination notice is final, it is possible to reinstate a terminated contract provided there is written consent by the contractor to reinstatement.

SUMMARY

- Nearly all contracts are completed in a manner satisfactory to the parties.
- Several less than satisfactory methods of completing contracts demand attention because they represent a departure from planned outcomes.
- Seven sources of complexity and delay in closing out physically completed contracts illustrate challenges to effective contract management.
- A contract closeout checklist provides excellent insight into the factors that contribute to error and oversight in making final payments on completed contracts.
- Adverse effects on contractors who are declared in default are summarized into four costly sanctions.
- Because of the adverse impacts of default action on contractors, programs, and communities, eight vital factors that bear on the

decision should be reviewed carefully.
- Breach of contract may occur as a result of wrongful acts by either party. This subject is made complex by the special duty of contractors to proceed with work pursuant to government contracts.
- The concepts of waiver and forbearance under conditions in which a contractor has breached his contract provide clear insight into the dynamic nature of contractual activity.
- Certain adverse effects of termination for convenience, particularly its policy ramifications when used widely during peacetime, lead to a consideration of those effects.

TOPICS FOR DISCUSSION

1. An invoice should contain certain information in order to facilitate prompt payment. Discuss these information elements.
2. Regardless of the care taken in preparing contract invoices, numerous issues may arise to delay payments. Summarize the issues most likely to cause problems in closing out a contract.
3. For what reasons might the absence of a final royalty report delay payment of final vouchers?
4. What are the three types of actions that signify a contract breach has occurred?
5. Discuss the implications of the seven methods of completing contracts other than normal deliveries of specified end items.
6. Summarize the specific consequences of default (or breach) on the supplier; on the purchaser.
7. Explain the implications of the contractor's duty to proceed under government contracts.
8. Compare forbearance and waiver as they pertain to circumstances in which a breach (default) has occurred.
9. Explain the policy implications of the power to terminate for convenience as it is currently implemented in peacetime.

CASE 15-1

Simplex "C"

In negotiating their cost sharing contract with ERDA for a coal oil mixture (COM), Simplex made a particular point regarding the ownership of any facilities that they might acquire while pursuing the contract's objectives. The company's concern with this issue developed because of economic pressures caused by the cost sharing arrangement asserted by ERDA during negotiations. A special agreement documented by a unique contract provision resulted from these concerns. The matter later became a major issue, as indicated by the following information.

Simplex's early work in coal oil mixtures as an alternative fuel source for industrial boilers led to negotiations with ERDA, but the company had reservations about the economic viability of demonstrating the practicability of the concepts. This matter led the company to resist cost sharing. Nevertheless, Simplex accepted a form of cost sharing in the COM contract. Specifically, their portion of cost sharing was to be delayed until Phase II of the effort, and part of their cost sharing obligation was structured to be dependent on sales of COM operating systems after the system was proven feasible.

Because the company had not sought cost sharing arrangements for the COM project and, in fact, had accepted the arrangements only as a necessary part of participating in the DOE programs, they sought other ways to protect their interests in the event that economic viability or other factors resulted in no revenues to compensate for their invest-ment. One factor in Simplex's calculations was title to property acquired as part of the project. The company viewed the prospect of acquiring title to property as a form of compensation for pursuing the project, and a particularly important one, if the final result were to be unsuccessful. Under this condition, the value of the property would reduce the com-pany's losses.

In April 1978, DOE refused to accept the Simplex plan for revision of their cost sharing and post-contract reimbursement obligations (see Simplex "B"). Protracted discussions ensued following the agreement on revised total performance costs reached in April 1978. The result was embraced in the following message sent on March 7, 1979 by the DOE contracting officer, Mr. Benjamin Able.

Simplex Aerospace
18 King Street
Palo Alto, California

Attention: Mr. Henry Lee, Vice President

Your contract No. EF-77-C-01-2563 is hereby terminated in its entirety pursuant to clause 34 of the general provisions of the contract entitled "Termination for Default or for Convenience of the Government (FPR 1-8.702)" effective immediately. Immediately stop all work, terminate subcontracts and place no further orders. Telegraph similar instructions to all subcontractors and suppliers. Letters and instructions follow.

This action was based on the DOE view of the contract status expressed in the following extract from a February 21, 1979 memorandum by the agency's program director.

> Simplex-Aerospace entered into a cost-share agreement with ERDA for a program to demonstrate COM firing in an industrial boiler. The contract called for a COM preparation plant at the host site and conversion of the host's boiler (Loveland Corporation, Danville, Virginia) from oil to coal-oil mixture. The original contract value of $1,982,195 was divided into two phases. Phase I was total Government funding and Phase II was to be shared 50-50 by the Government and the contractor. The amounts for these two phases were

> Phase I   - $1,131,645
> Phase II   - $ 850,550

> The up-front amount to be contributed to Phase II by Simplex-Aerospace was $297,692. Hence, the actual Government commitment to this contract was $1,684,503 of the $1,982,195 total. The contract allowed for contractor conditional reimbursement of the Government after contract completion as a means of satisfying the Phase II, PON FE-3, 50-50 cost-share requirement. The definitive cost-sharing contract also specified conditions for costs incurred in excess of $1,131,645 in Phase I and $850,550 in Phase II. These costs were to be shared 50-50 by the Government and contractor without allowances for conditional future payback by the contractor.

> In early 1978 it was apparent, via a detailed cost estimate, that the cost would be much greater than the original estimate. Negotiations to cost share the projected overruns were initiated in early spring of 1978. In May of 1978 project progress was virtually stopped by the contractor pending resolution of overrun funding.

> The relevant cost estimates for this project are:

> | | Contractor | DOE | Total |
> |----------------------------------|------------|------------|------------|
> | Present government estimates | $297,692 | $3,507,308 | $3,805,000 |
> | Original estimates | $297,692 | $1,684,503 | $1,982,195 |

> · · ·

> Of the increased contract cost, the contractor has indicated that he will provide none of the overrun cost sharing required, nor is he

amenable to other equitable adjustments offered by the Government. His requirement is that the Government fund the overrun completely, subject to partial future contingency reimbursement. The increased cost is 91 percent of the original contract value.

. . .

Several technical approaches to completing this project have been thoroughly explored. However, none of the approaches offer any significant economic relief. In light of this situation, and FY '79 and FY '80 budget constraints, we request the immediate termination of the Simplex-Aerospace contract.

After termination of the project, negotiations to settle cost issues and determine final payment were initiated. Simplex prepared inventory schedules, collected final cost information from subcontractors, and developed a proposal for settlement. After audit and negotiation with the TCO, all issues were resolved except one: treatment of costs associated with equipment purchased by Simplex during performance and, subsequent to termination, sold or donated by Simplex. The issue, formulated as seen by DOE's Termination Contracting Officer on September 2, 1981, is quoted, in part, below:

1. My letter of 31 July 1981 recommended initiation of a Unilateral Determination of the Contracting Officer. Summarized below is the Contractor's recent submittal of generated inventory values with associate derived disposal proceeds which can be used in your negotiation efforts or basis for further investigations.

2. On the surface (without DCAA Auditor Technical Evaluation as to accuracy) it appears from my knowledge of the coal-slurry program to be reasonable.

INVENTORY DISPOSAL CREDITS:			($79,141.00)
INV. DISPOSAL SETTLEMENT EXPS:			
DIRECT LABOR		$10,948.16	
ABATED FRINGE RATE (25.9%)		2,835.57	(a)
		$13,783.73	
TRAVEL & PER DIEM PLUS G&A		$ 3,846.07	(b)
		$17,629.80	
FREIGHT EXP. PLUS G&A		$ 1,445.80	
		$19,175.60	$19,175.60 (c)
NET DISPOSAL CREDIT DUE GOVERNMENT			($59,965.40)
NEGOTIATED SETTLEMENT PAYMENT DUE			$65,221.00
NET PAYMENT DUE SIMPLEX			$ 5,255.60

NOTES:

   (a) FPR 1-15-205.42 (f)(3) states that all settlement expense labor will bear only an abated fringe rate. Rate computed by DCAA, Ref. Report Schedule A-1, Page 4.

   (b) Applied G&A is appropriate since administrative effort was required to effect logging of travel and per diem costs and expensing to Books of Accounts.

   (c) Same as above.

   The TCO's view of the special provision incorporated into the original contract is stated below.

NOTE A. Article X of subject contract states that title to all material purchased under the contract shall rest exclusively with Simplex, to wit:

> Title to all equipment supplied or purchased under this contract shall rest fully and exclusively with the contractor.

> This termination settlement takes into consideration reimbursement for all materials and supplies purchased by the contractor. Pursuant to Article X, transfer of title to the Government of this material was not effected. The contractor disposed of the material, deriving sales proceeds that is suspected of being in excess of their acquisition cost. No appropriate credit was made to the U.S. Government as recognition for those sales. It is the opinion of this TCO that the contractor has been "unjustly enriched" through the application of Article X.

> Article X clause as drawn deviates from the normal "Title to Material" clause recognized under F.A.R., i.e., title normally rests in the Government and not with the contractor. The Termination for Default or for Convenience of the Government, FPR 1-8.702, the Standard clause, Paragraphs 6 and 7 of FPR 1-8.702 clearly conflicts with Article X. It is the opinion of this TCO that this conflict and its resulting application is not only detrimental to the U.S. Government but was undoubtedly not considered by the parties in the light of a termination environment.

> This TCO feels that one of the following courses of action should be imposed:

> (1) Title to all materials or supplies generated should be tendered

to the U.S. Government and appropriate disposition actions taken with resultant sales proceeds retained by the U.S. Government; or

(2) Simplex should be required to disclose and support all sales revenue for the disposition of acquired materials/supplies, and an appropriate credit recognized in the termination settlement; or

(3) All costs for the acquisition of materials and supplies with appropriate burdens and G&A expenses be excluded and not recognized in this termination settlement.

Inasmuch as resolution of this question rests with the PCO (signatory authority), cost recognition is hereby referred for appropriate action.

Simplex and the DOE contracting officer were unable to resolve the differences that had developed over their positions concerning the property. Each side felt its position was fully justified. Consequently, on December 16, 1981, through counsel, Simplex stated their position to the contracting officer (see attachment A). The DOE contracting officer's position was stated in a final decision under the "Disputes" clause of the contract (see attachment B). The contractor's appeal of the dispute was docketed on August 2, 1981.

* * * * *

1. Evaluate these events and factors. Show how this course of events could have been handled without litigation. How would you, as a negotiator, have handled this issue?

2. Formulate your view as to which party has the stronger case. Do you perceive any difference between what you feel is an appropriate and reasonable settlement, and the decision that you anticipate will result from litigation?

Attachment A - Simplex C

Contracting Officer
Office of Procurement Operations
United States Department of Energy
Washington, D.C. 20585

Re: Simplex Corporation Contract EF-77-C-01-2563

This firm represents Simplex in connection with its termination claim
under the above referenced contract. The purpose of this letter is to
respond to your letter of November 9, 1981, which sets forth the Department of Energy's analysis and proposal for settlement. Inasmuch as the
central issue preventing a final settlement relates to the treatment of the
equipment purchased in connection with the contract, and since the
government's position with respect to that equipment is summarized in
the Terminating Contracting Officer's letter to Simplex dated June 26,
1981, our response will address itself to the arguments raised in that
letter.

The contract was a negotiated, cost participation agreement for
Simplex to develop a Coal-Oil Mixture substitute for fossil fuel (COM).
The government's objective in this project was to obtain technical data
and develop the technology to create an alternate energy resource.
Simplex's interest in entering into the contract was the prospect of
participating in future sales of the technology developed should it prove
commercially viable.

In light of the uncertainties and the risks involved in the attempt
to develop an economically viable COM process, a cost participation
arrangement was specifically negotiated, in phases, to coincide with
separate and distinct phases of the contract. Phase I involved the initial
development of the process, and the government undertook full funding of
all program costs in this Phase. Cost participation in Phase I occurred
only in the event of "excess" costs. Cost participation in Phase II, the
demonstration phase, was structured ultimately to achieve a 50/50 ratio
by way of a "deferred payback" formula. Under this arrangement, the
government and Simplex shared a 65/35 ratio of costs incurred and
Simplex was to pay the government an additional 15% from future sales,
if any, ultimately resulting in a 50/50 cost ratio.

As an additional incentive to enter into the contract, Simplex
specifically required that it obtain title to all equipment purchased in
Phase I. The government was not interested in acquiring this inventory,
and Simplex would not have entered into the contract unless it acquired

title to the equipment. Therefore, the parties agreed that Article 10, "Equipment Title," would be expressly written into the contract. This Article provides that:

> Title to all equipment supplied or purchased under this contract shall vest fully and exclusively with the contractor.

Pursuant to the terms of the contract, Simplex proceeded to purchase and install equipment in its name. The equipment was the sole property of Simplex. When the contract was terminated for the government's convenience, Simplex had no further need for the equipment, sold it, and retained the proceeds.

In its settlement proposal the government has taken the position that, pursuant to Clause 55(b) "Limitations of Costs," Simplex and the government are required to negotiate an equitable distribution of property purchased under the contract, based upon the share of costs incurred by each. It argues further that since Simplex did not participate in the costs, equity dictates that title to all equipment should revert to the government. This position is unsupported by the history of negotiations of the contract and the intent of both parties in entering into it. Further, Clause 55(b) does not even apply to these facts since that clause relates only to property furnished or acquired by or *on behalf of the government,* and this was not the case here.

From a legal standpoint, title to the equipment was taken in Simplex's name. This was negotiated between the parties as part of Simplex's consideration. At no time did the government acquire, nor did the parties ever contemplate that the government would acquire, any interest in the equipment or the proceeds from its sale. That this was the specific intent of both parties could not have been more clearly nor more strongly stated than in the language in the contract that "Title...shall vest *fully and exclusively* with the contractor." This language was the direct result of specific negotiation on that point alone and, as such, totally supersedes any general language in the contract which might be construed to the contrary.

In addition to the general law of contract interpretation, which clearly supports Simplex's position in this contract, Clause 60 of the contract, "Order of Precedence," explicitly provides that the negotiated items in the schedule take precedence over the general conditions of contract so that Simplex's title to the equipment takes precedence over the government's claim to "equitable" return of all of the proceeds resulting from their sale.

From an equitable standpoint, the government's argument that Simplex did not participate in costs and therefore is not entitled to the equipment, is not accurate and ignores the realities surrounding this particular contract. Simplex did participate in costs and undertook the risk of incurring substantially more costs. According to the government's own audit report dated June 20, 1981, a cost sharing adjustment of $23,254 was applied against Simplex's share of the settlement representing a 50/50 participation in excess costs under Phase I which Simplex was contractually obliged to share.

With respect to Phase II, Simplex was contractually bound to participate in up to 50% of the costs. At the absolute minimum, Simplex's share was 35%. The remaining 15% was deferred and to be paid from future sales. Simplex assumed the obligation to share in these costs and was ready, willing, and able to proceed with all phases of the contract. The fact that Simplex was unable to participate to the full extent originally contemplated by the parties was the direct result of the government's unilateral decision to terminate this contract for its own convenience.

The contract reflects exactly what both parties wanted, needed, and negotiated and, as structured, complies fully with the meaning and intent of the Department of Energy's own regulations applicable to Cost Participation Contracts (DOEPR Sec. 9-4.5901), which specifically provide that the propriety, manner, and amount of cost participation must be decided on a case-by-case basis and that full funding may be provided in the early phases of development programs when technology has not been adequately evaluated or proven.

Simplex proposes an early resolution of this claim to avoid the necessity of additional proceedings, fees and settlement expenses. For that reason, Simplex has asked us to handle discussions with a view towards settlement. Consequently, I will make myself available to meet and talk with you, and the Department of Energy legal staff, if you believe it appropriate, at any time to explore settlement possibilities.

After you have had an opportunity to review this letter, I would appreciate hearing from you and would further ask that you direct any further responses to the undersigned.

(signed by counsel for Simplex)

Attachment B - Simplex C

Letter of August 24, 1982

Simplex Corporation
Aerospace Group
ATTN: General Manager, Administration
18 King Street
Palo Alto, CA 94042

    This letter constitutes the contracting officer's unilateral determina-
tion and final decision regarding contract DE-AC01-77ET10384 (formerly
contract number EF-77-C-01-2563). This final decision and unilateral
determination results from a claim by the Government against the Contractor for equitable reimbursement to the Government of proceeds
derived from the Contractor's sale of property acquired with contract
funds.

. . .

    The contract was terminated in its entirety for the convenience of
the Government, effective March 7, 1979. This termination occurred
during the first phase of the contract. Thus, at the time of termination
the Government was obligated to pay 100 percent of costs incurred to
fund the contract, except for $46,125, an amount contributed by Simplex
which represents the Contractor's one-half share of excess costs for
Phase I, for which share the Contractor is responsible under Article IV,
"Financial Provision," of the contract.

    Subsequent to termination, Simplex disposed of equipment acquired
under the contract with Government funds and retained the proceeds.
The Government notified the contractor of its position regarding the sale
of the property and the required distribution of the proceeds thereof, and
of its proposal for settlement by letter of November 9, 1981, in which the
Government requested that the Contractor list any substantive objections
in writing in the event the Contractor did not concur with the Government's position. Simplex responded, through counsel, by letter of December 16, 1981, in which it stated its position and argued the validity of
the Government's claim. The parties have been unable to reach agreement with respect to the Government's claim.

. . .

    All termination settlement matters have been resolved except for
those matters relating to the sale of property acquired with contract

funds and the required distribution of the proceeds thereof. Excluding these property matters, the final settlement amount agreed to by both parties was $65,221 owed to Simplex by the Government.

. . .

Decision

It is my unilateral determination and final decision, based on the above facts and for the reasons set out below, that Simplex must reimburse the Government in the amount of $76,248. This sum constitutes a debt due and owed the U.S. Government. Of the total proceeds received through the disposition of property ($79,141) Simplex is entitled to retain only $2,893 which is that fraction of the proceeds equal to the fraction (3.655%) of the total allowable costs contributed by Simplex ($46,125 of $1,261,944). Thus, the Government owes Simplex a net final settlement of $8,149. This amount is derived as follows:

$65,221	Negotiated settlement excluding property matters
+$19,176	Contractor's allowable property disposition costs
$84,397	Subtotal
-$76,248	Government's share of property disposition proceeds
$8,149	Total

Simplex's claim to title in the equipment is not in issue. The Government agrees that Simplex had legal title to the equipment by the terms of the contract. At issue, rather, is whether any portion of the proceeds of the sale of equipment acquired by the Contractor must be deducted from the amount otherwise due the Contractor under clause 34 of the General Provisions of the contract, and what constitutes an equitable distribution of property produced or purchased under the contract within the meaning of clause 55 B of the Alterations to the General Provisions of the contract.

Simplex argues that the rule of contract interpretation that specific language in a contract supercedes any general language and that the "Order of Precedence" clause preclude the Government claim to equitable reimbursement of the proceeds because Simplex has title. I find no merit in this argument for the reasons explained below.

As stated, the instant concern involves the propriety of deducting proceeds of the sale of Contractor acquired equipment from that amount otherwise owing the Contractor, and the equitable distribution of property in the settlement of a convenience termination, and not a question regarding title. Thus, the more specific language immediately pertinent to settlement is that language found in clause 34 and in clause 55 B, not the title provision.

By its very terms, the "Order of Precedence" clause applies only in the event of inconsistency between provisions of the contract. There is no inconsistency between the title clause and the "Termination Clause" or the "Limitation of Cost" clause since those clauses concern two separate and disparate matters; the one, title to property, the other, termination settlement.

The "Termination" clause clearly provides that proceeds from the sale of Contractor acquired equipment are to be deducted from those amounts otherwise owing the Contractor.

The "Limitation of Cost" clause clearly provides that proceeds from the sale of Contractor acquired equipment are to be deducted from those amounts otherwise owing the Contractor.

The "Limitation of Cost" clause clearly provides for "an equitable distribution of all property produced or purchased under the contract based upon the share of costs incurred by each [party]." Thus, the Government, having funded all but a minor portion of the contract at the time of termination, is entitled to all but a minor portion of the proceeds realized from the sale of such property, regardless of title status. To interpret the contract in the manner Simplex suggests would result in a transfer of property tantamount to a gift, which was not the Government's intent. Furthermore, the law recognizes that legal title is not dispositive of equitable ownership.

(Signed by the Contracting officer for DOE)

CASE 15-2

RAM Development Corporation, Pacific Operations[1]

The termination for convenience notice, dated August 20, 1982, had come as quite a surprise to Mr. Jim Garrison, Manager of Contractual Relations for RAM Development Corporation, Pacific Operations. Two weeks before RAM received the notice, the U.S. government had indicated

---

[1]Research and the original draft of this case were performed by Curtis Cook while a student at George Washington University.

that negotiations to definitize the letter contract would begin on August 23, 1982. Jim recalled the many months after the award of that contract in September, 1981. Four months after award, the government issued a stop work order to review technical changes to the specification that had been recommended by RAM. During the period of the stop work order, the government continued to issue changes to the contract and to request information from RAM.

Now that RAM's termination claim was finally being negotiated in August 1985, Mr. Garrison was informed by the contracting officer that the amount that RAM had spent between the stop work order date and the termination notice (in excess of $160,000) were not allowable costs. Jim wondered whether RAM had reacted properly to the stop work order. For that matter, it seemed to him that certain government actions and communications had led RAM to believe that the costs would be negotiated as part of the letter contract definitization. It now looked as though RAM could end up losing more than $160,000. Something had to be done--and soon.

General Company Background

RAM Development Corporation, Pacific Operations, which is located in California's Silicon Valley had sales in excess of $260 million in 1984, employed over 2,600 people, and projected double-digit annual growth over the next five years. Since the company specialized in electronic defense systems, electronic reconnaissance and active countermeasures systems comprised about 90 percent of their sales. Advanced laser technology and anti-intrusion systems were also important growth areas for the remainder of the 80s.

Contractual Relations Department

Jim Garrison, with a staff of 42, was responsible for managing over 250 contracts and 300 other contractual documents (orders against blanket ordering agreements, for example). These contracts ranged from a few thousand to several million dollars and involved RAM as both a prime and a subcontractor. Mr. Garrison reported to the Corporate Director of Administration.

The Story of a Simple Letter Contract

In September 1981, a DOD contracting activity issued a $2.6 million undefinitized letter contract to RAM Development Corporation for development of an improved microprocessor and dual antenna system for an essential defense weapon system. The contract included all the usual government provisions, including the changes and disputes clauses. The intention of both parties was to negotiate a cost-plus-fixed-fee contract within 180 days after award. Soon after contract award, RAM and DOD engineers and contracting officers met in a technical interchange to clarify the required effort--a necessary step preceding RAM's submission of a detailed cost proposal for negotiation. At the meeting it soon became evident that the government's statement of work (SOW) did not adequately reflect the level of effort needed to meet desired performance criteria. Furthermore, RAM and DOD personnel interpreted parts of the SOW differently, leading to confusion about the scope of work included under the contract. As a result of the meeting, RAM submitted two proposals to the government: one for $18.5 million that covered the work RAM *thought* DOD wanted and one for $2.6 million that covered the work as stated in the contract. The latter proposal included a caveat, telling DOD that a system that was developed in accordance with the current SOW would not accomplish the overall mission requirements stated in the contract.

During the next month, RAM and the contracting officer exchanged letters, phone calls, and visits in an attempt to resolve the issues. DOD extended the stop work order and issued a unilateral change order that reflected the DOD interpretation of the scope of work. RAM was asked to submit a revised proposal for the work as changed. Subsequently, the contracting officer extended the stop work order, one month at a time, through mid-September 1982, while revising the SOW four additional times. On several occasions RAM managers, including Mr. Garrison, traveled to the DOD contracting activity to apprise government managers of the situation and of RAM's efforts to help resolve the problems. In turn, government engineers visited RAM to view performance of prototype systems and to discuss RAM's perspective of what was needed to satisfy the government's requirement.

On July 30, 1982 RAM submitted a new cost proposal for $14.9 million. Upon receiving the proposal, the contracting officer indicated that negotiations would start on August 23rd.

On August 20, 1982 DOD terminated the contract for the convenience of the government.

RAM's Dilemma

The DOD terminating contracting officer (TCO) who was assigned to a central DOD contract administration office, and who had not been involved in the case previously, asked RAM to submit its termination claim. RAM's claim amounted to $540,000, $160,000 of which had been incurred after the first stop work order had been issued, but before termination. Government auditors recommended disallowing all of the latter amount. The original contracting officer for the contract had, long ago, taken another job. The current CO refused to discuss any costs incurred after the stop work order had been issued. The TCO was powerless to discuss that portion of the claim without delegation from the contracting officer.

On August 21, 1985 three years after the termination, the issue was still not resolved. Mr. Garrison wanted this case closed immediately, one way or the other, yet he was uncertain regarding exactly what action to take. As he sat in his office reviewing the case history with his staff, he considered the available alternatives.

CASE 15-3

Winning Requirements

Inland's marketing manager, Harry Markham, was extremely pleased at winning the DLA contract (a requirements contract) under which Inland would receive, for one year, the DLA depot's orders for corrugated fiberboard boxes. This was the third consecutive year that Inland had won the contract, but now, Harry thought, the business should really take off. In order to win this contract, Harry had to agree (at the urging of the contracting officer and other DLA officials) to open a branch plant near the depot. Shortly after award Inland opened the branch, although at substantial cost, which Harry figured would result in only a break-even contract for this year. He expected to do much better with the new plant in future years as business developed.

What Harry didn't know was that DLA issued forecasts of its corrugated box needs to GSA, and GSA bought, entirely independently, a rotating stock of most of the items demanded by the depot. Therefore, GSA was able to supply out of its inventory (and as it turned out, did supply) all of the depot's needs, except special difficult-to-make boxes.

Since GSA didn't stock special items, Inland received orders for them totaling $35,000. This resulted in total sales of $54,000 by Inland's new branch plant during the first six months of the year and also resulted in an operating loss of $35,000 for Inland--and a black eye for Harry, from his boss's viewpoint. At that point Inland closed the branch plant and continued contract obligations using its normal supply system.

Now Harry is perplexed about how to proceed. After several conferences with the contracting officer concerning his loss, he understands the system much better.

He is now aware that DLA holds these views:

1. Requisitioning off the shelf from a sister agency of the government is not a purchase within the meaning of the "requirements" contract.
2. GSA's purchases to replenish its stocks were not in fulfillment of any specific depot order.
3. Certain internal DLA regulations require the Depot to order from GSA regardless of requirements contract commitments, if in the best interest of the government.
4. Inland had frequently failed to meet its (timely) delivery obligations under the contract, GSA had a better record, and this justified purchasing from GSA.

* * * * *

Harry had thought he was a pretty good salesman and manager, but he needs help sorting out what happened to him, what he and DLA (or both) should have done differently, and what to do now.

CASE 15-4

Stimsons, Inc.

Because of their reputation in the field and their cooperative approach of helping to define requirements in collaboration with their customers, Stimsons, Inc., a medium-size electronics manufacturer, was successful in acquiring, as sole source, an Army contract to furnish voltage control oscillators (VCOs). The VCO functions as power source for a transponder used in several security devices by the U.S. Army. Stimsons had produced VCOs before, but because of the specialized application required in this case, the contract was governed by a performance specification. Shortly after award, Ralph Bergman, Stimsons' production manager, called in the chief engineer, Harry Preston, to discuss the technical problems he was encountering. As a result the two came to the conclusion that an isolator was required to meet performance requirements.

Alteration to include the isolator required contracting officer action, since the specifications had to be modified, and authority to incorporate the isolator was essential. Accordingly, Raymond Powell, Contract Administrator, presented Stimsons' proposal to the contracting officer, Newton Kendall. Surprisingly, Kendall offered little objection to this and modified the contract (FFP) accordingly. Since Stimsons was a major producer of both VCOs and isolators and very familiar with the requisite technology, it now appeared that everything would be O.K.

The customer was also quite pleased with Stimsons' work and placed an additional sole source RFP for 150 units in Stimsons' hands. While negotiations were going on, Stimsons' chief engineer called the production manager to advise that he was encountering some design problems associated with matching the isolator to the VCO for this application.   In fact he advised that he was authorizing intensive engineering effort to resolve the problems, and that he anticipated a loss on the deal.

Shortly afterward Stimsons and the government completed their negotiations for the new contract and executed the document.

Stimsons' design problems unfortunately grew worse, and substantial effort was expended on the needed match.   Since this greatly increased performance costs, general management became disgusted and demanded an accounting of contract status.   As a result of this review, it became clear to Stimsons that it was commercially impracticable to continue to perform without an adjustment of the contract.   The customer's technical staff concurred in Stimsons' assessment that current technology could not accomplish the specified performance. At this point the contract delivery schedule had passed, and Stimsons slowed its efforts to a virtual halt during the period of discussions with the customer.   Also, the company directed Ray Powell and the engineering staff to prepare a revision of the contract cost.   Ray submitted the claim for a price increase and time extension to the contracting officer.   At this point, however, relationships deteriorated.

Ray Powell was surprised and disappointed to receive a show cause notice five days after delivering his proposed modification to the contracting officer (and only two weeks after the contract review meeting).

* * * * *

1.   Specify the actions Ray Powell should initiate at this time.
2.   Specify the actions Newt Kendall should be planning at this time.
3.   Assess this situation.   What are the issues and likely outcome of these developments?

16

Contracting and
Logistics Improvement

Throughout this book comparisons of private sector and government practice in contract management have been important elements of the discussion. The primary source of data has been government-sponsored procurement and associated policy and practice. The work has treated those aspects of the processes that arise after a contract of purchase has been established. It has also focused on large contracts, ones with substantial post-award interaction between the parties. This emphasis has been intentional for two reasons. Most directly, the author's earlier text, *Government Procurement Management,* has treated pre-award management in some detail. Secondly, post-award activity, although often not given priority in the scheme of management, may actually offer greater potential for improvement in the acquisition process than pre-award matters. Since actual application of resources to work occurs post-award, effective management of that phase of the procurement process is critical. The art of managing through a contract, i.e., in accordance with the rules of the agreement, is particularly challenging. Government regulation and political perceptions add measurably to these interface challenges.

One facet of the contract management process seems important for attention in this closing chapter: is the process operated to secure the greatest economic potential for its participants and for the economy as a whole? A clear dichotomy has emerged between the public and private sector perception of how to achieve this potential. The dichotomy is concerned with competition, how it relates to achieving the potential, how it alters post-award management activity, and the strategies that will gain competition's fullest benefits. The author has observed that no consensus exists regarding these matters and that optimum solutions have not been approached.

Conflicting Trends in Contracting

Private sector and government personnel have developed sharply contrasting viewpoints regarding the best form of competition in procurement. The trend in government has been toward competition for every contract award. The trend in private sector procurement has been toward creating longer term contractual relationships with fewer invited competitions and exercise of management discretion as to the wisdom of each potential competitive procedure.

Authors in the fields of purchasing and materials management and logistics have also been active in attempting to recast the image of contract activities. Burt has adopted the concept of proactive procurement[1] and has emphasized the need for a role in strategic planning for purchasing managers. Bowersox has adopted the concept of integrated logistical management[2] and has given emphasis to systems analysis focused on customer service. Overall, the authors visualize participation by the buying community in strategic planning, fuller cooperation between internal management functions and more fully integrated operations as essential ingredients for advances in the art of buying. As part of this, they visualize longer term contractual relations, exchange of information, and cooperation in planning activities between contractual parties.

These perceptions are not shared by the government, especially by the Congress. Drastic actions have been taken by the Congress during the mid 1980s to correct perceived deficiencies in government procurement and contract management. Both pre-award and post-award measures have been introduced for this purpose. Increased competition has been mandated by the Competition in Contracting Act. Increased audit and investigatory activity and reduced collaboration between the parties concerning performance judgments have been imposed through both statutory and regulatory action. Regardless, a different type of revolution is occurring in corporate perceptions of the best way to achieve overall economy and efficiency.

These congressional and corporate pathways differ because Congress does not or cannot rely upon government personnel in matters that are basically judgmental. It places greater reliance on competition for

---

[1]Burt, David N., *Proactive Procurement,* Englewood Cliffs, NJ: Prentice Hall, 1984.

[2]Bowersox, Donald J., and others, *Logistical Management,* 3rd. Ed., New York, NY: John Wiley and Sons, 1985.

objective pre-award decisionmaking, and it has imposed increased audit, oversight and investigative practices to gain objectivity in post-award decisionmaking. This reliance may be essential in the political defense of governmental action, but it results in greater regulatory control and complication of the basic processes. This in turn increases the bureaucratic review and approval processes associated with procurement. This fact should be reexamined in light of recent doctoral research at George Washington University, in which Curtis Cook has demonstrated that complexity and bureaucratization reduce the likelihood that managers will seek optimum solutions in their decisionmaking.[1]

The corporate world is more likely to focus on productivity, innovativeness and overall efficient operations. Measures adopted include reduced inventory, renewed emphasis on quality, just-in-time (JIT) purchasing and production systems, and reliance on management discretion. The just-in-time concept has major implications for purchasing and contract management practice. Possibly the most significant implication is its reduction in the frequency of competitive purchases. The potential economies that JIT promises are focused on inventory. It promises to reduce inventory throughout the supplier system. This is accomplished by creating extraordinarily close coordination of supplier production at all levels. Inventory is reduced because it is not allowed to accumulate. Accumulations at all points are cut--incoming, in process, finished goods, etc. JIT stimulates improvement in efficiency provided product quality is sufficient to allow complete reliance on scheduled deliveries. Its promise of overall economy is also contingent upon adoption by the whole supplier system. If it achieves reduction of the purchaser's inventory only by pushing the stocking requirements back to the supplier, no overall economic gain is likely. JIT demands that the entire supplier system become closely coupled in every dimension to achieve long-term net economy. This places a premium on post-award management and demands cooperative interaction between buyer and seller.

Every dimension of a supplier system, including producers throughout the distribution channel, becomes a factor in effective JIT operations. This includes the production systems, quality programs, purchasing systems, traffic management and customer service systems. If JIT is to work, the entire system must be brought to a standard of excellence. To do this impacts competition. It specifically impacts the method of securing competition and the frequency of turnovers to new suppliers.

The stated objective of material managers at many top corporate enterprises in the United States is to establish long-term relationships

---

[1]Cook, Curtis R., *A Study of Decision-Making Processes in the Practice of Federal Contract Management,* unpublished doctoral dissertation, George Washington University, July, 1987.

with suppliers. They seek to build closer relationships. They want to monitor and assist their vendors to provide reliable, 100 percent acceptable quality. They want to share information with vendors, but in doing so they want the vendor to be a partner in creating the end result needed and desired by the customer. They want to treat materials in a way that creates a continuous flow, one that is tightly coupled so as to eliminate bottlenecks and static inventory. With all of this they do not want to become deeply involved in their suppliers' internal management processes. If anything, they want to design their procurement systems so that fewer personnel are needed. But their employees must understand and implement the kinds of working relationships implicit in JIT.

It is evident that these concepts of how to accomplish acquisition and logistics needs are widely at variance if not incompatible. Government policy is so strongly expressed in its statutory mandate for competition of each contract, that the question of whether the benefits of specific competition outweigh the costs of securing it is difficult even to ask. It is even more difficult to challenge the audit/investigation approach by which government has keynoted its current policy. Investigators consistently turn up some corrupt, abusive or wasteful example that cannot be defended. By contrast, industry focuses directly on the benefits to be achieved, not on competitive procedure and not on individually destructive abuses and fraudulent behavior. The effectiveness of the industrial system outweighs the losses incident to such practices. Industry is concerned with overall productivity, with total system cost optimization. If a 100 percent acceptable quality level pays off and obtaining it means staying with a proven source, that is what they do. If the administrative cost of mounting a competition exceeds foreseeable benefits, they proceed without the competitive expenditure. If they perceive that innovative concepts are being fed to them by long-term, close working relationships with suppliers, they preserve those relationships.

These contrasting viewpoints reflect significant differences in underlying work requirements as well as differences in political perceptions. Industry is in the business of procuring for production. They buy material to be incorporated into their own product which must then meet the test of salability in the open market. Government managers procure for a different purpose. They buy to consume, to build an inventory against some future threat, or to create a new capability. The concept of a total system cost is difficult for them to measure because the hardware and systems they buy face no further market test of valuation. These factors help but do not fully meet the challenge of harmonizing the conceptual differences between procurement by industry and by government.

It is important to reconcile these differences. If the industrial approach is correct in the sense of more fully advancing the nation's competitive position through lower total costs, and if the nature of government procurement is not so different as to justify its distinct techniques, then a system modification must be found.

Arguably this matter is less important in practice than in concept. Government clearly has developed a powerful and sophisticated contracting system that achieves important objectives. And it is fundamental to our economic system that competition, in whatever form is most effective, be free to drive the marketplace. It is also clear that extraordinary benefits have accrued to the nation because the market system is open to competition. But competition can be tested in many ways, and the contract-by-contract approach may not be the only way for government to proceed.

Elements of a Scheme for Improvement

The principal reason for the dichotomy of perception discussed above is the strong tendency for government procurement to be used for research, development, production of unique goods, and support of complex and unpredictable operations which are inherent in the work of the government. The United States' experience during and since World War II has demonstrated the need to mobilize the entire economy, private and public, to solve complex problems. The contractual method is the only available technique to achieve this level of concentration on public needs. Because of the nature of its work and these associated factors, a high proportion of government contract funding is expended using other than firm-priced contracts and is supported by unproven (but not invalid) requirements and specifications. These contracts require the comprehensive post-award management systems discussed in this book. The systems cannot be abandoned because standards for acceptance, assessments of cost, and management of delivery are subject to adjustment as a function of the work itself--they are not fully predetermined. Improvement could be achieved by reduced adversarial attitudes on the part of spokesmen and administrators at all levels. This could be facilitated by greater reliance on the administrator coupled with a willingness of government to accept some level of poor decisionmaking and even unethical conduct without adding systematic barriers to exercise of judgment. Administrative action and simple corrective measures would suffice in most cases. Reduction of current audit and investigatory capabilities coupled with greater emphasis on managers' skill and willingness to assume responsibility would facilitate greater reliance.

Appendix

Federal Acquisition Regulations

Subpart 42.302, Contract Administration Functions

(a) The following are the normal contract administration functions to be performed by the cognizant CAO, to the extent they apply, as prescribed in 42.202:

    (1) Review the contractor's compensation structure.

    (2) Review the contractor's insurance plans.

    (3) Conduct post-award orientation conferences.

    (4) Review and evaluate contractors' proposals under Subpart 15.8 and, when negotiation will be accomplished by the contracting officer, furnish comments and recommendations to that officer.

    (5) Negotiate forward pricing rate agreements (see 15.809).

    (6) Negotiate advance agreements applicable to treatment of costs under contracts currently assigned for administration (see 31.109).

    (7) Determine the allowability of costs suspended or disapproved as required (see Subpart 42.8), direct the suspension or disapproval of costs when there is reason to believe they should be suspended or disapproved, and approve final vouchers.

    (8) Issue Notices of Intent to Disallow or not Recognize Costs (see Subpart 42.8).

    (9) Establish final indirect cost rates and billing rates for those contractors meeting the criteria for contracting officer determination in Subpart 42.7.

    (10) Prepare findings of fact and issue decisions under the Disputes clause on matters in which the administrative contracting officer (ACO) has the authority to take definitive action.

    (11) In connection with Cost Accounting Standards (see Part 30)--

        (i) Determine the adequacy of the contractor's disclosure

statements;

    (ii) Determine whether disclosure statements are in compliance with Cost Accounting Standards and Part 31;

    (iii) Determine the contractor's compliance with Cost Accounting standards and disclosure statements, if applicable; and

    (iv) Negotiate price adjustments and execute supplemental agreements under the Cost Accounting Standards clauses at 52.230-3, 52.230-4, and 52.230-5.

(12) Review and approve or disapprove the contractor's requests for payments under the progress payments clause.

(13) Make payments on assigned contracts when prescribed in agency acquisition regulations (see 42.205).

(14) Manage special bank accounts.

(15) Ensure timely notification by the contractor of any anticipated overrun or underrun of the estimated cost under cost-reimbursement contracts.

(16) Monitor the contractor's financial condition and advise the contracting officer when it jeopardizes contract performance.

(17) Analyze quarterly limitation on payments statements and recover overpayments from the contractor.

(18) Issue tax exemption certificates.

(19) Ensure processing and execution of duty-free entry certificates.

(20) For classified contracts, administer those portions of the applicable industrial security program designated as ACO responsibilities (see Subpart 4.4).

(21) Issue work requests under maintenance, overhaul, and modification contracts.

(22) Negotiate prices and execute supplemental agreements for spare parts and other items selected through provisioning procedures when prescribed by agency acquisition regulations.

(23) Negotiate and execute contractual documents for settlement of partial and complete contract terminations for convenience, except as otherwise prescribed by Part 49.

(24) Negotiate and execute contractual documents settling cancellation charges under multi-year contracts.

(25) Process and execute novation and change of name agreements under Subpart 42.12.

(26) Perform property administration (see Part 45).

(27) Approve contractor acquisition or fabrication of special test equipment under the clause at 52.245-18, Special Test Equipment.

(28) Perform necessary screening, redistribution, and disposal of contractor inventory.

(29) Issue contract modifications requiring the contractor to provide packing, crating, and handling services on excess Government property.

When the ACO determines it to be in the Government's interests, the services may be secured from a contractor other than the contractor in possession of the property.

    (30) In facilities contracts--

        (i) Evaluate the contractor's requests for facilities and for changes to existing facilities and provide appropriate recommendations to the contracting officer;

        (i) Ensure required screening of facility items before acquisition by the contractor;

        (iii) Approve use of facilities on a noninterference basis in accordance with the clause at 52.245-9, Use and Charges;

        (iv) Ensure payment by the contractor of any rental due; and

        (v) Ensure reporting of items no longer needed for Government production.

    (31) Perform production support, surveillance, and status reporting, including timely reporting of potential and actual slippage in contract delivery schedules.

    (32) Perform pre-award surveys (see Subpart 9.1).

    (33) Advise and assist contractors regarding their priorities and allocations responsibilities and assist contracting offices in processing requests for special assistance and for priority ratings for privately owned capital equipment.

    (34) Monitor contractor industrial labor relations matters under the contract; apprise the contracting officer and, if designated by the agency, the cognizant labor relations advisor, of actual or potential labor disputes; and coordinate the removal of urgently required material from the strikebound contractor's plant upon instruction from, and authorization of, the contracting officer.

    (35) Perform traffic management services, including issuance and control of Government bills of lading and other transportation documents.

    (36) Review the adequacy of the contractor's traffic operations.

    (37) Review and evaluate preservation, packaging, and packing.

    (38) Ensure contractor compliance with contractual quality assurance requirements (see Part 46).

    (39) Ensure contractor compliance with applicable safety requirements, including contractual requirements for the handling of hazardous and dangerous materials and processes.

    (40) Perform engineering surveillance to assess compliance with contractual terms for schedule, cost, and technical performance in the areas of design, development, and production.

    (41) Evaluate for adequacy and perform surveillance of contractor engineering efforts and management systems that relate to design,

development, production, engineering changes, subcontractors, tests, management of engineering resources, reliability and maintainability, data control systems, configuration management, and independent research and development.

(42) Review and evaluate for technical adequacy the contractor's logistics support, maintenance, and modification programs.

(43) Report to the contracting office any inadequacies noted in specifications.

(44) Perform engineering analyses of contractor cost proposals.

(45) Review and analyze contractor-proposed engineering and design studies and submit comments and recommendations to the contracting office, as required.

(46) Review engineering change proposals for proper classification, and when required, for need, technical adequacy of design, producibility, and impact on quality, reliability, schedule, and cost; submit comments to the contracting office.

(47) Assist in evaluating and make recommendations for acceptance or rejection of waivers and deviations.

(48) Evaluate and monitor the contractor's procedures for complying with procedures regarding restrictive markings on data.

(49) Monitor the contractor's value engineering program.

(50) Review, approve or disapprove, and maintain surveillance of the contractor's purchasing system (see Part 44).

(51) Consent to the placement of subcontracts.

(52) Review, evaluate, and approve plant or division-wide small and small disadvantaged business master subcontracting plans.

(53) Obtain the contractor's currently approved company- or division-wide plans for small business and small disadvantaged business subcontracting for its commercial products, or, if there is no currently approved plan, assist the contracting officer in evaluating the plans for those products.

(54) Assist the contracting officer, upon request, in evaluating an offeror's proposed small business and small disadvantaged business subcontracting plans, including documentation of compliance with similar plans under prior contracts.

(55) By periodic surveillance, ensure the contractor's compliance with small business and small disadvantaged business subcontracting plans and any labor surplus area contractual requirements; maintain documentation of the contractor's performance under and compliance with these plans and requirements; and provide advice and assistance to the firms involved, as appropriate.

(56) Maintain surveillance of flight operations.

(57) Assign and perform supporting contract administration.

(58) Ensure timely submission of required reports.

(59) With the exception of changes in accounting and appropriation

data which must be issued by the contracting office, issue administrative changes (see 43.101).

(60) Cause release of shipments from contractor's plants according to the shipping instructions. When applicable, the order of assigned priority shall be followed; shipments within the same priority shall be determined by date of the instruction.

(61) Obtain contractor proposals for any contract price adjustments resulting from amended shipping instructions. ACOs shall review all amended shipping instructions on a periodic, consolidated basis to assure that adjustments are timely made. Except when the ACO has settlement authority, the ACO shall forward the proposal to the contracting officer for contract modification. The ACO shall not delay shipments pending completion and formalization of negotiations of revised shipping instructions.

(b) The CAO shall perform the following functions only when and to the extent specifically authorized by the contracting office:

(1) Negotiate or negotiate and execute supplemental agreements incorporating contractor proposals resulting from change orders issued under the Changes clause. Before completing negotiations, coordinate any delivery schedule change with the contracting office.

(2) Negotiate prices and execute priced exhibits for unpriced orders issued by the contracting officer under basic ordering agreements.

(3) Negotiate or negotiate and execute supplemental agreements changing contract delivery schedules.

(4) Negotiate or negotiate and execute supplemental agreements providing for the deobligation of unexpended dollar balances considered excess to known contract requirements.

(5) Issue amended shipping instructions and, when necessary, negotiate and execute supplemental agreements incorporating contractor proposals resulting from these instructions.

(6) Negotiate changes to interim billing prices.

(7) Negotiate and definitize adjustments to contract prices resulting from exercise of an economic price adjustment clause (see Subpart 16.2).

(8) Issue change orders and negotiate and execute resulting supplemental agreements under contracts for ship construction, conversion, and repair.

(c) Any additional contract administration functions not listed in 42.302(a) and (b), or not otherwise delegated, remain the responsibility of the contracting office.

Glossary

ACCEPTANCE: The act of an authorized representative of the government by which the government assumes for itself, or as agent of another, ownership of existing and identified supplies tendered, or approves specific services rendered as partial or complete performance of the contract on the part of the contractor.

ACQUISITION PLAN: A document which records program decisions, contains the requirement, provides appropriate analysis of technical options and the life cycle plans for development, production, training and support of materiel items.

ACTUAL COST: The sum of the direct and indirect costs incurred to produce a part, product, or service, and, for government contracts, that are allowable and allocable under the reimbursement rules.

ADVANCE PAYMENT: A deposit into a special bank account prior to, in anticipation of, and for the purpose of direct payment of the cost of performance under a contract or contracts.

ADVANCED DEVELOPMENT: Includes all projects which have moved into the development of hardware for experimental or operational test.

ALLOCABLE COST: A cost is allocable if it is assignable or chargeable to one or more cost objectives in accordance with the relative benefits received or other equitable relationships defined or agreed to between contractual parties

ALLOWABLE COST: A cost is allowable under a government contract if it meets the tests of reasonableness and allocability, is in consonance with standards promulgated by the Cost Accounting Standards Board (if applicable), or otherwise conforms with generally accepted accounting principles, with specific limitations or exclusions set forth in FAR Part 31, and with specific agreed-to terms between contractual parties.

ASSEMBLY: Two or more parts or subassemblies joined together to form a complete unit, structure, or other article.

ASSIST AUDIT: An audit performed by one audit office at the request of another audit office. The assist audit is usually an adjunct to or an integral part of an audit being performed by the requesting office.

AUDIT: The systematic examination of records and documents and the securing of other evidence by confirmation, physical inspection, or otherwise, for one or more of the following purposes: determining the propriety or legality of proposed or consummated transactions; ascertaining whether all transactions have been recorded and are reflected accurately in accounts; determining the existence of recorded assets and inclusiveness of recorded liabilities; determining the accuracy of financial or statistical statements or reports and the fairness of the facts they present; determining the degree of compliance with established policies and procedures relative to financial transactions and business management; and appraising an accounting system and making recommendations concerning it.

AUDITOR: A professional accountant responsible for systematic examination of records and documents. In government contract work acts as an advisor to contracting officers on contractor accounting and contract audit matters.

BALANCED LINE: A series of progressive related operations with approximately equal standard times for each, arranged so that work flows at a desired steady rate from one operation to the next.

BARCHART: A detailed graph depicting the work plan for an effort that reveals scheduled and actual time for each trackable task necessary for the job.

"BASED-ON" PRICE: A price that is based on established catalog or market prices of commercial items sold in substantial quantities to the general public. Considered a valid basis for price decision if the item being purchased is sufficiently similar to the commercial item to permit the difference between the prices of the items to be identified and justified without resort to cost analysis.

BID AND PROPOSAL COSTS: Costs incurred in preparing, submitting, and supporting bids and proposals.

BILL OF MATERIALS: A descriptive and quantitative list of materials, supplies, parts, and components required to produce a designated complete end-item of material or assembly or subassembly. The bill of materials may include estimated costs or fixed prices.

BUDGET: A planned program for a fiscal period that is stated in dollars. Includes estimated costs, obligations, and expenditures. Identifies source of funds including payments, reimbursements, debt, and other resources.

BURDEN: (See indirect cost.)

CALIBRATION: The comparison of a measurement system or device of unverified accuracy to a measurement system or device of known or greater accuracy to detect and correct any variation from required per-formance specifications of the unverified measurement system or device.

CAPACITY ANALYSIS: An analysis most frequently employed in a machine or process area to project capability for additional business.

CHANGE ORDER: A written order signed by the contracting officer, directing the contractor to make changes authorized by the Changes clause of a government contract.

COMMERCIAL ITEM: An item (which may be either supplies or services) of a class or kind that is (1) regularly used for other than government purposes, and (2) sold or traded in the course of conducting normal busi-ness operations. To qualify for the established catalog or market price exemption from the requirement for submission of cost or pricing data the item must be sold in substantial quantities to the general public.

COMPETITION: A market condition in which buyers and sellers freely solicit and offer to buy or sell. Potential buyers such as government may attempt to induce or stimulate competition under circumstances in which conditions in the marketplace appear to limit competitive interaction.

COMPETITIVE PROPOSALS: A competitive procedure used by government that is initiated by a request for proposals (RFP), specifies requirements and criteria for evaluation of offers, and contemplates the submission of timely proposals normally followed by discussion with those offerors found to be within the competitive range. The procedure is normally concluded by award of a contract to the offeror whose offer is believed to be most advantageous to the government, considering price and other factors specified in the solicitation.

COMPETITIVE RANGE: A group of offerors responding to an RFP whose offers are determined by the contracting officer on the basis of price, cost, technical, and other salient factors to have a reasonable chance of being selected for award of a contract. Normally the contracting officer must conduct written or oral discussions with all responsible offerors who submit proposals within the competitive range.

CONFIGURATION: The functional and/or physical characteristics of hardware and computer programs as set forth in technical documentation and achieved in a product.

CONFIGURATION MANAGEMENT: A discipline applying technical and administrative direction and surveillance to: (1) identify and document the functional and physical characteristics of a configuration item, (2) control changes to those characteristics, and (3) record and report change processing and implementation status.

CONSTRUCTIVE CHANGE: During contract performance, an oral or written act or omission by the contracting officer or other authorized government official, which is of such a nature that it is construed to have the same effect as a written change order.

CONTINGENCY: A possible future event or condition arising from presently known or unknown causes. The event or condition, if it occurs, is dependent on future events. Outcome may be defined but is not determinable based on present knowledge.

CONTRACT: A term descriptive of various agreements including ones for procurement of supplies or services. A contract is enforceable by law if mutual between two or more competent parties provided it calls for doing or not doing something not prohibited by law, for a legal consideration.

CONTRACT MODIFICATION: Any written alteration in the specification, delivery point, rate of delivery, contract period, price, quality, or other provision of an existing contract. It may be unilateral as with exercise of a contract option or in accordance with a contract clause such as a change order or notice of termination. It may be bilateral when based on a supplemental agreement.

CONTRACTOR-ACQUIRED PROPERTY (CAP): Under government contracts property procured or otherwise provided by the contractor for the contract. Title is vested in the government pursuant to contract terms.

CONTRACT PRICING: A series of actions directed toward making judgments regarding proposed prices. Includes steps to obtain, evaluate, assess, and verify cost and price information plus steps necessary to document the process. The purpose is to ascertain that prices are fair and reasonable prior to contract award.

CONTRACT PRICING PROPOSAL COVER SHEET: The vehicle for submitting to the government a price proposal supported by estimated and incurred costs by contract line item. The Standard Form 1411 (SF 1411) is to be used for this purpose. It is prepared in accordance with the instructions and formats of FAR Table 15-2.

CONTRACT TYPE: This term refers to specific pricing arrangements used for contract work. Type of contract determines the payment (or compensation) method for the contract including fixed-price and cost reimbursement arrangements. Contract types may involve incentive or award fees, fixed rates for labor, several ordering arrangements, either term or completion forms of executing obligations, and unpriced (letter) agreements. Allocation between the parties of the risks associated with performance is determined by the factors embraced in the contract type.

CONTRACTING OFFICER: A government employee who, either by virtue of position or by appointment is vested with the authority to enter into and administer contracts for the government and make determinations and findings with respect thereto, or is vested with any part of such authority. The duties assigned are similar to those of a purchasing agent in the private sector and may be limited in specific ways. In part, duties are reflected by three designated types of contracting officers: procurement contracting officer (PCO), administrative contracting officer (ACO), and termination contracting officer (TCO).

COST ACCOUNTING: A system of analysis and reporting that deals with costs of producing goods or services or of operating programs, activities, functions, or organizational units. The system also may embrace memorandum records, cost estimating, determination of cost standards based on engineering data, and comparison of actual and standard costs for the purpose of aiding cost control.

COST ANALYSIS: The review and evaluation of a contractor's cost or pricing data and of the judgmental factors applied in projecting from the data to the estimated costs. The purpose is to form an opinion leading to a position regarding the degree to which the contractor's proposed costs represent what contract performance should cost, assuming reasonable economy and efficiency. It includes appropriate verification of cost data, evaluation of specific elements of costs, and projection of these data to determine the effect on price factors like cost necessity, allowances for contingencies, and the basis used for allocation of overhead costs.

COST CENTER: Any subdivision of an organization comprised of workers, equipment areas, activities, or a combination that is established for the purpose of assigning or allocating costs. Cost centers are also used as a base for performance standards. Synonym: burden center, cost pool.

COST ESTIMATING: The process of forecasting a future result in terms of cost, based upon information available at the time.

COST INCURRED: A cost identified through the use of the accrued method of accounting and reporting or otherwise actually paid. Cost of direct labor, direct materials, and direct services identified with and necessary for the performance of a contract, and all properly allocated and allowable indirect costs as shown by the books of the contractor.

COST OBJECTIVE: A function, organizational subdivision, contract, or other work unit for which cost data are desired and for which provision is made to accumulate and measure the cost of processes, products, jobs, capitalized projects, and so forth.

COST OR PRICING DATA: Data consisting of all facts existing up to the time of agreement on price, which prudent buyers and sellers would reasonably expect to have a significant effect on price negotiations. Being factual, these data are types of information that can be verified. They do not reflect on the accuracy of the contractor's judgment about estimated future costs or projections; they do, however, reflect on the data upon which the contractor based his judgment.

COST OVERRUN (OR UNDERRUN): A difference between actual cost and the cost expected based on the contract price agreement that is caused by, or attributed to, factors under control of the contractor's management. Responsibility for financing or benefiting from the difference depends upon contract type. Other sources of differences between actual cost and originally estimated cost such as change orders or additions to deliverable work are not treated as overrun (underrun).

COST REIMBURSEMENT: Refers to a family of pricing arrangements that provide for payment of allowable, allocable, and reasonable costs incurred in the performance of a contract, to the extent that such costs are prescribed or permitted by the contract. In the case of a CPFF arrangement, costs may vary under or over the initially agreed-to estimate, but the fee remains fixed as an expressed dollar amount and is not subject to adjustment by reason of the contractor's cost experience during the life of the contract.

COST RISK: Monetary loss or gain associated with overrun (underrun). Allocation of the risk is one of the elements to be considered in the negotiation of a fair and reasonable price, and the key factor to be considered when agreeing to the type of contract under which performance will occur.

CRITICAL DESIGN REVIEW: In development projects this review determines whether the design satisfies the performance and engineering requirements of the contract. Based on the contract specification this review establishes compatibility of the contract item and other items of equipment, facilities, computer programs, and personnel. The review team assesses producability and risks associated with the preliminary product specifications.

DEFECTIVE COST OR PRICING DATA: Certified cost of pricing data subsequently found to have been inaccurate, incomplete, or noncurrent. Under its policy requiring submission of this data, the government is entitled to a downward adjustment of the negotiated price, including profit or fee, to remove from its payment obligation any significant sum by which price was increased because of the defective data, provided the data were relied upon by the government.

DIRECT COST: Any cost that is specifically identified with a final cost objective. Direct cost may include cost elements other than those for items that are incorporated in the end product as material or labor.

DIRECT MATERIAL: All material that enters into and becomes part of the finished product (including waste) or is consumed in its production, the cost of which can and should be identified with and assessed against the particular product accurately and without undue effort and expense.

DISCLOSURE STATEMENT (COST ACCOUNTING STANDARDS): The statement, prepared using form CASB-DS-1, that describes a company's cost accounting practices by providing data that are responsive to the form's requirements. Applies to all defense contractors who enter into negotiated national defense contracts in excess of $100,000, with certain exceptions applying to contracts where the price negotiated reflects or is based on (1) established catalog or market prices of commercial items sold in substantial quantities to the general public, or (2) prices set by law or regulation. The presumed or anticipated presence of a competitive environment does not constitute an exception or exemption for the submission of a disclosure statement.

EARNED HOURS: The time in standard hours credited to a worker or group of workers as a result of their completion of a given task or group of tasks.

ECONOMIC PRICE ADJUSTMENT: An alteration permitted and specified by contract provisions for the upward or downward revision of a stated contract price upon the occurrence of certain contingencies that are defined in the contract.

EQUITABLE ADJUSTMENT: A modification of an existing contract to compensate for the cost, profit and time effects of altered requirements for work. The adjustment may incorporate modifications of other terms and conditions as needed to return the parties to their relative positions as existing at the time the work requirement was altered. This type of adjustment is authorized by certain contract clauses in government contracts.

ESCALATION: A term traditionally used to indicate an upward or downward movement of price. "Economic price adjustment" is the contemporary term used to express the sense of escalation.

ESTABLISHED CATALOG PRICE: A price included in a catalog, price list, schedule, or other form that (1) is regularly maintained by a manufacturer or vendor, (2) is published or made available for inspection by customers, and (3) states prices at which sales are currently or were last made to a significant number of buyers constituting the general public.

ESTABLISHED MARKET PRICE: A current price, established in the usual and ordinary course of trade between buyers and sellers free to bargain which can be substantiated from sources independent of the manufacturer or vendor. Substantiation of a market price may be based on data supplied by the seller.

FACILITIES: Industrial Property (other than material, special tooling, military property, and special test equipment for production, maintenance, research, development, or test) including real property and rights therein, buildings, structures, improvements, and plant equipment.

FAIR AND REASONABLE PRICE: A price that is fair to both parties, considering the agreed-upon conditions, promised quality, and timeliness of contract performance. Although generally a fair and reasonable price is a function of the law of supply and demand, there are statutory, regulatory, and judgmental limits on the concept.

FAILURE: Pertinent to contract obligations, the event in which any part of an item does not perform as required by its performance specification.

FEE: In cost-reimbursement pricing arrangements, fee is an amount to be paid in lieu of profit. It is paid in addition to cost. Fee reflects a variety of factors, including risk, and is subject to statutory limitations. Fee is fixed in dollars at the outset of performance in cost-plus-fixed-fee contracts. It is an amount that varies as a function of the sharing agreement in incentive contracts, and varies within a contractually specified minimum-maximum range in award fee contracts.

FIELD PRICING SUPPORT: Analysis of contractor pricing proposals by government technical and other specialists in field offices, including plant representatives, administrative contracting officers, contract auditors, price analysts, quality assurance personnel, engineers, and legal and small business specialists.

FINAL COST OBJECTIVE: A cost objective that has allocated to it both direct and indirect costs and, in the contractor's system, is one of the final accumulation points.

FIXED PRICE: Refers to a group of pricing arrangements (contract types) characterized by a stated or ceiling price for which the contractor guarantees to deliver an acceptable end item. The purchaser expects to pay no more than that price. Final price is variable at an amount below the ceiling in incentive contracts, but in the case of a firm-fixed-price is not subject to any adjustment except for changes and similar actions by the purchaser.

FORMAL ADVERTISING: (See sealed bidding.)

FORWARD PRICING ARRANGEMENT: A written understanding negotiated between a contractor and the government to make certain rates (e.g., labor, indirect, and material usage) available for use during a specified period of time in pricing contracts or contract modifications.

FULL AND OPEN COMPETITION: The process by which all responsible offerors are allowed to compete. Available competitive procedures include sealed bids, competitive proposals, combination of competitive procedures (e.g., two-step), and other competitive procedures (e.g., A-E).

GANTT CHART: A graphic representation (bar chart) on a time scale depicting tasks and milestones for planned performance and completed work.

GENERAL AND ADMINISTRATIVE: Indirect expenses, including a company's general and executive offices, executive compensation, the cost of staff services such as legal, accounting, public relations, financial, and similar expenses and other miscellaneous expenses related to the overall business.

GOVERNMENT-FURNISHED PROPERTY (GFP): Property owned by the government and subsequently provided to a contractor.

GUARANTEED LOAN: A loan for which payment is guaranteed by the government. Essentially the same as other loans made by financial institutions. Funds are distributed, collected, and administered by the lending institution. Government funds are not involved except for the purchase of the guaranteed portion of the loan for the settlement of losses in cases of default.

INCENTIVE ARRANGEMENT: A negotiated pricing arrangement designed to motivate and reward the contractor dependent upon performance as measured in relation to the contract specification. Provides an incentive fee or profit or an award fee to be paid in addition to cost for superior performance. The incentive is payable based on a formula in the case of incentive contracts, and on evaluated performance in award contracts.

INCREMENTAL FUNDING: The obligation of funds to a contract in periodic installments. Payment is restricted to the amount actually funded which should be at or below the total price or estimated cost.

INDEPENDENT COST ANALYSIS (ICA): An analysis of program cost estimates conducted by an impartial body disassociated from the management of the program.

INDEX NUMBERS: Ratios, usually expressed as percentages, indicating changes in values, quantities, or prices. Typically, the changes are measured over time, each item being compared with a corresponding figure from some selected base period.

INDIRECT COST: Any cost not directly identified with a single final cost objective but identified with two or more final cost objectives or with at least one intermediate cost objective. Also referred to as overhead or burden.

INDIRECT COST POOL: A group of incurred costs identified with two or more cost objectives but not identified with any final cost objective.

INSPECTION: The examination and testing of supplies and services (including, when appropriate, raw materials, components, and intermediate assemblies) to determine whether they conform to specified requirements.

INVITATION FOR BIDS: The solicitation document used in sealed bidding and in the second step of two-step sealed bidding.

JOB ORDER COST SYSTEM: A cost system in which the contractor accounts for output and costs incurred by specifically identifiable physical units. A job order may cover the production of one unit or represent a composite of a number of identical units.

LETTER CONTRACT: A written preliminary contractual instrument that authorizes work to begin even though a final price agreement has not been reached. Specifies the maximum liability of the government pending definitization of a fixed-price or cost-reimbursement pricing arrangement for the contract. Designed to be superseded by a definitive contract within a specified time.

LINE OF BALANCE: A graphic display comparing scheduled units versus actual units passing a given set of critical schedule control points on a particular day.

MAKE OR BUY: Analysis performed by a contractor to determine whether an item should be made "in house" or purchased from an outside supplier.

MARKET ANALYSIS: The process of analyzing prices and trends in the competitive marketplace for the purposes of projecting product availability, offered prices in relation to market alternatives, and establishing the reasonableness of offered prices.

MARKET DATA: Any information concerning price, quality, or availability of products in a particular market. Includes information obtained from market surveys, price quotes, newspapers, trade journals, and other sources. Such data are used to establish the reasonableness of an offered price.

MARKET SURVEY: Studies to locate and qualify sources capable of satisfying a requirement. These studies may include written or telephone contact with knowledgeable experts regarding similar or duplicate requirements, review of recently undertaken market tests, sources-sought announcements in pertinent publications (e.g., technical/scientific journals or the Commerce Business Daily), and solicitations for planning purposes.

NEGOTIATION: A bargaining process between two or more parties, each with his own viewpoints and objectives, seeking to reach a mutually satisfactory agreement on, or settlement of, a matter of common concern.

NEGOTIATION OBJECTIVES: A range of goals, normally determined by analysis in advance of negotiation indicating the limits within which fair and reasonable contract provisions, including desired costs or prices, should be negotiated.

OVERHEAD: (See indirect cost.)

PARTIAL PAYMENT: A payment authorized under a contract, made upon delivery and acceptance of one or more contract end items (or one or more distinct items of service). Also a payment made against a termination claim upon prior approval before final settlement of the total termination claim.

PRICE: A monetary amount given, received, or asked in exchange for property or services, expressed in terms of a single item or unit of measure for such property or services.

PRICE ANALYSIS: The process of examining and evaluating a prospective price without evaluation of the separate cost elements and profit of the individual offeror whose price is being evaluated. It may be accomplished by a comparison of submitted quotations, a comparison of quotations with market prices of the same or similar items, a comparison of price quotations and contract prices with past prices or current quotations for the same or similar items, the use of yardsticks (dollars per point, for instance), or a comparison of proposed prices with independently developed government estimates.

PRICING: The process of establishing the amount or amounts to be received or paid in return for providing goods and performing services.

PRICING ARRANGEMENT: An agreed-to basis between contractual parties for payment for specified performance. Usually expressed as a specific cost-reimbursement or fixed-price type of contract.

PRICE NEGOTIATION MEMORANDUM (PNM): In government practice the document summarizing a negotiation. It is intended to support the reasonableness of the agreement reached with the successful offeror, and becomes a permanent record of the decisions the negotiator made in establishing that the price was fair and reasonable.

PRIORITY RATINGS - DO AND DX: The two types of priority ratings contained in Defense Priorities System Regulation that specify rules relating to the status, placement, acceptance and treatment of priority rated contracts and orders. DO ratings have equal preferential status and take priority over all unrated orders. DX ratings have equal preferential status and take priority over all DO rated and unrated orders.

PROBABILITY: A probability is a number between 0 and 1, inclusive, representing the chance or likelihood that an event will occur. A probability of 0 means that the event is impossible, while a probability of 1 means that the event is certain to occur. A probability may also be stated as a percentage (there is a 50 percent chance of this happening) or as an odds ratio (there is a 3 to 2 chance of this happening). The concept of probability assumes two things: an average over a long series of possibilities for an event to occur, and independence of events.

PROCESS COST SYSTEM: A system in which a contractor accounts for output by the process that is employed continuously to manufacture or produce an end-item. At the end of an accounting period, the costs incurred for a process are assigned to the units (both complete and incomplete) that the process has produced or is producing.

PROFIT: In contract pricing, profit represents a projected or known monetary amount realized by a producer or performer after the deduction from the contract price of cost (both direct and indirect) incurred or to be incurred in the performance of the contract.

PROFIT CENTER: A discrete, organizationally independent segment of a company, which has been charged by management with profit and loss responsibilities.

PROFIT OBJECTIVE: That part of the estimated contract price objective the negotiating party concludes is appropriate for the proposed contract. Where cost analysis is undertaken, a profit objective is developed by the government after a thorough review of proposed contract work and all available knowledge regarding the offeror as well as an analysis of the offeror's cost estimate, and a comparison of it with the government's estimate or projection of cost.

PROGRESS PAYMENT: A payment made as work progresses under a fixed price contract on the basis of percentage of completion (construction) or cost incurred (supply and service contracts).

PROSPECTIVE PRICING: A pricing agreement made in advance of per-formance, based on analysis of comparative prices, cost estimates, past costs, or combinations of such considerations.

PUBLIC LAW 87-653: Generally referred to as the Truth in Negotiations Act. Created for government contracts the requirement for submission, either actually or by specific identification in writing, of cost and pricing data, and certification of accuracy, completeness, and currency of the data. The requirement applies to the award of any negotiated contact expected to exceed $100,000. Certain exceptions apply that are tied to adequate price competition or other conditions reflecting a competitive marketplace.

QUALITY: The composite of material attributes including performance features and characteristics of a product or service to satisfy a given need.

QUALITY ASSURANCE: A planned and comprehensive system encompassing all actions necessary to provide confidence that adequate technical requirements are established, that materials and operations are under control and a record developed that ensures products and services conform with the established technical requirements to the end that satisfactory performance is achieved.

REASONABLE COST: A cost is reasonable if, in its nature or amount, it does not exceed what would be incurred by an ordinarily prudent person in the conduct of competitive business.

REQUEST FOR PROPOSALS: A solicitation document used in other than sealed bid procurement. When an RFP so states, the government reserves the right to award a contract based on initial offers received without any written or oral discussion with offerors.

REQUEST FOR QUOTATIONS: A solicitation document used in other than sealed bid procurement. An RFQ is a request for information. Quotes submitted in response to it are not offers that the government may accept without some confirmation or discussion with offerors.

REQUEST FOR TECHNICAL PROPOSALS: The solicitation document used in the first step of two-step sealed bidding.

RETROACTIVE PRICING: A pricing agreement made after some or all of the work specified under contract has been completed, based on a review of contractor performance and recorded cost data.

RISK: The likelihood of an outcome other than that planned and expected. In contracting, the risk bearer assumes possible monetary loss or gain associated with such outcomes. Allocation of risk between the parties is an important element to be considered in the negotiation of a fair and reasonable price, as well as in determining the type of contract under which performance will occur.

SAMPLING: A method of obtaining statistics from a large body of data without resorting to a complete census. Two broad methods of selecting samples are probability sampling (in which sample units are selected according to the law of chance) and non-probability sampling (in which personal choice, expert judgment, or some other non-probabilistic rationale is used to select sample units).

SEALED BID: A method of solicitation used in public contracting that uses competitive bids, public opening of bids, and award without negotiation. Previously known as formal advertising.

SHOULD COST: A concept that the objective of cost analysis and contract pricing is to base price agreements on what it should cost the offeror to produce, assuming reasonable economy and efficiency of operation. Should cost analysis is an attempt to remove inefficiencies otherwise accepted without critical analysis of better methods.

SHOULD-COST TEAM: An integrated team of government procurement, contract administration, audit, and engineering representatives. The team conducts a coordinated, in-depth should cost analysis at the contractor's plant. Its purpose: to identify uneconomical or inefficient practices in the contractor's management and operations, to quantify the findings in terms of their impact on cost, and to develop a realistic price objective for negotiation that reflects the outcome of the should-cost effort.

SINGLE SOURCE: The one source among others in a competitive marketplace which, for justifiable reason has predominant qualifications for selection for contract award. (Sometimes used interchangeably with the term "sole source".)

SMALL PURCHASE: A procurement action whose aggregate amount does not exceed a prescribed dollar value.

SMALL PURCHASE PROCEDURES: The methods prescribed for making small purchases using impress funds, purchase orders, and blanket purchase agreements.

SOLE SOURCE: The one and only source regardless of the marketplace, possessing a unique and singularly available performance capability for the purpose of contract award. (Sometimes used interchangeably with the term "single source.")

SUBSYSTEM: A subset of subassemblies or devices or an individual unit of hardware that constitutes a defined part of a system (e.g., the avionics of an aircraft system, the fire control mechanisms of a ship system, the transmission/receiving elements of an electronic system).

SUNK COST: A cost that is not recoverable.

SUPPLEMENTAL AGREEMENT: A modification to an existing contract that is accomplished by the mutual action of the parties.

SYSTEM: A group of subassemblies or devices or individual units of hardware (e.g., subsystems) which in concert with necessary software, personnel and other system elements meets or serves the total performance requirements of one or more defined mission or objective (e.g., an aircraft system, a ship system, a land vehicle system).

SYSTEM DESIGN REVIEW: Evaluates the design and functioning of a system including all data demonstrating performance of intended functions and risks associated with the allocated technical requirements.

TECHNICAL ANALYSIS: In support of pricing actions an evaluation of functions that cause costs to occur. Usually performed by engineering and technical personnel. Vitally important to understanding cost projections as they relate to the job to be done. Provides informed opinion about the validity of projections for direct materials; equipment usage; scrap; use of hand, semiautomatic, or automatic operations; the number and types of workers it takes to do a job; and differences between the estimated labor mix and planned operations.

TECHNICAL DATA PACKAGE: Specifications, drawings, reports, manuals, data lists, revisions, technical orders, and other documents (including magnetic media) used as an integrated unit as the controlling technical data for a contract. May also be the deliverable product of a development contract and therefore delineated as items on a Contract Data Requirements List (CDRL).

TESTING: An element of inspection. Generally denotes the determination by technical means of the properties or elements of supplies, or components thereof, including functional operation, and involves the application of established scientific principles and procedures.

VALUE ANALYSIS: A systematic and objective evaluation of the function of a product and its related cost. The analyst evaluates the product characteristics in terms of aesthetics, utility, and demand. As a pricing tool, value analysis provides insight into the inherent worth of a product and is oriented to reduce cost. It may be encouraged or required as a program under value engineering provisions of government contracts.

VARIABLE COST: A cost that changes with the rate of production of goods or the performance of services.

WEIGHTED GUIDELINES METHOD: A technique the government uses to ensure consideration of the relative value of appropriate profit factors in establishing a profit objective and conducting negotiations. Profit factors are subject to change periodically as perceptions of needs and changes in points of emphasis arises in government

WILL-COST: An approach to contract pricing based on the submission and evaluation of what an offeror estimates it will cost to do the job given established operations during a future period. As a concept, it is the opposite of should-cost. It is viewed as undesirable because it may ignore inefficiencies in contractor operations that should be eliminated.

Selected
Bibliography

General Purchasing and Materials Management:

Burt, David N. *Proactive Procurement.* Englewood Cliffs, NJ: Prentice-
Hall, 1984.
Dobler, Donald W.; Lee, Lamar Jr.; and Burt, David N. *Purchasing and
Materials Management*, 4th Ed. New York, NY: McGraw-Hill, 1984.
Heinritz, Stuart F.; Farrell, Paul V.; and Smith, Clifton L. *Purchasing:
Principles and Applications.* 7th Ed. Englewood Cliffs, NJ: Prentice-
Hall, 1986.
Leenders, Michiel R.; Fearon, Harold E.; and England, Wilbur B.
Purchasing and Materials Management. 8th Ed. Homewood, IL:
Richard D. Irwin, 1985.
Zenz, Gary J. *Purchasing and the Management of Materials.* 6th Ed. New
York, NY: John Wiley & Sons, 1987.

Logistics and Physical Distribution Management:

Bowersox, Donald J.; Closs, David J.; and Helferich, Omar K. *Logistical
Management.* 3rd Ed. New York, NY: Macmillan Publishing Company,
1986.
Johnson, James C.; and Wood, Donald F. *Contemporary Physical
Distribution and Logistics.* 3rd Ed. New York, NY: Macmillan
Publishing Company, 1986
Magee, John F.; Copacino, William C.; and Rosenfield, Donald B. *Modern
Logistics Management.* New York, NY: John Wiley and Sons, 1985.

446

U. S. Government Procurement and Legal Information Sources:

Armed Services Pricing Manual. Washington, DC: Government Printing
Office, 1986. Contract pricing approached primarily by analysis of
cost and pricing data in a manner consistant with government policy.

Board of Contract Appeals Decisions. Chicago, IL: Commerce Clearing
House. Full texts of Board of Contract Appeals Decisions. Includes
case tables and finding lists by BCA Docket Number.

Cibinic, John Jr.; Nash, Ralph C. Jr. *Administration of Government
Contracts.* 2nd. Ed. Washington, DC: George Washington University,
1985.

Cibinic, John Jr.; Nash, Ralph C. Jr. *Formation of Government Contracts.*
2nd. Ed. Washington, DC: George Washington University, 1986.

Comptroller General's Procurement Decisions. Washington, DC: Federal
Publications, Inc. Photographic reproductions of the Comptroller
General of the United States' procurement decisions concerning
protests against procurement actions. Contains indices by B number,
by government volume number and by subject.

Cost Accounting Standards Guide. Chicago, IL: Commerce Clearing House.
Published periodically as an information service concerning rules and
decisions pertinent to the U. S. Government cost accounting
standards.

Federal Contracts Report. Washington, DC: Bureau of National Affairs.
Weekly reports concerning federal contracts and grants. Summarizes
current decisions and rulings by administrative boards, courts and
the Comptroller General concerning federal contracts. Reports
developments in the contract field from all sources.

Federal Court Procurement Decisions, Washington, DC: Federal Publications, Inc. Photographic reproductions of government contract
decisions by the U. S. Claims Court and the U. S. Court of Appeals
for the Federal Circuit. The series began October 1, 1982.

Government Contractor. Washington, DC: Federal Publications, Inc.
Published every two weeks as a newsletter. Summarizes
administrative actions, statutes, and case decisions in the field of
government contracts. Indexed. Cumulative index since 1959
available.

Government Contracts Reporter. Chicago, IL: Commerce Clearing House.
Nine volume information service with updates periodically concerning
regulations, decisions, and policy actions in the field of government
contracts.

Quinn's Uniform Commercial Code Commentary and Law Digest. Boston,
MA: Warren, Gorham and Lamont, Inc. Updated annually since 1980.
Cumulative master index, 1986.

Sherman, Stanley N. *Government Procurement Management.* 2nd. Ed.
Gaithersburg, MD: Wordcrafters Publications, 1985.

Index

About the author:

Stanley N. Sherman, DBA, C.P.M., C.P.C.M.,
began his career as a navigator in the United
States Air Force. As a civilian his work was
devoted to procurement and contracting management at the Bureau of Naval Weapons, the
National Aeronautics and Space Administration,
and Harbridge House. He continued that emphasis as a member of the faculty of the School
of Government and Business Administration at
George Washington University. In 1986 he was
named the National Association of Purchasing
Management Professor at George Washington
University. Dr. Sherman is director of the
university's Logistics, Operations and Materials
Management Program.